Teaching Modern British and American Satire

Teaching Modern British and American Satire

Edited by

Evan R. Davis and Nicholas D. Nace

The Modern Language Association of America

New York 2019

Printed in the United States of America

Library of Congress Cataloging-in-Publication Data
Names: Davis, Evan R., editor. | Nace, Nicholas D. (Nicholas David), editor.
Title: Teaching Modern British and American Satire / edited by Evan R. Davis, Nicholas D. Nace.
Description: New York, NY: The Modern Language Association of America, 2019.
Series: Options for teaching; 45
Identifiers: LCCN 201902198
ISBN 9781603293792 (hardback)
ISBN 9781603293808 (paper)
ISBN 9781603293815 (EPUB)
ISBN 9781603293822 (Kindle)
Subjects: LCSH: Satire, English--Study and teaching. | Satire, American--Study and teaching. | English literature--Study and teaching. | American literature --Study and teaching. | Satire, English--History and criticism. | Satire, American--History and criticism. | BISAC: LANGUAGE ARTS & DISCIPLINES / Study & Teaching. | LITERARY CRITICISM / Humor.
Classification: LCC PR931 .T325 2019 | DDC 827.0071--dc23
LC record available at https://lccn.loc.gov/2019021986

Options for Teaching 45
ISSN 1079-2562

Cover illustration of the paperback and electronic editions:
Gian Lorenzo Bernini, *Anima Dannata* (*Condemned Soul*), 1619.
Credit: Spanish Embassy, Rome, Italy / Bridgeman Images.

Second printing 2019

Published by The Modern Language Association of America
85 Broad Street, suite 500, New York, New York 10004-2434
www.mla.org

Contents

Acknowledgments

Any volume about teaching is already an attempt to discharge longstanding but often untraceable debts to teachers and students who have—as allies, antagonists, accomplices, and agitators—influenced the way we teach. But with this particular volume, very specific debts have accrued as well during the book's long gestation, first under the generous and exacting direction of James Hatch and then under the care and precision of Erika Suffern.

Thanks, first of all, to our contributors, whose enthusiasm never flagged during the collection's wait-then-act phases. Two contributors, Mike Conlon and Jon Greenberg, gave advice on the introduction at crucial stages, as did our outside readers, especially one who, despite our brushing elbows on airplanes and in interview rooms, kept helping us while maintaining his secret identity. Thanks, then, to Brian Connery and to others we queried about bibliographical matters or not-yet-released satire work, particularly Joe Pappa and Yulia Ryzhik. And it would be a serious omission to speak of bibliographical matters without mentioning Michael F. Suarez, SJ, whose Rare Book School provided the occasion for the present editors to meet and, between sessions, to dish about satire.

There seem to be few satiristi who have not read, written, or corrected some of this book. For ideas and assistance at early stages and incarnations of this collection, we thank Pedro Garcia-Caro, Wanda Creaser, Michael Hames-García, Ted Gournelos, Jonathan Lamb, Katie Lanning, Steven Minuk, Zoja Pavlovskis-Petit, Vlastik Svab, and Reuben Quintero.

And, of course, there are our students. As unfair and misleading as it is to attach certain names to what was always a dynamic group effort, our e-mail archives tell the story of those who have either kept up their interest in satire after graduation or have deemed us unable to talk about anything else. We would therefore like to thank Stephen Brower, Sarah Budow, Patrick Madej, Rebecca Porath, and many other satire students at University of Massachusetts, Boston, Binghamton University, and Hampden-Sydney College. And on behalf of our contributors, we'd like to thank Eden Keller, Derian Pugh, and Imani Reid (for Robin Runia), as well as Ashlee Joyce and Rachael Wyatt (for John Clement Ball).

We owe an irredeemable debt to our respective families who have given so generously of their support, interest, and love. Thanks to Mary

Boodell, Ravenel Davis, and Benjamin Davis; and to Lynn and Kay Nace, as well as Chelsie Malyszek, formerly of New Haven, Connecticut, but now a proud resident of Farmville, Virginia.

And, finally, each editor would like to thank the other.

For all they have taught us about teaching, this book is dedicated to our colleagues in English and rhetoric at Hampden-Sydney College and to Charles Knight, formerly of University of Massachusetts, Boston.

Evan R. Davis and Nicholas D. Nace

Introduction

Satire itself is a form of pedagogy. It wishes to inform about a topic that has not been seen clearly, it worries over what constitutes its subject, it anticipates the responses of its audience and tailors its presentation accordingly, and it frames its interventions relative to what at any given time passes for knowledge.[1] Horace's very first satire in his *Sermones* even equates laughter-inducing satirists with wheedling teachers ("blandi doctores") who would bribe students with pastries in order to get them to learn their alphabet (6). It is no wonder that satire so often and so self-reflexively adopts the habits of pedagogy and offers to us educators of all sorts: scholarly annotators, passionate pedants, blinkered teachers, and egocentric newscasters. And yet, if satire teaches, it does so with an inviting wink. For millennials raised on *The Simpsons*, *The Onion*, *South Park*, *The Colbert Report*, and the documentaries of Michael Moore, satire is familiar, vibrant, and welcoming, even if the satiric texts they encounter in classes often prove to be more bewildering and wily than they anticipate.

Satire has been called "the cuckoo bird of the literary genres because it lays its eggs in other birds' nests" (Ellis 200). No less is it the cuckoo bird of the curriculum, laying eggs in other birds' courses. Satire has found its home most often in courses devoted to eighteenth-century

British literature, and an informal survey of several dozen satire syllabi indicates that Jonathan Swift, Alexander Pope, and John Dryden remain among the most frequently taught satirists, with Mark Twain and Kurt Vonnegut coming in at numbers three and five, respectively. But thanks to its present cultural popularity and to a number of penetrating studies of satire *outside* the eighteenth century (including several by contributors to this volume), satire is currently extending its curricular reach. Indeed, in the proposals we received in response to our call for papers for this volume, only Swift was mentioned more often than Stephen Colbert. Given its rhetorical nature and its attention to voice and audience, satire has found an easy home in composition courses, such as the one described below by Robin Runia. As David Mazella argues in his essay, because reading satire leads so quickly to issues of authorship, intention, irony, agency, reception, and historical context, it can effectively structure a gateway course for English majors. Similarly, as Edward Wesp suggests, insofar as it requires students to read closely without ever losing sight of historical contexts, satire can address two of the main concerns of instructors teaching survey classes. Far from leaving satire solely a province of eighteenth-century British courses, Darryl Dickson-Carr shows how instructors can place "satire and irony at the center of the American literature classroom, rather than at its margins as a virtual afterthought." Other essays in this book offer suggestions for the incorporation of satire—either as a primary focus or a unit—into courses that emphasize contemporary political activism (Day, McClennen), genre (Prescott, Alff), modernism (Greenberg), postcolonialism (Ball), film (Horowitz, Nace), gender (Ingrassia, Deutsch, Bobker, Stratton), and visual culture (Conlon, Palmeri, Soper, Henry), not to mention the long eighteenth century (Ingrassia, Weinbrot, Domingo, Bogel, Combe, Rounce).

Framing the Field of Satire

The increasing appearance of satire courses and of satiric texts within more general courses results not only from the popularity of mainstream satire in film and television but also from the quality and range of satire criticism in recent years. Following a heyday of satire criticism in the 1960s and 1970s, throughout the 1980s the study of satire narrowed as the discipline of literary study erected strong boundaries within itself; critical work as well as courses were largely focused on single authors and narrowly periodized studies.[2] By the mid-1990s satire became an especially fit subject through which to explore "postmodern concerns," and two collections, Brian A. Connery and Kirk Combe's *Theorizing Satire* and James E. Gill's *Cutting Edges* (both 1995), offered essays that would place satire under the light of high theory in order to see clearly the gap between signifier and signified that satire, with its skepticism and irony, seems always to widen.

In roughly the past fifteen years, influential monographs have investigated satire within African American, Chicanx, postcolonial, filmic, cartoon, and a variety of new media contexts.[3] Others have returned to assessing satire within a wide, often transhistorical view of the subject in order to elucidate the core aims and methods that the largest portion of satirical writing shares when not restricted to nationality or period.[4] Ruben Quintero's compendious *Companion to Satire: Ancient and Modern* (2007) is representative of this recent trend, with its tremendous scope of twenty-nine discrete essays, which range from "Ancient Biblical Satire" to "Satire in Modern and Contemporary Theater." Like the courses they inspire, many critical studies of contemporary satire use eighteenth-century authors and texts as models for framing the variety of satires found in the twenty-first century, with a new theoretical approach to media studies that enables such comparisons between different satirical media, including political cartoons, animated television, parodic news shows, mockumentaries, mash-ups, and various forms of what has recently been dubbed "culture jamming."[5] Very recent scholarly works demonstrate that multidisciplinary and transhistorical investigations of satire develop new narratives and open new possibilities that will determine the way satire is taught in the coming years. In drawing from a wide variety of scholars teaching at a wide variety of institutions, this volume hopes to contribute to this increasingly comprehensive notion of satire that weaves together various periods, nationalities, and genres.

If the profession's attention to satire over the past two decades has rivaled that of the 1960s, in one crucial regard it has fallen short: theoretical and critical insights have not been accompanied by the pedagogical tools necessary to bring those insights into the classroom. Alvin Kernan, whose *Cankered Muse* (1959) proved to be one of the most influential and durable works in the field, followed that work three years later with his anthology *Modern Satire* (1962), which even after going out of print remained on syllabi well into the 1990s. Between 1962 and 1975, the period of major works of criticism by Frank Ellis, Gilbert Highet, Edward Rosenheim, and Ronald Paulson, another ten anthologies of Anglophone satire appeared, shaping classroom practice alongside criticism. Today, however, despite—or perhaps because of—the richness of contemporary satire and the quality of satire criticism, there is only one significant anthology for college use on the market: *American Satire: An Anthology of Writings from Colonial Times to the Present*, edited by Nicholas Bakalar and introduced by Stephen Koch.[6] This oversight is perhaps a response to the ephemerality of much satire: looking back on those anthologies from the 1970s, it is their most up-to-date satires that now seem the most dated. Who remembers or now teaches "Freud on Football" or "Postal System Input Buffer Device"? Will the same fate befall *The Colbert Report*, which was mentioned frequently in proposals for this volume, but which went off the air before the prospectus had been accepted? The result is that instructors are left on their own to cobble together course packs, to teach from general anthologies whose satiric texts are sparse and often insufficiently annotated, or to focus on satiric novels that can be purchased individually.

General anthologies such as the Norton or Longman, designed as they are for survey courses, misleadingly favor satires that appear as parasites on canonical host texts. Take, for instance, the case of Sir Walter Raleigh, an excellent poet who often exists in anthologies mostly to offer a satirical response to Christopher Marlowe's "The Passionate Shepherd to His Love"; or Anthony Hecht, another excellent poet whose "The Dover Bitch" is canonized by its use in helping to teach Matthew Arnold. From this point of view that privileges parody as the epitome of the mode, the status of satirical texts might appear to be dependent on the constantly shifting canon of literature in general. But this has never been the way satire has worked. If anything, it usually works the other way around. We read Dryden's attacks on Thomas Shadwell, but not Shadwell himself; Pope's attacks on Richard Bentley or Colley Cibber, but not Bentley or Cibber themselves. And the individual targets of satiric news interviews—the minor politicians looking to promote themselves knowing that, even during the show's taping, they will be overshadowed by the host—matter less than the satiric opportunity they afford. Especially for newcomers to the field, the study of satire would be helped immeasurably by the development of a transhistorical and transcultural anthology of satire, as well as by the publication of collections of satires within more localized fields, chronological periods, and genres.

The paucity of anthologies is mirrored by a lack of concerted attention to the teaching of satire. Despite the methodological, historical, cultural, and linguistic challenges posed by satiric texts, there exist no more than a few essays about how to teach this collection of works. We hope that the essays collected here will begin to fill the pedagogical void. Specifically, it is our aim to bring together essays that offer both new and seasoned instructors suggestions about how to address some of the major challenges and opportunities posed by British and American satire from Renaissance Menippea to contemporary television satire. Given the scope, and in keeping with the parameters of the MLA *Options* series, our emphasis is less on tactics for teaching individual works—though of course most essays refer to single works as case studies—and more on teaching the issues that recur and that bind the tradition together.

Especially for newcomers, the sheer scope of satire can seem overwhelming: not only does its history span 2,500 years, but shifts of mode and genre, of technique, and of audience and medium all seem to raise the question of whether there is in fact a tradition of satire at all, or whether we are actually describing a series of unique, if overlapping, forms. Issues that seem paramount in a course on Renaissance verse satire might seem tangential at best in a course on contemporary performative satire. Five intractable questions, though, engage virtually all satires and have received special attention in the satire criticism of the last half century:

definition (what is satire?)
efficacy (does satire do what it claims?)
norms (does it require a set of agreed-upon assumptions, moral or otherwise?)
audience (how does it conceive of and approach its audience?)
politics (what is the relationship between satire and the world?)

Patricia Meyer Spacks has noted satire's "peculiarly troublesome demands on its readers, its insistent generation of uncertainties," warning that "[t]hose who proffer single-minded interpretations often seem victims of the joke" (408). In this introduction, we are not attempting to put these issues to rest but rather to indicate how they can be articulated and brought into the classroom, with particular reference to the essays that follow.

What Is Satire?

A course on satire, more than one on a specific historical period, author, or genre, begins with uncertainty about its object of study. As students soon realize, the works on a satire syllabus can seem an eccentric assortment of poems, prose fiction, drama, and, increasingly, television programs, cartoons, and film that ranges across diverse periods. The first questions that emerge in the classroom are those of definition. Just what is satire? On this matter, students are more apt to be permissive rather than exclusive, imagining satire as a very big tent in which we might find any manner of literary circus tricks—parodies, impersonations, morally transgressive gags, grotesque propositions, and biting critiques of social pieties. Instructors can, however, clarify matters by explaining satire's origins, particularly pointing to a time when satire was a fairly stable genre that itself involved different outlooks toward the world that corresponded to a particular author's unique self-presentation, or what we now see as different varieties of satiric personae.

In one view of its origins, satire seems to have emerged as an acknowledged verse genre. When, in the late first century CE, Quintilian claimed satire for the Romans ("satura quidem tota nostra est" [4: 52]), Lucilius had established its repertoire and reputation, Horace had stabilized it with lashings of urbanity in two books of *sermones*, and Persius had intellectualized it (later Juvenal would give it bite). However unique their development of the persona through which they speak, and however ironic their speech may become as it emerges through this persona, all these authors write in the same mode and in the same form of public and direct verse consisting of between one hundred and four hundred lines. The somewhat parallel Menippean tradition, however, given as it is to hybridity, fully establishes satire as an injectable form, to be introduced to any kind of work to enhance what M. M. Bakhtin calls its "experimental fantasticality" (116).

There are, as some students point out, moments of satire in many works that are not generally given the label of satire, and today, no genre whatsoever proves resistant to satire. We speak of satiric novels, plays, poems, essays, and even autobiographies, but we can also see examples of satiric e-mails, tweets, and Web sites; course descriptions, comment cards, and alumni class notes; films, cartoons, and television shows; and even various book paratexts such as jacket blurbs and notes on a book's author or typeface. Nor does satire now seem restricted to text- or script-based forms. Even the most expansive conception of creative writing as a category cannot contain all the examples of this mode. Satirical personae can be inhabited by real people and, when loosed on the world, can create scenarios in which satire becomes a real-life, real-time possibility. Not only can you get your news from a satirical persona, but you can buy an artisanally sharpened pencil from one or even get your morning latte from a "Dumb Starbucks."

Satire seems to be a victim of its own shape-shifting adaptability. It resists the kind of definition that might lead it to a settled place in a course catalog. As teachers of satire quickly discover, a tidy definition is as elusive as it might be convenient, and students who want clear boundaries around the object of study have to become accustomed to the protean nature of satire. While keeping in mind Charles Knight's admonition that "tight, rigid descriptions are inadequate to the variety and complexity of such forms, but loose, flexible descriptions tell us relatively little about the shape and content of the text we begin to read" (15), we often begin our courses by examining some of the more famous attempts at definition, including those by Northrop Frye ("satire is militant irony" [223]), M. H. Abrams and Geoffrey Galt Harpham ("the literary art of diminishing or derogating a subject by making it ridiculous and evoking toward it attitudes of amusement, contempt, scorn, or indignation" [352]), and Edward Rosenheim ("an attack by means of a manifest fiction upon recognizable historical particulars" [39]).

Offering up different definitions of satire helps make the point that the mode is still, at this moment in its long history, a contested thing. This point can be extended by proceeding by analogy and asking what satire is *like*. The satirist has been emblematized by a host of irritating animals: a porcupine (in satire 3 of Joseph Hall's *Virgidemiarum*), a wasp (in the irascible character Humphrey Wasp from Ben Jonson's *Bartholomew Fair*), and of course that hybrid creature that comes to the study of satire via a false etymology, the satyr. While the word *satire* does not, as many critics have proven, emerge from *satyr*, the false etymology has nonetheless insinuated itself deep into constructions of satire for so long as to now be an integral part of the mode, one that recognizes in the evolution of the mode an early convergence between Roman formal verse satire and the tradition of low Greek comedy. "There is," as one critic says, "satire in the satyric; the figure of the satyr saturates satire" (Gilbert 284). Giambattista Vico, in reasserting the primacy of the shaggy, goat-legged satyr figure, identifies its origin in the "rough and simple" practices of early social entertainments such as hock-cart riding and throwing grapes (331). The dithyrambic chorales of ancient satyr plays provide, for Nietzsche, "a rhetorical figure of disruption and disorder triggered by an overtly aesthetic relation between human beings and their created world" (119).

A 2013 satyr play film satire, *Clark: A Gonzomentary*, confirms that these impulses are still alive. As James Horowitz explains in his essay in this volume, there is a cinematic genealogy by which the figure of the disruptive, oversexed libertine can be traced back through the genre of sex comedy to the Restoration conjunction of satire, masculinity, and satyriasis.

Whether this lineage reveals a clean assimilation of the festive-aggressive mode to the direct and formal mode, the idea of the satirist as a trickster figure using crude methods to identify and test artificial social boundaries is something now ingrained in the way we teach satire. The lustful, dissolute satyr exposed something about the world by bringing his low perspective into higher culture and by refusing to exist comfortably within its constraints, including the constraints of genre. Satire therefore comes to be seen as a variety of reactive literary play that identifies and imitates what the world presents. It preys on anything constructed and contrived. It sits throbbing in the corners of literary history, waiting to absorb and digest from within other genres. It seems especially apt to invade what Bakhtin calls "small genres," such as diatribe, soliloquy, symposium, and romance. If satire is "pre-generic," as Frye would have it, it may be so in several ways: first, because choosing to be satiric is a decision made before the choice of a genre, and second, because as satire addresses a target it has the propensity to generate new genres such as admonition, burlesque, calumny, castigation, character assassination, defamation, derision, derogation, diatribe, exposure, invective, jeu d'esprit, jeremiad, libel, lampoon, pasquinade, philippic, provocation, travesty, screed, slur, squib, and snark. Would the novel have developed into what it has become if it had not satirically asserted itself against the romance and refined its notions of realism against satiric treatments of its earliest models in *Robinson Crusoe* and *Pamela*? If world-changing events are eventually cast as farce, as Karl Marx believed, it's also possible for satire to reverse this process and make its destabilizing absurdity the precondition for getting a genre on its feet.

As critics began to realize the limitations of etymology, definitions of satire began to proceed by epithet. Having largely let go of its claim to being a distinct genre, satire has been understood in the past several hundred years not so much as a thing in itself but an inflection. Failing to successfully account for it as a noun, we offer instead clues by which we may recognize it when we see it, usually through a thicket of affect-based adjectives. Offering to vivify satire rather than define it, Joshua Poole in 1657 proclaims that it is

> girding, biting, snarling, scourging, jerking, lashing, smarting, sharp, tart, rough, invective, censorious, currish, snappish, captious, barking, brawling, carping, fanged, sharp-tooth'd, quipping, jeering, flouting, sullen, rigid, impartial, whipping, thorny, pricking, stinging, sharp-fanged, injurious, reproachful, libellous, harsh, rough-hewn, odious, opprobrious, contumelious, defaming, calumnious. (176)

Twentieth-century thought on satire has largely followed this strategy, so much so that strands of adjectives might be seen to constitute satire's DNA. Satire is for George Test "tumultuous, crowded, aggressive, cynical, pessimistic" (1); for Brian A. Connery and Kirk Combe it is "messy, cluttered, and smelly" (1); for Wyndham Lewis it must be "unfair and single-minded" (452); for Kenneth Burke it is "admonitory, cautionary, curative, corrective, and idealistic" (Rueckert 280); for Ejner Jensen it is "biting, pricking, stinging, stabbing" (102); for Dustin Griffin it is "problematic, open-ended, essayistic, ambiguous in its relationship to history, uncertain in its political effect, resistant to formal closure, more inclined to ask questions than provide answers, and ambivalent about the pleasures it offers" (5). What proves interesting about these lists are not the appropriate subtleties of any particular adjective but that no single one ever seems sufficient. In its intentions and associated feelings, satire is compound and complex in ways that we have still not been able to grasp. Any clarity that can be produced from within this mass of adjectives comes not through further definition but association. Critics separate out the biting and snarling kind and proclaim it Juvenalian, whereas the witty and urbane—always urbane—comes to be seen as Horatian. What is left—the crowded, festive, and open—is often characterized as Menippean or Aristophanic. With these associations in place, what instructors might find most useful is to keep going back to definitions and associations offered at the beginning of the course and refine them against students' growing base of knowledge.

Satire's Moral Norms

As Frye famously asserted, satire's "moral norms are relatively clear, and it assumes standards against which the grotesque and absurd are measured" (223). For satire to attack vice, the thinking goes, it needs to be able to exaggerate, ridicule, and caricature; and how can we recognize distortion if we don't have an idea of clarity? More recent critics echo Frye's claim. As Ruben Quintero remarks, "Satire cannot function without a standard against which readers can compare its subject. We praise with delight what we admire, enjoy, or profit from, and we censure with indignation the despicable or what causes ill because we have an acquired sense of what the world should or might be" (3). This view of satire is perhaps especially alluring in the classroom, where some of satire's unruly energies can be tamed by emphasizing the binaries that satire often presents: William Hogarth's *Gin Lane* next to *Beer Alley*, Alexander Pope next to his dunces, the Houyhnhnms next to the Yahoos, the preacher of Twain's "The War Prayer" in front of the congregation to whom he preaches. In those cases where no positive norm readily announces itself—Nathanael West's *The Day of the Locust*, for instance, or George Saunders's "The Semplica-Girl Diaries"—dutiful students can infer the positive based on the negative, teasing out the *should be* from the satiric presentation of the *is*.

But if this approach to satire might seem to clarify things theoretically, there have always been limits to it in practice, and the notion of satire as embodying accepted norms about virtue and vice reflects not so much the mode of satire itself as the propensity of Augustan satirists in particular to represent themselves within this framework.[7] The division between virtue and vice, though often central to the satirist's self-presentation, frequently seems unsuited to explaining the thrust of many satires. The critical history of book 4 of *Gulliver's Travels* attests to the difficulty of making just these sorts of distinctions. Or as West wrote to the critic Edmund Wilson, "[T]here is nothing to root for in my work and what is even worse, no rooters" (793). Moreover, in the sixty years since Frye made his claim about the moral norms of satire, satires themselves have tended to move in the opposite direction, many of them staking out targets without proposing solutions or positing ideals. The postmodern novel, as Steven Weisenburger contends, "lacks a steady narrative voice, specific 'targets,' and fixed norms or corrective goals" (14); what values it contains are "nomadic and conditional, at best" (6). As John Clement Ball argues in his essay here, postcolonial fiction at times engages normative binaries specifically to undercut them, employing them "as a form of playful opposition and corrective resistance that holds the powerful and the dangerous to account."

Graphic satire often represents the interplay between moral norms and their satiric subversion especially forcefully, helping students understand how the dynamic operates in literary works. We sometimes introduce these issues by showing students the first two pages, one at a time, of volume 1 of Joe Sacco's *Bumf* (2014), a satire of United States' foreign policy so successful in its graphic offenses that images cannot be printed here.

Typically, as our students respond to the first page, their comments proceed from the identification of the text from Genesis and the Edenic panel to some of the odder features of the page: Who is this unshaven, sketchy character who seems to have usurped the role of Genesis's narrator? Is that two-dimensional ooze supposed to represent the spirit of God? What is the tonal effect of the word *Etc.*? Why do Adam and Eve look like a vacationing couple posing strategically behind a bush? The lion is lying down with something that might be a lamb, but the Bible surely doesn't mention a sloth, kangaroo, armadillo, or river otter, does it? Why is there a unicorn? But however confused the Edenic scene may appear, few students are prepared for the shock of the two-page spread that follows.

Many of our undergraduates, as they describe the image and consider Sacco's presentation of this fallen world, are initially drawn to the social ills: violence, squalor, sexual exploitation, alcoholism. But soon they realize the extent of the historical references: 9/11, the sexual abuse scandals of the Catholic Church, goose-stepping Nazis, environmental destruction, the 1968 murder of Vietcong operative Nguyen Van Lem by the South Vietnamese national police chief Nguyen Ngoc Loan. When we then show them Hogarth's *Gin Lane*, they are further intrigued to see how closely Sacco's spread imitates its eighteenth-century predecessor: the hanged man, the maimed and nearly dead drunk, the woman with the wailing child, the polluting chimneys, the urban squalor framed by two buildings, and the bishop and boy all have close equivalents in Hogarth's print. (One student has plausibly suggested that one of Sacco's most alarming additions—the central figure, wide-eyed in horror as his brains are shot out—stands in for the satiric reader.) Understanding satire, students begin to see, will mean taking into account general vices, historical particulars, and intertextual precursors.

At this point in the discussion, the satiric fall from an Edenic past to a squalid and depraved present is painfully obvious, a sequence that can illuminate any number of other satires, such as Evelyn Waugh's *Love among the Ruins*, in which an ancestral estate has been turned into a prison. But what about the unicorn? Just how seriously does Sacco take his Edenic norm? Isn't that vision of the past as illusory as the present is horrific? The question of moral norms is handled differently within different satires, and students need to be ready to see them treated reverentially, skeptically, sardonically, or dismissively.

A salient strain of satire criticism argues for recasting the terms, questioning the binaries upon which the discussion rests. Rather than imagining a satirist standing apart from the target of the satire ("Ask you what Provocation I have had? / The strong antipathy of Good to Bad" [Pope 701; from "Epilogue to the Satires, Dialogue II," lines 197–98]), we might consider what it is that binds them together. Michael Seidel's *Satiric Inheritance* (1979) was one of the first critical works to take this approach: "Satirists generate their own insecurities and then elaborate a fable in which they attempt to displace themselves from what they have generated. . . . By creating the impression that monstrosities are in front of and 'away' from him, the satirist tries to sustain the impression that the monstrous is different from him—that the tub is sufficient to stay the Leviathan. But rarely has that been the case" (11–12). The satirist, in other words, often serves himself in expressing his high-minded outrage, emphasizing his difference from the uncomprehending target. Satire is "the stranger that lives in the basement" (Test 6), the uncanny presence in our familiar spaces.

The most trenchant extension of this line of thought is Fredric Bogel's *The Difference Satire Makes*. "[I]nstead of taking the originating moment of satire to be the satirist's perception, across the gulf of utter rejection, of an object that exists prior to the satiric attack," Bogel suggests that we imagine an "alternative 'founding moment,'" one in which "satirists identify in the world something or someone that is both unattractive and curiously or dangerously like them, or like the culture or subculture that they identify with or speak for, or sympathetic even as it is repellent—something, then, that is *not alien enough*" (41). Bogel's argument has not yet been sufficiently absorbed into scholarship about satire; it is, however, one of the most important books about satire published in the last twenty years, with enormous utility in the classroom, giving students a compelling new way to think about where satire, and irony in particular, comes from. If students have the opportunity to write their own satires—a common assignment in many classes—it is instructive to have them consider their work in Bogel's light: Are your satiric targets essentially other than you, or does your satire create the difference from a target that would otherwise seem dangerously close? Is it distinct, or is it "not alien enough"? Does the satire express preexisting differences, or is it a vehicle for the production of those differences?

The first essay of this collection, by Nicholas Hudson, suggests that satiric texts be grouped according to their level of indeterminacy. As students can readily apprehend, some satires leave readers in little doubt about the target of the satire or the attitude that the satirist hopes to evoke toward it. Others call such normative certitude into doubt and demand a willingness to see the relationship between author and persona as varying and provisional. Other essays complicate the issue of satiric norms differently. As Jonathan Greenberg explains, reading novels such as Aldous Huxley's *Brave New World* (1932), Waugh's *Vile Bodies* (1930), and George Schuyler's *Black No More* (1931) can illuminate how satires present or resist moral norms; read in tandem, they can also point to satiric blind spots, enabling students to understand, for instance, that Huxley's novel almost completely occludes the racial satire that generates Schuyler's novel.

The Efficacy of Satire

Beginning in the lead-up to the 2000 US presidential election, a group calling itself "Billionaires for Bush (or Gore)" began stumping at campaign rallies, its members dressed in tuxedos and ball gowns and carrying signs that read, "Because Economic Inequality Is Not Growing Fast Enough," "Make Social Security Neither," and "Corporations Are People Too." Other groups such as the Yes Men (Jacques Servin and Igor Vamos), who have impersonated corporate spokespersons from Dow Chemical, ExxonMobil, and the World Trade Organization, and the Church of Stop Shopping, whose Reverend Billy (Bill Talen) has preached his gospel in malls, Grand Central Station, and a JP Morgan Chase bank branch, have similarly worked on the fringes of traditional media as they "borrow, beg, and steal the media spotlight if only for a fleeting moment as a means of forwarding their aims" (Day 145). Students are quick to recognize that the tactics and distribution of such culture jamming differ substantially from traditional literary satire, reconfiguring the relationship among satirist, target, and viewer. But the performances also rekindle the perennial question: What, if anything, is the practical effect of satire? What does it *do*?

In raising this question so insistently, satire departs from other literary forms whose social, moral, or political aims tend to be definitionally tangential to the form. With satire, such aims are usually the core of the definition. During the eighteenth century, the tradition of defining satire by its moral effects became commonplace. Notwithstanding the exceptional skepticism of Swift about the efficacy of satire, the clergyman John

Trusler is merely repeating conventional wisdom when in 1766 he defines satire as "a poem, in which, the folly and wickedness of the times, are severely, censured; written with an intent to reform" (Elkin 24). More recently, Howard Weinbrot describes Menippean satire as "a genre for serious people who see serious trouble and want to do something about it—whether to awake a somnolent nation, define the native in contrast to the foreign, protest the victory of darkness, or correct a careless reader" (xi). And Stephen Kercher, writing about 1950s liberal satire, restricts himself to "forms of humorous expression that, by definition, deploy irony to criticize vice and raise awareness. Spurred often by anger or scorn and informed by serious moral concern, satire is humor with a social purpose" (1). Indeed, we have found that for some of our students, often non-English majors, it is precisely this aspect of satire—its avowed aim of getting something done—that makes it appealing to them. Finally, they sigh, literature that *matters*.

But familiarity can also breed skepticism, and astute students will sometimes point out that it is not always clear whether the political punch of satire is heightened or compromised by the very thing that entices students in the first place: its value as entertainment. For Jon Stewart, who recognizes that his demographic consists of the already converted, *The Daily Show* during his tenure approached satire as a mode of expressivity that did not use laughter as a weapon but as a way to cover up the annoyance of offering social commentary. But if it is effective only in electrifying its base, as a politician might say, does it become a poignant emblem of its own impotence? Satire, Stewart comments, "can be sharp and it can be pointed and shaming, but at heart it's impotent and sort of feckless" (Bates 47). The satirist must follow Horace's dictum for all poetry and coat its pills with sugar, but has *The Daily Show* produced such a thoroughgoing combination of mirth and medicine that the former trumps the latter? Or perhaps, by offering up its comfortingly consistent politics in so obvious a way as to serve as a baseline by which to orient the events of the day, *The Daily Show* is as current, clear, and news-rich as prime-time network news broadcasts that persist in the fantasy that journalistic objectivity is achievable.

It is important that teachers not let students be seduced by the story that satire often tells about itself. For all the snarling duplicity with which we characterize satirists, satirists themselves often tell a profoundly sentimental story in which the altruistic author, afflicted by a high-minded outrage, attempts to lay bare, and thereby incite a desire to correct, the folly of the greatest percentage of mankind, appealing to a timeless, consistent, and unwavering sense of right and wrong, hoping that despite all the times satire has proved ineffectual in the past, this time will be different. Equipped with a mirror and a whip, the satirist cannot help but castigate the world that obtrudes all too insistently, clearly, and provocatively. Thus, for instance, H. L. Mencken wrote of the short story author Ambrose Bierce, "Doomed to live in a country in which, by God's will, honesty is rare and courage is still rarer and honor is almost unknown . . . he fell upon the mountebanks, great and small, in a Berserker fury, thus to sooth and secure his own integrity. That integrity, as far as I can make out, was never betrayed by compromise. Right or wrong, he always stuck to the truth as he saw it" (252).

Those satirists who claim to be reforming the world—a claim few satirists today would make without qualification—are not, of course, simply describing a state of affairs; they are crafting their own personae, and behind satirists' protestations of moral aims often lurks the desire to forestall criticism of their satire as spiteful, malicious, indecorous, or unchristian. Understood in the most reductive form, the claim that satire changes the world quickly becomes ridiculous. Has the tradition of Menippean satire lessened the amount of ponderous erudition? How many readers have become less prideful after reading *Gulliver's Travels*? Did *Dr. Strangelove* alter the proliferation of atomic weapons? Has Gary Shteyngart's *Super Sad True Love Story* retarded the loss of privacy, the addictive consumption of digital and visual stimulation, or the desire for eternal life? It is tempting to side with Wyndham Lewis, who states categorically that "the greatest satire *cannot* be moralistic at all: if for no other reason, because no mind of the first order, expressing itself in art, has ever itself been taken in, nor consented to take in others, by the crude injunctions of any purely moral code" (5). A survey of the history of satire theory and criticism reveals a tendency to approach the definition of satire at large with a level of credulity about its motives that few would grant to individual satirists.

Particularly when it comes to contemporary satires, students are likely to have strong opinions about what kind of work they perform. Though mistrustful of overly facile claims about satire's corrective potential, many of the essays in this volume suggest that rather than dismissing satire's political effect altogether, the terms of that effect be clarified. Amber Day and Sophia McClennen both argue that if individual satires may not have measurable outcomes—"any attempt to attribute that sort of causality to one isolated text—or conversely, to *expect* a political text to unilaterally start a revolution—is absurd" (Day 21)—one effect of satires like *The Colbert Report*, *The Daily Show*, the films of Michael Moore, and the culture jamming of the Yes Men has been to alter the terms of political debate. When Colbert establishes his own super PAC or testifies about immigration reform at a congressional hearing, he affects public perception of what is newsworthy. When, in the segment of his show called "The Wørd," he coins terms such as *truthiness* or *wikiality*, he joins earlier satirists who have bestowed to English other words and phrases—*utopia*, *yahoo*, *catch-22*, *newspeak*, *doublethink*, *brave new world*—whose origins most students could not identify but which help them understand their politics and society. Rather than futilely preaching to the choir, contemporary satirists can be seen as reinforcing and energizing already existent political groupings.

With satires that are more chronologically or culturally distant, by contrast, it can be difficult for students to appreciate the stakes of satire, and teachers will want to historicize claims about satire's efficacy, considering how both critical terms and satire itself has shifted. Several of the essays here, especially those by David Alff, Kirk Combe, and James Horowitz, offer suggestions for linking contemporary and historical satire to illuminate how claims about satire's moral, cultural, and political effects have developed over time.

That the world would respond to satire with contrition and self-correction is unlikely, as the most recent transhistorical discussions of the mode have noted. Griffin's influential "critical reintroduction" of satire rethinks precisely satire's moral dimension, what he feels is a commonplace of mid-century satirical criticism, choosing to emphasize instead its capacity for "inquiry and provocation" as well as "display and play"—authorial activities that are open-ended and ateleological. Several contributors to this volume note that satire's aim is often not to change behavior but to alter perception. Drawing on her experience teaching at Xavier University of Louisiana, a Catholic and historically black college, Robin Runia describes how her students explore "power differentials and inequality rooted in age, race, gender, or economic status" by writing an imitation of Jane Collier's *An Essay on the Art of Ingeniously Tormenting*. John Clement Ball, meanwhile, argues that in the context of postcolonial satire, "teaching satire as a mode of exploratory inquiry rather than a sure-footed answer—as a process of responding rather than the product of a response—can make it more palatable, more interesting, and more complex."

Laughter, Anger, Audience

In his *Naturalis Historia*, Pliny the Elder describes an admittedly dubious episode from the middle of the sixth century in which Hipponax of Ephesus, an aggressive verse satirist, so brutally savaged a sculptor who made an unflattering caricature of him that, upon reading Hipponax's bitter verses ("amaritudinem carminum"), the sculptor was compelled to end his life (10). The story constitutes a familiar fantasy of satire's potency: the physical underdog, tired of getting sand kicked in his face, finds in words a powerful weapon for redressing a power imbalance in the world and gets the last laugh. But words, however biting, seldom result in so final a form of retribution, and it may be that the fantasy of retribution is more alluring to the audience than it is worrisome to the target. Satire itself frequently appeals to the unspeakable pleasures humans take in witnessing vengeance enacted on others, in this case those who are guilty only of their own form of satire. In fact, satire presents us with unspeakability in several ways that impact our teaching. Often our responses are deeply troubling, whether students realize this or do not. Satire may offer something that is scandalous, grotesque, or vicious, and it may compound that problem by presenting scandalousness, grotesquerie, or viciousness in a risible manner that prompts a more or less uneasy laughter. Our laughter frequently shades into vindictiveness, and we take comfort in the notion that we are rooting for an underdog satirist in a real-world contest.

In this respect, little has changed in the past 1800 years since Pliny recounted this dubitable vision of satire's triumph in hazing. Consider the cartoon by Kevin Kallaugher in response to the 2015 attack at the offices of the satirical magazine *Charlie Hebdo* (fig. 1). Satire in this case places itself in the relatively innocent position of a hectoring nuisance, hurling a rock and a defiant laugh at the powerful guerrilla of Hate, who responds predictably, but still shockingly, with deadly force. The laughter itself, however, cannot be eradicated as easily as the satirist or disregarded as easily as his rock; it hovers in the air, impervious to violence until Hate is ironically crushed in the attempt to destroy the trace of laughter, and the resurrected Satire has the last laugh. A satire's effect—and in this case its associated affect—does not inhere simply within an interpersonal battle and therefore cannot be put back in the bottle. It is easy to overlook how such fantasies of satire's efficacy designedly portray the aggressor as victim. Just as Hipponax's satire responds decisively to another kind of satire, here one form of aggression responds to a different form of aggression. Neither

Figure 1. © Kevin KAL Kallaugher, *The Economist*, www.kaltoons.com.

entity is precisely innocent—nor is Kallaugher, who, with the pretense of attacking an abstract entity, appears to be speaking only about the general concept of hate, when nearly every reader would be able to apply the label "Hate" to specific agents in the world. (Interestingly, however much hatred might give rise to satire, it is a relatively infrequent target.)

When satire presents a target smaller than humanity in general, it necessarily gives offense. Most satire constitutes a surgical strike against a narrowly defined target, the very precision of which is understood as hostility, at which point laughter comes to be seen as a process of defamation or even humiliation leveled against certain social groups. When satire thus becomes sharper, so do our metaphors for describing it. For Joseph Addison and Richard Steele, satire conceals "a dagger under her garment" (63); for Abrams and Harpham, it "uses laughter as a weapon" (352); for Edward and Lillian Bloom, it slices "calculatingly like a surgeon wielding his lancet" (146). Other definitions get across a similar point by using the words *deride* and *ridicule*, which, though they acknowledge the idea of a maligned target, already contain in their etymological makeup the idea of directed laughter. "Savage indignation" motivates satire as much as other forms of aggression, and though there is a tradition of satirists insisting that one "must not think that a satiric style allows of scandalous and brutish words" (Dillon 213), more typical is Nathaniel Hawthorne's characterization of satire as the devil's spit. David Worcester describes satire as the "engine of anger" (18), by which we might be able to more clearly see it not only as a form that runs on anger but also a producer or generator of that anger; "satire is by nature hostile" (Elkin 1), making an individual's enjoyment of it suspect. Perhaps it is the case, as W. H. Auden claims in "Heresies," that "we are not, any of us, very nice" (208).

In the classroom, however, the truism that satire uses laughter as a weapon can confuse the roles of author and audience. Whose laughter is inflicting the damage, the satire's or the reader's? And through what model of agency can our responses be thought of as a weapon at all? Dryden articulates this untoward pleasure when he claims that Juvenal, with his sneering attacks on persons and groups, "is of a more vigorous and Masculine Wit [than Horace], he gives me as much Pleasure as I can bear" (2: 84). When we laugh, it is in response to watching a rhetorical weapon be used on another—one who, though fictionalized, resembles some person or thing in the world that the satirist wishes to attack.

We may recognize, with varying degrees of pleasure, what satire attacks, but who are "we"? Because satire focuses our view toward or against something in the world we inhabit, students need a more precise sense of audience, identity, and the ethical dimensions of the role they occupy relative to the ridiculed target. On the one hand, satire seems to consolidate a readerly community. As Edith Wharton comments regarding her friendship with Henry James, "The real marriage of true minds is for any two people to possess a sense of humor or irony pitched in exactly the same key, so that their joint glances on any subject cross like interarching searchlights" (qtd. in Booth 13). At the same time, of course, satire is also working as a solvent upon our notion of audience, creating a gap between those who get the joke and those who don't, between those who laugh and those who do not. The laughter (or lack of it) is not reducible to politics or ideology. Barry Blitt's July 2008 *New Yorker* cover, entitled "The Politics of Fear," which depicts then United States presidential candidate Barack Obama as a Muslim and his wife, Michelle, as a black militant, is a case in point; the cartoon divided the magazine's loyal readership, prompting longtime subscribers to cancel their subscriptions and generating deep disagreements even among people who shared a political outlook.

Audiences, as we know, are not monolithic entities; they are plural and politically diverse, particularly in the age of globalization, in which satire's reach can exceed its audience's grasp. Satire is ubiquitous and transnational, but responses to it can identify divergences in cultural norms.

Audiences change depending on location and historical moment, and they possess a knowledge rooted in those particularities; the "awareness" that satire raises constitutes a distinct perspective on the world against existing and notoriously perishable ideas that are, in their specificity, difficult to reproduce for students. Our sense of the importance of understanding the diversity of audiences in teaching satire is reflected in our penultimate section of essays, "Satire, Affect, and Student Response." There is pedagogical value in forcing the recognition that students may be included in satire's construction of its foolish victims. In fact, as Peter Schmidt believes, such recognition is especially necessary when discussing the portions of our humanity that we have ceded to technology. And Christopher Vilmar demonstrates just how resistant students can be to satires about possessive individualism.

But what do we do when satire alienates a portion of its audience? Given that offensiveness is tactical in many satires, in many cases specifically designed to elicit laughter, how do we deal with offense in the classroom? What do we do when one student's laughter is met by another's scorn, discomfort, or anger? Are Swift's scatological poems funny? What does the laughter (or unease) elicited by a work such as Schuyler's *Black No More* reveal about students' understandings of race and African American history? In her essay on the subgenre of the "rape joke," Danielle Bobker takes on such challenges directly, positioning her argument first in Restoration works that deal with rape and then in our present pedagogical moment, in which satire's humorous presentation leaves it unable, in the view of many, to approach serious concerns about sexual violence, particularly in the classroom. Because so-called rape jokes are not always satirical, the student must be in a position to determine and sort through the purposes of subtle kinds of affective response that pass under the name of "humor."

Politics and Representation

Our own general satire classes have tended to attract students who are as interested in politics as in literature, so it is not surprising that they are attuned to the political leanings of the satirists they find on the syllabi. Depending on the films and television shows they watch, the magazines they read, and the Internet sites they visit, many of them enter class with the preconception that satire will bend reliably to the left or the right. We sometimes introduce the issue by sharing with them the *Doonesbury* strip from 3 August 2014, in which the radio commentator Mark Slackmeyer poses the question, "Ever wonder why conservative comedy is so unfunny?" His answer, that "the point of satire is to comfort the afflicted by afflicting the comfortable" is the same that Garry Trudeau has given: "Satire punches up, against authority of all kinds, the little guy against the powerful. Great French satirists like Molière and Daumier always punched up, holding up the self-satisfied and hypocritical to ridicule. Ridiculing the nonprivileged is almost never funny—it's just mean" ("Abuse"). Students are not hard-pressed to think of examples of satirists from John Oliver to Stephen Colbert who engage in the sort of satire Trudeau advocates. (Most students these days have not seen Warren Beatty's 1998 film *Bulworth*, but it is worth playing excerpts for them.) But no matter how satisfying (or infuriating) Trudeau's certainty might seem, courses on satire need to make clear that the historical record is much murkier. Teachers can point to individual conservative satirists such as William Gifford, editor of the *Anti-Jacobin*; Evelyn Waugh, a staunch opponent of the Second Vatican Council; or Wyndham Lewis, an attacker of "left-wing orthodoxy." They can examine a single period such as the eighteenth century, in which, as Ashley Marshall claims, "we can find both defenses and fierce denunciations of the status quo" (297).

Perhaps most fruitfully, teachers can pose the question of how, if satire always "punches up," as Trudeau claims, we are to understand the long and conflicted tradition of antifeminist satire from Juvenal's sixth satire onward, along with the relative exclusion of women from the satiric canon. Female wits such as Aphra Behn, Mary Wortley Montagu, and Dorothy Parker have appeared sporadically on satire syllabi for some time, particularly when their wit is engaged in ongoing satiric debates about gender, but most critical narratives and syllabi still include few women.[8] Important and accessible women writers with satirical leanings—such as Mary Jones (1707–78), Mary Leapor (1722–46), Ivy Compton-Burnett (1884–1969), Dawn Powell (1896–1965), Elizabeth Bowen (1899–1973), Stella Gibbons (1902–89), Mary McCarthy (1912–89), and Bernardine Evaristo (1959–)—are infrequently taught, while more canonical figures, including Jane Austen, Virginia Woolf, Djuna Barnes, Flannery O'Connor, Margaret Atwood, and Doris Lessing, tend to be overlooked within the satirical context. Catherine Ingrassia's essay here focuses on the dialogue form of satire, as it constitutes a way of understanding the place of women in the satiric construction of gender and helps to identify the contributions of female satirists who have largely been left out of the history of the mode, and Matthew Stratton's essay considers how works by Dorothy Parker and Anita Loos demonstrate how "authors can repurpose satire's conservative gender norms to serve a literary and political feminism that demands both economic and sexual equality."

One way to introduce students to the real-world implications of satire is for teachers to explore instances in which satire has found itself at odds with the law or has, as Frank Palmeri's essay shows, contorted itself into acceptable forms so as to avoid censorship. Flagitious published satires in early modern London, for example, were burned in the wake of the Bishops' Ban of 1599, which did not last a year before "satire" again began to appear unabashedly on the title pages of printed drama. More often, it has been not the work but the satirist who has been censored. While satire's ability to achieve its implied ends is questioned by most scholars, it is true that satire can bring real-world consequences, primarily for those who create it. Most in peril at present are those drawing and publishing satirical cartoons: Remon Wang in China, newspaper editor Ali Reza Eshraghi in Iran, Ali Ferzat in Syria, Kudzanai Chiurai in Zimbabwe, Kurt Westergaard at *Jyllands-Posten* in Denmark, and, of course, the Parisian cartoonists at *Charlie Hebdo.* Satire's indirection has at times made it resistant to prosecution. Legal proceedings against satirists reveal a perception that satire's harm must be clear, including in cases of defamation. The criminal case against the British satirist Michael Breen for defamation of the Korean electronics company Samsung was ultimately dismissed by the judge on the grounds that there was "no victim." The aggression of satire has been regulated by censorship and libel laws, the constraints that give satire its indistinct shape and account for its protean nature. Even the label "satire" can itself constitute a defense. We now see legal protection accorded in the United States to satire and any other "distorted imitation" under the First Amendment.

But addressing the question of politics requires instructors to raise the vexed question of satiric mimesis: what exactly is the relationship between satire and the world it represents? Very broadly, one might distinguish between two competing strands of satire scholarship that emerged in the two decades after World War II. As Griffin has usefully characterized them, the Chicago and Yale schools took fundamentally different approaches. On one side, Yale critics, including Maynard Mack, Alvin Kernan, Robert C. Elliott, and Ronald Paulson, presented satire as a rhetorical work of art, a self-contained imaginative space with its own logic and formal structure. Such an approach rewarded close reading, brought a certain respectability to satire, and proved especially productive in the classroom, where the wit and imagery of a work could be appreciated without extensive knowledge of a satirist's biographical or historical context. On the other side, critics associated with the University of Chicago, especially Sheldon Sacks and Edward Rosenheim, responded that it was precisely this historical context that gives satire its energy and historical punch.

Needless to say, it would be a mistake to teach satire as if it were *merely* rhetorical or *simply* historical (and none of the critics just mentioned was so formulaic). The very pleasure of the form emerges from the slippage between the one and the other, from watching Pope's dunces or Trudeau's presidents call to mind real individuals while they simultaneously stand in for foibles, vices, and waywardness that exceed historical referent. Of course, making students aware of both rhetorical art and historical reference, not to mention theorizing the relationship between the two, is easier said than done. In many cases, it is the artful nature of contemporary satire and the historical context of earlier satire that can be especially challenging for students, and the essays in the fourth section of this volume suggest ways to raise students' understanding of history without embalming satire as an ephemeral timepiece.

Students who have considered these questions of satiric mimesis will be in a better position to think critically about an especially vibrant form of satire: the satiric news programs they often already enjoy. Ever since it was a possibility, we have wanted our satire delivered as regularly and freshly as our news. For the conscientious Londoner, Addison and Steele's *Spectator* papers were to be presented "as a part of the tea-equipage" and consumed along with breakfast (40). Satiric news was an inevitability, especially as news and opinion became more obviously different, if still for many interchangeable. Given its emphasis on politics and history in progress—its intense presentness—satire has, not surprisingly, insinuated itself into our news genres, starting with newspapers such as France's *Le Canard enchaîné* and extending from Canada's *The Whistler Answer*, Ireland's *Waterford Whispers News*, and America's *The Onion* to far-reaching online satirical news blogs such as *The Daily Currant*. As current events began to arrive even more immediately than print could offer them, we began to get our reports live from the mouth of a broadcast journalist.

Satire, sensing the opportunity to work through a more vivid persona, quickly followed suit in the borrowed livery of the news anchor, starting with the so-called satire boom in 1960s England and its seminal program *That Was the Week That Was*, which inspired Canada's *This Hour Has Seven*

Days and, later, *Saturday Night Live*'s "Weekend Update" in the 1970s and HBO's *Not Necessarily the News* in the 1980s. The form became most stable, and to some insidious, with *The Daily Show*, out of which emerged *The Colbert Report* and *Last Week Tonight with John Oliver.* Radio programs devoted to a satirical presentation of news events are, paradoxically, more recent than their equivalents on television, from BBC Radio 4's *Week Ending*, *On the Hour*, and *The Now Show* to CBC's *This Is That* to NPR's *Wait Wait . . . Don't Tell Me!* in which a segment called "Bluff the Listener" challenges contestants to distinguish between fictional and genuine news stories. The urgency of quickly dealing with certain topics makes these programs as transitory and perishable as the news they fixate on. Satire's sell-by date creeps ever earlier, and once it is past its prime, the historical moment of its first airing needs to be actively re-created, a task increasingly more difficult to do as social media unmoor satires from their original context, shorten them into device-ready formats, and splinter the very idea of viewership into tiny demographic niches.

The Way Satire Is Taught Now

Readers familiar with other volumes in the MLA Options series may notice the lack of a section labeled "Texts," which generally offers guidance about teaching specific literary works that fall within the volume's purview. We have chosen instead to foreground specific techniques, obstacles, challenges, and issues that emerge in a wide range of works, asking our contributors to introduce texts as case studies, not as ends in themselves. Thus, though the index will point toward specific works, readers will find the names of individual satires or satirists in few of the essay titles. To understand the logic behind this organizational choice, it is helpful to understand the composition of most current syllabi.

In an examination of forty-two satire syllabi that we conducted in 2012, we found a few extremely canonical satires clustered at the front, followed by a statistical "long tail" of satires that appear only on one or two syllabi (fig. 2). For purposes of legibility, we have limited this chart to satires that appear on at least ten percent of the syllabi, omitting another 270 satires that appear less frequently. The first thing that catches attention here is that the top eight satires all come from the long eighteenth century, Rochester to Byron, with Swift and Pope accounting for six of them. Even when we extend the count out to twenty-two, we find that of those, only six fall outside the long eighteenth century: Bierce's *The*

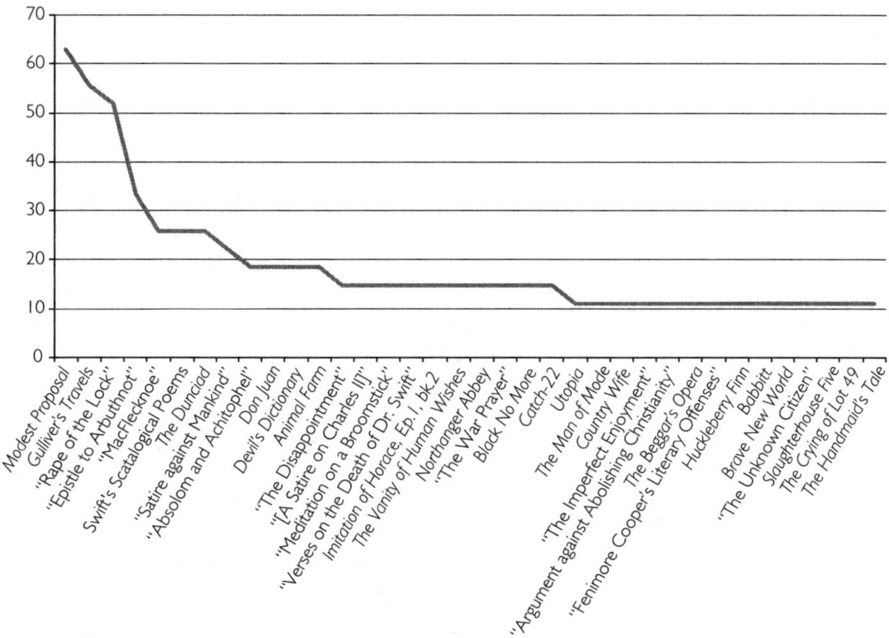

Figure 2. Frequency of texts on syllabi of satire courses, expressed as a percentage. Based on a survey conducted by the editors in 2012.

Devil's Dictionary, Orwell's *Animal Farm*, Twain's "The War Prayer" (his shortest and, perhaps not coincidentally, most popular work in our sampling), Schuyler's *Black No More*, and Joseph Heller's *Catch-22*. From this vantage, the eighteenth century begins to seem not just a high point of satire in English but the only point.

And yet, while the Restoration and eighteenth century undeniably loom large in the satiric pantheon, when we turn from satires to *satirists*, the picture is differently nuanced. Here, Swift continues to dominate the scene, appearing nearly 85 percent of the time, followed by Pope at 59 percent and Twain at 44 percent (fig. 3). Long eighteenth-century British satirists are now outnumbered by satirists from other periods and evenly numbered by Americans. Indeed, what becomes clear is that the canon of satire is less dominated by eighteenth-century satires than by a small number of eighteenth-century satirists: Rochester, Dryden, Pope, Swift, and sometimes Samuel Johnson. Significant satirists such as John Oldham (1653–83) and Charles Churchill (1731–64) are almost unheard

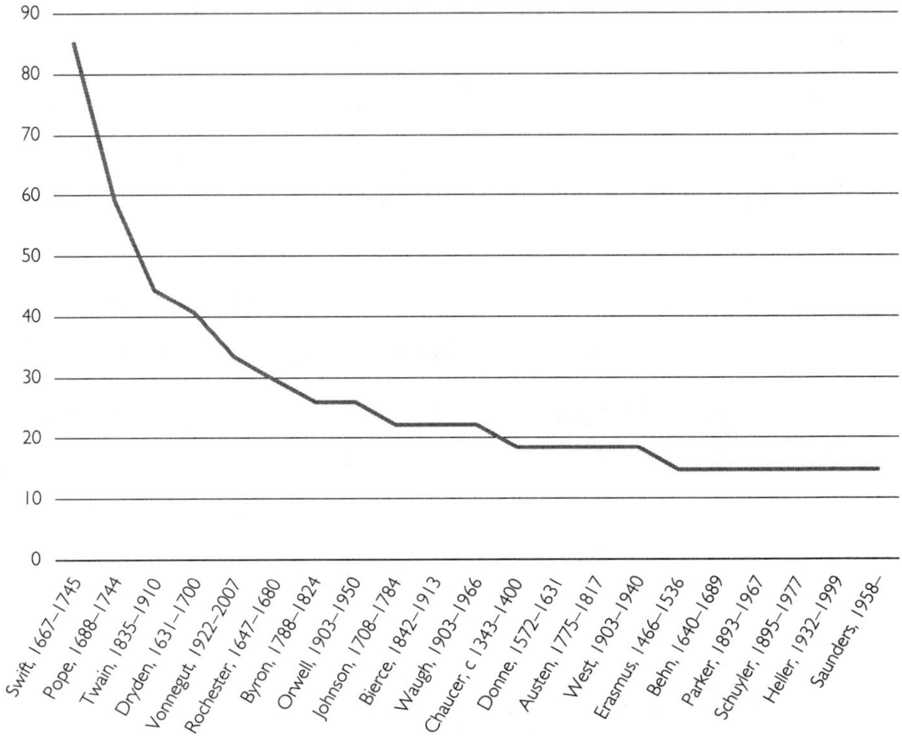

Figure 3. Frequency of satirists on syllabi of satire courses, expressed as a percentage. Based on a survey conducted by the editors in 2012.

of, and even major figures like Henry Fielding (1707–54) and John Gay (1685–1732) appear less often than one might expect. We can also see that for writers like Twain, there is little consensus about which works to teach, so that, though none of his satires appears on more than four syllabi, his works taken together appear near the top of the charts.

Compared with survey courses or genre courses, satire-specific courses remain wedded to a relatively small number of texts and authors with a rich critical tradition, while allowing themselves idiosyncratic excursions into relatively uncharted textual waters. Given the cluster at the fore-end and the long tail at the rear, a volume organized around texts would be only moderately useful. Instructors interested in the major satirists, including Swift and Pope, can refer to MLA volumes devoted exclusively to their works, and any attempt to address works in the long tail would inevitably touch on only a few of the many selections that instructors find compelling. Often, and for good reason, those idiosyncratic additions to a syllabus come from contemporary satires, whether literary or visual; yet it is the contemporary satires that become dated most quickly, even as the problems they pose reemerge in other works. Moreover, as extensive as this volume's scope seems, we are acutely aware of major omissions in terms of texts represented. By its very scope it excludes a direct discussion of Roman verse satire and early Menippean forms, seventeenth-century French satire, and twentieth-century Russian satire, to name just a few prominent occasions of thc mode, and the call for submissions yielded no proposals in Asian American, Chicanx, and British Romantic literature.

Volume Contents and Structure

The essays in this volume are disposed into six parts: "Definitions and Techniques," "Genre and Mode," "Historical, Political, and Cultural Contexts," "Visual Satire," "Satire, Affect, and Student Response," and "Satire across the Curriculum." The structure will allow teachers different entry points. Given the challenges of recognition inherent to satire, the contributors in part 1, "Definitions and Techniques," offer insights for framing classroom discussions of satire by establishing some pedagogically effective categories (open vs. closed, public vs. private), analyzing some common techniques (parody, irony, burlesque), and locating specific sites of meaning (the page, the body, the dialogue). Because satire has a complex relation to genre as it is traditionally understood within the study of poetry, the teachers in part 2, "Genre and Mode," seek to approach satire as it manifests within performative genres (film, drama), subgenres (romance, dystopian novel), and modes or approaches characteristic of satire that call our categories of genre and subgenre into question (Menippeanism, apocalyptic visions). Part 3, "Historical, Political, and Cultural Contexts," examines the networks of power that satire always engages or reveals. These essays are framed by the tension between the critical methodologies of formalism and historicism, which themselves can be elucidated by satire and its early staging of materialism in contrast to spiritualism. Because its distribution is uneven and its uses so subject to abuse, political power, broadly conceived, both innervates and enervates a good portion of the best satire and dictates the parameters within which truth is conceived and run to exhaustion. This part offers approaches to conspicuous forms of politics, such as that which upholds or challenges nation-states and empires, as well as the less visible forms that govern gender relations, cultural access, and knowledge production.

Part 4, "Visual Satire," proceeds from the assumption, asserted by its lead essay, that satire is fundamentally connected to vision, not exclusively in the obvious ways that have precipitated certain visual forms (comic strips, cartoon sitcoms, satiric news), but also in the ways that satire approaches certain mediums (novels, newsprint, television) and places their ideological commitments into view. Part 5, "Satire, Affect, and Student Response," follows from the previous section in that it foregrounds the issue of perspective that satire often addresses visually, but the focus of this section is on audience and even more specifically on helping students realize their place in viewing satire, especially when that view is from within the satire. If part 2 discusses how we identify satires, this section examines how we identify with satires, either with the author or victim, categories that are often troublesome when used to structure courses. Teachers here tear down the myth of the monolithic audience by imposing distinctions that separate out classes of audience and redrawing the boundaries in ways that allow students to understand their own ideological position relative to victimology, offense, taste, elitism, technology, etc. The vectors of this realization are determined by affect, the examination of which helps to clarify where we stand when we experience mirth, offense, confusion, or irritation. Our sixth part, "Satire across the Curriculum," gives recommendations for a variety of courses that can benefit from incorporating satirical texts: composition courses, gateway courses for beginning literature students, historical period survey courses, the upper-level American literature course.

How to Read This Book

When read in order, the essays in this book move from general issues relevant to the widest range of teachers to specific contexts in which teachers present satire as a way of supplementing the goals of courses structured by other means. Contributors may approach a topic with specific test cases that emerge in a certain historical period, but the pedagogical discussions in each are relevant across boundaries. We have attempted to structure individual sections by this same logic, with the most general essays followed by those specific to certain common pedagogical aims and settings. The number of categories imposed on these essays reflects what we feel are the most relevant concerns that emerge in the classroom when satire is, in whatever proportion, the object of study.

Given our emphasis on large-scale pedagogical issues, there are many smaller conversations taking place across the volume. While the table of contents lays out what we feel is the most intuitive structure of the volume, we believe some readers will be served by following alternative paths through the book. Several essays offer framing concepts and useful binaries for imposing structure on an entire course or individual discussion: opened vs. closed (Hudson), human vs. inhuman (Deutsch), public vs. private (Ingrassia), spiritual vs. material (Bogel), manifest vs. latent (Fulton), word vs. image (Conlon), intent vs. effect (Day), Horatian vs. Juvenalian (Henry), norm vs. deviation (Ball), class vs. the individual (Vilmar), getting it vs. not getting it (Nace), trivial vs. nontrivial (Day, Bobker), fiction vs. discourse (Greenberg). Readers may find it helpful in lieu of a definition of satire to contrast satire itself with certain forms, subsets, and even techniques with which it is often indistinguishable. Thus we have satire positioned within and/or against mockery (Stevens, Alff, McClennen), carnivalesque and Menippea (Prescott, Stevens, Soper, Schmidt), commentary (Combe, McClennen), and caricature (Conlon, Palmeri, Vilmar, Runia). While there are essays directly on parody (Stevens) and satiric norms (Hudson), one might begin with Stevens on parody and follow by exploring the topic as it emerges in essays by Henry, Alff, and Day; or one might, after reading Hudson on satire's relation to norms, follow the thread that goes through Deutsch, Stratton, and Ball.

One might, alternatively, follow conversations that occur at different points in the teaching experience: some pose questions for students to consider within a class (Davis, Ingrassia, Greenberg, Bobker, Mazella, Day), while others pose questions about what instructors can accomplish in a class (Domingo, McClennen, Nace, Dickson-Carr). Other essays propose specific assignments and classroom exercises that can function within many different course structures (Domingo, Greenberg, Schmidt, Santesso, Nace, Runia). Some focus on close reading/critical thinking (Davis, Domingo, Stratton, Mazella, Wesp), while others aim to help situate satire within literary history (Prescott, Stratton, Dickson-Carr) or intellectual history (Combe, Bogel).

While this collection at large looks to deemphasize period specificity in teaching satire, some readers nonetheless may find it helpful to enter into the discussion from familiar ground and follow the variety of pathways laid out. Thus early modernists may wish to begin with Prescott, Horowitz, Bobker, and Combe; eighteenth-centuryists with Ingrassia,

Weinbrot, Bogel, and Rounce; nineteenth-centuryists with Fulton and Palmeri; twentieth-centuryists with Greenberg, Stratton, Soper, Vilmar, and Dickson-Carr; and those interested in twenty-first-century satires with Day and Nace. Certain essays may appeal to readers focusing on British contexts (Stevens, Weinbrot, Prescott, Alff, Domingo, Deutsch), those focusing on American contexts (Fulton, Ball, Day, Schmidt, Palmeri, Soper, Henry, Vilmar, Stratton, Wesp, Dickson-Carr), or those looking for useful ways and examples to combine both national contexts (Hudson, Conlon, Bobker, Greenberg). Still other readers may want to begin with satirists who, according to our studies, appear frequently on syllabi: Swift (Deutsch, Ingrassia, Domingo), Pope (Stevens, Weinbrot), Twain (Fulton), and Colbert (McClennen, Santesso, Day).

Those teaching courses that do not focus exclusively on satire might find ways to include satire in classes or units that take up common course-structuring concerns: race (Stevens, Greenberg, Dickson-Carr, Ball, Schmidt), gender (Ingrassia, Deutsch, Bobker, Stratton), sexuality (Prescott, Horowitz, Greenberg, Henry, Bobker), critical theory (Hudson, Combe, Ball, Conlon), cultural studies (Alff, Greenberg, Bogel, Combe, Stratton, Ball, Soper, Day, Wesp, Dickson-Carr), globalization (Schmidt, Combe, Ball, Runia), media studies (Conlon, Henry, Greenberg, Day, McClennen), and history of the book (Fulton, Domingo, Rounce, Palmeri). Those who teach courses on the novel can be enriched by Prescott, Greenberg, Stratton, Ball, Palmeri, and Vilmar; those teaching poetry by Deutsch, Ingrassia, Rounce, and Combe; film by Hudson, Horowitz, Henry, Combe, and Nace; and those teaching performance in general by Horowitz, Bobker, and Nace. Whatever the purview of their course, we hope instructors will benefit from the series of bibliographies they can find in the resources section.

Notes

1. For a discussion of satire as public pedagogy, particularly as that concept emerges in the work of Henry Giroux, see Sophia A. McClennen, *America According to Colbert: Satire as Public Pedagogy* (2011).

2. Dustin Griffin provides a very useful account of this history of satire criticism in *Satire: A Critical Reintroduction*, pp. 28–34.

3. See Darryl Dickson-Carr's *African American Satire* (2001), Dana Williams's *African American Humor, Irony, and Satire* (2007), Glenda Carpio's *Laughing Fit to Kill* (2008), Derek Maus and James Donahue's *Post-Soul Satire* (2014), Ball's *Satire and the Postcolonial Novel* (2009), Johan Nilsson's *American Film Satire in the 1990s* (2013), Robin Mookerjee's *Transgressive Fiction* (2013),

David Gunkel and Ted Gournelos's *Transgression 2.0* (2012), McClennen's *America According to Colbert* (2011), McClennen and Remy M. Maisel's *Is Satire Saving Our Nation?* (2014), Amber Day's *Satire and Dissent* (2011), Kerry Soper's *Garry Trudeau* (2008) and *We Go Pogo* (2012), Guillermo Hernández's *Chicano Satire* (1991), Geoffrey Baym and Jeffrey P. Jones's *News Parody and Political Satire across the Globe* (2012), Jonathan Greenberg's *Modernism, Satire, and the Novel* (2011), and Matthew A. Henry's The Simpsons, *Satire, and American Culture* (2012).

4. See Fredric V. Bogel's *The Difference Satire Makes* (2001), Christopher Yu's *Nothing to Admire: The Politics of Poetic Satire from Dryden to Merrill* (2003), Charles Knight's *The Literature of Satire* (2004), Howard D. Weinbrot's *Menippean Satire Reconsidered: From Antiquity to the Eighteenth Century* (2005), and Frank Palmeri's *Satire in Narrative: Petronius, Swift, Gibbon, Melville, and Pynchon* (1990).

5. Amber Day likens culture jamming, which was first theorized by Mark Dery in 1993, to the situationists' technique of *détournement*. She explains, "*Culture jamming* roughly refers to the repurposing, deconstructing, or hijacking of mass culture, using the media as means to critique the media. The term was first coined by Negativland, which has become known since the late 1980s for cutting up songs and subverting their original meanings, for instance, using snippets of advertising jingles for Pepsi to disparage the product in an album called *Dispepsi*" (159).

6. Jane Ogborn and Peter Buckroyd's slim Cambridge Contexts in Literature volume, *Satire*, contains excerpts that are so short as to be unhelpful in the classroom. At the other end, Joe Queenan's *The Malcontents: The Best Bitter, Cynical, and Satirical Writing in the World* presents fuller excerpts of canonical works but, lacking annotations, aims at a general audience, not students.

7. This point is made most forcibly by P. K. Elkin in *The Augustan Defence of Satire*. See too Michael Seidel: "The satirist as a moral scourge is the imposition of an ethical fabrication upon a literary structure, perhaps an indication of how things may be forced into proper form but hardly a guarantee of how things necessarily shake up" (3).

8. The most extensive critique of the existing canon of eighteenth-century satire is Ashley Marshall's *The Practice of Satire in England, 1658–1770*. Other scholars have made a more sustained critique specifically on the grounds of gender. See especially Felicity A. Nussbaum's *The Brink of All We Hate* (1984), Paula R. Backscheider and Catherine Ingrassia's *British Women Poets of the Long Eighteenth Century* (2009), Claudia Thomas Kairoff's "Gendering Satire: Behn to Burney" (2007), and Devoney Looser's *Women Writers and Old Age in Great Britain, 1750–1850* (2008).

Works Cited

Abrams, M. H., and Geoffrey Galt Harpham. *A Glossary of Literary Terms*. 11th ed., Cengage Learning, 2015.

Addison, Joseph, and Richard Steele. *Selected Essays from* The Tatler, The Spectator, *and* The Guardian. Edited by Daniel McDonald, Bobbs-Merrill, 1973.

Auden, W. H. "Heresies." *New York Review of Books*, 17 Feb. 1966, pp. 202–09.
Backscheider, Paula R., and Catherine Ingrassia, editors. *British Women Poets of the Long Eighteenth Century: An Anthology*. Johns Hopkins UP, 2009.
Bakalar, Nicholas, editor. *American Satire: An Anthology of Writings from Colonial Times to the Present*. Meridian, 1997.
Bakhtin, M. M. *Problems of Dostoevsky's Poetics*. Edited and translated by Caryl Emerson, U of Minnesota P, 1984. Theory and History of Literature 8.
Ball, John Clement. *Satire and the Postcolonial Novel: V. S. Naipaul, Chinua Achebe, Salman Rushdie*. Routledge, 2009.
Bates, Eric. "Jon Stewart: The *Rolling Stone* Interview." *Rolling Stone*, 29 Sept. 2011, www.rollingstone.com/tv/features/the-rolling-stone-interview-jon-stewart-20110929.
Baym, Geoffrey, and Jeffrey P. Jones, editors. *News Parody and Political Satire across the Globe*. Routledge, 2013.
Beatty, Warren, director. *Bulworth*. Twentieth Century Fox, 1998.
Blitt, Barry. "The Politics of Fear." *The New Yorker*, 21 July 2008, cover.
Bloom, Edward Alan, and Lillian D. Bloom. *Satire's Persuasive Voice*. Cornell UP, 1979.
Bogel, Fredric V. *The Difference Satire Makes: Rhetoric and Reading from Jonson to Byron*. Cornell UP, 2001.
Booth, Wayne C. *A Rhetoric of Irony*. U of Chicago P, 1974.
Carpio, Glenda R. *Laughing Fit to Kill: Black Humor in the Fictions of Slavery*. Oxford UP, 2008.
Connery, Brian A., and Kirk Combe, editors. *Theorizing Satire: Essays in Literary Criticism*. St. Martin's Press, 1995.
Day, Amber. *Satire and Dissent: Interventions in Contemporary Political Debate*. Indiana UP, 2011.
Dickson-Carr, Darryl. *African American Satire: The Sacredly Profane Novel*. U of Missouri P, 2001.
Dillon, Wentworth (Earl of Roscommon). *Poems by the Earl of Roscommon*. London, 1717.
Dryden, John. *Essays of John Dryden*. Compiled and edited by W. P. Ker, Clarendon Press, 1926. 2 vols.
D.W., Daniel, director. *Clark: A Gonzomentary*. *Funny or Die*, www.funnyordie.com/gonzomentary/webseries.
Elkin, P. K. *The Augustan Defence of Satire*. Clarendon Press, 1973.
Ellis, Frank H. *The ABC of Lit Crit: Aspects of Craft and Creation in the Critical Enterprise*. Academica Press, 2003.
Frye, Northrop. *Anatomy of Criticism: Four Essays*. Princeton UP, 1957.
Gilbert, Christopher J. "Toward the Satyric." *Philosophy and Rhetoric*, vol. 46, no. 3, 2013, pp. 280–305.
Gill, James E., editor. *Cutting Edges: Postmodern Critical Essays on Eighteenth-Century Satire*. U of Tennessee P, 1995. Tennessee Studies in Literature 37.
Greenberg, Jonathan. *Modernism, Satire, and the Novel*. Cambridge UP, 2011.
Griffin, Dustin H. *Satire: A Critical Reintroduction*. UP of Kentucky, 1994.
Gunkel, David, and Ted Gournelos. *Transgression 2.0: Media, Culture, and the Politics of a Digital Age*. Continuum, 2012.

Hall, Joseph. *Virgidemiarum: First Three Bookes*. London, 1598.
Henry, Matthew A. The Simpsons, *Satire, and American Culture*. Palgrave Macmillan, 2012.
Hernández, Guillermo E. *Chicano Satire: A Study in Literary Culture*. U of Texas P, 1991.
Highet, Gilbert. *The Anatomy of Satire*. Princeton UP, 1962.
Horace. *Satires, Epistles, The Art of Poetry*. Edited and translated by H. R. Fairclough, Harvard UP, 1926. Loeb Classical Library 194.
Jensen, Ejner J. "Verse Satire in the English Renaissance." Quintero, pp. 101–17.
Jonson, Ben. *Bartholomew Fair*. Edited by Eugene M. Waith, Yale UP, 1963.
Kairoff, Claudia Thomas. "Gendering Satire: Behn to Burney." Quintero, pp. 276–92.
Kallaugher, Kevin. Cartoon. *The Economist*, 10 Jan. 2015, p. 6.
Kercher, Stephen E. *Revel with a Cause: Liberal Satire in Postwar America*. U of Chicago P, 2006.
Kernan, Alvin B. *The Cankered Muse: Satire of the English Renaissance*. Yale UP, 1959. Yale Studies in English 142.
———. *Modern Satire*. Harcourt, Brace and World, 1962. Harbrace Sourcebooks.
Knight, Charles A. *The Literature of Satire*. Cambridge UP, 2004.
Lewis, Wyndham. *The Apes of God*. 1930. Black Sparrow Press, 1984.
Looser, Devoney. *Women Writers and Old Age in Great Britain, 1750–1850*. Johns Hopkins UP, 2008.
Marshall, Ashley. *The Practice of Satire in England, 1658–1770*. Johns Hopkins UP, 2013.
Marx, Karl. *The Eighteenth Brumaire of Louis Bonaparte*. Translated by David De Leon, Charles H. Kerr, 1907.
Maus, Derek C., and James J. Donahue, editors. *Post-Soul Satire: Black Identity after Civil Rights*. UP of Mississippi, 2014.
McClennen, Sophia A. *America According to Colbert: Satire as Public Pedagogy*. Palgrave Macmillan, 2011. Education, Politics, and Public Life.
McClennen, Sophia A., and Remy M. Maisel. *Is Satire Saving Our Nation? Mockery and American Politics*. Palgrave Macmillan, 2014.
Mencken, H. L. "Bierce Emerges from the Shadows." *The American Mercury*, Feb. 1930, pp. 251–52.
Mookerjee, Robin. *Transgressive Fiction: The New Satiric Tradition*. Palgrave Macmillan, 2013.
Nietzsche, Friedrich Wilhelm. *The Nietzsche Reader*. Edited by Keith Ansell-Pearson and Duncan Large, Blackwell, 2006. Blackwell Readers.
Nilsson, Johan. *American Film Satire in the 1990s: Hollywood Subversion*. Palgrave Macmillan, 2013.
Nussbaum, Felicity A. *The Brink of All We Hate: English Satires on Women, 1660–1750*. UP of Kentucky, 1984.
Ogborn, Jane, and Peter Buckroyd. *Satire*. Cambridge UP, 2001.
Palmeri, Frank. *Satire in Narrative: Petronius, Swift, Gibbon, Melville, and Pynchon*. U of Texas P, 1990.

Paulson, Ronald. *The Fictions of Satire*. Johns Hopkins UP, 1967.
———. *Satire and the Novel in Eighteenth-Century England*. Yale UP, 1967.
———. *Satire: Modern Essays in Criticism*. Prentice-Hall, 1971. Prentice-Hall English Literature Series.
Pliny the Elder. *Naturalis Historia* [Natural History]. Translated by D. E. Eichholz, vol. 10, Harvard UP, 1963. Loeb Classical Library 419.
Poole, Joshua. *The English Parnassus; or, A Helpe to English Poesie*. 1657. Scolar Press, 1972.
Pope, Alexander. *The Poems of Alexander Pope: A Reduced Version of the Twickenham Text*. Edited by John Butt. Yale UP, 1963.
Queenan, Joe, editor. *The Malcontents: The Best Bitter, Cynical, and Satirical Writing in the World*. Running Press, 2002.
Quintero, Ruben, editor. *A Companion to Satire: Ancient and Modern*. Blackwell, 2007. Blackwell Companions to Literature and Culture 46.
Quintilian. *The* Institutio Oratoria *of Quintilian*. Translated by H. E. Butler, Harvard UP, 1920–22. 4 vols. Loeb Classical Library.
Rosenheim, Edward W. *Swift and the Satirist's Art*. U of Chicago P, 1963.
Rueckert, William H. *Kenneth Burke and the Drama of Human Relations*. 1963. 2nd ed., U of California P, 1982.
Sacco, Joe. *I Buggered the Kaiser*. *Bumf*, vol. 1, Fantagraphics, 2014.
Seidel, Michael. *Satiric Inheritance: Rabelais to Sterne*. Princeton UP, 1979.
Soper, Kerry D. *Garry Trudeau:* Doonesbury *and the Aesthetics of Satire*. UP of Mississippi, 2008.
———. *We Go Pogo: Walt Kelly, Politics, and American Satire*. UP of Mississippi, 2012.
Spacks, Patricia Meyer. "Uncertainties of Satire." *Modern Language Quarterly*, vol. 40, no. 4, 1979, pp. 403–11.
Test, George A. *Satire: Spirit and Art*. U of South Florida P, 1991.
Trudeau, Garry. "The Abuse of Satire." *The Atlantic*, 11 Apr. 2015, www.theatlantic.com/international/archive/2015/04/the-abuse-of-satire/390312.
Vico, Giambattista. *The New Science of Giambattista Vico*. Translated by Thomas Goddard Bergin and Max Harold Fisch, Cornell UP, 1968.
Weinbrot, Howard D. *Menippean Satire Reconsidered: From Antiquity to the Eighteenth Century*. Johns Hopkins UP, 2005.
Weisenburger, Steven. *Fables of Subversion: Satire and the American Novel, 1930–1980*. U of Georgia P, 1995.
West, Nathanael. *Novels and Other Writings*. Edited by Sacvan Bercovitch, Library of America, 1997.
Williams, Dana A., editor. *African American Humor, Irony, and Satire: Ishmael Reed, Satirically Speaking*. Cambridge Scholars, 2007.
Worcester, David. *The Art of Satire*. Harvard UP, 1940.
Yu, Christopher. *Nothing to Admire: The Politics of Poetic Satire from Dryden to Merrill*. Oxford UP, 2003.

Part I

Definitions and Techniques

Nicholas Hudson

"Open" and "Closed" Satire: Levels of Indeterminacy in Satiric Texts

"Like the god Mercury," write Edward and Lillian Bloom, "satire is elusive and variable, wearing many disguises and satisfying many expectations" (15). For the teacher, the amorphous and heterogeneous nature of satire presents major problems of organization and presentation. Even the definition of *satire* presents major difficulties, for satire seems more of a mode than a genre, parasitic on other genres such as the heroic or the romance, intruding into other literary forms, and often difficult to distinguish from associated genres like comedy, tragedy, and the novel. What follows is a method for organizing one's presentation of satire that will help make this literary genre or mode clearer and more comprehensible for students, suggesting the range of its possibilities along a scale marked by the extremes of "closed" satire on one side and "open" satire on the other.

The terms *open* and *closed* are borrowed from a recent scholar of the nature of satire, Dustin Griffin, who himself reflects a recent point in the evolution of theoretical reflections since the 1950s. Griffin defines satire as "rather an 'open' than a 'closed' form, both in its formal features (particularly in its reluctance to conclude) and in its more general rhetorical and moral features, in its frequent preference for inquiry, provocation, or playfulness rather than assertion or conclusiveness" (186). Writing in the 1990s, Griffin was reacting against two preceding waves of critical reflection. The first was the New Critical school that prevailed in the early 1960s, including scholars such as William K. Wimsatt and Cleanth Brooks, who stressed the purely formal properties of satire in distinction from both the intentions of the author and the historical context of the literary work. In reaction to the New Critics, a group of scholars, including Edward Rosenheim and Alvin Kernan, insisted instead that satire is typified, even by definition, by its reference to outside historical events and people. It is a persuasive mode, attempting to reform society and setting out clear distinctions between right and wrong. Griffin represents a third way of understanding satire, rejecting the normative or persuasive function of this mode and insisting instead that it is "an open and exploratory form, designed to pose questions and raise problems" (Knight 14). As Fredric V. Bogel argues, the referential gestures of satire should be understood as formal conventions that create, rather than reflect, the normative differences that satire typically undermines by showing their mutual cancellation, implicating both the putative author and the reader in its deconstructive ironies (11; see also Seidel 263).

One unifying feature of all these theories is that they rely heavily on evidence drawn from the great age of satire, the eighteenth century, and especially the work of Jonathan Swift, whose interpretation as either a paradigmatically "open" satirist, endlessly undermining any fixed moral position, or as a "closed" satirist, finally endorsing the ideals exemplified by the Houyhnhnms or the Portuguese captain in *Gulliver's Travels* (1726), has provided a locus classicus for theories of satire in general. This focus on the eighteenth century has been highly restrictive (an opinion I offer as primarily a scholar of that age). Satire is a tradition that extends not only back through millennia to the Greeks and Romans but also forward from the eighteenth century to the present moment. Widening our perspective from the eighteenth century suggests that even the more recent theories, which militate against all closed or normative ideas of satire, are too narrow, diminishing the range of this form as exhibited by different authors at different times.

For satire certainly *can* be historically specific and normative, having definite external targets and reforming purposes—what I here define as *closed*. And it may come as some surprise that this kind of satire became more common in the twentieth century, an age that, in the common view, tended to disrupt the moral certitudes of previous eras. As an example of closed satire, consider Bertolt Brecht's *The Resistable Rise of Artuo Ui* (written 1941; first performed 1953). The normative and referential status of this satirical play is exemplified not only by its burning political hostility to Adolf Hitler, whose historical rise to power after 1933 is allegorized event by event through the thuggish ascendance of Ui's gangsters over the Chicago vegetable trade. In addition, Brecht was quite aware of the tendency of a literary work or performance to isolate itself from historical particulars. In reaction against recent formalist tendencies in both literary art and criticism, Brecht's "alienation effect" was specifically designed to draw the audience's attention back toward history by laying bare the play's mere theatricality. The demonic buffoonery of Artuo Ui, introduced as a mere character at the beginning of the play, reminds us of the real clown who should have been resisted but was not in his brutal domination of Germany and Europe. Brecht's impatience with the notion of satiric art as mere "playfulness" reflected his moral passion in the face of events of tangible material urgency, a context that explains the similarly sinister comedy of Charlie Chaplin's *The Great Dictator* (1940).

It is indeed an irony of literary history that the New Criticism, with its rejection of historical context, grew up in the shadow of satires that stressed more than ever their normative value and reformist aims. While Wimsatt and Brooks were cordoning off literary art and the artist in noble isolation from historical catastrophe, satirists were linking their work ever more directly with concrete historical particulars. A reader who mistakes George Orwell's *Animal Farm* (1945) for the "fairy story" announced on the title page is simply missing its satirical attack on Stalinist totalitarianism. The ironic inversions of madness and sanity in Joseph Heller's *Catch-22* (1961) become less laughable toward this novel's dark and murderous conclusion, because the author's intention was always to expose the insanity of the American military bureaucracy and its commercial exploitation of war. The comedy of Stanley Kubrick's *Dr. Strangelove, or: How I Learned to Stop Worrying and Love the Bomb* (1964) gave vent to real and worrying bewilderment in the face of official assurance that a nuclear apocalypse could never happen. Recent suggestions that satire is never normative, or that it playfully deconstructs the difference between right and wrong, arguably imply modern complacency as well as a tendency to focus on satiric works of the past whose historical urgency is now difficult to recover. Although we may now detect disruptive uncertainties in John Dryden's *Absalom and Achitophel* (1681) or Henry Fielding's *Jonathan Wild* (1743), they had a historical directness for their original audience comparable to the directness of *Artuo Ui* or *Catch-22* for theirs. More obviously, Percy Bysshe Shelley's *The Mask of Anarchy* (written 1819, published 1832) has lost none of its satiric sting in being an unambiguous unmasking of the government's excuse for the Peterloo massacre. Indeed, it seems important to affirm that closed satire is not for that reason "bad" satire: its enduring impact lies in the effective pillorying of an opponent who is made to look immoral and absurd, especially when the ethical or political stakes are undeniably high.

Nevertheless, not all satire, even in the twentieth century, has been clearly referential or normative in this way. As suggested by Bogel and others, satire becomes open when its putative binaries of right and wrong overlap and dissolve, typically because of the lack of some authoritative perspective secured by the narrator or main characters. But a satire may approach this limit of indeterminacy without fully reaching it. Hunter S. Thompson's *Fear and Loathing in Las Vegas* (1971) is a serious satire of the degradation of the American dream, as embodied by Las Vegas and, finally, a burned-down nightclub, formerly the Psychiatrist's Club, on the outskirts of town. The narrator, Raoul Duke, seems mostly the spokesman for the author, though Thompson preserves a margin of difference: Duke at one point receives a telegram from Thompson and appears to have gone insane in the episode where he discovers the American dream. More generally, Duke's comically excessive drug use implicates him in the phantasmagoric excesses of the Strip. He is attempting, like the gamblers and impresarios, to find a shortcut to the American dream. Such undermining of the figure of moral authority, problematically associated with what is satirized, also characterizes Evelyn Waugh's *The Loved One* (1948). The putative center of authority in this novel is Dennis Barlow, an English exile and failed Hollywood scriptwriter, who recognizes as sharply as Waugh the soulless artificiality of Los Angeles, exemplified by the meretricious and exploitive cemetery Whispering Glades. Nevertheless, Barlow has not only taken employment in an equally absurd pet crematorium, Happier Hunting Ground, but views the world of Whispering Glades with a morbid and predatory fascination, fixating on an absurd yet tragically unfulfilled mortician named Aimée Thanatogenos. Barlow is an internal "satirist," yet his cynical manipulation of Aimée, "the Loved One," whom he tries to seduce with plagiarized poetry, leads instead to her suicide. What Barlow lacks is the author's sense of tragedy, his traditional Catholic sense that the failure of American society to face mortality has the terrible and corrosive consequence of spiritual emptiness. Thus *The Loved One* is far from canceling out all alternatives to its satirized objects. Yet this alternative is left largely to the mind of the reader, who will find no explicit guidance in the satire itself.

One might well ponder whether much satire is quite so value-free or deconstructive as recent commentators have suggested. Where comic works verge toward the total lack of normative standards, their status as satire becomes problematic. For example, can we define Oscar Wilde's *The Importance of Being Earnest* (1895) as satire? Certainly Wilde is showing up the self-important hypocrisy of late Victorian upper-class society. Yet the enduring delightfulness of this play lies in its joyful rejection of any deeper or "earnest" meaning, its willful indulgence in superficial and sparkling repartee, and its acceptance that hypocrisy, including "Bunburying," at least facilitates the freedom to do what one wants. If Jack's accusation that Algernon "never talk[s] anything but nonsense" is apt, then so is Algernon's reply: "Nobody ever does" (273). The rejection of earnestness in Wilde's play makes it more difficult to teach as satire than its close contemporary, George Bernard Shaw's *Major Barbara* (1905). In many respects, Shaw's play questions confident normative stances as aggressively as Wilde's. Shaw achieves this openness by empowering his most immoral, even demonic character, the arms dealer Andrew Undershaft, with the play's most compelling critique of ruling-class English society. As Shaw confirms in his preface, Undershaft is essentially correct that values such as "honor, justice, truth, love, mercy, and so forth" are "the graces and luxuries of a rich, strong, and safe life" (93)—a luxurious and hypocritical ideology that Undershaft bestows on the poor by building a model arms factory. This critique is finally accepted by both the eponymous Major Barbara, who has doled out salvationist platitudes to a cast of unattractive plebeians, and her fiancé, Cusins, who finally joins the arms dealership while recognizing Undershaft's essential evil. Equally with Wilde, Shaw has exposed the emptiness of the prevailing morality. But this work is more easily defined as satire rather than comedy because it is genuinely earnest, leaving the audience with a troubled sense of tragic disorder.

Indeed, one might well say that satire bridges the gap between tragedy and comedy. Even in its most open forms, where normative values are most fully called into question, satire differs from comedy by cultivating the belief that its critique has a broader social import, whether or not it delivers solutions. In shifting back to the golden age of satire, we find that this sense of social import links all forms of satire along the scale from closed to open. John Gay's *The Beggar's Opera* (1728) has a good claim to being an open satire, offering no evident escape route from what John

Bender has called its "total irony" (153). All of this work's characters—Macheath, Mr. Peachum, Lockit, Polly—seem implicated in Gay's portrait of society corrupted from top to bottom by criminality and injustice. In this respect, *The Beggar's Opera* differs from Henry Fielding's *Tom Jones* (1749), which, for all its double and even triple ironies, offers the serious alternative of benevolence and sympathy, what Fielding called "the Good Heart," in opposition to the self-interest and hypocrisy of Master Blifil or Thwackum. Brecht was famously inspired by Gay's opera, and one might ponder whether the eighteenth-century writer prefigured the alienation effect of *Artuo Ui.* The difference seems to lie in Brecht's implication that resistance is possible and that only cowardice explains the ascendance of either Ui or Hitler. Gay, on the other hand, makes no suggestion of a moral alternative to the world he describes. Even in directing the play's finale toward comedy rather than tragedy (the hanging of Macheath, his inevitable fate in the real world), he draws the audience into complicity with the nation's fall from grace, a decline highlighted by the opera's nostalgic songs of pastoral innocence.

According to many scholars, however, the eighteenth century's paradigm of the open satire is the work of Swift. We might, indeed, note the similarities between Swift's satires and the techniques that we have considered in later works that undermine moral certainty. Like Thompson, Waugh, and Shaw, Swift deprives the reader of a secure center of moral authority, for his many personas are persistently implicated in the absurdities or immoralities that they describe. The narrator Strephon in "The Lady's Dressing Room" (1732) is as much the butt of Swift's satire for his absurd idealization of Celia as Celia is the apparent target of the author's misogynist attack on female vanity and disguise. Most famously, Gulliver transforms into a Yahoo vaunting madly against the total depravity of Yahoos, able to identify with the rational Houyhnhnms only by whinnying hypocritical diatribes against human pride. Against the view that Swift is ultimately offering a positive vision over the head of his persona, as perhaps exemplified by the generosity of Pedro de Mendez, Claude Rawson has powerfully contended that Swift relentlessly entraps the reader in the satire's accusatory ironies: "The book's prevailing tone is quarrelsome and disorienting, programmed to 'vex' rather than divert, and it is quite the antithesis of more conventional satiric styles which purport to engage the reader's solidarity" (130). According to Rawson, the weight of evidence for human depravity is too heavy to be relieved by either the Portuguese captain or our awareness of Gulliver's madness. But not all have accepted this reading even to the present day. Ashley Marshall has recently insisted that Pedro de Mendez's humanity provides a serious ethical alternative to Gulliver's insane misanthropy (223–24).

It is not the purpose of this essay to decide on the rightness of either reading. Whatever our judgment of Swift or the other satirists mentioned, we can usefully present our students with a schema that arranges the satiric tradition along its varying range of indeterminacy. The most recent scholarship has possibly underrated the extent to which satires, right into the twentieth century, can be closed in the sense of offering positive moral alternatives and identifying examples of evil in the world that can and should be resisted. Such satires may indeed be described as "persuasive." But satirists can also employ various strategies, often involving the removal of a reliable or uncompromised viewpoint, for disrupting norms and ideals. Such open satire differs from its near neighbor, comedy, in its earnest engagement with ethical and political problems, a feature it has in common with its neighbor on the other side, tragedy. Neither comedy nor tragedy commits satire to moral certainty. By means of this scheme, we may not be able "to domesticate the shaggy, obscene, and transgressive" beast of satire (Griffin 6). But we can reduce our inspection of this beast to some order.

Works Cited

Bender, John. *Imagining the Penitentiary: Fiction and the Architecture of the Mind in Eighteenth-Century England.* U of Chicago P, 1987.

Bloom, Edward, and Lillian D. Bloom. *Satire's Persuasive Voice.* Cornell UP, 1979.

Bogel, Fredric V. *The Difference Satire Makes: Rhetoric and Reading from Jonson to Byron.* Cornell UP, 2001.

Griffin, Dustin. *Satire: A Critical Reintroduction.* UP of Kentucky, 1994.

Knight, Charles A. *The Literature of Satire.* Cambridge UP, 2004.

Marshall, Ashley. *The Practice of Satire in England, 1658–1770.* Johns Hopkins UP, 2013.

Rawson, Claude. *Swift's Angers.* Cambridge UP, 2014.

Seidel, Michael. *Satiric Inheritance: Rabelais to Sterne.* Princeton UP, 1979.

Shaw, George Bernard. *Major Barbara.* Edited by Dan H. Laurence, Penguin, 1960.

Wilde, Oscar. *The Importance of Being Earnest.* Penguin, 1948.

Anne H. Stevens

Parody

Teaching parody can present a unique set of challenges in the classroom. As Wayne C. Booth has argued, parody, more than any other type of irony, "dramatizes . . . the difference between experienced and inexperienced readers" (72). At every level of teaching, one is likely to encounter a mix of both experienced and less experienced readers, and thus teaching works of parody can highlight the disjunctures in skill levels among students. In order to make sense of a parodic work, students must be familiar with or at least recognize the target of the parody. If they are unfamiliar with the target they may well miss the satiric "point" of the parody or not recognize a work as parodic at all. This essay suggests a few strategies for teaching parody in the undergraduate and graduate classroom, including using popular culture as a way to introduce the topic, providing background on the target of a parodic work in order to better equip students to recognize it, and introducing critical concepts that highlight parody's subversive potential.

The topic of parody arises in many different types of classes: courses on satire, film, visual art, or literary periods or genres. When I introduce the topic of parody in any class, I often begin with a short writing exercise. I ask the students to define satire, parody, and irony and to give an example for each. After giving them some time to think and write, the class will discuss as a group their responses to the questions and begin to delineate the relationships among the three terms. Oftentimes in this exercise students are able to define parody the most precisely, while they struggle a bit more with the broader, more nebulous category of satire. They often also provide the clearest and most apt examples of parody, usually drawn from popular culture. Over the last ten years or so, my students' examples of parody have included Stephen Colbert's persona on *The Colbert Report*, Tina Fey's *Saturday Night Live* sketches as Sarah Palin, moments from *South Park* and *Family Guy*, "Weird Al" Yankovic's parodies of popular songs, and the Wayans brothers' movie parodies from *Scary Movie* to *Fifty Shades of Black*. Beginning the discussion with student-provided examples rather than literary works or examples of the instructor's choosing can provide a fun and nonintimidating avenue into the topic of parody and consequently to irony and satire more broadly. Because students can clearly recognize how parody functions through imitation and exaggeration when dealing with more recent and familiar examples, this can provide a model for identifying parodic strategies when studying literary works from earlier periods that employ parody and where the models being imitated and exaggerated may be less familiar to students.

I employ Gérard Genette's distinction between *hypertext* and *hypotext* as a means to distinguish a work of parody and the work it is parodying. In his highly influential *Palimpsests*, Genette delineates five different types of relationships between texts: intertextuality (which includes allusion as well as plagiarism), paratextuality (the relationship of a text and paratextual elements such as prefaces), metatextuality (the relationship between a text and commentary about it), architextuality (which concerns issues of genre), and, finally, hypertextuality (1). Hypertexuality is the "relationship uniting a text B (which I shall call the *hypertext*) to an earlier text A (I shall, of course, call it the *hypotext*) upon which it is grafted in a manner that is not that of commentary" (5). Within this category of hypertexuality Genette describes a number of forms this grafting can take, including pastiche, burlesque, travesty, and parody. I usually do not bombard students with a full range of Genettian vocabulary and fine-grained distinctions, particularly at the lower levels of the curriculum, but the basic binary of hypertext and hypotext can be useful in getting students to think about how parody operates at a basic level.

Using these terms, I further distinguish between works of parody where the hypotext functions as an object of satire and works where the hypotext is being parodied in order to satirize something else entirely. Here too popular culture examples can help to disentangle this relationship between the object of parody and the target of satire: Colbert is parodying a certain type of cable news presenter (Bill O'Reilly in particular) in order to satirize them, and Fey is certainly sending up Palin for political effect. By contrast, Weird Al parodies songs for comic effect rather than to lampoon the songs themselves: "White and Nerdy" isn't making fun of its hypotext (Chamillionaire's song "Ridin'") but rather sending up/celebrating nerd culture by rewriting Chamillionaire's lyrics. Similarly, the rapid-fire, often absurdist use of parody in shows like *The Simpsons*, *30 Rock*, *Family Guy*, and many others can function as a way to layer references to popular culture without those references necessarily functioning as critique of the hypotext.

In *A Theory of Parody*, Linda Hutcheon defines parody as "repetition with critical distance" that uses "ironic inversion" (6). Hutcheon's concise wording translates well into the classroom, and popular culture examples can help to illustrate strategies of ironic inversion. Moving from student examples to older works of parody where students may be unfamiliar with the hypotexts, though, can present some obstacles to teaching. For example, as someone who specializes in eighteenth-century British literature, I often teach the works of the Augustan satirists Alexander Pope and Jonathan Swift, generally in period courses, courses on satire, or required surveys of British literature. Both Pope and Swift parody a wide range of authors and genres, both those they venerated and those they held in contempt. Swift's works provide a rich array of examples where the hypotext serves as an object of satire. In "A Modest Proposal," for example, he adopts the voice of a modern "projector" to ironic, even absurd effect in a way that parallels Colbert's parody of O'Reilly and other cable news pundits. Similarly, in *Gulliver's Travels*, Swift uses travel literature as a hypotext, mocking travel writers' tendency to stretch the truth. In that latter example, Swift does not restrict his satire to travel writing but takes in politics, religion, science, and, indeed, human nature. But to at least some extent the hypotext serves as one of his many satiric targets. In contrast, Pope's works provide clear examples where the hypotext is not an object of satire. To analogize with my Weird Al example above, *The Rape of the Lock* : *The Iliad* :: "White and Nerdy" : "Ridin'." That is, the mock epic uses Homeric epic as a template but not a target—Pope "rewrites the lyrics" of the epic to mock fashionable society, not to mock the epic, just as *Peri Bathous; or, The Art of Sinking in Poetry* uses Longinus's *On the Sublime* as a hypotext in order to satirize modern writers.

A further useful distinction can be drawn between works parodying a genre or type and those that parody individuals, be they people or works. These categories certainly overlap, as a parody of an individual can shade into parody of the larger type. Pope parodies Homer but also the ancient and modern epic more generally, while Weird Al parodies both individual songs and musical genres such as hip-hop.

On some occasions, I have devoted classroom time to introducing students to an unfamiliar hypotext (a work or a genre) so that they can better appreciate a work of satire. I turn once again to Swift and the collection of documents known as the Bickerstaff Papers, which target an astrologer and almanac maker named John Partridge. In order to fully appreciate Swift's vicious satire, students need to understand what Partridge's series of almanacs, titled *Merlinus Liberatus*, were like. Because my institution subscribes to the Eighteenth Century Collections Online (ECCO) database, this can become a fun and easy exercise: I will pull up some of Partridge's almanacs on ECCO in the classroom and highlight a few passages. The 1708 *Merlinus Liberatus*, for example, contains, alongside a wealth of astrological symbols and an advertisement for "Partridge's Purging Pills" (2), a series of increasingly vague predictions about the coming year: "If peace is not yet Concluded, there will be occasion for spilling more Humane blood" (13); "News from the West Parts of the World, that seem to please many People" (17); "Many Robberies, and Casualties about this time" (31). Spending a few minutes paging through this text thus helps to contextualize Swift's critique of Partridge in *Predictions for the Year 1708*, published under the pseudonym Isaac Bickerstaff, and to show his model for such predictions as "On the 15th, news will arrive of a very *surprising event*, than which nothing could be more unexpected" (197). Doing this kind of contextual work can run the risk of "spoiling the joke," as it were, which is perhaps why Swift's Bickerstaff Papers are much less frequently taught than *Gulliver's Travels*, though equally scathing.

In the case of the Bickerstaff Papers, providing students with background about the hypotext can help them to better appreciate Swift's satire. At other times, however, hypotext can be nearly impossible to contextualize because of historical distance or the obscurity of a particular object of parody. For example, in a graduate seminar on the Enlightenment, I once attempted to teach Pope's *The Dunciad Variorum*, a remarkably complex work of mock-epic that parodies both the classical epic and the conventions of classical scholarship. Getting graduate students to identify the mock-epic elements of the poem, such as its scenes of funeral games and the voyage to the underworld, was an easy enough task. However, the variorum edition sends up scholarly erudition in an extensive series of multilingual footnotes, and here the hypotext proved to be too inaccessible and the humor too obscure even to graduate students. In general, I have found that parodies of erudition tend to fall flat with most students, and the effort required to explain a joke in the tradition of "learned wit," from Desiderius Erasmus to Laurence Sterne to Thomas Carlyle, has seldom seemed worth it.

One final strategy for getting students to appreciate works of parody is to highlight theoretical and especially political stakes. M. M. Bakhtin's notion of the carnivalesque as a "temporary suspension, both ideal and real, of hierarchical rank created during carnival time[,] a special type of communication impossible in everyday life," and of parody as one of the central features of the carnivalesque provides one lens for seeing parody as a tool for subversion (10). Here a work like *Gulliver's Travels* could serve as a very simple example of this type of upending. Swift subverts the hierarchy of the Great Chain of Being in book 4, where the equine Houyhnhnms appear to be far superior beings to the humanoid Yahoos. Further classroom discussion could then serve to complicate that perhaps overly simplistic example. Likewise, Homi Bhabha's notion of postcolonial mimicry, "a complex strategy of reform, regulation, and discipline, which 'appropriates' the Other as it visualizes power" (86), could be used to discuss the ways that colonial subjects can use parody to question and even to subvert power structures. Swift's Irish writings, such as "A Modest Proposal" and the Drapier's Letters, could illustrate this idea, as could later texts by Salman Rushdie, Percival Everett, George Saunders, and many others.

This brief essay began by discussing contemporary popular culture, then turned to look back at two eighteenth-century satirists, Pope and Swift. The strategies outlined here, however, could work just as well for parodic works from any era. While satirists of each generation find new objects to parody, their basic strategies of irony, subversion, and imitation persist.

Works Cited

Bakhtin, M. M. *Rabelais and His World.* Translated by Helene Iswolsky, MIT P, 1968.

Bhabha, Homi K. "Of Mimicry and Man: The Ambivalence of Colonial Discourse." *The Location of Culture*, Routledge, 1994, pp. 85–92.

Booth, Wayne C. *A Rhetoric of Irony.* U of Chicago P, 1974.

Genette, Gérard. *Palimpsests: Literature in the Second Degree.* Translated by Channa Newman and Claude Doubinsky, U of Nebraska P, 1997.

Hutcheon, Linda. *A Theory of Parody: The Teachings of Twentieth-Century Art Forms.* Methuen, 1985.

Partridge, John. *Merlinus Liberatus: Being an Almanack for the Year of Our Blessed Saviour's Incarnation 1708.* London, 1708.

Swift, Jonathan. *Predictions for the Year 1708. Major Works*, edited by Angus Ross and David Woolley, Oxford UP, 2008, pp. 193–200.

Evan R. Davis

Verbal Irony

On the first page of *A Rhetoric of Irony* (which remains, after more than four decades, an indispensable text for instructors), Wayne C. Booth describes an experience teaching *Pride and Prejudice* in which a bright student tells him that Mr. Bennet is "really quite stupid . . . because he says toward the end that Wickham is his favorite son-in-law." The student has missed Mr. Bennet's irony, and Booth states assuredly, " [H]e made a flat mistake, and I feel a great deal of confidence that everyone who has read *Pride and Prejudice* attentively will agree with me" (2). Putting aside the question of whether Jane Austen's irony is as stable as Booth suggests, his pedagogical vignette is suggestive. On the one side sits the master teacher who confidently identifies irony; on the other, the bright but inattentive student who has failed in his reading. Given that irony generates this kind of imbalance between experienced and inexperienced readers, it's not surprising that some students seize irony as a sort of master key to their professors' domain, while others shy from it as a rhetorical trap, a snare that enables the professor to measure how far a student's skills (or, in Booth's terms, "attentiveness") fall short.

Indeed, Northrop Frye's definition of satire as "militant irony" (223) suggests that a weak understanding of irony can befuddle students as they read satire, leading them to mistake attack for approbation, chiding for charity, calumny for compliment. Unlike readers who misconstrue allegory, who overlook the source of a parody, or who miscalculate satiric hyperbole, thereby diminishing the depth of their understanding, those who misread irony run the danger of getting the whole point backward, or at least seriously askew, as if Jonathan Swift really wanted to serve babies in a "Fricasie, or Ragoust" ("Modest Proposal" 297). In the satire courses that I teach at a small liberal arts college, I therefore devote several days early in the semester to building students' familiarity with irony: what it is, how it functions, and how it invites their affective response. Introducing irony also gives me a chance to explore with students various forms of satiric exclusion. It lets me introduce distinctions—insiders vs. outsiders, knowing vs. unknowing, said vs. unsaid—that will recur throughout the course and that, if left unexamined, can undermine students' enjoyment and understanding of satire in general.

My initial classroom focus is on sentence-level irony, which lays the groundwork for later discussions of situational, cosmic, or Romantic irony: without understanding the discrete verbal ironies of Swift, Mark Twain, Flannery O'Connor, or Gary Shteyngart, students' grasp of their grander satiric views is likely to remain muddy. Focusing on sentence-level irony also quickly demonstrates why the definition that many students bring with them from high school—that irony is saying one thing while meaning the opposite—comes up short when applied to those Möbius-strip-like ironies that resist revealing their opposite. (We would probably all label as ironic Swift's famous sentence, "This is the sublime and refined point of felicity, called, *the possession of being well deceived*; the serene peaceful state, of being a fool among knaves" [*Tale* 84], but what would its opposite be?) I tackle verbal irony in two steps: first, helping students identify it, and second, helping them understand that irony is something other than the rigged game that they might expect. While the two theorists I introduce—Booth and Linda Hutcheon—disagree about the stability of irony and the importance of affect, each is immediately applicable to classroom practice, perhaps a reflection of both critics' presentation of irony as a deeply humane enterprise.

In class, I often introduce students to irony with simple sarcasm. Pointing to a student, I quip, "Nice T-shirt." With a mild edge, the statement puts students on guard. I ask for a show of hands: "How many of you think I'm seriously complimenting that T-shirt?" And then, "How can you tell?" As they rattle off reasons, we assign them to categories that we later name: tone ("Your clipped tone of 'nice shirt' sounds more sarcastic than a more even-tempered 'That's a nice shirt'"), gesture ("Didn't your eyebrows move ironically?"), speaker's knowledge ("You don't know anything about basketball, so why would you compliment a Lakers T-shirt?"), the nature of the referent ("That T-shirt is really ugly; no one would compliment it"), the context of the utterance ("We're in the middle of class; it doesn't make any sense that you would suddenly be talking about T-shirts if you didn't have an ulterior motive"), the ethos of the speaker ("You're a nice guy; why would you insult someone in the middle of class?"). The discussion of course fails to establish conclusively how I feel about the T-shirt, but it helps students recognize their ability to spot potential irony and to articulate some of the means by which they interpret it. Rarely does a student say, "I simply cannot imagine a situation in which 'Nice shirt' means something other than 'Nice shirt.'"

A relatively simple piece of sarcasm like "Nice shirt" invites the kind of analysis that Booth describes for stable irony, and as a starting point, students find it helpful to walk through Booth's four "steps of reconstruction":

1. "The reader is required to reject the literal meaning" (10). Professor Davis wouldn't suddenly compliment that ugly shirt in the middle of class, and he doesn't like basketball, so he must mean something else.
2. "Alternative interpretations or explanations are tried out" (11). Maybe he doesn't see how ugly the shirt is, or maybe he actually likes ugly shirts, or maybe he was referring to someone else. Doubtful.
3. "A decision must therefore be made about the author's knowledge or beliefs" (11). He can't actually believe what he just said.
4. "Having made a decision about the knowledge or beliefs of the speaker, we can finally choose a new meaning or cluster of meanings with which we can rest secure" (12). His words really mean, "For some reason that I'm not bothering to explain, I don't like the shirt you're wearing, or at the least, I don't like it in the way that my words suggested I do."

Irony, even in the case of sarcasm, is rarely quite as stable as these four steps suggest, and the ironies in literary satires seldom fully jettison the said as they conjure the unsaid. But as an opening gambit, Booth's steps help students appreciate irony's temporal and discursive aspects: ironic meaning, they see, resides not in the words by themselves but in the full social context of their delivery and reception.

Why is it then that students who employ and interpret irony in their daily lives (one study confidently estimates that American conversation exhibits irony once every two minutes [Gibbs]) stumble when confronted with irony in more literary works? The problem is not that students are unfamiliar with irony per se, but rather that they misconstrue the norms and expectations that govern the discursive communities in which irony functions. When my students have grappled with the cartoons from *Charlie Hebdo*, for instance, the interpretive difficulties arise because of students' uncertainty about the assumptions behind the magazine's discursive context, not because they are unfamiliar with irony. But it is also the case that literary works signal the presence of irony differently from the way it is signaled in everyday speech. I give students a handout of Booth's categorization of those signals, updated here with more recent examples:

Straightforward warnings in the author's own voice

Titles

Any editorial whose title begins "A Modest Proposal for . . ."
Little Failure (Shteyngart)
I Am America (and So Can You!) (Stephen Colbert)
IQ84 (Haruki Murakami)

Epigraphs to famous satirists

Margaret Atwood's *The Handmaid's Tale*: "But as to myself, having been wearied out for many years with offering vain, idle, visionary thoughts, and at length utterly despairing of success, I fortunately fell upon this proposal" (Swift, "A Modest Proposal").

Jeffrey Eugenides's *The Marriage Plot*: "People would never fall in love if they hadn't heard love talked about" (paraphrased from François de La Rochefoucauld).

Other direct clues of ironic distance between speaker and author

"Many of my Republican friends have said to me, 'George, why are you voting for Barack Obama?' They assume it is because I believe in his radical socialist agenda of being fair to everyone, even the poor. But that's not it at all. I could actually care less about the poor. We have some living near us, and pee-yew. They are always coming and going to their three or four jobs at all hours of the day and night. Annoying! No, the reason I am voting for Obama is more complicated" (George Saunders, "I Was Ayn Rand's Lover").

Known error proclaimed (speaker violates expectations of knowledge)

Popular expressions

Colbert: "Give a man a fish, he'll eat for a day. Give a man a subprime fish loan and you're in business, buddy!" (*The Colbert Report*, 14 May 2008).

Historical fact

"As everyone knows, banks have historically been second-class citizens in America" (Donald Barthelme, *Here in the Village* 53).

Conventional judgment or knowledge

"I said I knew they had all been single since childhood and I could see how this might make them feel 'unmarried' and 'on their own,' but I said John Milton and Vachel Lindsay and James Dickey had all been single at one time or another and that writing words in lines of uneven length on a piece of paper had helped them to stop running" (Veronica Geng, "Teaching Poetry Writing to Singles").

Conflicts of facts within the work

"Alone, adj. In bad company" (Ambrose Bierce, *The Devil's Dictionary* 22).

"'I am the most generous man in the world,' I said aloud as I looked at the sleeping Russians, their stomachs filled with the expensive food I had bought them. 'And anyone who doesn't understand that is a stupid, ungrateful bitch'" (Shteyngart, *Absurdistan* 79–80).

Clashes of style

"[F]or our sakes who adore Thee, Lord, blast their hopes, blight their lives, protract their bitter pilgrimage, make heavy their steps, water their way with their tears, stain the white snow with the blood of their wounded feet! We ask it, in the spirit of love, of Him Who is the Source of Love, and Who is the ever-faithful refuge and friend of all that are sore beset and seek His aid with humble and contrite hearts. Amen" (Twain, "The War Prayer" 655).

"Ample parking day or night / People spouting, 'Howdy, neighbor'" (Primus, "South Park Theme").

Conflicts of belief

"Last week I saw a woman *flayed*, and you will hardly believe how much it altered her person for the worse" (Swift, *A Tale of a Tub* 84).

> "Is that a lot or a little? I haven't been keeping up with Mexico's crime stats" (Veronica Bronski, responding to a reporter's question, "On an abandoned ranch just south of the U.S. border, members of the Mexican navy discovered 21 rifles, four trucks, bulletproof vests, and 72 corpses. What do *you* think?" (*The Onion*, 27 Aug. 2010).

As Aaron Santesso explores in his essay in this volume, many, if not most, discussions of satire emphasize the divisions that the form creates: between insiders and outsiders, the knowledgeable and the ignorant, the elite and the hoi polloi, ironists and literalists, the informed and the naive, the sophisticated and the unsophisticated. A certain amount of "spot the irony" is probably therefore inevitable in any satire class. And yet there is a pedagogical problem if the discussion of irony stops there, for while some students might feel they have become part of a priestly initiate, others will inevitably be frustrated that they "just don't get it" or that they "get it only after you explain it." So as students use Booth's descriptions as a way to help them recognize irony, and as they work with a range of texts from Shakespeare's *Julius Caesar* ("Brutus is an honorable man") to Siegfried Sassoon's "They" or Stephen Crane's "Do Not Weep, Maiden, for War Is Kind," I also push them to move beyond the recognition of irony to ask, What does it do? Why would an ironist want to use this roundabout form of speech? And, crucially for the classroom, what role does the reader play in completing the ironic gesture?

To introduce these questions, I show students an image of the ironic columns on the rear of the Williams College Museum of Art, designed by Charles Moore in 1986 (fig. 1). If I'm lucky, at least one student in the class will know what an ionic column is and will recognize the visual pun of ionic/ironic.[1] But even without that knowledge, students have an easy time seeing that the columns are clearly not doing what they are supposed to be doing: they gesture toward one purpose—supporting an addition to the building—while also flaunting the fact that they are nothing more than decorative. I then ask the question "So how does that strike you?" A few students like the playfulness of the gesture; others find it self-indulgent. For some, it is clever; for others, gratuitous. A single ironic statement, as the students' responses demonstrate, can be evaluated in multiple ways. Indeed, this is part of the appeal of irony as a trope: that even when a statement is accepted as ironic, it can be valued quite differently, and that difference can then become the central contention.

Figure 1. Charles Moore, Williams College Museum of Art, 1986.

In locating that appeal, I draw on Hutcheon's *Irony's Edge*, whose classroom value arises from its central claim about the importance of affect. Her book is worth requiring for graduate students; for my undergraduates, I emphasize several main points:

That reading irony means, inescapably, responding to what Hutcheon calls its "affective edge," which in turn implies that ironic meaning must involve the agency of the student/reader.

That irony is as much about attitude as about meaning: "Irony is the intentional transmission of both information and evaluative attitude other than what is explicitly presented" (11). That attitude is not inherent within the ironic statement itself, for irony, she claims, is transideological: "Which evaluative position you hold usually depends as much on your perspective on the issue under review as on your personal view of irony" (28).

That the relationship between irony and community is more complex than other theories have allowed: "It is not so much that irony *creates* communities or in-groups; instead, I want to argue that irony happens because what could be called 'discursive communities' already exist and provide the context for both the deployment and attribution of irony" (18).[2]

That "[i]ronic meaning is simultaneously double (or multiple), and . . . therefore you don't actually have to reject a 'literal' meaning in order to get at what is usually called the 'ironic' or 'real' meaning of utterance" (60). Exploring the unsaid while not rejecting the said encourages a more expansive response to the question of why someone would use irony at all.

The following exercise helps students to understand these principles in practice. First, I give them a chart from Hutcheon's book, and we discuss how it works: the center column describes various functions that irony can serve, from those with "minimal affective charge," such as irony that merely reinforces a preconceived notion or that complicates an otherwise clear binary, to those with "maximal affective charge," such as those that assail someone or something (fig. 2). For each function, there are multiple ways that a reader might respond. Thus, for instance, while some readers might applaud oppositional irony as transgressive and subversive, others might censure the same irony as insulting and offensive. The chart gives students a way to think about irony's different functions; additionally, it provides them with an expansive vocabulary with which to discuss irony and satire throughout the semester.

Once they understand Hutcheon's basic framework and terminology, I put students into groups and offer them a set of randomly ordered ironic statements. Some come from literary works we have already read and whose contexts they will therefore recognize; others are new to them. Each group is charged with assigning the statements to one level of the chart and with selecting the adjective that they think best describes the irony. Here, for instance, are some of the examples I gave my most recent class:

"I ain't sayin' you treated me unkind / You could have done better but I don't mind / You just kinda wasted my precious time / But don't think twice, it's all right" (Bob Dylan, "Don't Think Twice, It's All Right").

"[W]e value your interest much more than our own. If your little finger be sore, and you think a Poultice made of our *Vitals* will give it any Ease, speak the Word, and it shall be done" (Swift, *A Letter from a Member of the House of Commons in Ireland* 14).

"Her collars and cuffs were white organdy trimmed with lace and at her neckline she had pinned a purple spray of cloth violets containing a sachet. In case of an accident, anyone seeing her dead on the highway would know at once that she was a lady" (Flannery O'Connor, "A Good Man Is Hard to Find" 3).

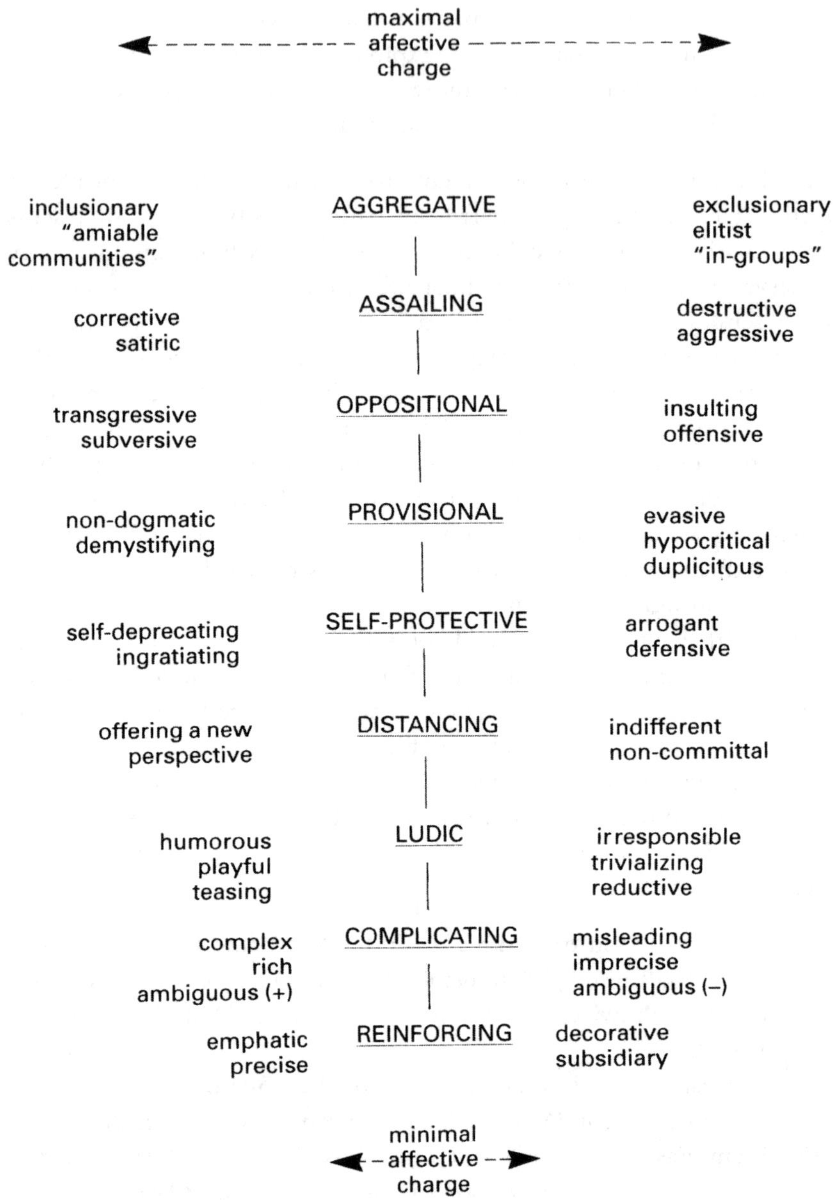

Figure 2. Chart on the functions of irony. Source: Linda Hutcheon, *Irony's Edge: The Theory of Politics and Irony.* © 1995 Routledge, reproduced by permission of Taylor and Francis Books UK.

"For some years, he [Shostakovich] had always made the same New Year's toast. For three hundred and sixty-four days of the year the country would have to listen to Power's insane daily insistence that all was for the best in the best possible of worlds, that Paradise had been created, or would be created quite soon when a few more logs had been chopped and a million more chips had flown, and a few hundred thousand more saboteurs had been shot. That happier times would come—unless they already had. And on the three hundred and sixty-fifth day, he would raise his glass and say, in his most solemn voice: 'Let's drink to this—that things don't get any better!'" (Julian Barnes, *The Noise of Time* 88–89).

"It was a close place. I took it up, and held it in my hand. I was a trembling, because I'd got to decide, forever, betwixt two things, and I knowed it. I studied a minute, sort of holding my breath, and then says to myself:

"'All right, then, I'll *go* to hell'—and tore it up.

"It was awful thoughts, and awful words, but they was said. And I let them stay said; and never thought no more about reforming. I shoved the whole thing out of my head; and said I would take up wickedness again, which was in my line, being brung up to it, and the other warn't. And for a starter, I would go to work and steal Jim out of slavery again; and if I could think up anything worse, I would do that, too; because as long as I was in, and in for good, I might as well go the whole hog" (Twain, *Adventures of Huckleberry Finn* 270–71).

"Nothing is more evident than that Nature hates Mind. Thinking is the most unhealthy thing in the world, and people die of it just as they die of any other disease. Fortunately, in England at any rate, thought is not catching. Our splendid physique as a people is entirely due to our national stupidity" (Oscar Wilde, "The Decay of Lying" 291).

"These sorrowful meditations fastened upon his mind; he past (sic) four months in resolving to lose no more time in idle resolves, and was awakened to more vigorous exertion by hearing a maid, who had broken a porcelain cup, remark, that what cannot be repaired is not to be regretted" (Samuel Johnson, *History of Rasselas* 48).

The payoff comes in the group discussion that follows. Students quickly realize that though this is not an exercise with single answers, neither is irony a free-for-all: they can often nudge one another toward tentative agreements about irony's charge and how it might be evaluated. They understand (or sympathize with) the self-protective role of irony in the Dylan quote (while disagreeing about whether the speaker is self-deprecating or just defensive), and they recognize the more aggressive irony of the Swift quotation. They can begin to articulate the multiple reasons that a speaker would want to use irony in these contexts.

These suggestions for introducing verbal irony are, of course, only opening salvos in a longer consideration of irony. But by slowing down the analysis, by providing critical vocabulary, and by underscoring the significance of their own affective responses, we can help students become more confident that if irony is a game, it is one in which they too are players.

Notes

1. As one reviewer of this essay noted, the columns also form a double set of the irony markers (upside-down exclamation points) proposed by John Wilkins in *An Essay towards a Real Character and a Philosophical Language* (1688).

2. The essays in part 4 of this volume all address the issue of introducing students to discursive communities.

Works Cited

Atwood, Margaret. *The Handmaid's Tale*. Random House, 1986.

Barnes, Julian. *The Noise of Time*. Knopf, 2016.

Barthelme, Donald. *Here in the Village*. Lord John Press, 1978.

Bierce, Ambrose. *The Devil's Dictionary*. The World Publishing Company, 1941.

Booth, Wayne C. *A Rhetoric of Irony*. U of Chicago P, 1974.

Colbert, Stephen, performer. *The Colbert Report*, season 4, episode 66, 14 May 2008.

Dylan, Bob. "Don't Think Twice, It's All Right." *The Freewheelin' Bob Dylan*, Columbia Records, 1963.

Eugenides, Jeffrey. *The Marriage Plot*. Farrar, Straus, and Giroux, 2011.

Frye, Northrop. *Anatomy of Criticism*. Princeton, 1957.

Geng, Veronica. "Teaching Poetry Writing to Singles." *The New Yorker*, 12 June 1978, www.newyorker.com/magazine/1978/06/12/teaching-poetry-writing-to-singles.

Gibbs, Raymond. "Irony in Talk among Friends." *Metaphor and Symbol*, vol. 15, nos. 1–2, Apr. 2000, pp. 5–27.

Hutcheon, Linda. *Irony's Edge: The Theory and Politics of Irony*. Routledge, 1995.

Johnson, Samuel. *The History of Rasselas, Prince of Abissinia*. Penguin, 1976.

La Rochefoucauld, François de. *Collected Maxims and Other Reflections*. Oxford UP, 2008.

O'Connor, Flannery. "A Good Man Is Hard to Find." *"A Good Man Is Hard to Find" and Other Stories*, Harcourt Brace, 1955, pp. 1–22.

Primus, "South Park Theme." *Chef Aid: The South Park Album*. Columbia Records, 1998.

Saunders, George. "I Was Ayn Rand's Lover." *The New Yorker*, 28 Oct. 2012, www.newyorker.com/humor/daily-shouts/i-was-ayn-rands-lover.

"72 Bodies Found on Mexican Ranch." *The Onion*, 27 Aug. 2010, www.theonion.com/72-bodies-found-on-mexican-ranch-1819560662.

Shteyngart, Gary. *Absurdistan*. Random House, 2006.

Swift, Jonathan. *A Letter from a Member of the House of Commons in Ireland. Swift's Irish Writings*, edited by Carole Fabricant and Robert Mahoney, Palgrave Macmillan, 2010.

———. "A Modest Proposal." *The Essential Writings of Jonathan Swift*, edited by Claude Rawson and Ian Higgins, W. W. Norton, 2010, pp. 295–301.

———. *A Tale of a Tub*. Oxford, 1986.

Twain, Mark. *Adventures of Huckleberry Finn*. Edited by Walter Blair and Victor Fischer, U of California P, 1988.

———. "The War Prayer." *Collected Tales, Sketches, Speeches, and Essays, 1891–1910*. Library of America, 1966.

Wilde, Oscar. "The Decay of Lying." *The Artist as Critic: Critical Writings of Oscar Wilde*, edited by Richard Ellmann, U of Chicago P, 1969, pp. 290–320.

Wilkins, John. *An Essay towards a Real Character, and a Philosophical Language*. Gellibrand and John Martyn, 1668.

Joe B. Fulton

Teaching Burlesque with Twain

"It was a crisp and spicy morning in early October," Mark Twain writes in "A Double-Barreled Detective Story." In one long, florid sentence, Twain piles up references to "lilacs and laburnums," "the glory-fires of autumn," and "a fairy bridge provided by kind Nature" before arriving at the final delicious thrust of the burlesque: "far in the empty sky a solitary œsophagus slept upon motionless wing; everywhere brooded stillness, serenity, and the peace of God" (312–13). One sees here an illustration of Robert Falk's definition of burlesque as "incongruous imitation and deflationary treatment" (88), but the paragraph became one of Twain's most notorious burlesques because it tricked so many people. "A Double-Barreled Detective Story" was a burlesque of Sir Arthur Conan Doyle's *A Study in Scarlet* and *The Hound of the Baskervilles*, but it can be read alongside any Sherlock Holmes story, for Holmes himself appears in Twain's story and provides one of those characteristic instances of deduction identifying the assassin as left-handed based on abstruse clues (349). What provoked letters to the editor and to the author was not the exaggerated spoof of detective fiction; readers simply wondered what sort of bird was this "œsophagus."

Twain discussed one such letter writer, amazed that "nothing in the paragraph disturbed him but that one word" (313).[1] What shocked Twain was that some read his story as a detective story, rather than as a burlesque of detective stories. True to burlesque exaggeration, the paragraph teemed with nonsensical lunacy beyond the "solitary œsophagus." Opinions at the time were divided, with some readers agreeing with the review in *Public Opinion* that "it will be difficult for the average reader to see where the joke comes in" and others siding with the review in the *Cleveland Plain Dealer* that considered Twain's burlesque to be "most admirable fooling" (Budd 516–17).

The solitary œsophagus took flight in 1902, but this was by no means the first time Twain's burlesquing muse tricked readers. Twain's use of burlesque began early in his career, with notable examples being "Petrified Man" (1862) and "A Bloody Massacre Near Carson" (1863). In the first instance, Twain wrote a fake news article about a petrified man supposedly found near Carson City, Nevada, an article reprinted by some newspapers as true reportage. In the second instance, Twain described a manifestly unbelievable massacre that was accepted by many as authentic. In both cases, Twain adopted journalistic style but provided clues the events were fabricated. As Twain recalled the reception of the two articles in "A Couple of Sad Experiences" (1870), many were fooled because of a difficulty inherent to the art: "To write a burlesque so wild that its pretended facts will not be accepted in perfect good faith by somebody, is very nearly an impossible thing to do" (388–89).

In most traditional definitions, burlesque is a comic imitation of a particular style of work or of the work of a particular author. In *Burlesque*, John D. Jump defines parody as "the high burlesque of a particular work (or author)" (2). Jump provides the apt example of Henry Fielding's *Shamela*, a parody of Samuel Richardson's *Pamela*; by contrast, Fielding's novels *Joseph Andrews* and *Tom Jones* are burlesques of the larger Richardsonian school of sentimentalism. In this definition, parody is a subset of burlesque. Contemporary parodies students might be familiar with are "Weird Al" Yankovic's numerous spoofs of pop songs, while burlesque is broader than parody, "freer" in its approach, as Falk phrases it (88). *The Century Dictionary* (1889–91) traces burlesque to its Italian origins, with *burla* meaning "jest" or "mockery" (Whitney 1: 727). Classic examples include Horace's *Satires*, Francesco Berni's *Opere burlesche* (1550–55), Miguel de Cervantes's *Don Quixote* (1605–15), Samuel Butler's *Hudibras*

(1663–78), and such later American contributions as Washington Irving's *Knickerbocker's History of New York* (1809), which purports to tell the history of Walter the Doubter, William the Testy, and Peter the Headstrong in the early years of New Amsterdam.

Burlesque is undeniably comic, but it is often satirical as well. Historically, burlesque has often seemed to be just low humor. Horace used the phrase *musa pedestris* to define his own approach in book 2, satire 6 of *Satires*, at least in part because of the low language he used, low burlesque being the mocking of something high with low language and high burlesque directing inflated language toward something prosaic. One might translate Horace's phrase as "pedestrian muse" or, as H. R. Fairclough does in the Loeb edition, as "prosaic muse" (211). Burlesque might even be coarse and profane, but it should not be confused with the vaudeville version of burlesque, for by the late 1880s a divergence had occurred in American usage, with burlesque acquiring "in modern use often specifically a theatrical piece, a kind of dramatic extravaganza," according to *The Century Dictionary* (Whitney 1: 727). Those extravaganzas grew bawdier, and burlesque came to be associated with the striptease, so that by 1909, the *Cambridge Tribune*, the "Saturday Morning Record of Cambridge and Harvard Affairs," declared in the article "The Evolution of Burlesque" that the entertainment had "reached such a degree of coarseness that the very word 'burlesque' had become synonymous with everything that was vulgar in theatricals" (12). Nevertheless, the satirical nature of much burlesque means that it aims not just to destroy through anarchic humor, but to construct something new and better on top of the rubble. This is true whether one is reading Alexander Pope's *The Rape of the Lock* (1712–14) or any of Twain's many burlesques.

A very effective introduction to burlesque is to read Twain's early burlesques "Petrified Man" and "A Bloody Massacre Near Carson" alongside his recollection of their reception in his sketch "A Couple of Sad Experiences," which contains the author's explanation of why people failed to detect the "'nub' or moral of the burlesque" (389). Twain claimed his joke was "so broad and so perfectly palpable that even a one-eyed potato could see it," yet fooled many people because of the "superior glare of something in the body of the burlesque itself" (389). In the case of the "Petrified Man" sketch, he explains that the readers missed the "string of roaring absurdities," including the fact that the petrified man was thumbing his nose (390). Here, the petrified man was the "superior glare" that hid such details. Intended to be satire of both the "petrifaction mania" and a local judge, G. T. Sewell, with whom Twain had many disagreements, the work failed, for "nobody but me ever discovered and comprehended the peculiar and suggestive position of the petrified man's hands" (389, 391).

Similarly, with "A Bloody Massacre Near Carson," Twain wrote a burlesque news article about a man who horribly massacres his family after despairing over his investments in a water company, the satirical target of the article. Although Twain included many indications that the article was not true, he watched in dismay as a farmer, described as a "heedless son of a hay-mow," scanned through the article, entirely missing the revelatory hints at burlesque as he hungrily devoured the lurid details, the "superior glare" that hid the real object (388). Both "Petrified Man" and "A Bloody Massacre Near Carson" had a satirical point and illustrate Gilbert Highet's definition of satire in *The Classical Tradition* as "joking in earnest" (305). One reason Twain found these experiences "sad" is that readers missed his larger point. It is as if one were to read Jonathan Swift's "A Modest Proposal," a satire of English policy in Ireland that mimics the language and style of dry political proposals, as an actual scheme to eat babies.

Just as Twain strove to make the burlesque obvious enough that it could be detected while subtle enough to be humorous, it is the educator's role to make manifest burlesque's "roaring absurdities." I have found a number of methods, responding to Twain's own concerns, to be effective. Reading Twain's "A Couple of Sad Experiences" is a great start, for it provides the author's own explanation of his tricks and how they fooled readers. Another technique is to begin with a direct parody, as a means of illustrating the distinction between parody and burlesque. The "superior glare" Twain complained of is reduced when the parody is obvious. Lane Cooper, a family friend of Twain's in-laws, the Langdons, revealed chapters 15 and 26 of Walter Besant and James Rice's *The Seamy Side* (1880) as the original for the notorious paragraph from "A Double-Barreled Detective Story" (86). Placing the sources alongside Twain's paragraph provides a direct parody that helps students see what Twain was doing with the paragraph. One could also read any of the Sherlock Holmes stories to see the broader burlesque, an exercise that clarifies the relationship between parody and burlesque, the former being a comic imitation of a particular text and the latter spoofing an entire category of texts. The teacher can also discuss the relationship between the burlesque and the original, what Twain scholar James Cox has referred to as "a double vision, half of which imitates the parent form, the other half which mocks it" (44). For this reason, Cox, like many other scholars, has argued that "burlesque is parasitic in a way that epic and tragedy are not" (44). Burlesque's parasitism is one reason people are often tricked by it, mistaking it for an example of the genre it mocks. This is why, as K. N. Macfarlane has pointed out, Horace's burlesque poem "Integer Vitae" has found a home "solemnly adorning graduation exercises and funerals" (23). One does not know whether to laugh or cry at this absurdity, but Horace would have us laugh.

With Twain's most frequently taught works, *The Adventures of Tom Sawyer* (1876) and *Adventures of Huckleberry Finn* (1885), understanding burlesque is similarly essential. In many respects, these two works are best understood as burlesques of Sunday school books, a genre that Twain described in "The Christmas Fireside" (1865) as "mild little books with marbled backs," books that show bad little boys and girls suffering for their sins and good little boys and girls triumphing over temptation (408). Twain's burlesques of the genre include "The Christmas Fireside," often anthologized by its subtitle, "The Story of the Bad Little Boy That Bore a Charmed Life" (1865); "Advice for Good Little Boys" (1865); "Advice for Good Little Girls" (1865); "Christian Spectator" (1865); "Colloquy between a Slum Child and a Moral Mentor" (1868); "The Story of Mamie Grant, the Child-Missionary" (1868); "The Story of the Good Little Boy Who Did Not Prosper" (1870); and "Little Bessie" (1908–09), among many others. Twain created these burlesques, or "antigenre," by deviating comically and satirically from books that sought to instruct children in moral precepts of Christianity, often from particular denominational perspectives.

The lunacy of Twain's spoofs is easily made manifest by comparing them with examples of the class of book he was burlesquing. One might compare *The Polite Boy* (c. 1860), whose author is ostensibly "Uncle Madison," with Twain's "The Christmas Fireside," which purports to be by "Grandfather Twain." Many of these Sunday school books are available online in searchable texts, facilitating comparison of structure or particular words or phrases. For example, Twain wrote in "The Story of the Good Little Boy Who Did Not Prosper" that "no boy, good or bad, ever starts a remark with 'Oh, Sir!'" (377–78). Some variant of "Oh! Mother" and "Oh! Father" are used ad nauseam in *Willy Graham; or, The Disobedient Boy* (1844), and the inevitable "Oh, Sir" occurs in *Frank Harper; or, The Country-Boy in Town* (1847). Twain's "The Story of the Good Little Boy Who Did Not Prosper" embraces "all the Sunday-school books" as the pattern to which it responds, but in this burlesque, "there was a screw loose somewhere, and it all happened just the other way" (374, 376). By adopting an entire genre and then making things happen "just the other way," Grandfather Twain burlesques Uncle Madison and all the other moralistic relatives with their goody-goody fictions.

Sydney Krause accurately contends that Twain's writing was typically provoked by "an animus against *some*thing. His motive, like that of all fellow satirists, implied the Juvenalian pretext, 'si natura negat, facit indignation versum'" (21), which one might loosely translate as "although nature has left one weak, indignation allows one to write." Sunday school books were not just poorly told tales; they were immoral because they lied about children and lied about Calvin's ideas about providence, a lifelong preoccupation of Twain's. They rewrote the Book of Job to side with his "comforters" by implying that bad things happen only to bad people: Job must have done something. In *Willy Graham*, the father ascribes the death of Willy's siblings to his parental neglect of Christian duties, citing the Book of Job as an example. Had the father (or the author) actually studied the Book of Job, the absurdity of that parallel would be obvious, for Job was "perfect and upright, and one that feared God, and eschewed evil" (*Bible*, Job 1.1). Depicting a world in which the wicked are always punished and the virtuous always rewarded (albeit sometimes with a victorious death scene) is more than bad art, Twain argues; it is bad theology.

For the classroom, the best examples of the flowering of this burlesque treatment of Sunday school books are *Tom Sawyer* and *Huckleberry Finn*. *Tom Sawyer* is the story of a bad boy who makes good; Leslie Fiedler famously labeled Tom the "Good Bad Boy" (270), but in fact when compared with the genre's typical bad boys, Tom really is bad. He hangs out with low people like Huck Finn and visits low places like bars and prisons, and he even declares, "[C]hurch ain't shucks to a circus" (83). The entire work can be viewed as a burlesque of the Sunday school book plot. The book's first word is Tom's name yelled in anger, yet *Tom Sawyer* ends with Tom triumphant: rich and embraced by Judge Thatcher, who declares that even his lies are "noble" because of the purpose to which he put them (232–33). For the classroom, *Tom Sawyer* is a great choice because, generally, fewer college students have read it than have read *Huckleberry Finn*.

For immediate comparison and to reveal the mature artistic burlesque, compare chapters 2–4, covering the famous whitewashing scene and its aftermath. These chapters show in microcosm the burlesquing structure of the story. Twain actually pairs the whitewashing scene, which is Tom's punishment for playing hooky from school, with a scene in the Sunday school, where Tom uses the treasure he has gained by conning other boys into whitewashing the fence to obtain the tickets necessary to gain the coveted Bible—and the attention that comes with it. Even today, the motto of many Sunday schools emphasizes memorization with the verse "Thy word have I hid in mine heart, that I might not sin against thee" (*Bible*, Ps. 119.11), but Tom, as we see in the first pages of chapter 4, cannot remember his verses. Mary tries to guide him through the simplest verses but finds him unwilling and unable, so he converts the wealth he was "literally rolling in" from the whitewashing episode into the tickets (awarded for having memorized verses) necessary to get a Bible. When asked what they think of Tom at this point, most students will respond negatively. Discussing him as the antitype of the Sunday school book protagonist who sins, converts sin into reward, and converts that reward into a biblical reward in church reveals what Twain is up to. Of course, the collapse is inevitable as Tom lacks the knowledge to back up his claim that he had learned the verses. As he proclaims the first two disciples were "DAVID AND GOLIAH!" at the end of the chapter, the narrator quietly intrudes—"Let us draw the curtain of charity over the rest of the scene"—with language drawn from the genre, here harnessed to comedy (65). Class discussion at this point can focus on which character is the vehicle of satire and which are the objects of it. As much as Tom is revealed as a con man, the society devoted to style, rather than substance, seems the target of the satire.

Twain's masterpiece *Huckleberry Finn* likewise shows its burlesque origins with the narrative reversing Sunday school book logic and theology. One sees it in an obvious way when Tom justifies stealing: "I don't care shucks for the morality of it, nohow. When I start in to steal a nigger, or a watermelon, or a Sunday school book, I ain't no ways particular how it's done" (307). Another example is the famous scene where Huck debates whether to turn Jim over to the authorities as an escaped slave, which follows the generic moral crisis, a scene in which a character has to make the decision for once and always. "Willy's first step in disobedience was taken when he rebelled in his heart against his mother's commands," the narrator of *Willy Graham* intones (15). His decision is fateful, for his wickedness nearly leads to his drowning and does end the life of another boy. Huck's downward slide begins early and accelerates with such humorous inversions as his discussion with Jim about the morality of stealing, leading them to "drop crabapples and p'simmons" but continue to "borrow" watermelons and cantaloupes (80). Huck's conscience quickens as the book progresses, with the moral crisis of chapter 31 and his declaration, "All right, then I'll *go* to hell" (271). Huck's vow to go to hell rather than turn Jim in is the apex of American burlesque, an example of dramatic irony that reveals to the reader the corruption of society in its own corrupt terms. This particular scene is often misread by students and critics alike. Putting it into conversation with the Sunday school book restores the social context in which Twain wrote the work and highlights the fact that Huck, like those goody-goody protagonists, thinks through his moral crisis in terms society has provided. Society has taught Huck that slavery is righteous, so his moral crisis highlights how morally bankrupt society is. Comparing Huck with Willy Graham helps students comprehend the object of the satire when this boy with "a sound heart and a deformed conscience," as Twain called him, shows that he has been grievously mistaught by a society whose moral code is bankrupt.[2]

Burlesque has often been characterized as having a democratic, antiauthoritarian spirit. As Twain's contemporary Richard Grant White wrote, "[B]urlesque casts down all the gods from their pedestals" (256). Among the great artists he included in this band of vandals were Aristophanes, with his comedies *The Birds* (414 BCE) and *The Frogs* (405 BCE); Butler, with *Hudibras*; and Swift, with *Gulliver's Travels* (1726). Twain's shorter burlesques provide a clear introduction to burlesque, allowing the teacher to lead discussion toward clarifying the relationship among burlesque, parody, and satire. Teaching Twain's masterworks *Tom Sawyer* and *Huckleberry Finn* as burlesques illuminates those works even while illustrating how extraordinarily productive burlesque has been in American and world literature. The best burlesques achieve life apart from their hosts, but understanding the dynamic relationship between literary "parasite" and "host" deepens our understanding of the artist's work in destroying one view of the world and substituting a new one.

Notes

1. Quotations from the letters and Twain's responses to them are from an extended footnote in the 1903 edition of "A Double-Barreled Detective Story," pp. 312–15.

2. The phrase is from Twain's notebook and is quoted in the 2003 U of California P edition of *Adventures* (619).

Works Cited

The Bible. The Authorized King James Version, edited by Robert Caroll and Stephen Prickett, Oxford World Classics, 2008.

Budd, Louis J., editor. *Mark Twain: The Contemporary Reviews.* Cambridge UP, 1999.

Cooper, Lane. "Mark Twain's Lilacs and Laburnums." *Modern Language Notes,* vol. 47, no. 2, Feb. 1932, pp. 85–87.

Cox, James M. *Mark Twain: The Fate of Humor.* Princeton UP, 1966.

"The Evolution of Burlesque." *Cambridge Tribune,* 30 Oct. 1909, p. 12.

Falk, Robert P. "Burlesque." *Princeton Encyclopedia of Poetry and Poetics,* edited by Alex Preminger, Princeton UP, 1974, pp. 88–89.

Fiedler, Leslie A. *Love and Death in the American Novel.* Criterion Books, 1960.

Frank Harper; or, The Country-Boy in Town. American Sunday-School Union, 1847.

Highet, Gilbert. *The Classical Tradition: Greek and Roman Influences on Western Literature.* Oxford UP, 1949.

Horace. *Satires, Epistles, The Art of Poetry.* Translated by H. R. Fairclough, Harvard UP, 1926. Loeb Classical Library 194.

Jump, John D. *Burlesque.* Methuen, 1972.

Krause, Sydney J. *Mark Twain as Critic.* Johns Hopkins UP, 1967.

Macfarlane, K. N. "'Integer Vitae': A Wolf by the Ears." *The Classical Journal,* vol. 77, no. 1, Oct.–Nov. 1981, pp. 23–26.

Twain, Mark. *Adventures of Huckleberry Finn.* Edited by Victor Fischer et al., U of California P, 2003.

———. *The Adventures of Tom Sawyer. The Works of Mark Twain: The Adventures of Tom Sawyer; Tom Sawyer Abroad; Tom Sawyer, Detective,* edited by John C. Gerber et al., U of California P, 1980, pp. 31–237.

———. "The Christmas Fireside. For Good Little Boys and Girls. By Grandfather Twain. The Story of the Bad Little Boy That Bore a Charmed Life." *The Works of Mark Twain: Early Tales and Sketches, Volume 2, 1864–1865,* edited by Edgar M. Branch and Robert H. Hirst, U of California P, 1981, pp. 407–10.

———. *Collected Tales, Sketches, Speeches, and Essays, 1852–1890.* Edited by Louis J. Budd, Library of America, 1992.

———. "A Couple of Sad Experiences." Twain, *Collected Tales,* pp. 388–95.

———. "A Double-Barreled Detective Story." *"The Man That Corrupted Hadleyburg" and Other Essays and Stories,* Harper and Brothers, 1903, pp. 292–367.

———. "The Story of the Good Little Boy Who Did Not Prosper." Twain, *Collected Tales,* pp. 374–78.

White, Richard Grant. "The Age of Burlesque." *Galaxy,* vol. 8, Aug. 1869, pp. 256–66.

Whitney, William Dwight, editor. *The Century Dictionary: An Encyclopedic Lexicon of the English Language.* Century Company, 1889–91. 6 vols.

Willy Graham; or, The Disobedient Boy. American Sunday-School Union, 1844.

Helen Deutsch

Disgust and Embodiment

The biggest challenge I've faced as a teacher was English 10B—the second course in a three-part introduction to the English major covering *Beowulf* to Virginia Woolf (and beyond) at the University of California, Los Angeles, a course so demanding that it boasted its own T-shirt declaring, "I Survived the 10 Series." It was the first and has remained the only large lecture course I've ever taught, and I found my position behind the podium more frightening than empowering. This was not just because I preferred discussion to lecturing (indeed the longer I taught the course, the more I realized that the two formats were much more permeable than I'd assumed). My material—Restoration and eighteenth-century literature—was a particular source of anxiety.

The Renaissance, I tell my students, may have been the great age of tragedy, and others may identify the Enlightenment with the rise of the novel, but my eighteenth century is the age of satire. Satire, I argue, is tragedy turned against the reader. Stereotypes of the polite eighteenth century notwithstanding (often gleaned by students from filmic adaptations of Jane Austen's novels), I traffic in texts that are neither polite nor friendly to their readers, that expose human nakedness in an effort to cut beauty down to size, that revel in excrement, that delight in cruelty toward the particular objects of their opprobrium in order to excoriate general humanity.[1] By the time my students get to Austen, they realize that controlled as she may be, she is as vehement and skilled a hater as her fellow satirist Alexander Pope, whose poetry she admired and whose couplets' intricate balance of oppositional forces we can hear not only in the titles of *Sense and Sensibility* and *Pride and Prejudice* but in each novel's complex unsettling of easy binaries. I call my course "Paradox 10B," and our conversation revolves around the paradox at the heart of satire itself: between elegant polished form and uncivil and often revolting deformity.

"SATYR is a sort of Glass, wherein Beholders do generally discover every body's Face but their Own" (Swift, *Essential Writings* 95). The opening line of the preface to Jonathan Swift's "The Battel of the Books" perfectly and politely articulates the impetus behind satire's violent attempts to reform by replacing self-love with the painful shock of readers' self-recognition. At once prideful and abject, idealistic and despairing, godlike and powerless, the satirist strives to humble human pride by holding up a beastly mirror. The passivity of Swift's metaphor belies the ways in which this mirror is a weapon that wreaks havoc with the reader's consciousness. Irony at its simplest, I tell my students, makes the reader want to be in on the joke rather than its butt; it is the art of hearing the invisible quotation marks around words. In the case of Swift—who dominates this essay as he does the satiric tradition in English—I have had students tell me that they would rather be behind him at a cocktail party listening to him impersonate the voices of his enemies than confront him face-to-face. Swift's satire insists upon the confrontation. Consider book 4 of *Gulliver's Travels*, in which Gulliver is stranded on an island populated by savage hominids (Yahoos) and ruled by reasonable horses (Houyhnhnms). Gulliver is forced, most definitively after having suffered the advances of a young female Yahoo (who he later admits was not quite as disgusting as the rest of her kind), to deem himself "a real Yahoo, in every limb and feature" (2444). He repudiates the Yahoos by fervent identification with the master equine race, making clothing and the canoe in which he leaves the island from Yahoo skins and finally, upon his forced exile to England, escaping the stench of his human family through the comfort of a stable. While he redounds from one extreme to the other, we remain unmoored in the uncomfortable limbo that irony provides, tethered to our bodies by the inescapable recoil of disgust. If satire's wit frees the reader from unthinking acquiescence to convention, such freedom comes with a price.

The reader of satire has nowhere to come home to, not even, indeed especially, his own body.

While eighteenth-century travel narratives entertained audiences by bringing the exotic home, Swift's satire in *Gulliver* inverts this project by making the familiar strange. Intending to vex the world rather than divert it (Swift, *Essential Writings* 676)—an angry take on Horace's influential credo that literature delight and instruct—book 4 forces the reader to identify the savages, whose place on the Great Chain of Being (a hierarchy at risk of falling apart in an age of discovery and revolution) was somewhere between human and animal, with herself. Students in my class learn to be comfortable with thinking of themselves as lesser animals. Gulliver's Houyhnhnm master appraises the "gentle Yahoo's" body from a horse's perspective and finds much to be lacking. Noting Gulliver's tender feet and lack of 180-degree vision, the horse's voice seems to merge with Swift's own when observing that since Gulliver walks unsteadily on his hind legs, he "must inevitably fall" (2430). While I point out to students the pun on the Christian fall and original sin (from which the virtuous Houyhnhnms might appear to be exempt, until Gulliver's singular case brings them to contemplate Yahoo genocide), in a recent course they did Swift's irony, so firmly grounded in the material world and its physicality, one better. Several biology majors, a few of whom grew up on or near farms, pointed out that horses, bred to race and run straight, in fact fall very easily, and when they fall they often can't get up again and have to be shot. The Houyhnhnms too have their pride.

The experience of reading Swift forces the abjectly disabled being he defined, through his ironic mouthpiece Gulliver, in an echo of Shakespeare's *Richard III*, as "a lump of deformity, and diseases both in body and mind, smitten with *pride*" and the human reader into identity (2462). Swift's irony is the most extreme yet representative example of satire's ability to undermine both dominant protocols of representation and standard ethical categories. The reader of eighteenth-century satire is forced to embrace madmen, monsters, and the savage others known as Yahoos as himself, "in doubt to deem himself a god, or beast," as Pope puts it in his meditation on the nature of the human that opens book 2 of *Essay on Man* (2548, line 8). To read satire is to be at once humbled by and freed from the limits of the human.[2] Once again Swift provides us with a defining example: a gendered object lesson in the perils of rejecting the body. The speaker of Swift's "The Lady's Dressing Room" makes a point of separating himself from the pitiable "wretched Strephon, blind / to all the charms of womankind" (2593, lines 129–30). Strephon's disillusionment stems from his discovery, in a gendered reversal of the Pandora myth, of the reeking remnants of his beloved Celia's beauty routine (a routine Swift's friend Pope celebrated as both divine self-worship and epic arming for battle in his more affectionately satirical, feminine miniature mock-epic *The Rape of the Lock*). His scientific "survey" of Celia's closet runs the gamut from puppy urine to dirty socks to a magnifying glass that tellingly leads him to imagine Celia's pimple extractions by looking at his own face to, finally, a chamber pot disguised as a cabinet (a great opportunity for visual aids readily available through *Google Images*, since eighteenth-century chamber pots were often witty pieces of artifice), in which Strephon "foul[s] his hands in search of hope" (2592, line 94). Refusing the opportunity to find hope in excrement, Strephon is doomed, like Gulliver, to madness. In a parody of the Lockean association of ideas, he ends the poem, again like Gulliver, woefully compelled to associate "each dame he sees with all her stinks" (2592, line 122). By contrast Swift's speaker demonstrates the difference between satiric wit and tragedy, stopping his nose and marveling at feminine art. "Should I the queen of love refuse," he asks, "Because she rose from stinking ooze?" (2593, lines 131–32). This couplet wittily balances the classic icon of beauty—think Botticelli's *The Birth of Venus* on the half shell—with redolent slime (the goddess of love was born from blood and semen when Saturn castrated his father, Caelus, and threw the cast-off genitals into the sea) and repellent rhyme, perfectly exemplifying Swift's urbanely scatological wit, genteelly declining to transcend the stink of the body and reversing the proper ascent of humanity above its shit that Sigmund Freud outlined in *Civilization and Its Discontents.* As he does in all his satire, Swift makes it impossible to rise above the filthy world that he futilely tries to change.

I am a firm believer in reading literature out loud with students. When you teach satire, this exercise becomes more essential and more risky. I therefore begin each iteration of 10B (and there have been many) with a satire on myself as teacher of satire. I do this to demonstrate the ways in which the period's satire not only focuses on the body in all its aberrancy, but also implicates the reader through the power of its performative utterance. I recount my experience as a beginning assistant professor at Northwestern University, invited to an event called Frivolous Readings sponsored by a humanities-oriented (non-frat) house of bookish students, who called upon their professors to entertain them with lighthearted humorous selections.

Somewhat perversely, it seems to me now, I decided to read "The Imperfect Enjoyment," a poem of failed masculinity, by John Wilmot, the Earl of Rochester. Like any of Pope's or Swift's satiric targets, I was proud and oblivious: I hadn't read the poem recently and figured Rochester's bawdy account of an experience of premature ejaculation would make me a hit. As I began to read to a group of senior male colleagues and dutiful young undergraduates, I realized I had seriously miscalculated. I was a young woman appearing to be referring to my penis as "the all-dissolving thunderbolt below" (2169, line 10). This wonderful line, in which the allusion to Zeus's proverbial lightning bolt and his destruction of his human lover Semele when appearing to her in his true form merges with the destruction of the pentameter's customary caesura, definitely earned a laugh (and a laugh even more pointed when provoked by a woman). But when I seemed to be praising my former erotic prowess by nostalgically recalling how my "dart of love" "where'er it pierced, a cunt it found or made" (2170, line 43)—thus forced to utter a word I had never before spoken out loud, much less in public—I knew I was in trouble. Things got only worse when I got to the poem's conclusion, a vitriolic and obscene curse of the penis, now disowned and disavowed, condemning it to disease and low company, finally demanding that "may ten thousand abler pricks agree / to do the wronged Corinna right for thee" (2171, lines 71–72). On that closing image of gang rape (one that in the context of 10B I was later able to connect to Edmund Burke's unironic image of ten thousand swords leaping to defend Marie-Antoinette from the French revolutionaries in *Reflections on the Revolution in France*), I left the stage to the dropped jaws and disoriented looks of the students, immersed in consternation and shame. I still don't know if I felt better or worse when Jean Hagstrum, a much-admired and extremely senior scholar of eighteenth-century eroticism, kindly reassured me how much he enjoyed my performance.

I recover from this story in the classroom by giving students enough background to understand that Rochester's purported subject, the experience of premature ejaculation, is in fact a learned exercise in poetic showmanship as well as a sophisticated philosophical meditation on the mind-body problem and the nature of the human. I stress above all that the speaker's "I" is not identical to Rochester himself. I describe Rochester's transformation of the genre of the impotence poem, which began with the Roman poet Ovid's sexually and politically transgressive *Amores* and flourished in the licentious, sophisticated, and theatrical court of the libertine king Charles II. (Rochester's two most important innovations are the unprecedented length and intensity of the concluding curse and his substitution of premature ejaculation for impotence—even the satirist has his pride.) I explain that libertines linked freedom of body with freedom of mind, rebelling against conventions that they thereby reinforced (to shit on an altar, as one Restoration libertine did, is to give credence to religion's power). I note the political dimensions of the period's pornography by turning to Rochester's satire on King Charles: "his sceptre and his prick are of a length; / And she that plays with one may sway the other" (Wilmot, *Selected Works* 17, lines 11–12). I explain the Epicurean philosophy of atoms and void revived by Restoration thinkers (most important, for my purposes, the political philosopher Thomas Hobbes), which rejected the afterlife for the lived body and which Rochester took to unprecedented extremes. I turn to John Dryden by way of contrast, whose *Mac Flecknoe* introduces students to a satire of ironic praise that, unlike Swift's and Rochester's, reinforces and links aesthetic, political, and religious values and, with its timeless phrase "relics of the bum" (2114, line 105), referring to the ultimate fate of bad writing, presages Pope's excremental mock-epic of intellectual chaos, *The Dunciad*. I linger on the phrase as an example of Dryden's prowess as a master of epic diction's periphrasis, the "speaking around" in its literal sense, that grounds materiality with abstraction and that Pope takes to new heights in his mock-epics.

In his frank translation of the fourth book of Lucretius's *De Rerum Natura* on love, Dryden enters Rochester's territory. For Lucretius, love is a disease of the imagination that tragically separates humans from animals, and is therefore the one appetite that can't be satisfied. (In his "Satire against Reason and Mankind," Rochester declares he'd rather be "a dog, a monkey, or a bear / Or anything but that vain animal / Who is so proud of being rational," who eats not when he is hungry but when the clock dictates [Wilmot, "Satire" 2173, lines 5–7].) Lucretius's advice to the young man to whom he addresses his poem is to dispel desire's illusions—"discharge thy loins on all the leaky kind" (Dryden, *Selected Poems* 199, line 20)—in a misogynistic periphrasis that haunts Celia's dressing room and future satirical masculine fantasies of disembodied impenetrability. "The Imperfect Enjoyment," I tell my students, is an object lesson in the pitfalls of being a human animal, one that Aphra Behn, in her own version of the impotence poem, "The Disappointment," narrates from the woman's perspective and from within the confines of the period's sexual double standard. All of this context notwithstanding, students still have a difficult time separating Rochester from what is, ironically enough, a shameful experience of separation from one's own body.

For the teacher of satire, the body in all its excess and immediacy, within and without the text, is at once key and obstacle to student engagement. It is even harder for our students to recognize their face in satire's glass when history has made the genre's topicality almost illegible: the ugly particulars that mar *The Dunciad*'s pages and the elaborate political allegories of *Gulliver's Travels*, just to name two possible examples, are nearly untranslatable to most readers today. As the eighteenth-century catalog of literary monsters known as the canon demonstrates, what endures beyond the page and continues to surprise students is the body of the satirist himself, which can never be fully separated from the objects he reviles. Homer's misshapen hunchback Thersites—whose name was hurled at the similarly deformed and socially disenfranchised Pope (who both translated the *Iliad* and mocked ancient heroes by casting them as modern ladies in his *Rape of the Lock*) and whose satiric excesses provoked a vicious circle of brutal responses (including Lady Mary Wortley Montagu and Lord John Hervey's cruel characterization of him in their "Verses Address'd to the Imitator of Horace" as both "resemblance and disgrace" of the human form rendered in the divine image [Fairer 189, line 15])—is literature's original abusive satirist and abject object of satire. While the ever-elusive Swift's weapon is the glass in which readers recognize themselves in general deformity, Pope inverts the mirror to force readers to see themselves in his ugly particularity (Deutsch, *Resemblance*). For Pope, satire is a weapon wielded as a sword or whip, and in the character portraits that animate his poetry, he attacks his opponents by rendering them as versions of himself: the portrait of the fierce Atossa (Duchess of Marlborough), in "Epistle to a Lady," who "finds all her life one warfare upon earth" (2600, line 118), borrows the phrase from Pope's own correspondence, and when Pope insists upon breaking the butterfly John Hervey upon a wheel in his *Epistle to Arbuthnot*, the hybrid creature he terms "one vile antithesis" (2557, line 325) resembles nobody more than himself. Yet even this master of negation, in his final imitation of Horace, makes himself, in all his disorderly imperfection, emblematic of common humanity, reproaching his patron Lord Bolingbroke for his unreflective laughter at Pope's unseemly form while ignorant of his own moral disarray (Deutsch, "Bolingbroke's Laugh").

Despite or perhaps because of my Rochester-induced trauma, I always ask students to ponder the author's case, both body and example, as crucial to satire's effectiveness. Whether I discuss Rochester's syphilis and deathbed conversion in relation to his libertine conservatism, Anne Finch's battle with melancholy in elucidation of her self-doubting feminism in "The Spleen," Swift's vertigo and lifelong fear of madness in the context of his dizzying irony, Montagu's disfigurement by smallpox in contemplation of the alternating irony and sincerity of her mock-eclogue "Saturday," Samuel Johnson's nervous tics in explication of the unconcluded conclusions of *Rasselas* and "The Vanity of Human Wishes" (Deutsch, "Author"), or Mary Leapor's weak and ungainly body and career in service as informing her "Essay on Woman," envisioning the satirist's body allows the student to experience history viscerally, holding the glass up to the author and/as herself. When I show the class the African American artist Kehinde Wiley's 2009 reimagination of Joshua Reynolds's 1769 portrait *Johnson Arguing*, from Wiley's Black Light series, they immediately grasp the game that eighteenth-century satire is asking them to play. Reynolds's dark portrait balances a realistic depiction of a wigless Johnson's singular gesticulations with neoclassical idealization. By portraying a young African American man in a baseball hat and polished streetwear in the same pose against a brightly colored, patterned background, Wiley translates eighteenth-century paradox into twenty-first-century wit, casting a transformative "black light" over the original.

Taking them back in time to Reynolds's neoclassical take on Johnson as the figure of Socrates in Raphael's *School of Athens* and forward to twenty-first-century hip-hop iconography, these images allow the Greek philosophical tradition's famously ugly original satirist, whose irony was likened by Alcibiades in Plato's *Symposium* to the half-human, half-animal Silenus doll inside of which hides a golden Apollo (an apt personification of the genre of satire), to speak to them in their own embodied present. Socrates' impossible injunction is satire's vexing and variable challenge: know thyself.

Notes

1. For a definitive study of the period's comic literature, which documents a culture wherein laughing at cripples was common and aristocratic entertainments such as the old lady race (as depicted in Frances Burney's *Evelina*) a familiar reality, see Dickie.

2. Eighteenth-century satire thus reorients George Test's reading of the genre as "a legitimate aesthetic expression of basic human emotions—anger, shame, indignation, disgust, contempt—that are aroused by universal human behavior" by questioning the nature of the human itself (5).

Works Cited

Deutsch, Helen. "The Author as Monster: The Case of Dr. Johnson." *"Defects": Engendering the Modern Body*, edited by Helen Deutsch and Felicity Nussbaum, U of Michigan P, 2000.

———. "Bolingbroke's Laugh: Alexander Pope's *Epistle I* and the Rhetoric of Embodied Exemplarity." *Studies in the Literary Imagination*, vol. 38, no. 1, Spring 2005, pp. 137–61.

———. *Resemblance and Disgrace: Alexander Pope and the Deformation of Culture.* Harvard UP, 1996.

Dickie, Simon. *Cruelty and Laughter: Forgotten Comic Literature and the Unsentimental Eighteenth Century.* U of Chicago P, 2011.

Dryden, John. *Mac Flecknoe.* Lipking and Noggle, pp. 2111–17.

———. *Selected Poems.* Edited by Steven N. Zwicker and David Bywaters, Penguin Books, 2001.

Fairer, David, and Christine Gerrard, editors. *Eighteenth-Century Poetry: An Annotated Anthology.* 2nd ed., Blackwell, 2004.

Lipking, Lawrence, and James Noggle, editors. *The Restoration and the Eighteenth Century. The Norton Anthology of English Literature*, vol. C, 8th ed., Norton, 2006.

Pope, Alexander. "Epistle to a Lady." Lipking and Noggle, pp. 2598–604.

———. *Epistle to Dr. Arbuthnot.* Lipking and Noggle, pp. 2548–59.

———. *An Essay on Man.* Lipking and Noggle, pp. 2540–48.

Reynolds, Joshua. *Johnson Arguing.* 1769. *Tate*, www.tate.org.uk/art/artworks/reynolds-doctor-johnson-arguing-n04506.

Swift, Jonathan. *The Essential Writings of Jonathan Swift.* Edited by Claude Rawson and Ian Higgins, Norton, 2010.

———. *Gulliver's Travels.* Lipking and Noggle, pp. 2323–462.

———. "The Lady's Dressing Room." Lipking and Noggle, pp. 2590–93.

Test, George A. *Satire: Spirit and Art.* U of South Florida P, 1991.

Wiley, Kehinde. *After Sir Joshua Reynolds' "Portrait of Samuel Johnson."* Black Light series, 2009. *Artnet*, www.artnet.com/artists/kehinde-wiley/after-sir-joshua-reynolds-portrait-of-samuel-QIP2aYR5C9Xa_bxMLYSqSQ2.

Wilmot, John (Earl of Rochester). "The Imperfect Enjoyment." Lipking and Noggle, pp. 2169–71.

———. "A Satire against Reason and Mankind." Lipking and Noggle, pp. 2172–77.

———. *Selected Works.* Edited by Frank H. Ellis, Penguin, 2004.

Catherine Ingrassia

Gendered Satires in Dialogue

Anne Finch's verse fable "The Critick and the Writer of Fables" (1713), an imagined dialogue between a poet and critic, satirizes the fashionable poetic attempts to "please the Men of Taste." The critic accuses the poet of seeking "to purchase Fame by childish Tales" (e.g., fables) and urges him to pursue other genres. "[E]asily persuaded," the poet moves through epic ("old Bombast . . . I'm sick of Troy") and pastoral ("Th' Eternal Hush, the Lullaby of Streams") but without success: "both the Writers, and the Readers sleep." "If thou would'st move our Thoughts," the critic advises the poet, "urge thy Pen, . . . To show us private, or the publick Faults"—that is, write satire.[1] As Mary Savage notes in "On the Use—Abuse of Poetry," satire allows poets to " say that in rhime, / Which they dare not in prose attempt to define" (9–10). That female poets assert the corrective, entertaining, and potentially subversive possibilities of satire runs counter to the persistent misapprehension that women had limited engagement with the genre in the long eighteenth century. In fact, during the so-called age of satire, women consistently contributed to this form, actively engaged contemporaneous male satirists, and addressed key issues of the day.

Commercial literary anthologies construct women's involvement in eighteenth-century satire as limited, often adversarial, and primarily reactive. *The Norton Anthology of English Literature*, for example, suggests women's inability to "resist the urge to reply" to their male counterparts prompted their satiric forays (Lipking and Noggle 2589).[2] Consequently, the voices of the male satirists, such as Alexander Pope and Jonathan Swift, emerge as dominant, and too few poems by too few women (always paired with a male contemporary) serve as proxy for the dozens of female poets writing satiric verse. Aphra Behn's "The Disappointment" inevitably appears with Rochester's "The Imperfect Enjoyment"; Mary Wortley Montagu's "The Reasons That Induced Dr. Swift to Write a Poem Called 'The Lady's Dressing Room'" with that Swift poem; and Mary Leapor's "An Epistle to a Lady" with Pope's poem of the same name. These familiar pairings, centered on gender or sexuality, provide an opportunity to discuss the cultural expectations shaping heteronormative interactions and their particular effects on women—an important subject to be sure. But while editorially and pedagogically tidy, such pairings flatten the unremarked differences among the poets in question (eliding, for example, Behn's desires to be a court poet and casting her as a disgruntled provocateur) and artificially limit the topics of women's poetry (Montagu, like other women, wrote satiric poems that extended far beyond issues of gender and sexuality). Consequently, anthology-bound instructors unwittingly present an incomplete vision of the diversity of satire in the period, ultimately diminishing the complexity of the poems by women and men.

While this brief essay cannot construct a complete literary history of women's contributions to satire, I suggest some pedagogical strategies for more richly presenting the culture of eighteenth-century satire and for exploring gendered dialogues beyond those anthologies construct. Teaching dialogues between poets Pope and Swift and contemporaries such as Mary Barber, Mary Jones, and Montagu provides opportunities to explore the nature of the genre, its gendered implications, and the contrasting verse that results. Carefully supplementing the anthology enables instructors to engage issues beyond the establishing lens of gender and to see how men and women also satirically wrote about topics such as class, marriage, and the literary marketplace.

Montagu's "Reasons That Induced Dr. Swift" and Swift's "The Lady's Dressing Room" remain a staple of British literature anthologies. If instructors begin with this important if perhaps overexposed pairing, they should remind students that it presents Montagu as vindictive and reactive and forecloses the ability to think about Swift's treatment of women as more nuanced than pure misogyny. (Swift's satire is more complex than even Montagu acknowledges, its subject as much the unrealistic Strephon as Celia and the consumer culture from which she springs.) However, to complicate that discussion with a focus on class, instructors might integrate canto 1 of *The Rape of the Lock*, Mary Leapor's "Epistle to a Lady," and Swift's ironically titled "A Beautiful Young Nymph Going to Bed." Each poem also presents a woman's dressing room but reminds students how economics determine the nature of that space.

Pope's Belinda, dreaming of a glittering youth (her sylph in disguise), is awakened by her lapdog Shock and her "Eyes first open'd on a *Billet-doux*" (1.18).[3] Canto 1 continues with the highly teachable and deeply resonant dressing table scene that allows instructors to discuss empire, commerce, and gender. Swift, himself perhaps satirizing Pope, presents the private space of the prostitute Corinna. Rather than potential lovers, Swift's Corinna dreams instead of imprisonment, exploitation, or transportation to the colonies:

> Or if she chance to close her eyes,
> Of Bridewell and the compter dreams,
> And feels the lash, and faintly screams.
> . . . .
> Or to Jamaica seems transported. (40–42, 45)

Awake, she greets "the Ruins of the Night," the consequences of the cannibalization of her few possessions by the animals around her. Leapor, herself a kitchen maid, meaningfully draws on both those poems. "Mira," Leapor's pen name, "dreams, as slumbring Poets may," of "Books and Pictures in Bright Order" (21, 23) (suggestive of Belinda's toilet, with "Each Silver Vase in mystic Order laid" [1.122]). Yet, like Corinna rather than Belinda, Mira's reality is confined by work and the limitations of class: "She awakes, alas! To Business and to Woes, / To sweep her Kitchen, and to mend her Clothes" (31–32). Adding these distinct scenes of private space to a discussion of Swift and Montagu can extend the classroom conversation beyond sexuality to a consideration of class, forms of female labor, and consumer culture. These poems also illustrate that the dialogue among poets and their poems extends far wider than perhaps originally realized.

Pope's *Rape of the Lock*, like "Epistle to a Lady," remains a touchstone for many instructors who might teach it with Leapor's "Epistle to a

Lady," with which it is frequently anthologized. However, also integrating Charlotte Lennox's "The Art of Coquetry" offers rich possibilities for discussing both coquetry as a social performance and the literary marketplace. Better known as a satiric novelist, Lennox published the poem in *The Gentleman's Magazine* in November 1750 and also in her collection of poems. The *Internet Library of Early Journals* (www.bodley.ox.ac.uk/ilej/), an open-source collection of eighteenth-century periodicals that includes *The Gentleman's Magazine*, makes is possible for students to read Lennox's poem in facsimile, providing instructors with the opportunity to discuss the emergence of print culture, the role of poetry within periodicals, and the significance of women's poetry within such a popular publication. Considering "The Art of Coquetry" within its original context also reminds students that verse satire was a popular, accessible form.

The poem, centered on the figure of the coquette, invokes both *Rape of the Lock* and "Epistle to a Lady," with allusions recognizable to an eighteenth-century reader (and to twenty-first-century college students, as a well-designed classroom assignment demonstrates). Written for the "lovely maid" who has "Ne'er felt the Force of Love's resistless Darts" (1–2), the poem addresses women "Who o'er Mankind wou'd fain exert [their] sway" (5). The term *sway* immediately invokes "Epistle to a Lady," where Pope defines women as driven by "The Love of Pleasure and the Love of Sway" (210).[4] Lennox's coquettes are women with "Power all your Wish, but Beauty all your Arms" (4), a line that simultaneously summons Pope's assertion that women operate with "Pow'r all their end, but Beauty all the means" (220), as well as the moment in *Rape of the Lock* when Belinda's "awful Beauty puts on all its Arms" (1.139).

Lennox offers a satiric primer for the social performance of women with recommended practices that mimic the attributes Pope ascribes to the feminine creatures who populate *Rape of the Lock*. Like Pope's female figure Spleen who "sighs for ever on her Pensive Bed" (4.23), Lennox's coquette lies with "The pensive Head upon the Hand reclin'd" (41). Just as Pope's Belinda creates "her Charms, / Repairs her Smiles, awakens ev'ry Grace, / And calls forth all the Wonders of her Face" (1.140–42), so too Lennox's coquette, "Proud of her charms, and conscious of her Face, / . . . calls forth ev'ry Grace" (19–20). In *Rape of the Lock*, Affectation "Faints into Airs, and languishes with Pride" (4.33–34), while Lennox's coquette's "Dark rolling Eyes a Languish may assume" (39). Significantly, Lennox reverses the gendered power dynamic when she describes how a coquette "By Force she wins, by Force she keeps the Heart" (22), an image drawing on the Baron's determination "By Force to ravish, or by Fraud betray" (2.32). Lennox's poem, especially when taught in facsimile, expands the discussion of all three poems and provides a perspective on female performance of gender.

Female satirists also turn their attention to men's private behavior. For example, Pope and Montagu each write an epistle to Allen, Lord Bathurst. Pope's "Epistle to Bathurst" valorizes his use of riches with the idealized portrait of the Man of Ross, the cautionary tale of Sir Balaam, and an unwavering message of moderation, balance, and boundaries. Bathurst becomes a public model for those values. Montagu's more satiric portrait presents Bathurst's visible improvements to his estates ("With study'd Art on Nature you Refine—" [19]) but does so in the context of the private man, one easily diverted from "the dull rewards of Future Fame" to more libidinous pursuits: ". . . while yet you have to live: / And Love is all the Blessing Heaven can give; / Fir'd by new passion you address the fair" (39–41). Not only does Montagu actively complicate Pope's portrait by presenting the private man, but she also appropriates Pope's own language, creating a "Bellinda" by whom Bathurst's "Soul [is] by fond Desire possess'd" (48). Like Pope's Belinda, who "smil'd, and all the World was gay" (2.52), or his coquette Chloe, who can "kill . . . with a Frown" (5.68), Montagu's Bellinda "A smile she gives, and with a smile can wound" (55). Yet upon Bathurst's heart, "However deeply made no long Impress remains" (62). In Montagu's portrait his character shares the malleability Pope ascribes to women who are "Matter too soft a lasting mark to bear" ("Epistle to a Lady" 3). Bathurst, "So yielding the Warm temper of [his] Mind," is "So touch'd by every Eye; so toss'd by every Wind" (65–66) as to remained unmoored. The cultural dialogue about the characters of men and women is captured within these poems.

Men's fickle nature contributes to the marital discord Montagu and other female satirists often depict. For example, Montagu's frequently anthologized "Epistle from Mrs. Yonge to Her Husband" or "The Lover: A Ballad" explicitly detail the consequences of men's diminishing emotions. Other female poets also interrogate this topic. For example, Mary Jones's "Matrimony" imagines a female "author" filling in the blanks of twenty-four lines, each ending with a "rhyme first put down by a gentleman." The gentleman's conventional rhymes (which appeared in italics), designed for a predictable paean to marital bliss, instead become fodder for a subversively satiric dialogue about the poem's title subject. Thus

Cloe, coquet and debon *air*,
Haughty, flatter'd, vain, and *fair*;
. . . .
. . . took the husband to her *arms*,
Resign'd her freedom and her *charms*. (1–2, 5–6)

However,

At length she found the name of *wife*
Was but another word for *strife*.
That cheek, which late out-blush'd the *rose*,
Now with unwonted fury *glows*. (11–14)

The internal dialogue within "Matrimony," marked typographically, also exposes the larger cultural dialogue about the social expectations that position marriage as women's primary objective.

Marriage, famously, was not part of Swift's or Pope's own life. When, in *An Epistle to Dr. Arbuthnot*, Pope examines the cost of a literary career, he wistfully observes, "The Muse but serv'd to ease some Friend, not Wife" (131). Female poets similarly explore the price their marriages paid for their literary pursuits. Mary Barber's "The Conclusion of a Letter to the Rev. Mr. C——" imagines what the Rev. Mr. C—— would say to her husband, "poor *Barber*," who "has surely a terrible Life; / . . . [with] a verse-writing Wife" (19–20): "What Good's in a Dame, that will pore on a Book? / No!—Give me the Wife, that shall save me a Cook" (33–34). Similarly, Susanna Centlivre's "A Woman's Case" ventriloquizes her own husband, who complains not only that Centlivre's writing takes up her time ("Deuce take your scribbling Vein, . . . / What did it ever get for me?" [110–11]) but that it's not remunerative:

Two Years you take a Play to write,
And I scarce get my Coffee by't.
Such swingeing Bills are still to pay
For Sugar, Chocolate, and Tea,
I shall be forc'd to run away. (112–16)

In addition to presenting gender tensions, Centlivre's poem, like other contemporaneous satires, also captures the financial vagaries of the commercialized world of print culture.

Female poets such as Elizabeth Hands and Barber take up the perils of the print culture in their own satires, narrating the challenging paths to publication for women, the resistance to women's writing, and the often negative reception of the same. Incorporating their poems allows instructors to talk about the persistent cultural dialogue centered on the commercialization of the literary marketplace and its attendant gender and class hierarchies. For example, Hands's "A Poem, on the Supposition of the Book Having Been Published and Read" imagines the after-dinner discussion of "the new book (that we talk'd of that day, / At your house you remember) of Poems, 'twas said / Produc'd by the pen of a poor Servant Maid" (19–21)—that is, Hands herself. The poem undermines the pretentious reaction to a servant writing ("Most servants can cook for the palate I find, / But very few of them can cook for the mind" [70–71]) by revealing the upper classes' own hypocrisy and limited intellectual pursuits. "Mrs. Routella," having purchased the book, "thought to have read it myself, but forgat it; / In short, I have never had time to look at it. / Perhaps I may look it o'er some other day" (26–28). The book's title, *The Death of Amnon*, comes from "A Scripture Tale," yet no one present recognizes the reference ("Of Amnon, of Amnon, Miss Rhymer, who's he?" [42]). Miss Gaiety vows to "borrow / My house-keeper's Bible, and read it to-morrow" (48–49), and the Reverend "blush'd for the laity" (51). By satirically ventriloquizing the voices of the gentry, Hands highlights her own elevated intellectual pursuits. Hands's companion piece, "A Poem, on the Supposition of an Advertisement Appearing in a Morning Paper, of the Publication of a Volume of Poems, by a Servant Maid," captures the resistance to her publication among a group of women. They express incredulity at the possibility of poetic production by a servant: "Pray what is the subject?—a Mop, or a Broom? / . . . I suppose we shall see / An Ode on a Dishclout—what else can it be?" (12–14). The poems provide a different perspective to the same class antagonisms Pope explores in *The Dunciad*.

Similarly, Barber's "To a Lady, Who Commanded Me to Send Her an Account in Verse, How I Succeeded in My Subscription" details the cultural and material obstacles she encounters seeking sufficient readers to publish a volume by subscription; it allows instructors to discuss the newly available publishing mechanisms. Women scorn her request because of their own resistance to women writing (". . . *I hate a Wit*; / Women should to their Fate submit, / Should in the Needle take Delight; / 'Tis out of *Character* to write" [11–14]), their greed ("*Olivia* loses oft at Play; / So will not throw her Gold away" [23–24]), or their envy ("Sylvia, of the haughty Tribe: / She never ask'd me to subscribe, / Nor ever wrote a Line on me, / I was no Theme for Poetry!" [25–28]). Barber's use of iambic tetrameter, a meter preferred by Swift, intensifies the poem's satiric approach. This poem, like Hands's, complements *The Dunciad*, providing the perspective from the class of writers Pope largely excoriates.

Mary Jones's "An Epistle to Lady Bowyer" similarly chronicles her path to publication and the challenges of the literary marketplace, dispelling the idea "The knack of writing is an easy trade" (3). Drawing on the question of Pope's apologia *Epistle to Arbuthnot* ("Why did I write?" [125]), Jones questions her own motivation for writing: "And yet you'd have me write!—For what? for whom?" (13). She envisages her poems becoming the kind of scrap paper forecast in Dryden's *Mac Flecknoe*, used "To curl a Fav'rite in a dressing-room? / To mend a candle when the snuff's too short? / Or save rappee for chamber-maids at Court?" (13–15). Seeking sponsorship from the aristocracy, Jones realizes the upper classes provide neither patronage nor intellectual leadership. The servant reveals that "Alas! His lordship seldom reads: . . . / . . . / Reads not ev'n tradesmen's bills" (72, 75). Although urged to leave her poems with him, Jones departs with her manuscript, "Resolv'd no more to offer up my wit, / Where footmen in the seat of critics sit" (83–84). Yet she "cannot put [her] trust / In lords; smile lies, eat toads, or lick the dust" (124–25), the last phrase directly quoting Pope's description of Sporus as someone with "Pride that licks the dust" (*Epistle to Arbuthnot* 333). Like a good satirist, she seeks only "an honest heart" (127), a gentleman "too honest to be great" (95). Her final lines also echo *Epistle to Arbuthnot*, as she simultaneously celebrates the autonomy her situation provides ("I can be no man's slave" [98]) and the humble origins and modest ambitions she possesses ("I ask no more, but in some calm retreat, / To sleep in quiet, and in quiet eat" [114–15]).

As this brief discussion illustrates, the opportunity to expand the prefabricated pairings in commercial textbooks adjusts the gendered satiric dialogue between the sexes and enlarges the topics for discussion. The strategic use of additional texts, all available electronically, complicates our received understanding of eighteenth-century satire and begins to more fully reconstruct the period's gendered dialogues.

Notes

1. All poems by women cited here appear in Backscheider and Ingrassia, *British Women Poets of the Long Eighteenth Century*. All poetry references will be parenthetical and by canto (if applicable) and line number.

2. The three dominant commercial textbook publishers for British literature anthologies—Norton, Longman, Broadview—all include the exact same poems mentioned in the body paragraph. Even contemporary critics discount women's involvement. Ashley Marshall, mentioning eleven writers in one footnote (314n43), claims "only a relatively tiny number of women tried their hands at satire in the eighteenth century" (28).

3. All poems by Pope cited here appear in *The Twickenham Edition of the Poems of Alexander Pope*.

4. Sway is also, of course, a central power of the goddess Dulness in *The Dunciad*.

Works Cited

Backscheider, Paula R., and Catherine E. Ingrassia, editors. *British Women Poets of the Long Eighteenth Century*. Johns Hopkins UP, 2009.

Lennox, Charlotte. "The Art of Coquetry." *The Gentleman's Magazine*, vol. 20, Nov. 1750, pp. 518–19. *Internet Library of Early Journals*, www.bodley.ox.ac.uk/cgi-bin/ilej/image1.pl?item=page&seq=1&size=1&id=gm.1750.11.x.20.x.x.518.

Lipking, Lawrence, and James Noggle, editors. *The Norton Anthology of English Literature, Volume C: The Restoration and Eighteenth Century*. W. W. Norton, 2006.

Marshall, Ashley. *The Practice of Satire in English, 1658–1770*. Johns Hopkins UP, 2013.

Pope, Alexander. *The Twickenham Edition of the Poems of Alexander Pope*. General editor, John Butt, Yale UP, 1939–63. 6 vols.

Swift, Jonathan. *Jonathan Swift: The Complete Poems*. Edited by Pat Rogers, Yale UP, 1983.

Darryl P. Domingo

The Satiric Page

It is one of the paradoxes of the literary period still labeled by many teachers and scholars as the "age of satire" in England that some of the most celebrated (and canonical) satiric works of the first half of the eighteenth century tend also to be among the least teachable in the twenty-first-century classroom. Although satires such as Jonathan Swift's *A Tale of a Tub* (1704–10), Alexander Pope's *The Dunciad* (1728–43), and Henry Fielding's *The Author's Farce* (1730–34) are rich with meaning and usually reward attentive reading, they are also conspicuously difficult and seem often to take rhetorical delight in befuddling interpretation. Indeed, recent editors of these satires have acknowledged both the complexity of their scholarly task and the challenge facing novice readers at three centuries' distance from the literary and cultural issues at stake. Marcus Walsh characterizes the dizzying paratext with which Swift surrounds his *Tale of a Tub* (hereafter *Tale*) as a "theatre of obfuscation," conceding that the work's competing narrative voices, reflexive digressions, and typographical oddities render it tricky to "establish determinate meanings" (xxxii, lii). Valerie Rumbold admits that *The Dunciad*'s hundreds of topical references can make it seem "bafflingly complex and offputtingly alien" and observes that Pope's elaborate apparatus of prefaces, appendixes, and variorum notes only cause the work to become "vastly more complicated" for readers, whose eyes are "diverted into negotiation between poem and surrounding prose" (1–2). And Thomas Lockwood, analyzing Fielding's deep implication in the popular entertainments that he satirizes, describes *The Author's Farce* as an "ambivalent exhibition of contemporary cultural nonsense," but also a work belonging "so completely to its time as to make historical scholarship as it were the default approach" (188, 209). If we do not effectively contextualize the historical content and, as I argue in this essay, the printed form of these works, our students are liable to feel like the victims of the satire—the hacks and dunces and tasteless pleasure seekers who pervade the pages of Swift, Pope, and Fielding. How then might we go about convincing students to engage with satires that refuse to grant them an easy read?

Swift's *Tale*, Pope's *The Dunciad*, and Fielding's *The Author's Farce* "thematize" difficulty, boasting of their calculated obscurity or irrationality, teasing through their shifting ironies, and confronting students new to satire or to the eighteenth century with their lack of knowledge and apparent insufficiency as critical readers. When I teach these satires, I begin by directing my students' attention to the various ways in which satirists foreground the problems of interpretation and the pitfalls of hermeneutic indeterminacy. I ask students to identify passages in which Swift, Pope, or Fielding examines the causes and effects of right and wrong reading. Swift has the Grub Street hack who narrates *Tale* discriminate between the "*superficial*" or "*ignorant*" reader and the "*learned*" reader, suggesting that the former will be "provoked to *laughter*" or "disposed to *stare*" at his work, while the latter will find "sufficient matter to employ his speculations for the rest of his life" (89). In an attempt to assist his readers, the hack explains that "where I am not understood it shall be concluded that something very useful and profound is couched underneath" (21). Yet he expresses considerable skepticism that readers will comprehend "the sublime mysteries that ensue" (25). The bookseller warns in his prefatory letter that the author's intentions in *Tale* are "*like to remain a secret*" (13), and the footnotes added to the fifth edition contradict their explanatory function by questioning the very possibility of interpretation: "I cannot guess at the author's meaning here, which I would be very glad to know because it seems to be of importance" (93). *Tale* is about the corruptions in religion, the abuses of learning, and the consequences of a relative freedom of the press, but it is also about the difficulty of interpreting any work regarded for being "wondrous *deep*, upon no wiser a reason than because it is wondrous *dark*" (102). In a similar way, *The Dunciad* ironically praises "Chaos, Night, and Dulness," realizing its themes through the obscurity of the dunces whom Pope believes will bring about his apocalyptic vision (419). In the "Letter to the Publisher" prefixed to *The Dunciad Variorum*, Pope cautions that writers like James Ralph, John Oldmixon, and Giles Jacob are persons "too *obscure* for satire," and he employs his pseudonymous editor, Martinus Scriblerus, to provide extensive commentary on the rationale that the published works of his satiric objects are so ephemeral that "scarce one is known . . . by sight" (415–16). *The Author's Farce* begins as a mildly humorous comedy of manners but descends abruptly into a theatrical extravaganza after Witmore persuades Luckless, Fielding's impecunious playwright, to appeal crassly to the taste of the town and "write nonsense, write operas, write entertainments, write *Hurlothrumbos*" (1788). The result is a chaotic third act, featuring a "puppet show in a playhouse" that even the Player admits he can "make neither head nor tail of" (1801). How might those of us who teach eighteenth-century satire go about assigning sense to works that gleefully exemplify nonsense? What strategies might we use to make these satires more accessible to students who are unfamiliar with, for example, the editorial methods of Richard Bentley, the printing and publishing tactics of Edmund Curll, or the theatrical regimes of John Rich or Colley Cibber? How might we demonstrate the perceived cultural consequences of the debate between the "ancients" and the "moderns," the lapse in 1695 of the final press licensing act, or the commercialization of leisure?

Since it is not always practical to answer such complicated historical questions in detail—lest we become what Fielding derides in *The Welsh Opera* (1731) as "a sort of walking Notes" (35)—I have found that one of the most efficacious ways of dealing with the difficulty of eighteenth-century satire is to encourage my students to engage visually and materially with some of the features of *Tale*, *The Dunciad*, and *The Author's Farce* that seem most to defy meaning. In particular, I ask students to consider how these satires *look* and what their appearance on the printed page can tell us about the satirists' broader themes. Instead of immersing students in topical references, I contextualize these representative works of prose, verse, and dramatic satire in terms of the contemporary print culture they both exploit and expose to ridicule. Drawing upon current trends in textual studies and book history, I open our discussion by way of D. F. McKenzie's influential claim that "forms effect meaning" (13). I then challenge students to think about how this claim might apply to satires in which printed form frequently breaks down, surprises, or physically obtrudes and gets in the way of content. Although we usually understand print as simply the material means through which authors document and disseminate their ideas, during the eighteenth century, I point out, the devices of print came to assume what McKenzie classifies as an "expressive function" (17). Satirists especially elide the distinction between verbal text ("the linguistic code") and visual context ("the bibliographical code") in order to make their arguments on the very surface of the printed page. As critics such as J. Paul Hunter, James McLaverty, Christopher Fanning, Janine Barchas, Christopher Flint, Katherine Mannheimer, and myself have recently shown, eighteenth-century satirists mobilize printer's ornaments, idiosyncratic typography, and mise-en-page as their primary methods of attack. Because one of their main objects of attack was the publishing industry itself, Swift, Pope, and Fielding exaggeratedly parody the conventions of the "modern" book trade, making perceptible their satiric point about the dangerous proliferation of print and the plight of literature in an increasingly commercial culture.

These satirists indict what they view as a degraded literary marketplace, where literature is valued only to the degree to which it can gratify what Swift calls "the pleasure and delight of mortal man" (29). *Tale* is a work whose substance and structure alike reproduce what Swift regarded as some of the worst features of the contemporary publishing industry: its tendency to swell volumes with extraneous material like digressions or self-congratulatory preliminaries; its hasty publication of works that are obviously imperfect, having, for instance, defects in the manuscript marked by printed lacunae; and, most damningly, its brazen commercialism. Swift's hack protests that he is "too much a servant of the *modern* way" to neglect any lucrative opportunities to publish, and so regardless of whether he has anything worthwhile to say, he strenuously attempts "*to write upon nothing*" (102–03). Though he confesses that his treatise was conceived in desperate circumstances—"in a garret" and under "a great want of money" (20)—the hack boasts that "fate has flung me into so blessed an age for the mutual felicity of *booksellers* and *authors*, whom I may safely affirm to be at this day the two only satisfied parties in England" (88). As such, his fragmentary *Tale* is able to achieve "preferment and sanction in *print*," not because it is coherent or meaningful, but because of "the liberty and encouragement of the press" (103). In *The Dunciad*, Pope contextualizes what he views as the disastrous consequences of an unlicensed press by having Scriblerus account for the "occasion" of his poem:

> [The author] lived in those days, when (after Providence had permitted the invention of printing as a scourge for the sins of the learned) paper also became so cheap, and printers so numerous, that a deluge of authors covered the land: whereby not only the peace of the honest unwriting subject was daily molested, but unmerciful demands were made of his applause, yea of his money, by such as would neither earn the one, nor deserve the other. (420–21)

Like Swift, Pope satirizes the mercenary motivations of commercial publishers and hack writers, whom he portrays as residing in "the cave of poverty and poetry" (436) and condemns for writing down to "the taste of the rabble" (434n2). I emphasize that because professional hacks wrote for a living, they had to be especially sensitive to the requirements of booksellers, who, in their turn, were sensitive to capricious public taste. This is why Pope opens his mock-epic poem by invoking not one of the classical muses but the "Smithfield muses," glossing "*Smithfield*" as "the place where Bartholomew Fair was kept" and implying that the literature produced in Grub Street has its counterpart in London's popular "shows, machines, and dramatical entertainments" (434n2). In *The Author's Farce*, Fielding also dramatizes what happens to literary standards when authors are subjected to the economic laws of supply and demand and patronized only if they "please the Town" (1793). Since he is lacking in "interest," Luckless struggles to get his sentimental comedy performed or published. When he appeals to Bookweight for assistance, the bookseller mocks him for his belletristic idealism: "I do think writing the silliest thing that man can undertake" (1790). Yet Bookweight makes a living on the backs of those who "write hackney for bread" (1795), and the unscrupulous habits he cultivates in his stable of hacks illustrate what Fielding, Pope, and Swift understood to be the fundamental problem with a literary culture less interested in edifying than in entertaining readers and giving them something at which to stare.

Each of these satirists suggests that the commercial opportunism of the modern publishing industry is manifested, first and foremost, in the physical appearance of books and the printed disposition of their pages. Fielding's bookseller encourages his hacks to take advantage of the sensual appeal of printing, and Dash advises the aptly named Blotpage that "a title page is to a book what a fine neck is to a woman—therefore ought to be the most regarded as it is the part which is viewed before the purchase" (1795). Pope's dunces employ gaudy techniques to catch the eyes and, ultimately, secure the purses of readers:

> Hence bards, like Proteus long in vain tied down,
> Escape in monsters, and amaze the town.
> Hence miscellanies spring, the weekly boast
> Of Curll's chaste press, and Lintot's rubric post. (436–37, lines 37–40)

And Swift's archetypal Grub Street hack compares the commercial publishing practices of "*modern authors*" to the devious marketing strategies of "*monster-mongers* and other *retailers of strange sights*," whose "*moving* and *standing* piece of rhetoric" is at odds with the "fair large picture" they hang "over the door" (63). According to Mannheimer, eighteenth-century satirists censured the "imaginative and moral reductionism" they believed was the result of a "visually-addicted culture." However, they did so ironically by engaging in "a careful typographical engineering" and performing "a kind of visual pedagogy on the reader" (1–2). When teaching *Tale*, *The Dunciad*, and *The Author's Farce*, I remind my students that these satires do not merely describe the plight of literature and culture in an age of commercial expansion, but they exemplify it as well through textual and paratextual devices that both foreground the materiality of print and function self-consciously as visual keys to interpretation. For Swift, "the liberty and encouragement of the press" threatened to reify the imagination, reducing writing to a mechanical act and literature to a material object. In *Tale*, the "*principal Productions of* Grub Street" are thus degraded to "immense bales of paper" (16), and in attempting to evaluate these works Swift's hack offers to delineate their "beautiful externals for the gratification of superficial readers" (31). I propose that students adopt an analogous approach when struggling with the difficulty of eighteenth-century satire, since it is often through these very printed surfaces that satirists discriminate between judicious and genuinely superficial readers.

Deriving a mode of reading from Swift's "*modern* way" of writing, I devise simple in-class exercises that invite students to *read* the satiric page and to pay attention to the rhetorical effect of "beautiful externals." For example, I suggest at the outset of our discussion of *Tale* that students take seriously the hack's prefatory claim that "whatever word or sentence is printed in a different character shall be judged to contain something extraordinary of *wit* or *sublime*" (21). I then ask the class which parts of the satire stand out visibly and how they might contribute to Swift's meaning.

We proceed to examine *Tale*'s erratic use of italics and its ubiquitous rows of printed asterisks, and we debate what these disruptive devices might have to do with Swift's satire on indiscriminate publishing and the modern obsession with novelty. Because mass-market textbook editions, with their standardized layout and typography, cannot always reproduce the striking "character" of such devices, I distribute facsimile pages from the original period editions of these satires in order to allow my students to engage the "visual dynamism" and "rambunctious materiality" that Barchas views as typical of eighteenth-century texts (6). I pass around page 184 from the fifth edition of *A Tale of a Tub* (1710) and challenge students to make sense of the fifty asterisks that boldly stand in for the hack's aborted explanation of the physiological foundations of madness (fig. 1). I go on to observe that this "*Hiatus*," marked in the printed text with a marginal note that "*Hic multa desiderantur*" ("Here there is much wanting"), appeared as well in the first edition of *Tale* (1704), and I ask students why they think the missing material was not restored in subsequent editions. We discuss the fact that though the author expresses his desire to "unravel this knotty Point," *Tale*'s mock-annotator once again rejects the possibility of interpretation: "Here is another Defect in the Manuscript, but I think the Author did wisely, and that the Matter which thus strained his Faculties, was not worth a Solution; and it were well if all Metaphysical Cobweb Problems were no otherwise answered." In such a passage, my students come to realize, the exaggerated presence of print paradoxically signifies the absence of meaning. At the same time, the materiality of the page itself promotes hermeneutic indeterminacy, revealing in readily observable ways how the publishing industry confounds abstract thought, interferes with critical argument, and diminishes literature to printed marks at which readers can gawk as at one of London's "strange sights."

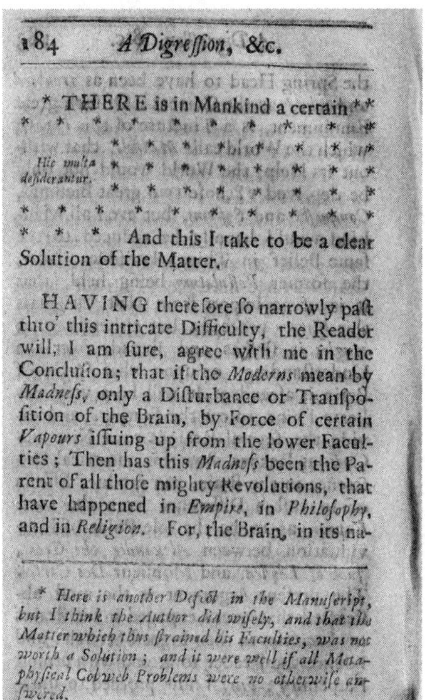
184 *A Digression, &c.*

* THERE is in Mankind a certain * *
* * * * * * * * * *
* * * * * * * *
Hic multa desiderantur. * * * * * * * *
* * * * * * * *
* * * * * * * * * *
* * * And this I take to be a clear Solution of the Matter.

HAVING therefore so narrowly past thro' this intricate Difficulty, the Reader will, I am sure, agree with me in the Conclusion; that if the *Moderns* mean by *Madness*, only a Disturbance or Transposition of the Brain, by Force of certain *Vapours* issuing up from the lower Faculties; Then has this *Madness* been the Parent of all those mighty Revolutions, that have happened in *Empire*, in *Philosophy*, and in *Religion*. For, the Brain, in its na-

* *Here is another Defect in the Manuscript, but I think the Author did wisely, and that the Matter which thus strained his Faculties, was not worth a Solution; and it were well if all Metaphysical Cobweb Problems were no otherwise answered.*

tural

Figure 1. Jonathan Swift, *A Tale of a Tub*. London, 1710, p. 184. Author's collection.

When analyzing the themes of *The Dunciad*, I employ a similar approach in grounding classroom discussion in the material appearance of Pope's page. I provide students with a sample page from either *The Dunciad Variorum* (1729) or *The Dunciad in Four Books* (1743) and suggest that they turn the page upside down to get a sense of both the disproportion between poem and notes and the profusion of words that represent spatially the perils of a world deluged by print (fig. 2). My students invariably observe that Pope's heroic couplets are drowned out by the pedantic footnotes of Scriblerus et al., and they complain that the variorum apparatus distracts them from the "Progress of Dulness." I maintain that this is exactly Pope's intention. The annotated *Dunciad* achieves at a textual level the burlesque inversion that the satire seeks at a formal level through its sustained parody of epic conventions. Just as Pope's dunces transgress social and aesthetic decorum by bringing the "Smithfield muses to the ear of kings," so too do his notes and paratext complicate the primacy of verse over commentary, exaggerating trifling observations on the career of "Edward Ward" or the significance of the "letter *E*" at the expense of the poem's broader vision of "Chaos, Night and Dulness." Like Swift, Pope adopts the very print technologies he attacks and adapts them for his own

THE
DUNCIAD.
Book the First.
BOOKS and the Man I sing, the first who brings
The Smithfield Muses to the Ear of Kings.

Figure 2. Alexander Pope, *The Dunciad Variorum*. London, 1729, p. 1. Courtesy of The William Andrews Clark Memorial Library, University of California, Los Angeles. (Intentionally inverted here.)

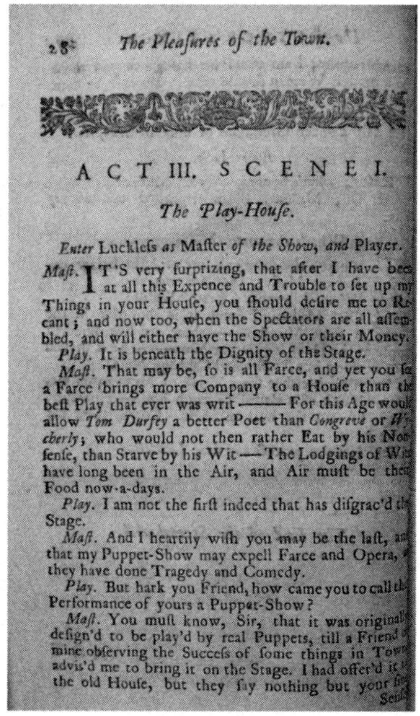

28 *The Pleaſures of the Town.*

A C T III. S C E N E I.

The Play-Houſe.

Enter Luckleſs *as* Maſter *of the Show, and* Player.

Maſt. IT'S very ſurprizing, that after I have bee at all this Expence and Trouble to ſet up my Things in your Houſe, you ſhould deſire me to Re cant; and now too, when the Spectators are all aſſem-bled, and will either have the Show or their Money.

Play. It is beneath the Dignity of the Stage.

Maſt. That may be, ſo is all Farce, and yet you ſe a Farce brings more Company to a Houſe than th beſt Play that ever was writ——For this Age woul allow *Tom Durfey* a better Poet than *Congreve* or *Wy-cherly*; who would not then rather Eat by his Non-ſenſe, than Starve by his Wit—The Lodgings of Wi have long been in the Air, and Air muſt be the Food now-a-days.

Play. I am not the firſt indeed that has diſgrac'd th Stage.

Maſt. And I heartily wiſh you may be the laſt, an that my Puppet-Show may expell Farce and Opera, they have done Tragedy and Comedy.

Play. But hark you Friend, how came you to call th Performance of yours a Puppet-Show?

Maſt. You muſt know, Sir, that it was original deſign'd to be play'd by real Puppets, till a Friend mine obſerving the Succeſs of ſome things in Tow advis'd me to bring it on the Stage. I had offer'd it the old Houſe, but they ſay nothing but your

Sen

Figure 3. Henry Fielding, *The Author's Farce; and, The Pleasures of the Town.* London, 1730, p. 28. Courtesy of The William Andrews Clark Memorial Library, University of California, Los Angeles.

satiric purposes, becoming, as Hunter puts it, "Smithfieldian" almost in spite of himself (65).

Even *The Author's Farce*, a play that was performed forty-one times in its opening season and that seems to have succeeded on account of its theatrical exuberance, was able to extend its satiric effects through a crafty manipulation of the printed page. In endeavoring to explain to my students why act 3 of Fielding's *Farce* is so different in tone from acts 1 and 2, I illustrate the curious fact that when the play was first published on 31 March 1730 (the day after its initial theatrical performance), Luckless's speeches, from the beginning of act 3 to the absurd denouement (at line 767), are headed not with "*Luck.*" but with "*Mast.*" for "Master *of the Show*" (fig. 3). I then invite students to consider how this name change, indicated in the printed text in a manner that would not have been possible during the live performance at the Little Haymarket Theatre, might contextualize the nature of Luckless's (and perhaps Fielding's) condescension to "*The Pleasures of the Town*," which, not coincidentally, is made the running title for the entirety of act 3. To what degree, I ask, does the evidence of the page (rather than the stage) signal a transformation in Luckless's identity from an impecunious playwright to a commercial impresario who literally and figuratively pulls the strings? And in what ways does page 28 of Fielding's first edition help the audience of readers make sense of a theatrical spectacle featuring Monsieur Pantomime, Sir Farcical Comic, Signior Opera, and other devotees of the Goddess of Nonsense? What my students come to see is that the published version of *The Author's Farce* captures the distinction that Bookweight draws between "acting plays" and "reading plays," insofar as the play stands "substantive" on its own merits thanks to its use of print conventions that convey Fielding's "wit and meaning" (1790).

In the classroom we necessarily focus our energies on teaching students to *read* literary works in a thoughtful and engaged way. Yet when confronted with the difficulty of satires like *A Tale of a Tub*, *The Dunciad*, and *The Author's Farce*, traditional literary-rhetorical methods of interpretation often fail us, frustrating students who understandably begin to feel that the humor might be at their expense. This essay has recommended that we encourage students to *look* at eighteenth-century satires, given that it is frequently through the visual and material appearance of the printed page that authors like Swift, Pope, and Fielding guide response and show readers how best to navigate the literary marketplace. A row of asterisks, an intrusive footnote, a running title—each of these devices needs to be seen clearly before the satire in which it appears can be coherently read. By teaching my students to make the satiric page legible, I ensure that they will be able to perceive the meaning of eighteenth-century satire, even if they do not as yet fully comprehend it.

Works Cited

Barchas, Janine. *Graphic Design, Print Culture, and the Eighteenth-Century Novel.* Cambridge UP, 2003.

Domingo, Darryl P. *The Rhetoric of Diversion in English Literature and Culture, 1690–1760.* Cambridge UP, 2016.

Fanning, Christopher. "Small Particles of Eloquence: Sterne and the Scriblerian Text." *Modern Philology*, vol. 100, no. 3, Feb. 2003, pp. 360–92.

Fielding, Henry. *The Author's Farce.* Edited by Jill Campbell. *The Broadview Anthology of Restoration and Early Eighteenth-Century Drama*, general editor, J. Douglas Canfield, Broadview Press, 2001.

———. *The Welsh Opera. Plays: Volume II, 1731–1734*, edited by Thomas Lockwood, Clarendon Press, 2007.

Flint, Christopher. *The Appearance of Print in Eighteenth-Century Fiction.* Cambridge UP, 2011.

Hunter, J. Paul. "From Typology to Type: Agents of Change in Eighteenth-Century English Texts." *Cultural Artifacts and the Production of Meaning:*

The Page, the Image, and the Body, edited by Margaret J. M. Ezell and Katherine O'Brien O'Keeffe, U of Michigan P, 1994, pp. 41–69.

Lockwood, Thomas, editor. *Plays: Volume I, 1728–1731*. By Henry Fielding, Clarendon Press, 2004.

Mannheimer, Katherine. *Print, Visuality, and Gender in Eighteenth-Century Satire: "The Scope in Ev'ry Page."* Routledge, 2011.

McKenzie, D. F. *Bibliography and the Sociology of Texts*. Cambridge UP, 1999.

McLaverty, James. *Pope, Print, and Meaning*. Oxford UP, 2001.

Pope, Alexander. *The Dunciad*. *The Major Works*, edited by Pat Rogers, Oxford UP, 2006.

Rumbold, Valerie, editor. Introduction. *The Dunciad in Four Books*, by Alexander Pope, rev. ed., Pearson/Longman, 2009.

Swift, Jonathan. A Tale of a Tub *and Other Works*. Edited by Angus Ross and David Woolley, Oxford UP, 1986.

Walsh, Marcus, editor. Introduction. A Tale of a Tub *and Other Works*, by Jonathan Swift, Cambridge UP, 2010.

Part II

Genre and Mode

Howard D. Weinbrot

Apocalyptic Satire

Satire is less a genre than a large and cluttered group home in which many species live more or less comfortably. Often they share the same room and look alike, but preserve their own features. The more precisely we define satire in theory, the less accurate the definition becomes in practice. The shifting form nonetheless has a few reliable traits: something appears wrong to the satirist; it needs correction or at least it requires exposure by someone who cares. The satirist can correct gently (Horace), sternly (Juvenal), grimly and philosophically (Persius), raucously (Rabelais, Swift), brutally (Rochester, Swift), elegantly and wittily (Boileau, Dryden, Pope), or thoughtfully (Johnson). At times satirists might combine some or all of these options. Teachers can help students to flesh out the representative terms and authors I have suggested, confound rigid definitions by showing how varied modes can overlap, and acknowledge that different satirists see different kinds of vice or folly to satirize.

For example, formal verse satire derived from Roman ancestors in a blame-and-praise pattern. It attacked one vice and praised the opposite corrective virtue: vain human wishes are harmful but religious human wishes are helpful, financial excess is harmful but sensible use of money is helpful, and so on. These satirists assume an at least marginally corrigible world in which readers listen to a persuasive voice that offers a sensible way to improve. Another kind of satire is less interested in correction than in punishment. Punitive satire humiliates and punishes a victim for any or no reason.

Different satiric kinds share at least one trait: the satirist is in control and his world is reasonably secure. Students will see this in John Dryden's *Mac Flecknoe* (written 1678; published 1682), as Dryden punishes the poet and playwright Thomas Shadwell for literary incompetence. Shadwell, or Mac Flecknoe, "never deviates into sense" (l: 20). Sense is like a nation whose borders are secure and whose army, epitomized by Dryden as satirist, is loyal. In *An Epistle to Dr. Arbuthnot* (1735), Alexander Pope converts his "adversarius," the friendly but disagreeing opponent, to his point of view regarding literature and politics: "Thus far was right. The rest belongs to Heav'n" (line 419).[1] In *The Vanity of Human Wishes* (1749), Samuel Johnson says, "Enquirer, cease, petitions yet remain, / Which heav'n may hear, nor deem religion vain" (*Poems* 107–08 [lines 349–50]). The satirist has the answer(s) we seek and that he demonstrates, perhaps by his own behavior in the work before us.

What if students find that the satirist has no answers? Or that possible answers are ignored? Or that whoever is being satirized neither listens nor cares and has the power that the satirist lacks? What if instead of speaking confidently to an Augustus or Maecenas or Arbuthnot or our own better selves seeking to improve, the satirist speaks to an indifferent, hostile, and malign world that he can only describe and lament? Cherished values are devalued; stable norms no longer are stable or normative; families no longer are familial; established religion is disestablished or marginalized; illustrious national culture is annihilated. Such a world could be portrayed by a speaker apparently unaware of the darker implications, as in Rochester's *A Letter from Artemisia in the Town to Chloe in the Country* (written 1675; published 1679). Ask students to discuss how Artemisia treats her hellish world of moral, sexual, and domestic corruption as amusing gossip, with her version of "whatever." Students also can compare and contrast Pope's dealings with his adversarius in *Arbuthnot* and the adversarius in the final dialogue of *Epilogue to the Satires* (1738). Pope's excellent arguments once convinced Arbuthnot to change his mind. The *Epilogue*'s adversarius represents the corrupt Walpole government and is indifferent to political pollution. He tells Pope: "Alas! Alas! pray end what you began, / And write next winter more *Essays on Man*" (lines 254–55). This unthreatening philosophical *Essay* argues that whatever *is* is right.

Students may find apocalyptic depiction of triumphant evil both challenging and depressing. After all, it is losers' satire in a nation of rubble. It is kin to Old Testament Jeremiads and prophets' complaints. It is related to "hearts of darkness" tales like Joseph Conrad's in the novella of that name and to those other texts that force us to see ourselves and what we prefer not to see. Witness King Lear, whose daughters expel him and who realizes that we are nothing but poor, naked, forked animals. He goes mad. The formal verse satirist knows that "petitions yet remain." The apocalyptic satirist knows that the petition may remain but that no one cares to do anything about it. He draws the collapse of a once-thriving political, moral, religious, and intellectual world now in darkness and chaos.

This kind of satire easily blends with other kinds of satire and other genres. Pope's *The Dunciad in Four Books* (1743) is punitive satire that savages his enemies and literary inferiors; it is a mock-epic that inverts the *Aeneid* and its epic of the rise of Roman civilization; it is a Menippean satire through its prose notes; and it is an inversion of *Paradise Lost* as well as an apocalyptic satire in which Dulness and disorder triumph. In such a case, teachers will want to guide students through historical, narrative, and analytical processes. How is a good warrior like Aeneas displaced by someone Pope thought a pedant and a bad cultural warrior like Richard Bentley (who in fact was a great classical scholar)? How does Pope show the Judeo-Christian god of light and creation displaced by the Hanoverian-Walpolean god of darkness and uncreation? The layering of satiric modes complicates and enriches our reading. As an apocalyptic satire it also includes central points.

Apocalyptic texts vary but have recognizable traits shared by opposing groups. Apocalyptic satire is an equal-opportunity hater. In the eighteenth century virtually all groups, whether Whig, Tory, Anglican, or Dissenter, used apocalyptic devices when presumably appropriate. Each side saw hordes of opponents ready to destroy, deluge, and overwhelm the remnants of national decency and intelligence, whether in church, state, or university. Henry Pendlebury lamented the "Deluge of many . . . corrupt Doctrines and Practices" introduced by ninth-century Catholic procedures (2). Radical lower Church Edmund Hickeringill saw that "by Priest-Craft, floods of Blood and Ruine have deluged Christendom" (26).

Teachers should alert students to the imagery of floods and masses of evil men who bring illness. Hickeringill insisted that brutish priests "may *infect* the Kingdom *all over*" (26). High Church Charles Leslie hated Dissenters and those not part of his kind of Anglican world. These deviants and their omnipresent pamphlets spread around London, and the leaflets "*Infect*" once they are "in every Body's Hand" (29). By 1740 Pope's unpublished fragment "One Thousand Seven Hundred Forty" used a yet darker image that recalled the bubonic plague of 1665–66 and some one hundred thousand deaths in London: "The plague is on thee Britain, and who tries / To save thee in th' infectious office *dies*" (336 [lines 75–76]).

Hordes of enemies, inundations of vice, and infections in the moral, political, and religious nation sap the foundations of received wisdom and virtue. Gilbert Burnet, soon Bishop of Salisbury, bitterly opposed James II's Catholic religion and political absolutism. In 1688 James used his royal dispensing power, independent of Parliament, to demand that Anglican clergymen read his Declaration of Indulgence to their Anglican parishioners. James granted unprecedented new rights to Dissenters and to Catholics. Burnet and most Protestants feared that this would intimidate congregants, allow James to force other innovations, extirpate the Church of England, and overturn "the whole Foundations of this *Government*, and all the most sacred part of it" (7). For Burnet, James II regarded the Church of England as a "*Pestilent Heresy*" to be rooted out (8). In 1702 the fiercely High Church Tory Henry Sacheverell also turned to an apocalyptic result if lower Church Anglicans and their friends the Dissenters from the Church of England should gain power. Sacheverell's apocalyptic language paints these false friends as treacherous, villainous, murderous vipers who seek to degrade the church and destroy the state: "*the One [is] Undermin'd through the Foundations of the Other*" (sig. A2v). Teachers can seek out these and other texts that use comparably powerful images.

An army can build bulwarks against invaders and provide hospitals against a plague, but the apocalyptic satirist sees himself as among the few or even only brave resister of tyranny, stupidity, heresy, and the like. In 1701 Francis Atterbury, later Bishop of Rochester, thought himself an isolated defender of High Church power. He lamented to Sir Jonathan Trelawny, bishop of Exeter, "What can be done by one poor hand and head, by the blessing of God, I will do, towards stemming matters" (54). Nonetheless, "it is a little uncomfortable to be left to work alone, without any assistance, or any body to bear a part in the same cause" (55). Some satirists turned to the Bible for imagery. For example, God sees rampant evil within Israel and "sought for a man among them, that should make up the hedge, and stand in the gap before me for the land, that I should not destroy it; but I found none" who could defend the endangered land

(Ezekiel 22.30 [*Book of Common Prayer*]). Jonathan Swift used this image ironically in his *Argument against Abolishing Christianity* (written 1708; published 1711): that state religion lends "its Name to stand in the Gap, and to employ or divert" dissenting ministers who violate "the publick Peace" (35). Elimination of Christianity eliminates defenses against evil. In 1738 Pope complained in the first dialogue of the *Epilogue to the Satires* that in his Walpole world "Nothing is Sacred now but Villany" (line 170). He then adapts the apocalyptic pose of the brave lone warrior who futilely resists: "there was one who held it in disdain" (lines 171–72). Ask students to read Pope's grim second and final Dialogue. Pope's "sacred weapon" to defend Truth is useless. He thus draws "the last Pen for Freedom" as "Truth stands trembling on the edge of Law." No true Britons are alive, so he can only "praise the Dead" (lines 248–51).

Students need both to recognize apocalyptic satire's traits and determine where and why they develop. The teacher can suggest two theories of causation (other than the perceived corruption itself necessary for such darkness). One is the vital connection of parts: destruction of the church destroys the state. Burnet's *An Enquiry into the Measures of Submission* (1688) encapsulates this sense of broken connections and collapse when power removes restraints upon itself. James II's Declaration of Indulgence suspended old law, made new law, and thereby made it impossible for English subjects to depend upon law as a restraining power: "The Authority of the *Law* is indeed all in one word, so that if the *King* pretends to a Power to *Dispence* with *Laws*, there is nothing left, upon which the *Subject* can depend." Illegal suspension of laws "is plainly a repealing of them." This breaks "the whole Constitution," removes administration of justice, and "is really a *Dissolution* of the *Government*" that nullifies trials and sentences (6). Burnet combines frightening words like *nothing left*, *dissolution*, *null and void*. This breaking happens, or will happen, because the monarch abuses his power and the law that restrains it. "The Authority of the *Law* is indeed all in one word. . . ." Debase and defy that word and moral, political, and legal chaos result. As Burnet soon adds, government will become so anarchic "that there is not any one part of it left sound and entire" (7). Swift portrayed this apocalyptic world in his *Argument against Abolishing Christianity*. Institutions require such close relationships among parts that destruction of one denotes the destruction of all. Elimination of religious requirements for public office will eliminate restraint, true Christianity, and episcopal Protestant churches from England and Ireland. Freethinkers thus attack Christianity "as a Sort of Edifice, wherein all the Parts have such a mutual Dependance on each other, that if you happen to pull out one single Nail, the whole Fabrick must fall to the Ground" (38).

The second apocalyptic theory of causation to suggest to students relates both to connection among parts and to the lone warrior: the fragility of culture. Pull out one nail and all collapses. Swift isolated that fragility in his *Verses on the Death of Dr. Swift* (written 1731; published 1739), which also laments Queen Anne's death and the end of the Stuart dynasty. There once were "golden Dreams" (line 372) regarding national greatness and the Queen's benign power; but there were no royal heirs. The dream "Was all destroy'd by one Event. / Too soon that precious Life was ended, / On which alone, our Weal depended" (*Poems* 567–68 [lines 376–78]. England's fate depended upon Queen Anne's fate. Destruction follows her death. Key words immediately thereafter depict a chaotic and fallen moral and political world with terms that connect the collapse of the established church and the established state: religion becomes a fable, the nation a Babel. Swift mourns far more than his own pending death. This mingled disappointment, defeat, and anger typify apocalyptic satire.

Students will need such historical context and training to recognize satiric conventions. Teachers also will need to deal with students who admire the satire's energy but reject its conclusion. The teacher can point out that they are not alone. Earlier readers also often were not convinced that the apocalyptic satirist had it right. Many of Swift's readers, for example, refused to accept either his dark judgments or his human decency, as made clear in frequent hostile responses to *Gulliver's Travels.* Much of the public then as now denied that human beings are what the king of Brobdingnag called "the most pernicious Race of little odious Vermin that Nature ever suffered to crawl upon the Surface of the Earth" (189 [pt. 2, ch. 6]). Many insisted that we are not the brutish Yahoos that Swift describes in part 4. Even Swift's friend Patrick Delany rejected that insult to human creation: the Yahoos are "too offensive to be copied, even in the slightest sketch," for Swift debases "the human form to the lowest degree of a defiled imagination" (162). *Gulliver's Travels* was "among the follies of his life" (172). Students who agree with Delany may find themselves leaning toward the "soft" school reading of *Gulliver's Travels*, which regards the Spanish sea captain Don Pedro as Swift's view of the good human being. Teachers and other students can counter with the "hard" school of apocalyptic satire and almost guarantee a lively discussion.

Writers of such satire often were defensive and presumed victims of troubling alterations in culture. Sometimes they were right regarding the changes without being right regarding the danger within those changes. Sacheverell correctly saw that the High Church of England was under stress and would lose power. The High Church's demise, however, was not near, and the English crown would not sit on Beelzebub's head. This is a good opportunity to ask students to consider the advantages and disadvantages of an established national church as opposed to pluralist national religions. Alternatively, there were and are times when darkness of vision is appropriate, necessary, and frankly depressing. Ask students to read both the final book of Pope's *The Dunciad in Four Books*, or at least its last three paragraphs, and William Butler Yeats's "The Second Coming" (1919). This grim poem was written after the Irish Easter Rebellion against the British (1916), the Russian Revolution (1917), and World War I (1914–18), which together produced some twenty-eight million deaths. Here are the poems' final couplets. Pope: "Thy hand, great Anarch! lets the curtain fall; / And Universal Darkness buries all" (360 [4.655–56]). Yeats: "And what rough beast, its hour come round at last, / Slouches towards Bethlehem to be born?" (187). Discussion of these dark visions may cast light on the nature of cultural decline and the satirist's response to it.

Students tend to be keen on celebrity and on films. Nathanael West's *The Day of the Locust* (1939) is a bracing antidote to that youthful passion. Its final chapter includes several apocalyptic conventions: massive crowds, deluges of vice, and an individual's fruitless defense of decency. Interested students should read both Exodus 10.1–11 and the prophetic Book of Joel. In the first, Moses calls down a horde of locusts when Pharaoh refuses to liberate the Israelites. It then narrates the horrors of the plague and calls for repentance to appease an angry God. The second demonstrates the blessings available to the people should they indeed repent. West alludes only to the darkest parts of Exodus and Joel. How would his book be different if, for example, he also suggested the modern equivalent of safely crossing the Red Sea or safely repenting and changing conduct?

Apocalyptic satire has a noble biblical ancestry. It forces us to look at serious weaknesses in our culture, in ourselves, and in other dark places that need exposure. Like all satirists, the apocalyptic satirist selects and embellishes his data, finds high virtue in resisting bad power, and probably thinks he fights a lonely battle against overwhelming odds. He fears moral infection, cultural collapse, and ruined foundations should he fail, as he almost invariably does—though he also almost invariably impresses us for at least going down fighting. Along the way, he reminds us that great art, and especially great satiric art, need not consist of sweetness and light when bitterness and darkness are appropriate. His not-so-secret hope is that by convincing you of how bad things are, they might, maybe, perhaps, possibly, conceivably, prayerfully, miraculously, get better.

Note

1. This essay cites Pope's *Epistle to Arbuthnot*, *Epilogue on the Satires*, and "One Thousand Seven Hundred and Forty" in Imitations of Horace*: With an* Epistle to Dr. Arbuthnot *and the* Epilogue to the Satires (the Twickenham Edition of the Poems of Alexander Pope).

Works Cited

Atterbury, Francis. *Epistolary Correspondence, Visitation Charges, and Miscellanies of the Right Reverend Francis Atterbury, D. D. Lord Bishop of Rochester*. Edited by [John Nichols], vol. 3, London, 1784.

Book of Common Prayer and Administration of the Sacraments and other Rites and Ceremonies of the Church, According to the Use of the Church of England. Oxford, 1728.

Burnet, Gilbert. *Enquiry into the Measures of Submission to the Supream Authority*. London, 1688.

Delany, Patrick. *Observations upon Lord Orrery's Remarks on the Life and Writings of Dr. Jonathan Swift*. London, 1754.

Dryden, John. *Poems 1681–1684. Works of John Dryden*, edited by H. T. Swedenberg, Jr., and Vinton A. Dearing, vol. 2, U of California P, 1972. The California Edition of the Works of John Dryden.

Hickeringill, Edmund. "Priest-Craft, Its Character and Consequences." *Miscellaneous Tracts, Essays, Satyrs, &c. in Prose and Verse*, London, 1707, pp. 1–91.

Johnson, Samuel. *Poems*. Edited by E. L. McAdam, Jr., with George Milne, vol. 6, Yale UP, 1964, pp. 107–08. The Yale Edition of the Works of Samuel Johnson.

Leslie, Charles. *The New Association of Those Called Moderate-Church-Man, With the Modern-Whigs and Fanaticks, to Under-Mine and Blow-Up the Present Church and Government. . . . By a True-Church-Man*. London, 1702.

[Pendlebury, Henry]. *A Plain Representation of Transubstantiation, As It Is Received in the Church of Rome: With the Sandy Foundations It is Built Upon, and the Arguments That Do Clearly Avert and Overturn It*. London, 1687.

Pope, Alexander. *The Dunciad in Four Books*. Edited by Valerie Rumbold, Longman, 1999.

———. Imitations of Horace*: With an* Epistle to Dr. Arbuthnot *and the* Epilogue to the Satires. Edited by John Butt, Methuen and Yale UP, 1961. Vol. 4 of The Twickenham Edition of the Poems of Alexander Pope.

Sacheverell, Henry. *The Political Union: A Discourse Shewing the Dependance of Government on Religion in General; and of the English Monarchy on the Church of England in Particular*. London, 1702.

Swift, Jonathan. *An Argument to Prove, That the Abolishing of Christianity in England, May . . . be attended with Some Inconveniencies, and Perhaps Not Produce Those Many Good Effects Proposed Thereby. Bickerstaff Papers and Pamphlets on the Church*, edited by Herbert Davis, Blackwell, 1939. Vol. 2 of *Prose Works of Jonathan Swift.*

———. *Gulliver's Travels.* Edited by David Womersley, Cambridge UP, 2012. The Cambridge Edition of the Works of Jonathan Swift.

———. *The Poems of Jonathan Swift.* Edited by Harold Williams, 2nd ed., vol. 2, Oxford UP, 1958, pp. 567–68.

West, Nathanael. *The Day of the Locust.* Random House, 1939.

Yeats, William Butler. "The Second Coming." *The Collected Works of W. B. Yeats: Poems*, edited by Richard J. Finneran, vol. 1, Macmillan, 1989.

Jonathan Greenberg

Dystopia and the Near Future

Dystopia is so pervasive a cultural trope today that most college students already possess a rudimentary understanding of the genre. Many have been consuming dystopian narratives since childhood in the form of movies, television, comics, and adolescent fiction. What the college classroom offers such seasoned readers is a critical understanding of the genre, its history, its ideological content, and the popular appeal that has helped it to achieve its ubiquity. Helping students to attain such a critical perspective—on the genre as a whole and on the imaginative achievements of individual works—is my overarching goal in teaching dystopian fiction. I aspire to draw out, organize, and contextualize what students already know, in the process forging higher-level, more nuanced understandings. Here the satiric aspect of dystopian fiction becomes paramount, since a focus on dystopia's satiric potential leads naturally to broader discussion of the relationship between the imaginative work and the social conditions from which it emerges.

This essay provides an overview of the genre's history followed by attention to two novels, Aldous Huxley's *Brave New World* (1932) and George Schuyler's *Black No More* (1931). The lessons, techniques, and discussion questions described are specific to these texts but can be modified to other dystopian or near-future texts. I have taught these books occasionally in tandem and frequently apart in courses on modern British and modern American fiction. And while they may appear an odd pairing, there are significant points of contact. Published only a year apart, they are both set in the future, Schuyler's in 1933, Huxley's in 2540. Both rely on imagined scientific developments, specifically biotechnological ones. In Schuyler's novel the "black-no-more" treatment that turns black people white relies on a vague process of "electrical nutrition and glandular control" (27), while Huxley's introduces a slew of innovations including the "Bokanovsky process," by which human ova fertilized in vitro are cloned on a mass scale. Huxley's novel more clearly fits the canonical model of dystopia, yet Schuyler's imaginary future also has much to say about utopian hopes and their dystopian realization.

A more hidden but equally pertinent connection is the influence of H. L. Mencken. Mencken esteemed Schuyler as "the best writer the Negroes have ever produced," published Schuyler's work in *The American Mercury*, and coached the younger writer in his own style of sardonic social commentary (Mencken 419, 349). The young Huxley, meanwhile, was influenced, in *Brave New World* and elsewhere, by Mencken's diatribes against consumerism and bourgeois taste, and he hailed the Sage of Baltimore's "brilliant, masterfully vulgar style" (qtd. in Bradshaw 2). The Mencken connection points to broader satiric attitudes and themes shared by the two novels. Both display scorn for and distrust of a society in which mass media and entertainments have produced a dysfunctional public sphere, where popular sentiment dangerously resembles mad religious enthusiasm.

Genres and Histories

While the genre of dystopia will be familiar to students, its history will probably not. I therefore provide a historical run-up to the emergence of near-future dystopia as a major satiric genre of the twentieth century. Whether this takes the form of a twenty-minute presentation or an hour-long discussion supported by critical readings will depend upon the level of the course and the pace of the syllabus, but in all cases I minimize direct lecture time by asking students to share their own ideas and learning. I collaborate with students to build understanding from our collective knowledge and insights. Below, I describe a series of discussion questions, each one followed by some pedagogical points underscored in discussion.

What is a utopia, and how is it satirical?

In addressing this question, I draw out both the overt meaning of the Greek term ("no place") and the covert one ("good place," or *eutopia*), and we examine how utopia can function as satire. In my rendition, Thomas More's *Utopia* emerges as an irony-laden critique of early modern Europe, in which the imagined society offers an implicit alternative to existing sociopolitical arrangements (Elliott 22). I make at least passing mention of *Gulliver's Travels*, whose fourth book can be understood as both following More's template and satirizing it. I describe the late Victorian boom in literary utopias and discuss the utopia as a genre positioned between rhetoric and representation (Paulson 4). Like much satire, literary utopia mediates between the rhetorical or discursive (e.g., political theory) and the representational or fictional (e.g., the form of the novel). I also stress that the genteel socialism of Edward Bellamy and William Morris (where sharp Swiftian ironies are minimized) reproduces as much as it critiques the manners and ideologies of its own time and class (Manuel and Manuel 759). The Victorians help us see that neither utopia nor dystopia is exclusively critical, and that even radical imagined futures are products of their time (Jameson 171).

Why do we read more dystopias than utopias today?

Addressing this question allows us to examine the historical shift from utopia to dystopia around the beginning of the twentieth century. Students can usually identify the role of communism and fascism in bringing about this shift, but I generally have to point out that while the novels of Yevgeny Zamyatin, Huxley, and George Orwell respond to the totalitarianisms of Lenin, Stalin, and Hitler, several earlier works—H. G. Wells's *The Time Machine* (1895), Jack London's *The Iron Heel* (1908), and E. M. Forster's "The Machine Stops" (1909)—antedate the Russian Revolution and satirize general conditions of modernity (monopoly capitalism, rationalization, industrialization, imperialism) rather than the regimes of particular despots. This question also allows us to see the relative plotlessness of utopias and the greater potential of dystopias for dramatic tension.

Why are dystopias set in the future?

Along with the shift from utopia to dystopia comes a shift from space to time. Utopias are usually located in alternate *places*, but around the beginning of the new century, the displacement from the here and now becomes a temporal one. I aim to prompt the recognition that the Victorian utopia and the twentieth-century dystopia both derive from a new conception of historicity. The imaginary future is not just an alternative world; it is an alternative world *somehow arrived at from our own*. And the mechanism of transformation from the present to the future is some form of historical progress, whether or not that term is placed in scare quotes. For this reason authors of dystopian fiction often make explicit the causal links between the time of the writing and the time of the text. In teaching dystopia, I encourage students to inquire into how the novels that we study account for the historical transformations that they envision.

What are the features of a dystopian society?

With this question student brainstorming works especially well, since students are quite able to identify features of dystopian societies. These include an all-powerful state; the repression of individuality, dissent, and other basic rights and freedoms; widespread surveillance; an emphasis on the language of the new society (Orwell's Newspeak, Anthony Burgess's Nadsat); new terminology for new classes of people (Huxley's freemartins, Margaret Atwood's Marthas); the regulation of sexuality and reproduction. Students also usually recognize that the protagonists of dystopia are dissidents, moved to resistance against the state.

How are utopia and dystopia related?

I want students, finally, to recognize not merely the antithesis but the continuity between genres; the dystopia is often a utopia gone wrong.[1] The innovations that were supposed to usher in a better world are the very technologies of standardization, efficiency, and control that make the world oppressive and dangerous. In Irving Howe's words, "Not progress denied but progress realized is the nightmare haunting the anti-utopian novel" (14). Historically, satiric mock-versions and parodies have always followed hard on the heels of any articulation of utopian politics—as Aristophanes and Lucian followed Plato, or Joseph Hall and Jonathan Swift followed

More. The dystopia, however, brings a second level of critique: utopia contrasts the real world with the ideal, but dystopia can satirize both contemporary reality and the imagined future that it threatens to become.

Huxley's *Brave New World*

With an overview of dystopia established, I move to in-depth discussion of individual novels. *Brave New World* is a fruitful text for many reasons, but especially because, unlike *We* and *Nineteen Eighty-Four*, it attacks not only Soviet Communism but also American-style mass production and consumerism. I initiate discussion by asking students to use a graphic organizer to map their observations about various features of the world that Huxley represents. The organizer includes the following categories: government; class and social hierarchy; family; sex, love, and gender relations; economics; race and ethnicity; reproduction; work and labor; birth and death; recreation, leisure, and entertainment; language; religion; architecture and environment; transportation, communication, and technology; hygiene; and literature, culture, film, and the arts. This exercise encourages analysis of particular aspects of the world and reveals how these different features interlock and support one another. I let discussion of the novel follow student interests and insights, while the framework of the exercise ensures that multiple features of the imagined world remain available for our collective analysis.

Still working from the organizer, we move from understanding the practices of Huxley's future society to analyzing its governing values. Those may be summed up in the slogan "Community, Identity, Stability," but they encompass both the culture's emphasis on easy pleasures, sexual freedom, and economic efficiency and its rejection of passionate emotional attachment, high art and literature, and intellectual dissent. Historical context is important here: I fill in discussion with background on topics such as assembly-line production, the sexual freedoms of the Jazz Age, the economic crisis of the Depression, and pre-Holocaust belief in eugenics. I stress that Huxley is looking west to the United States much more than east to the USSR. And rather than simply lament the picture of a hedonistic, utilitarian modernity that Huxley offers, I ask students to consider its attractions.

I try to resist the easy and false assumption that Huxley successfully "predicted" the condition of the world today. I use the graphic organizer to direct attention to areas in which Huxley failed to foresee large-scale cultural and political changes. Race and gender are glaring blind spots: higher education seems to be open to men only in *Brave New World*, while Africans and African Americans appear only as servants. Meanwhile, the cinema and jazz that Huxley scorned have become the objects of cultural prestige for his readers today. Students might note that Huxley's future world still uses twentieth-century data-storage technologies such as the telephone book or the card catalog. They may also be amused at what passes for sexual radicalism: in the book's orgy scene, promiscuity is actually compelled by the state. Through such failures of foresight, a dystopia like Huxley's dates itself, making visible its own historicity.[2]

The topics in the organizer open a virtually endless series of avenues into the novel, but as we move toward conclusions, I emphasize two questions in particular. First, I inquire about the novel's representation of its dissidents, those characters who chafe against the values of the brave new world—Bernard, Lenina, Helmholtz, John—and ask how they differ from the other inhabitants of their society. Lenina is perhaps most interesting of all, since she begins the novel by resisting the governmental strictures against monogamy but transforms into a crude emblem of threatening modern (female) sexuality. Huxley squanders her potential as a critic of patriarchy when John takes over the role of upholding traditional sexual mores. Bernard's rebellion, meanwhile, is undercut by insecurity that stems from his physique, in contrast to the robust Nordic types of Helmholtz and John. Whether or not one agrees with Adorno's diagnosis of the representation as anti-Semitic, Bernard's inferiority complex certainly reveals a belief in eugenic hierarchies (Adorno 106).

The second area of focus is the final dialogue between John the Savage and Mustapha Mond. This clash of ideas, modeled on Dostoyevsky's parable of the Grand Inquisitor, has become almost a generic necessity for dystopian fiction, echoed in the climactic conversation between Winston Smith and O'Brien in *Nineteen Eighty-Four*. Such an extended exposition of ideas can feel didactic, yet this sequence is balanced enough that different students will place "Huxley" on different sides of the debate. Keith Johnson puts it well when he writes, "[I]t is only Mond who grasps both sides of the situation . . . and this is partly why his disquisition is quite strangely, given our sense of Huxley's ostensible thesis, more persuasive than John's flimsy protestation" (183). To pin down Huxley's own position in this dialogue becomes only more difficult with rereading and continued discussion, and if students conclude their reading with a sense of uncertainty or unease, then the analysis of the novel has succeeded.

Schuyler's *Black No More*

For all his perspicacity on particular anxieties of his day, Huxley engages the topic of race mainly through regressive frameworks of eugenics and racial swamping. A powerful counterweight, Schuyler's hilarious *Black No More* makes plain the degree to which existing racial injustice was a topic available for satire in the 1930s. When teaching *Black No More*, I begin with the preface, where the author links the fictional treatment described in his novel to real-life commercial hair-straightening products and to scientific experiments promising racial transformation. It establishes two key points: the rootedness of even highly fantastical satire in the conditions of the existing world and the question of an oppressed group's internalized self-hatred or identification with the oppressor.[3]

The novel's opening scene, in which Max Disher is called "nigger" by a white woman whom he asks to dance, announces a concern with the intersection of race and sex: how sex is regulated in order to maintain politicized racial categories. Students recognize Max and his friend Bunny's preference for "yellow women" (19) and how Max's decision to undergo the black-no-more treatment is driven by a vengeful desire to take sexual "possession" of the woman who humiliated him.[4] The temporal location of the opening scene—New Year's Eve 1933—hints at imminent change and helps us to see how Schuyler's near-future gives us a world already in the midst of historical transformation, in stark contrast to Huxley's "end of history." (*Black No More* seems to share this dynamic quality with other American antifascist dystopian or alternative-history texts: London's *The Iron Heel*, Sinclair Lewis's *It Can't Happen Here*, Nathanael West's *A Cool Million*, Philip Roth's *The Plot against America*.) The canonical dystopias like *Brave New World* and *Nineteen Eighty-Four* posit a society with no room for change, but Schuyler presents a future in radical flux.

Because Schuyler's novel represents this flux, it also offers an explicit contrast of the world before and after the proliferation of the black-no-more treatment. I therefore modify the graphic organizer exercise, instead asking students to note as many changes to the world as they can that result from the whitening of the black population. I ask them to identify how different characters and groups of people within the novel respond to those changes: northern plutocrats, southern white supremacists, black political leaders, black-run businesses, white union workers, and so forth; the self-interested response of Max/Matt himself is of course worth analyzing too. Such an exercise shifts responsibility for analysis onto the students, prioritizes their own observations and concerns, and allows discussion to ramify in multiple directions. It also reveals that in Schuyler's analysis, different racial attitudes exist across different classes and domains of society. Schuyler spares no individual or group; all have their own ideological and economic investments in race.

As with *Brave New World*, an exercise like this generally produces more "material" than can be covered in a few class meetings. The novel is rife with passages in which Schuyler unmasks the ways that race and racism play out in American society. If time permits, I like to discuss the lynching of the white supremacists Snobbcraft and Buggerie, how the violence and grotesque figuration make the reader of the satire complicit in its sadism. This scene also provides a point of comparison with crowd scenes in *Brave New World*, such as the thwarted revolt of the Epsilons and the spectators' riot turned orgy outside John's lighthouse at the novel's end. But as we move toward our conclusions, I return to questions of satire and utopia. Schuyler's novel acknowledges the power of utopian hope. Max, for example, is prone to imagining, in utopian rhetoric, that whiteness will eliminate his troubles: "No more jim crow. No more insults. As a white man, he could go anywhere, be anything he wanted to be, do most anything he wanted to do, be a free man at last" (26). On a broader scale, the whitening of America means that authorities must treat their (now-white) populations better: the railroads can no longer run unsafe wooden coaches, towns must supply sewers and sidewalks to once-black neighborhoods, landlords must pay for long-needed repairs, schoolteachers (now teaching white children) must be paid a proper wage (133–34). For all its comedy, this passage implies that the elimination of race will lead to the elimination of social evils.

But if near-future fiction often imagines a utopian society free from social antagonism, it also satirizes utopianism itself. Schuyler's contrarianism prompted him to mock not only racism but the pieties of white liberals and the black intelligentsia. Thus even as Schuyler exposes the contradictory and self-interested thinking behind our constructions of race, he also suggests that it is naive to expect that racial division can be eradicated from American culture. The novel's ending, in which racial difference is reinstated after its temporary elimination, implies that the ideological need for racial hierarchies is too stubborn to eliminate. Like *Brave New World*, *Black No More* ultimately posits a tension between the utopian and dystopian sides of its imagined future. The teacher's job is to recognize and analyze rather than to resolve that tension.

Notes

1. An exception is the postcatastrophe or postapocalyptic dystopia, such as J. G. Ballard's *The Drowned World* or Cormac McCarthy's *The Road*, which focus more on brute human survival in extreme conditions.

2. See Greenberg for a fuller articulation.

3. Schuyler repeatedly suggests that the desire for whiteness may be both rational and expedient: "A lifetime of being Negroes had convinced them that there was great advantage in being white" (57).

4. These intersections of race and sexuality also afford the opportunity to look at Schuyler's satirical comments on the idea of passing.

Works Cited

Adorno, Theodor W. *Prisms.* 1955. Translated by Samuel Weber and Shierry Weber, MIT P, 1967.

Bradshaw, David. "Chroniclers of Folly: Huxley and H. L. Mencken 1920–26." *Between the Wars: Essays and Letters*, by Aldous Huxley, edited by David Bradshaw, Ivan R. Dee, 1994, pp. 1–30.

Elliott, Robert C. *The Shape of Utopia: Studies in a Literary Genre.* U of Chicago P, 1970.

Greenberg, Jonathan. "What Huxley Got Wrong." Greenberg and Waddell, pp. 109–26.

Greenberg, Jonathan, and Nathan Waddell, editors. Brave New World*: Contexts and Legacies.* Palgrave Macmillan, 2016.

Howe, Irving. "The Fiction of Anti-Utopia." *The New Republic*, 23 Apr. 1962, pp. 14–16.

Huxley, Aldous. *Brave New World.* 1932. Harper Collins, 2006.

Jameson, Fredric. *Archaeologies of the Future: The Desire Called Utopia and Other Science Fictions.* Verso, 2007.

Johnson, Keith Leslie. "Ethics in the Late Anthropocene." Greenberg and Waddell, pp. 169–88.

Manuel, Frank E., and Fritzie P. Manuel. *Utopian Thought in the Western World.* Belknap Press, 1979.

Mencken, H. L. *Letters.* Edited by Guy J. Forgue, Knopf, 1961.

Paulson, Ronald. *The Fictions of Satire.* Johns Hopkins UP, 1967.

Schuyler, George S. *Black No More: Being an Account of the Strange and Wonderful Workings of Science in the Land of the Free, A.D. 1933–1940.* 1931. Northeastern UP, 1989.

Anne Lake Prescott

Menippos in the Classroom

I offer the following paragraph to students in my course Wit and Humor in the Renaissance, which focuses on English literature but includes a few classical and Neo-Latin texts as well as François Rabelais:

> Trigger warning: The "Menippean" satires we will read contain offensive sexual and scatological humor. The 1565 picture I tried to use on the required description posted near the sign-up sheet was rejected because it included a huge codpiece stuck full of pins: "We may receive complaints." Likewise rejected was an early modern figure sporting a cannon in the relevant place, just as Freud would want. The texts on our syllabus, though, are often written in that same spirit, so be warned: this material is almost as dirty as *South Park*, say, or that carnival of a movie *Trading Places.* But remember that the authors are often laughing at themselves as much as at snooty ladies, jargon-spouting lawyers, fat rich guys, foppish courtiers, religious opponents, and closed-minded professors clutching out-of-date books.

I add that some years ago Rabelais was expelled from a required Columbia University course and that, despite official explanations, I heard from someone present that a passage in *Pantagruel* was thought too sexist. It's that imaginary wall around Paris made of vulvas, I was told. I objected that it's also made of monks' penises: the best defense of a kingdom is making kids, not firing guns. The issue is real, though, and much Renaissance satire is indeed misogynist, often with racial or religious bias. And yet, as students have reminded me, we live in a dirty-mouthed age with stand-up comics who live to offend.

How then to handle Menippean satire's sexual jesting and delight in what M. M. Bakhtin more solemnly calls the "lower bodily stratum" (38; cf. Herrick)? Teaching risqué or misogynist humor, often deployed against a religious "other," requires different approaches, sometimes according with the teacher's gender and age. Blue language is more comfortably taught by blue-hairs, but other ages and genders can find ways of putting students at partial ease. The chief pedagogical trick, students tell me, is to explain confidently, but not solemnly, that early modern satire can both offend, dealing with issues hardly funny in real life, and yet amuse the self-confident. True, teaching texts pockmarked by racist or snobbish wit is harder.

What made humor so valuable for early modern writers? Hurting "others," of course, and solidifying "us," but one can also explain such traditional views as found in Laurent Joubert's 1579 book *Traité du ris* (*Treatise on Laughter*). Laughter, runs the argument, results from joy mixed with grief. What pleasure to see a prank played on Shakespeare's grumpy Malvolio, but what sorrow to see a fellow human being hurt! So as the heart alternately swells and constricts with joy and grief, it shakes the diaphragm, and we say, "Ho, ho," getting air into the blood and increasing the sanguine humor. Laughter can even cure the sick. Doctors in the audience would agree with Beaumont and Fletcher's Merrythought in *The Knight of the Burning Pestle* that "'Tis mirth that fills the veins with blood, / More than wine, or sleep, or food" (act 2, scene 8; Strachey 420). Do you cringe at a text's bias while laughing at its wit? Good—you'll improve your health.

Defining the Menippea is another challenge, for this is a messy genre (see Kirk).[1] Allusions to the style/genre are few in early modern England, but modern scholars note its supposed derivation from the perhaps mythical ancient Greek satirist Menippos. Such a satire offers a *lanx satura*, a "heaped platter." To write effective heroic couplets such as those by John Dryden and Alexander Pope takes an ability to pack words tightly, excising anything needless. Menippean satirists, though, prefer linguistic spillage that amuses through a refusal to sit down and shut up. True, much of it learnedly aims at the learned, so unless we know the spurious erudition, assumptions, or structures at which the satirist aims, it is hard to identify the reversals—good reason to find helpful editions and provide background. Such satire, moreover, is associated with carnival and festival; we enjoy fleshy Mardi Gras (Fat Tuesday) today, knowing that Lent's fish arrive tomorrow. Such satire can aim at a mistimed fast, at those who insist on cultural fish *now*, on a respectable restraint that denies greenness, fullness, present mirth. To show Fast's tension with Carnival (or with such midwinter feasts as pagan Saturnalia or Christian Twelfth Night), one might distribute the title page of John Taylor's *Jack a Lent* (1620): skinny Lent, armed with a pike and astride a large fish (presumably a pike—ouch), trails a chubby Tuesday armed with a roasting spit. The text fattens Carnival through fake etymology, typographical variety, imaginary books, silly words, puns, anecdotes, and nonsense verse. Alliteration? Taylor is even-handed: "Friendly, frolicke, franke, free-hearted, famous flourishing *Fish-mongers*; And brave, bold, battring, Beefe-braining, *Butchers*," he begins, in either case inviting us to feast from dishfuls of comic discourse. Thomas Nashe's *Lenten Stuffe* (1599), to cite another example, is not about much of anything, seemingly, except Nashe's ability to toss around words (some a parody of Christopher Marlowe's "Hero and Leander"), until his discussion of fish becomes verbal Carnival. And what happens after a feast? Sir John Harington's *Metamorphosis of Ajax* (1596) postpones its promised transformation of the privy until almost the end of the text, a retention and release that may be the text's subtlest scatological joke.

Choosing Menippean texts to teach can be difficult, however, because some great ones were not originally in English and because so many offer only partial platters. I will briefly recall some relevant ancient and Continental texts and then move to England.

Among the classical Menippea read in England is the *Satyricon* by Petronius Arbiter, probably the elegant arbiter of taste under Nero whom that emperor forced into suicide. Its famous "Trimalchio's dinner" was lost until the late seventeenth century (and that phrase was F. Scott Fitzgerald's first title for *The Great Gatsby*), but enough remained to allow a sense of the genre: lawless sex, scatology, travel, literary parody, social reversals, and feasting. Students may be amused to read a flaccid penis described as casting its eye on the ground in words taken from Virgil's account of a grieving Dido—it can be Menippean satire's job to degrade the epic, that noblest of genres.[2]

Lucian, the Syrian satirist who wrote in Greek under the Roman Empire in the second century CE, played a large role in early modern satire.

Students might recognize in his *True History* anticipations of the *Oz* books, *Pinocchio*, and modern sci-fi, while his dialogue recounting Menippos's descent to Hades, where the once mighty suffer carnival reversals, inspired imitations (see Boyce). Lucian can also be learnedly anti-intellectual—witness "Philosophies for Sale" (imitating it makes a good assignment)—and his taste for such paradoxes (e.g., claiming at the start of *A True History* that everything he says is a lie) makes him useful for thinking about modern physics and number theory. Nor is assigning him a novelty: Thomas Elyot's *Governour* advises that teachers give students, if cautiously, some of his "quycke and mery dialoges" (D5). The African Apuleius's *The Golden Ass* may not be Menippean (opinions differ) but can likewise inspire interest, not least because its tale of Cupid and Psyche lies behind C. S. Lewis's *Till We Have Faces.* Students can enjoy the protagonist's adventures as a donkey (a beast famed for penile size), scatology, and embedded tales. Macrobius's *Saturnalia* has jokes, and a useful work with Renaissance parallels is Seneca's *Apocolocyntosis divi Claudii* (translated as *The Gourdification* or *Pumpkinification of Claudius*), which tells what happens when that emperor reaches the afterworld. Printed in 1513 and translated in 1664, it inspired Erasmus's *Julius Exclusus e Coelis* (1514) on the troubles Pope Julius II encounters at heaven's gate. A related, if yet more violent and potentially offensive, satire is the Italian Protestant Pier Paolo Vergerio's *Wonderfull Newes of the Death of Paule the III* (translated into English by William Baldwin).[3] Here students can meet versions of the famed Roman statues Pasquil and Marforius, on whom, in a proto-Twitter system, citizens could post satirical squibs. Here "P. Esquilles" (Pasquil) sees Pope Paul's trip to hell, clerical fornication, and a transgendered pontiff shedding menstrual blood into a chalice. Those wishing to watch dirt fly the other way can read the jokes, dialogues, fake letters, and rhetorical fireworks that propel Thomas More's assaults on Martin Luther and William Tyndale, whether in English or Latin.

Early modern European satires often scoff at conservative scholars uneasy with the new learning, not least a revived Greek and a humanist stress on Hebrew. *Letters of Obscure Men* (1515–17) by Ulrich von Hutten and others, available in translation, demonstrates this tension. Students enjoy seeing professors satirized, even if needing some explanations, and passages scorning extreme anti-Semitism have modern poignancy. As interest in ancient Menippea surged, imitations surged as well, and one might at least mention those by such learned men from the Low Countries as Justus Lipsius, Petrus Cunaeus, and Erycius Puteanus, all known in England, and especially the wittily polemical *Beehive of the Romish Church* (1569;

trans. George Gilpin, 1579) by the statesman Philips van Marnix, whose parrot was said to become snarky when drunk.

Of all vernacular early modern Menippea, though, the greatest must be *Gargantua and Pantagruel* by Rabelais, admirer of Erasmus, editor of ancient medical texts, and evangelical-minded monk who made his Gargantua king of Utopia. Thomas Urquhart's partial translation (1653) is a triumph of wrestling English into more shapes than one would think possible, lengthening Rabelais's lists, swinging sentences around so fast they squeal, and inventing words; Peter Motteux's edition (1693/94) is almost as good. Modern translations are easier to follow but less imaginative. The work was so famed in England that one might offer at least a few pages of this assortment of dialogues, feasts, paradoxical encomia (e.g., of debt), imaginary books, anecdotes, strange lands, talkative lawyers, lusty monks, poems, puns, reversals (such as the narrator's trip down his own giant's throat), a search for the best "arse-wiper" (try a soft feathery goose), and a Lucianic visit to Hades. The imaginary library in *Pantagruel* has jokes often now hard to detect but that can inspire students to create their own (I treasure one student's suggestions for the Columbia University library). Here and elsewhere Rabelais's point can be serious, and indeed at one point he fled France for safety; the current consensus is that much of his satire supports an Evangelical Catholicism that stresses the Bible over tradition and such distractions, in this view, as saints, theological minutiae, and ecclesiastical display.

For a fully Anglocentric course, though, one might start with More's *Utopia*, perhaps in its 1551 translation by Ralph Robinson. Cleverly satiric—something those many who toss around the word *utopian* often forget—More's text may not be fully Menippean, for its brilliance lies more in subtly ironic commentary on England than in heaped-up language. Nevertheless it has carnival touches. Utopians use gold for slaves' chains, for example, whereas we Europeans use them to dignify courtiers who serve the king . . . but oh, wait. Is there much difference? Who is the more demeaned slave? Gold for chamber pots? Paging Freud. Fully Menippean or not, moreover, *Utopia* includes sardonic marginalia, imaginary languages (including Utopian), playful paratexts, voyages, self-mockery, wittily invented names, passages that almost edge into indecency, and, in some early editions, a frontispiece that itself, like a paradox, plays with perspective and nothing, for "Utopia," meaning "nowhere," if also punning on *eutopia*, a "good where," is also round, a zero (a concept then still recent in Europe).

Moving ahead some decades, one might assign William Baldwin's *Beware the Cat* (1553). The scary "Cat" and its friends are implicitly "*Cat*holics" (then probably pronounced *Cat-licks*), for Baldwin injects his satire into England's often savage religious debates: Can mere words change matter's substance? How does mere feline hearsay seemingly relate to tradition, and does that tradition go back to Scripture? Do listen when cat[holic]s speak, although there is danger in their very secrecy—remember priest holes?—and in the meantime come scatology, tales, witchcraft, lists, imaginary books, verse, magic (which "cats" doubtless call the Mass, Baldwin may imply), legends, gossip, transformations, parodically fine writing, spells, illustrations, and marginal comments with, for example, the dubious claim that "the spring and neaping [ebbing] of the sea causeth the moon to wax and wane" (35). The modern editors wisely retain these notes' position in the margin so they can glance sidelong at the text while snuggling next to it.

A generation or two later came Sir John Harington's *Metamorphosis of Ajax* (1596; *Ajax* puns on "a jakes," meaning "privy"; Elizabeth Donno's edition [1962] includes vital associated texts). Godson of Queen Elizabeth and author of clever epigrams, and supposed inventor of the flush toilet, Harington translated Ariosto's *Orlando Furioso* (1591) and the medieval *Regimen sanitatis Salerni* ("Medical Advice from the School of Salerno," 1607), with its reminder to "Use three Physitians still, first Doctor *Quiet*, / Next Doctor *Mery-man*, and Doctor *Dyet*" (A7). *Ajax* offers verse, varied voices, pictures (one shows a toilet), chats with the reader, music, journeys, loquacious margins, lists, fake etymology, puns, wordplay (and self-referential comments such as a parenthetical phrase referring to parentheses [61]). There is cheerful obscenity, as when the narrator, dictionary in hand, tries to locate a verb beginning with *f* (the Latin, we read, is "fornicor") and searches another dictionary for a noun related to *con*, indecent French for "vagina" (135). Although the satire often aims at the court, Harington's deeper suggestion is that squeamishness denies our humanity—"what we are, and whither we must" (161). Earthy, we return to earth. A flush toilet makes smelly stuff vanish faster, but we remain descended from Adam ("red earth"), which is Menippean satire's deepest implication. No wonder Harington often alludes to Rabelais. *Ajax* is not quite a paradoxical encomium, a genre related to the Menippea, for its suggestion is that we clean up the world, not that we learn to love the unlovable, yet the effect is the same.[4] Shyer students might hesitate to discuss it in class, despite what they may watch on their cell phones, but they might appreciate Harington on the disapproving: "Yf one name a merd [turd] they thinke they are mard, but a fylthyer thing then that mard them. What doe they with Rables and Aretyne in theyre studyes?" (200). The question reminds us not to gaze so hard at stars that we forget where we come from.

Another fully Menippean text is Joseph Hall's *Mundus Alter et Idem* (c. 1605), a four-part satiric dystopia published in London, despite "Frankfurt" being on the title page, and translated by John Healey as *The Discovery of a New World* (c. 1609). Healey's version dissatisfies some, but Huntington Brown's edition (Harvard UP, 1937) retains the marginalia where they can talk to the main text. Although John Millar Wands's translation (Yale UP, 1981) is more faithful to the Latin, it has a modern flavor; his helpful introduction, noting the debt to Lucian and parodic travel literature, has a section on Menippean satire, and Richard McCabe's *Joseph Hall: A Study in Satire and Meditation* considers the Menippean context and Hall's discomfort with utopian aims. Hall's "New World," set in a yet unexplored Antarctica but reachable on the ship *Phantasia*, includes lands ruled by gluttons, women ("Viraginia, or [horrible pun] New Gynia"), fools, and crooks. The obvious joke is that these worlds are less England's antipodes than its reality. Even imagining a land ruled by women goes well with the age's many jokes about wives' power, for official hierarchies seldom work smoothly in real life.[5] There is much else in Hall's Antarctica for students to relish, including the imaginary books (often Healey's additions), which are entertaining to set next to those in *Pantagruel* or John Donne's *The Courtier's Library* (1930), as well as illustrations, lists, witty marginalia, reversals, puns, send-ups of scholarship, grotesqueries, parodies of travel literature, and food. Most relevant now might be Tenter-belly, ruled by the grotesquely fat, in which one candidate for office promises "that hee would . . . preserve us as wee were now, and make us as wee would bee" (Hall, *Discovery* 42): our nation is perfection—but I will improve it.

Many other texts offer a Menippean dish or two: dialogues, for example, or such imaginary voyages as that in the proto-sci-fi *The Man in the Moone* (1638) by Francis Godwin or the translation by "W.P." of Celio Curione's anti-Catholic *Pasquine in a Traunce* (1566), with its nose-thumbing marginalia and show-off narrator. Polemics are often Menippean, and indeed *Englandes Bright Honour* (1595) translates the French *Satyre Ménippée* by Pierre Pithou and others in support of the "politique" side in France's civil wars; the 1602 preface offers a page defining *Menippean*. Many polemics, like the verbal gunfire between Thomas Nashe and poor out-Menippized Gabriel Harvey, may be better suited to a graduate course, but they can still be excerpted to show undergraduates how techniques familiar from Menippean satirists—such as gushing or strutting verbosity, playful if still wounding lists, puns, pictures, anecdotes, jests, marginalia, a rhetoric that leaps from the printed page to grab the reader's elbow—could be aimed at the enemy in a religious or personal controversy. Such satire, to which one might add pages from *Apologie pour Hérodote* by the Huguenot printer/scholar Henri Estienne (1566; *The Stage of Popish Toyes*, trans. George North, 1581), shows how print culture added to satire's ancient weaponry by exploiting various typefaces, for example, or lists of errata in ways writers before Gutenberg could not manage. Just as lively, if subtler, is Donne's anti-Jesuit *Ignatius His Conclave* (1611) and its cluster of dubious superstars in the underworld. Indeed, although Donne never wrote a fully Menippean satire, *Ignatius His Conclave*, the verse *Metempsychosis*, formal satires, parodic "characters," *The Courtier's Library*, and his dazzling if mean poems before *Coryate's Crudities* (1611) add up to a fine, if scattered, Menippean satire.[6]

Satirical proto-novels (semi-Menippea), such as Nashe's *The Unfortunate Traveller*, can work, and the daring might add Nashe's obscene *Choice of Valentines*, for good reason unprinted in its own day; even now it can raise eyebrows, although as a literary send-up—the start of the poem flashes words from Chaucer and the end does the same from Virgil—and with a humiliated man and all-too-self-sufficient woman who competently plies her dildo, it is undeniably carnivalesque. One can give students the option of skipping it, although for those made of sterner stuff one can add some French parallels and the Restoration poem "Signior Dildo." Carrying less sexual than religious shock are the pamphlets deployed in the Martin Marprelate controversy, which Joseph Navitsky explicitly associates with the Menippea.

Longer texts that may not deserve an entire undergraduate class can still be useful. Thomas Coryate is no Rabelais or Harington, but the multiauthored prefatory material before his *Crudities*, some by such wits as Donne, Ben Jonson, and Michael Drayton, is delicious, not least a poem in Utopian by the emblematist Henry Peacham. This long verbal banquet, largely in verse, sports with puns, (pseudo)learning, insults, (pseudo)compliments, ironic alphabets, images, music, shaped poems, multiple languages and that mixture we call "macaronic," play with typeface, and a donkey. Pages from the Web or from the 1905 Glasgow edition (though it calms down the original's boisterous typography) are well worth circulating to show again the early modern taste for insults as a literary genre. Menippean? Certainly, although prose and verse arrive in separate dishes (see Craik).

This brief survey has omitted much, from a 1595 dialogue by Maroccus Extaticus (John Dando) between one Bankes and his sometimes verse-snorting horse—typical of the age's taste for satirical back-and-forth—to such paradoxical encomia, another ancient genre that saw revival, as Willibald Pirckheimer's *The Praise of the Gout* (trans. William Est, 1617) and much else. If teaching Menippean satire, it is good to remember that for the educated, including some women, a taste for a clever *lanx satura* and its side dishes extended from the Mediterranean world north and can now time travel from the ancients to a modern classroom, where, one can hope, students can still simultaneously take pleasure, grieve, and, says the old theory, become more sanguine.

Notes

1. For the genre's history and definitions see in particular Blanchard. On classical precedents (with some disagreement as to what counts) see Relihan, De Smet, Weinbrot, and Musgrave. Freudenburg has a chapter on the Menippea, and Renner cites recent scholarship in "From *Satura* to *Satyre*."

2. There was no good English edition until William Burnaby's 1694 translation. Federico Fellini's film version, marginally cleaner, omits some hijinks.

3. Overell and Lucas discuss the work's authorship.

4. Rosalie Colie's *Paradoxia Epidemica* describes such exercises in ambiguous irony. *Utopia*, praising "nowhere," may be one.

5. Ian Munro's *A Woman's Answer Is Never to Seek* offers such jests.

6. On Donne's Menippea, see Brown; Korkowski; Prescott.

Works Cited

Bakhtin, M. M. *Rabelais and His World*. Translated by Helene Iswolsky, MIT P, 1968.

Baldwin, William. *Beware the Cat: The First English Novel*. Edited by William A. Ringler, Jr., and Michael Flachmann, Huntington Library, 1988.

Blanchard, W. Scott. *Scholars' Bedlam: Menippean Satire in the Renaissance*. Bucknell UP / London Associated UP, 1995.

Boyce, Benjamin. "News from Hell: Satiric Communications with the Nether World in English Writing of the Seventeenth and Eighteenth Centuries." *PMLA*, vol. 58, no. 2, June 1943, pp. 402–37.

Brown, Piers. "'Hac ex consilio meo via progredieris': Courtly Reading and Secretarial Mediation in Donne's *The Courtier's Library*." *Renaissance Quarterly*, vol. 61, no. 3, Fall 2008, pp. 833–66.

Colie, Rosalie L. *Paradoxia Epidemica: The Renaissance Tradition of Paradox.* Princeton UP, 1966.

Craik, Katharine. "Reading *Coryat's Crudities* (1611)." *Studies in English Literature, 1500–1900*, vol. 44, no. 1, 2004, pp. 77–96.

De Smet, Ingrid A. R. *Menippean Satire and the Republic of Letters, 1581–1655.* Droz, 1996.

Donne, John. *The Courtier's Library.* Translated by Percy Simpson, edited by Evelyn Mary Spearing Simpson, London, 1930.

Elyot, Thomas. *The Boke Named Governour.* London, 1537.

Freudenburg, Kirk, editor. *The Cambridge Companion to Roman Satire.* Cambridge UP, 2005.

Hall, Joseph. *Another World and Yet the Same: Bishop Joseph Hall's "Mundus Alter et Idem."* Translated and edited by John Millar Wands, Yale UP, 1981.

———. *The Discovery of a New World (Mundus Alter et Idem).* Translated by John Healey, edited by Huntington Brown, Harvard UP, 1937.

Harington, John. *A New Discourse of a Stale Subject, Called the* Metamorphosis of Ajax. Edited by Elizabeth Story Donno, Routledge / Kegan Paul, 1962.

———. *Regimen sanitatis Salerni; or, The Schoole of Salernes.* London, 1634.

Herrick, Marvin T. *Comic Theory in the Sixteenth Century.* U of Illinois P, 1964.

Joubert, Laurent. *Treatise on Laughter.* Translated by Gregory de Rocher, U of Alabama P, 1980.

Kirk, Eugene P. *Menippean Satire: An Annotated Catalogue of Texts and Criticism.* Garland, 1980.

Korkowski, Eugene. "Donne's 'Ignatius' and Menippean Satire." *Studies in Philology*, vol. 72, no. 4, Oct. 1975, pp. 419–38.

McCabe, Richard. *Joseph Hall: A Study in Satire and Meditation.* Clarendon Press / Oxford UP, 1982.

Munro, Ian, editor. *A Woman's Answer Is Never to Seek: Early Modern Jestbooks, 1526–1635.* Ashgate, 2007.

Musgrave, David. *Grotesque Anatomies: Menippean Satire since the Renaissance.* Cambridge Scholars, 2014.

Nashe, Thomas. *Lenten Stuffe.* 1599. *The Works of Thomas Nashe*, edited by R. B. McKerrow, vol. 3, Oxford, 1966.

Navitsky, Joseph. "Disputing Good Bishop's English: Martin Marprelate and the Voice of Menippean Opposition." *Texas Studies in Literature and Language*, vol. 50, no. 2, Summer 2008, pp. 177–200.

Overell, Anne, and Scott C. Lucas. "Whose Wonderful News? Italian Satire and William Baldwin's *Wonderful Newes of the Death of Paul the III.*" *Renaissance Studies*, vol. 26, no. 2, Apr. 2010, pp. 180–96.

Prescott, Anne Lake. "Menippean Donne." *The Oxford Handbook of John Donne*, edited by Jeanne Shami et al., Oxford UP, 2011, pp. 158–79.

Relihan, Joel C. *Ancient Menippean Satire.* Johns Hopkins UP, 1993.

Renner, Bernd. "From *Satura* to *Satyre*: François Rabelais and the Renaissance Appropriation of a Genre." *Renaissance Quarterly*, vol. 67, no. 2, Summer 2014, pp. 377–424.

Strachey, J. St. Loe, editor. *The Plays of Francis Beaumont and John Fletcher*. Vol. 1, A. A. Wyn, 1949.

Weinbrot, Howard D. *Menippean Satire Reconsidered: From Antiquity to the Eighteenth Century*. Johns Hopkins UP, 2005.

David Alff

Satirical Drama in History

I open my undergraduate survey British Drama: 1660–1730 with an apology and an invitation. First, I apologize that we are late—too late to attend the performances that made Restoration theater a popular venue for poetry, spectacle, and the deliberation of cultural values. Drama, I explain, consists of writing and enactment: prompt books and playtexts as well as mouth sounds and limb gestures. Therefore, we cannot experience old plays with the sense of immediacy that we might derive from browsing a novel or scanning a lyric from the same era. While students with access to early editions can grasp the same books held by seventeenth-century readers, no equivalent artifact will help us understand how it felt to sit in the gallery of Dorset Garden on 24 March 1677, when Aphra Behn's *The Rover* premiered. The playtext will not show us how Thomas Betterton played Belvile, what hecklers shouted from the pit, whether any sunlight filtered through the windows, or how the chandelier's mutton candles smelled. Given our limited access to the multisensory experience of Restoration playgoing, I invite students to approach its drama under the auspices of a salvage project. Our goal is to learn everything we can about a show we missed.

Belatedness poses special challenges for the study of dramatic satire. Here students need not only reconstruct the performative event, but they must know something about the early modern world that satirists sought to infiltrate, ridicule, and perhaps correct. Because satire is prone to doing other than what it says, its relationship to this world can seem frustratingly indeterminate. Inferring whom or what a play sets out to mock, and through what means and to what ends, requires both careful attention to textual detail and an appreciation of how nonrhetorical layers of meaning could be introduced onstage through the posture, inflection, attire, and positioning of actors. The text in our hands tells only a partial story of satire's "inquiry and provocation," its tendency toward irony and resistance to literal-minded decoding (Griffin 71). Therefore, we must read closely, often against the grain, while also reaching beyond the words contained within our Broadview anthologies to discern the motives behind a given performance.

This essay outlines several strategies I use to help students appreciate satiric comedy of the Restoration as a corpus of writings and repertoire of enactments. It describes approaches to teaching some particularly challenging (and rewarding) dramatic passages and explains how my students acquire sufficient historical knowledge to deduce what drove particular playwrights to satire. A fifteen-week course hardly permits exhaustive mapping of the relationships between a body of theatrical literature and its multitudinous cultural referents. It is, however, enough time to assess satirical drama's impact upon one singular period of English history and, in so doing, to reconceive literary interpretation itself as a project for recovering old ways of declaiming and disguising thought.

Since satire operates on page and stage, the first task is to have students distinguish between the writing and performance of plays. Scholars of seventeenth-century drama have long recognized the inadequacy of New Critical approaches that reduce drama to script and script to "verbal icon" (Sauer and Tribble 35). This critical conventional wisdom can come as a shock to undergraduates habituated to making sense of literature through close reading. Getting students to look beyond the book in front of them can seem all the harder when the text it contains is so difficult. Basic comprehension of a Restoration play like John Dryden's *Marriage à la Mode* or William Congreve's *The Way of the World* requires the fortitude to follow complex plots, fluency in archaic idioms, and familiarity with the society that provoked its humor. One needs to remember which one is

Witwoud, that horns signal cuckolding, and that the line between modern and modish, fashion and foppery, shifted from year to year. Satire not only draws upon its cultural context but embarrasses its prevailing wisdoms and pretenses to style. It challenges students to place themselves in the position of a Restoration audience *and* be in on the joke—to know when to laugh with or at certain characters; to detect which views of morality, citizenship, sex, and commerce are undercut; and to recognize which modes of conduct are silently endorsed.

To surmount this complexity, I present performance as an aid to interpretation. What can seem dauntingly cryptic in text was often self-evident onstage. The seventeenth-century playgoer obviously would not have needed to flip to the dramatis personae to recall Witwoud's biographical details—the aspirant rake and self-proclaimed wit would have manifested through William Bowen, actor for the United Company. We do not need to see Bowen's performance for ourselves to understand how it made palpable Witwoud's grating attempts to impress those around him. I emphasize this point by showing clips of a modern production of *The Way of the World*, such as the one John Selwyn Gilbert directed for the BBC in 1975. Then I ask students how seeing Witwoud onstage clarifies his role in Congreve's plot, particularly in relation to more adept figures, like Mirabell, who possesses the intelligence Witwoud merely pretends to. Returning to the text, we ask why this adaptation foregrounds certain ironic possibilities while leaving others latent. The figure of Witwoud most obviously mocks stale jokes and unwelcome gallantry, but I ask whether his behavior might also satirize Restoration London's overinvestment in verbal dexterity as a criterion for judging personal worth. How might one badly socialized character indict not only those like him but the customs and values governing an entire society?

Watching performances on-screen makes clear that playtexts capture only a fraction of the dramatic events they guide and record. In my experience, students usually grasp the extrarhetorical nature of satire and of humor more broadly: the phrase "you had to be there," for instance, casually grieves the loss of experiential detail that occurs when an amusing incident is retold secondhand. This sense of being there is vital to satire, which can rely upon savvy enactment to sort out its double meanings and conflicting propositions. In this vein, my students undertake several exercises designed to help them navigate between playtext and performance. Before discussing each play, I pass out a photocopy of its entry in William van Lennep's *The London Stage, 1660–1800*, which catalogs who played what parts for what company and at what venue. Students will see, for instance, that Dryden's Leonidas and William Wycherley's Harcourt in *The Country Wife* were both performed by Edward Kynaston, who also played a female lead in the 1661 revival of Ben Jonson's *Epicene*. I ask how the appearance of well-known repertory actors established its own metatheatrical subtext based upon those players' previous roles. My point is that casting could involve its own comic decisions—decisions that could give observant audience members the pleasure of recognition. We then discuss these tactics in relation to the appearance of celebrities within modern comedy and cinematic conventions like the cameo.

In keeping with their penchant for self-reflection, Restoration comedies often reference the conditions of their own production. Prologues and epilogues, spoken by characters in costume, offer important evidence for how playwrights understood the relationship between their projects and the society they made light of. These speeches often bemoan the lowly status of drama, a complaint made ironic by its address to theatrical patrons. Within the plot, we pay special attention to scenes that take place in theaters. For instance, in Wycherley's *The Country Wife*, Pinchwife tries to conceal his spouse, Margery, from the rake Horner by watching a show from the "eighteen-penny place," an inconspicuous middle gallery sandwiched between the raucous pit and aristocratic boxes (Canfield 1047). This failed stratagem exploits the actual audience's knowledge of their own partition by class and behavior. Wycherley then presents his spectators with a boorish version of themselves in the character of Sparkish, a railing hack who disrupts plays and fancies himself the "poet's rival" (116). What, I ask, does Wycherley achieve by targeting members of the audience who paid to see his show? How might this censure have been received? Such scenes point to a current of self-satire in Restoration comedy, which sometimes prefaces its attacks on society by ironically disclaiming its powers of critique.

We can compare these dramatic reflections with actual accounts of playhouses excerpted within John McCollum's *The Restoration Stage* (1961). These writings include memoirs by Lorenzo Magalotti, a Tuscan count who observed that London's theaters mixed male and female spectators indiscriminately, and Samuel Sorbière, a French physician who chided English playwrights for ignoring the classical unities. The diarist Samuel Pepys further illuminates the patent theaters by evaluating dozens of plays on points of plot development and production quality, while singling out particular players who were cheered and hissed. Pepys's candid meditations on his own frequent drunkenness and smoldering attraction to the mistresses of Charles II present humorous episodes that we can contrast with the comic intrigue taking place on the stage. I open another class by passing around a 1673 royal proclamation condemning spectators who "rudely press, and with evil Language and Blows force their way into Our Theatres." That Charles II made the behavior of playgoers a matter of state concern suggests to students both the unruliness of London theaters and their importance to England's self-perception. The theater, it becomes clear, served both as outlet and object of criticism: audiences consumed dramatic satire while speaking and acting out in ways that compromised performance and lent it future fodder.

Just as valuable as these documents are the forms of knowledge we can produce ourselves within the classroom by acting out old plays. Following Diana Taylor's suggestion that performance can function as a "nonarchival system of transfer" (xvii), I make students read plays aloud with their ears attuned to parodic intent. Where text is silent, satire is auditory, bodily, and "gestic," to use Elin Diamond's term for the "contradictory interactions of text, theater apparatus, and contemporary social struggle" (519). While it's nothing new to have students act out parts, turning the classroom into impromptu theater, I find that even when routinized, this practice sounds out tonal shifts, half-hidden puns, and other aspects of satire's acoustical subterfuge, features that silent reading can leave buried. Vocalization forces students to make on-the-spot interpretive decisions regarding the motives behind a given piece of speech: What does a character want? Do her words agree with her motives? How is this verbal performance received? (Riggio 2). Reading aloud simultaneously gives the rest of the class an opportunity to hear drama through its back-and-forth, whether it's Wycherley's Horner duping a dully serious London citizen or the dialectic repartee that balances and binds Mirabell and Millamant in Congreve's *Way of the World*.

For a few especially sound-rich scenes, I divide the class into groups of four that work among themselves to devise a reading they perform before the class. Acting out the letter-writing scene in *The Country Wife*, for instance, makes students decide whether their Margery will betray genuine rural naïveté or mobilize that impression to resist her husband. They have to figure out whether Pinchwife's wielding of the penknife is truly frightening or comic excess, whether sympathy is possible for this expectant cuckold or whether he is a justly punished tyrant. Students quickly perceive that Wycherley leaves them great leeway in interpreting their roles, a degree of latitude that members of the King's Company also would have enjoyed when they first brought those roles to the stage in 1675. After students perform, we reassemble to discuss the differences between their adaptations and how acting itself entails interpretive work. Then I show them the same scene, as performed by Helen Mirren and Bernard Cribbins in a 1977 production of *The Country Wife*, to see how another set of actors resolved these same questions. At stake in this exercise is an ability to identify the target of Wycherley's satire: Is he merely poking fun at the Hampshire-born country bumpkin Margery and the covetousness of her husband? Or does Margery's rapid accumulation of know-how and eventual undermining of Horner threaten the self-assured and sophisticated Londoner of the sort who would have been attending *The Country Wife*? These conclusions rest upon performances (including our own) and not just Wycherley's language.

Another way to induce interpretive decision making is to have students illustrate particular scenes. Each semester, I invite class members to draw on the board act 2, scene 1 of Thomas Shadwell's *The Virtuoso*, in which the amateur natural philosopher and industrialist Gimcrack lies flat on a wooden plank and attempts to simulate the act of swimming by imitating the arm and leg motions of a frog in a basin. Where an overhasty reading might gloss over the ridiculousness of Gimcrack's project for "speculative swimming," and thereby underestimate Shadwell's sardonic attack upon the Royal Society's institutionalization of speculative knowledge, student drawings capture the depth of his madness. The flamboyant Fopling Flutter in George Etherege's *The Man of Mode* is another rewarding target for ekphrasis. Students can fix upon his rich attire, overwrought speech, or reported inability to dance. Their illustrations guide our subsequent discussion of the anxieties that motivated this caricature, including sentiments of Francophobia that we encountered in other plays like *Marriage à la Mode* and Susanna Centlivre's *A Bold Stroke for a Wife*. I also challenge students to draw scenes that opened to a wider public. How, for instance, would Behn's *Rover* have captured the impression of Naples in carnival season, with its attendant masquers and illicit liaisons? Does her comedy cement the role of southern Europe in a cavalier imaginary or lampoon its masculine fantasy? Given Behn's minimal use of stage direction, students must reimagine this scene by inferring details from dialogue. Only by scrutinizing speech can they establish the features and purpose of its setting.

Near the end of the semester, the class reads a nondramatic work, Behn's novella *Oroonoko; or, The Royal Slave* (1688). Turning to a non-satirical fiction at this point in the course makes visible by absence those stage conventions and ironic overtones to which students have become accustomed. The sudden transition from dialogue and scene divisions to paragraphs and third-person narration simultaneously reveals the distinguishing characteristics of prose, particularly its capacity to describe the world it imagines. Fiction, students see, requires no performance. I drive home this point by dividing them into groups and having each one choose an incident from Behn's plot. Working together, they transpose this action into ten to twenty lines of drama, which must consist entirely of dialogue and contain no stage directions. The challenge of boiling down redolent prose into spoken lines foregrounds the labor of playwrights, who must imply almost everything about their setting through the speech of actors.

We then read Thomas Southerne's *Oroonoko, a Tragedy*, which was performed at the Theatre-Royal in 1695. This play transforms Behn's narrative into a satire of courtship, greed, and managerial incompetence. Knowing the basic plot enables students to see the effects of its dramatization. The content that Behn conveyed through prose is now borne by bodies onstage, which partly explains why Southerne's play is about five thousand words shorter than the novella it adapts. This reduction implies the wealth of information that a stage performance conveys. Students will recognize how Southerne's play ironizes its New World setting by making it the site of madcap amatory plots and how Southerne recasts Behn's stoic hero as faltering and afraid. The performance functions not merely as postscript to dramatic composition, but it makes human its central figures and, in so doing, advances the play's independent comedic aims. Reading *Oroonoko* alongside *Oroonoko* enables students to see how drama and satire can be made from a source text that is neither. Given our semester's focus on drama's conjuncture of writing and enactment, Southerne's Suriname is the perfect place to grasp how satirical drama plays out between words and motion and to appreciate how such refashioning can complicate and refine our interpretive process.

Works Cited

Canfield, J. Douglas, editor. *The Broadview Anthology of Restoration and Eighteenth-Century Comedy*. Broadview, 2001.

Diamond, Elin. "*Gestus* and Signature in Aphra Behn's *The Rover*." *ELH*, vol. 56, no. 3, Autumn 1989, pp. 519–41.

Gilbert, John Selwyn, director. *The Way of the World*. Films for the Humanities and Sciences, 2004.

Griffin, Dustin. *Satire: A Critical Reintroduction*. UP of Kentucky, 1994.

McCollum, John I., editor. *The Restoration Stage*. Houghton Mifflin, 1961.

Mirren, Helen, and Bernard Cribbens, performers. *The Country Wife*. BBC Video, 1977.

Riggio, Milla Cozart. *Teaching Shakespeare through Performance*. Modern Language Association, 1999.

Sauer, David Kennedy, and Evelyn Tribble. "Shakespeare in Performance: Theory in Practice and Practice in Theory." Riggio, pp. 33–48.

Taylor, Diana. *The Archive and the Repertoire: Performing Cultural Memory in the Americas*. Duke UP, 2003.

van Lennep, William, editor. *The London Stage, 1660–1800: A Calendar of Plays, Entertainments, and Afterpieces: Part 1, 1660–1700*. Southern Illinois UP, 1965.

James Horowitz

Libertine Satire on Stage, Page, and Screen

Each year, students in my courses on Restoration and eighteenth-century satire are treated with a trip to Beverly Hills. This refreshing respite from the gloom and grime of Augustan London comes courtesy of Hal Ashby's celebrated 1975 screen comedy *Shampoo*, in which Warren Beatty, cast squarely in type, plays a shaggy hairdresser whose amorous adventures with a host of neurotic Angeleno women collapse into a puddle of suds on Election Day 1968. Described by its director as "a satiric swipe at the Hollywood community in which everyone has too much money, too much time, too much everything" (qtd. in Biskind 181), the film could profitably be taught alongside other sun-dappled satires on California materialism and moral vacuity such as Nathanael West's *The Day of the Locust* and Evelyn Waugh's *The Loved One*. I have found, however, that Ashby's film also provides fruitful opportunities to instructors in satire of the long eighteenth century. This is partly because, in a surprisingly little-known piece of trivia, *Shampoo* has its origins in a landmark of Restoration comedy from exactly three centuries earlier, William Wycherley's *The Country Wife* (1675), which the film's screenwriters, Beatty and the industry legend Robert Towne, were inspired to adapt after seeing a 1969 production of the play in Chichester, England.

As Towne recounts, he and Beatty were immediately struck by the satirical potential of updating and relocating Wycherley's central conceit of affected emasculation:

> [*The Country Wife* is] a wonderful play about a man named Horner who lets it be known throughout all of social London that his doctor, Doctor Quack, has rendered him a eunuch. Consequently, all husbands trust Horner with their wives, a big mistake. He's in fine shape. We talked about it, and Warren said, "Well, what would be the contemporary equivalent? An actor?" I said, "No, it would be a hairdresser." And he said, "You're right." (qtd. in Biskind 83–84)

This reported banter, which I read aloud to students from Peter Biskind's anecdote-rich biography of Beatty, offers a road map of the masculine identities that Wycherley's comedy and Ashby's film together subject to satirical scrutiny—doctor, rake, actor, author, cuckold, hairdresser, eunuch, and, implicitly, homosexual—in addition to suggesting some of the complex personal investments that the filmmakers themselves, as celebrity participants in the homosocial contests of the 1970s studio system, might have had in interrogating those social roles. To teach *Shampoo* and *The Country Wife* jointly, especially alongside other Restoration-era libertine writing, is to invite conversations not only about the genre and legacy of Wycherley's perennially controversial play but also about the place of gender and sexuality in satirical practice from the 1670s to the 1970s and beyond. Topics for discussion might include the relationship between the satirical impulse and masculine sexual aggression or anxiety; the ambivalence with which satirists typically approach eroticism, especially in forms perceived as socially deviant; and the use of sexually frank narratives, which might strike modern students as merely farcical or pornographic, as vehicles for incendiary commentary on structures of power and privilege.

Both *The Country Wife* and *Shampoo* belong to a tradition of what I describe to students as "libertine satire," an umbrella term that encompasses satires *on* libertinism, satires *by* libertines or written in a propriety-defying libertine voice, and, more common than we might expect, satires that are both at once. As John O'Neill describes this paradox as it appears in Restoration verse, "most of the poems written by members of the court circle about the life of the rake satirize, rather than praise, that life" (201), often by comparing what their authors saw as their own harmless indiscretions with the more brazen and destructive excesses of the reigning monarch, Charles II, whose public love affairs with actresses, Catholics, and foreign nationals were sources of widespread concern.

These tensions are especially evident in the work of John Wilmot, the notorious second Earl of Rochester, who died of complications from venereal disease five years after the premiere of Wycherley's comedy. In his breathtakingly rude erotic poetry, which is studded with profanities that students are surprised to discover antedate the twentieth century, Rochester at once attacks and immortalizes a London beau monde that thrives on hedonism and lurid gossip ("grave discourse, / Of who Fucks who, and who does worse" ["Ramble," lines 1–2]), while also displaying his penchant for excoriating self-deprecation and even self-disgust (one lyric that tends to be a hit in the classroom, "The Imperfect Enjoyment," recounts a case of erectile dysfunction in painful detail). If my students have strong stomachs, I also distribute Rochester's "Satyr" on Charles II, which describes the monarch both as every inch a king and as a political victim of his own incontinent lust ("His Scepter and his Prick were of a length, / And she may sway the one who plays with t'other" [lines 11–12]), or else an excerpt from the infamous and unattributed closet drama *Sodom and Gomorah*, where Charles appears as the overreaching pansexual tyrant Bolliximian, who vows in a Rochesterian argot that "with my Prick I'lle gouerne all the land" (1.1.8).

This ambivalent treatment of sexual freedom by Rochester and his fellow libertine wits prepares students to appreciate the famously unstable tone and agenda of *The Country Wife*, which has, in the words of Peggy Knapp, proved "so pliant to interpretation over the years that the genre of the play has seemed to oscillate between satire and romantic comedy, and its central character, Mr. Horner, between brilliant spokesman for the satiric mode and sinister predator, himself the object of dismissive critique" (452). *Shampoo*, I have found, throws into relief for students just those elements of *The Country Wife* that have made it both so flexible in the hands of scholars and so provocative to audiences, not least its raw treatment of sexuality (both the play and the film were considered shocking in their own time, and the latter still requires trigger warnings) and its almost unseemly degree of self-reflexivity (Wycherley, like Beatty, had a highly publicized sex life, eventually earning the soubriquet "Manly Wycherley").

The highly fraught characterization of Beatty's George Roundy, the hairdresser whose assumed homosexuality veils his liaisons with female clients, allows instructors to pose questions that have long plagued scholars about the comic genus and psychological makeup of George's theatrical antecedent. As many studies of *The Country Wife* have described (see Owen for a helpful survey), Horner's name has at least four resonances, at once suggesting his vocation as a cuckold-maker, his goatish libido, his potential as a Satanic tempter and trickster, and his status as what a grateful Lady Fidget calls a "generous . . . man of honour," chivalrously willing to sacrifice his reputation in order to protect those of his female companions (2.1.503–04). Depending on which of these traits a scholar chooses to emphasize, Horner can be characterized as anything from a joyous personification of unbridled Eros to an avatar for Wycherley as unsparing satirist (thanks to a false etymology with a long history, satire was associated in this period with the uncouthness of the horned satyr) to an addict whose pursuit of sex is compulsive and denuded of pleasure, especially as compared to the companionate monogamy supposedly modeled by a subplot involving Horner's friend Harcourt. Whether it is a sign of the subtlety or of the cross purposes of *Shampoo*'s three auteurs, who famously warred on set, George becomes a one-man gallery of these varied methods for interpreting and embodying Wycherley's faux eunuch. George purports to be a principled hedonist of the Rochesterian school, insisting that unlike everyone else he knows, "I don't fuck anybody for money, I do it for fun," but students rightfully tend to be suspicious of this claim. George almost never seems to enjoy himself in his frantic attempts to cater to the needs of his clients and lovers, and his private encounters with women often appear no less mechanical than his businesslike handling of them at the salon; he has effectively become a gigolo without realizing it. The lack of self-awareness that students typically see as fatal to George's moral authority, however, is precisely what can make the film serve as a textbook example of satirical invective, which in its canonical forms, from Juvenal to Jonathan Swift to Martin Amis, rarely maintains a secure distinction between its targets and its spokesmen.

Yet George's status as a compromised satyr-ical truth-teller hardly exhausts the ways in which his creators adapted the model of the Restoration rake hero and the self-reproaching ethos of libertine satire. George, for instance, has shades of the endearingly self-denying "man of honour" that some commentators have seen in Horner. As Pauline Kael observes in her perceptive review of *Shampoo* for *The New Yorker*, George is oddly ascetic for a hedonist: "He doesn't smoke tobacco or dope; he doesn't pop pills; outside of soft drinks, the only beverage he takes in the whole film is a little white wine" (582). Kael goes on to call George a kind of "sexual saint" who absorbs the frustrations of unsatisfied women across the city (583), and she might have added that he also appears as a self-styled health care provider. In the film's opening scene, George disguises a planned assignation as a visit to a sick friend (something to do with her "pancre-*ass*"), prompting a testy reminder from the woman he's leaving that he's "not a doctor." Whether or not this is a ghostly reference to Horner's confidant Doctor Quack, the exchange suggests that, in George's eyes and perhaps those of the filmmakers, his house calls represent a form of genuine care in an uncaring world. Interestingly, though, upon arriving at his latest tryst, George jokingly assumes the role of a homicidal housebreaker, in an episode that would in 1975 have conjured up memories of Charles Manson: here, however briefly, is Horner in his incarnation as horned devil.

At times, however, George is more like Wycherley's putatively monogamous Harcourt than the indiscriminately randy Horner, several times claiming that he yearns for the security of a conventional marriage and even for fatherhood, although students naturally tend to doubt George's sincerity or at least his ability to act on these desires, given that he makes these declarations to two different women. In a study published a year after *Shampoo*, Robert Hume suggests that if Wycherley had wanted to punish Horner he would have rendered him poxed and truly impotent at the play's end (99). This may not quite happen to George, but his fate isn't much sunnier: gazing at a freeway from a smoggy Mount Pisgah, as his former lover Jackie Shawn (played by an old flame of Beatty's, Julie Christie), to whom he has just directed a last-ditch proposal ("I don't trust anybody but you"), rides off to a loveless elopement with a tiresome sugar daddy. An earlier hint that she and George will recommence their affair after she returns should not be seen as a consolation for this self-loathing Lothario.

Targeted questions about the film's presentation of George—is he a satirical mouthpiece or a satirical target? do the filmmakers endorse his libertinism or punish it?—can lead to broader discussions about the sexual morality of the satirical tradition in which Wycherley participates, as well as providing groundwork for a conversation about Horner, as the film has effectively dramatized the range of interpretive possibilities outlined by half a century of scholarship on the character. One piece of critical writing that students nonetheless find valuable, however, is Eve Sedgwick's concise chapter on Wycherley's "Anatomies of Male Homosocial Desire," which influentially describes cuckolding as "a sexual act, performed on a man, by another man," although I explain that her argument was anticipated by a number of studies from the 1960s and '70s of masculinity in Wycherley

(49). The central conceit of *Shampoo* can help to bring the undercurrents of homosocial rivalry, or even mediated homoerotic attraction, to the surface of Wycherley's text. A careful viewing of the film reveals that, unlike Horner's active promulgation of rumors about his impotence, George almost never consciously plays up the reputation that he knowingly exploits, instead simply dodging questions about his sexual preferences, and the film's portrayal of one of his fellow salon employees as a gross homosexual stereotype highlights George's more conventionally macho affect. Only very briefly, when he is nearly caught in flagrante delicto in a steam room with Jackie, does he appear conspicuously swishy, suggestively insisting that the intruding cuckold-in-the-making "either come in or stay out," and George's subsequent look of abashment indicates that this performance is not a habit for him. I am in sympathy with students who consider the film homophobic in its suggestion that George's adoption of an outwardly gay lifestyle represents rock bottom in his sex addiction, but *Shampoo* can also be seen as satirical commentary on the overdetermined perception of gay men as both emasculated and hyper-virile, not to mention as arbiters of style with special expertise about women. In any case, George's socially precarious status is driven home in an early scene in which he is denied a loan by a smug and uptight banker, whom George ends up calling, in what students have seen as a projection of his own feelings of vulnerability, an "asshole."

The film's surprisingly deft exposure of heterosexuality as a fragile and defensive construction can serve as a gateway to discussing an aspect of libertine satire that is easily overlooked. This is its treatment of high politics, often as a sublimated expression of a desire for sexual pleasure or domination. George has two unlikely doubles among his fellow male characters. The first is Lester Karpf (Jack Warden), a blusteringly oblivious magnate and backer of the Republican ticket whose wife, daughter, and mistress all go to bed with George over the course of Election Day. The second is the presidential candidate Lester is supporting, Richard Nixon, whose familiar face and voice recur with ominous regularity throughout the film and whose election had, by 1975, come to seem as much of a death knell for '60s idealism as the Manson murders. Despite all the apparent differences between the counterculture George, zooming across town on his Triumph motorcycle with a giant hair dryer stuffed in his jeans, and the establishment Lester, who rumbles around in a black Rolls-Royce that emits a chorus of stock quotes and who brings his lover a wrapped trinket he calls his "little something," the film slyly suggests that the rake and the man of business have more in common than meets the eye, not least the complacency with which they enjoy their different forms of male privilege. In the film's penultimate scene, the two men meet after a wakeful night, gazing bleary-eyed at Nixon's televised acceptance speech and briefly coming to recognize the emptiness of their respective belief systems (George insists that he's not antiestablishment, but it's not clear what he does believe in), although in a piece of heavy-handed historical irony, Lester expresses an idle hope that Nixon will be "different" from all the other Washington "jerks."

As several of my students have argued in class essays, the mendacious specter of Tricky Dick, whose address to America's silent majority is framed between these self-deluding doppelgängers, can be seen to haunt the entirety of *Shampoo*, tainting even the most seemingly sincere exchanges with shabby inauthenticity, much as the recklessly libidinous spirit of Charles II infuses the plot and ethos of *The Country Wife*. It may be the fools in Wycherley's comedy, Sparkish and Sir Jaspar Fidget, who curry favor with the king, but, according to a long-standing critical commonplace, it is Horner who sets up a mock court in which he ends up replicating both Charles's pleasures and their unintended consequences. As one scholar put it in 1972, "This possessor of a seraglio finds himself, like King Charles II, dominated by his wenches" (Rogers 73). I feel that I have done my job effectively if a student connects George's earlier confession to a betrayed lover—"Let's face it: I fucked them all"—not only to the future skulduggery of the Nixon administration but also to Charles II and his tyrannical double in *Sodom and Gomorah*, who boasts that he has "fuckt and buggered all ye land" (3.5.107). Although this echo of an anonymous manuscript lampoon is clearly not an intentional allusion, to note the resemblance is to spot vestiges of Charles's Whitehall in Nixon's White House and to hear the rugged music of a satyr song in a Beatles-era celluloid satire. It is also to recognize the continuing viability of libertine satire, an abrasive but relentlessly self-questioning mode now perhaps most familiar from activist hip-hop and politically inflected stand-up comedy, which dares to ask if every claim to innocent pleasure or moral high-mindedness might conceal the insidious potential for self-aggrandizement and exploitation.

Works Cited

Ashby, Hal, director. *Shampoo*. Columbia, 1975.

Biskind, Peter. *Star: How Warren Beatty Seduced America*. Simon and Schuster, 2010.

Hume, Robert D. *The Development of English Drama in the Late Seventeenth Century*. Clarendon Press, 1976.

Kael, Pauline. "Beverly Hills as a Big Bed." *Reeling*, Warner Books, 1976, pp. 577–86.

Knapp, Peggy A. "The 'Plyant' Discourse of Wycherley's *The Country Wife*." *Studies in English Literature, 1500–1900*, vol. 40, no. 3, Summer 2000, pp. 451–72.

O'Neill, John H. "Oldham's 'Sardanapalus': A Restoration Mock-Encomium and Its Topical Implications." *Clio*, vol. 5, no. 2, 1976, pp. 193–210.

Owen, Susan J. "Comedy I: William Wycherley's *The Country Wife*." *Perspectives on Restoration Drama*, by Owen, Manchester UP, 2002, pp. 42–64, 177–83.

Rogers, Katharine M. *William Wycherley*. Twayne, 1972.

Sedgwick, Eve Kosofsky. "*The Country Wife*: Anatomies of Male Homosocial Desire." *Between Men: English Literature and Male Homosocial Desire*, by Sedgwick, Columbia UP, 1985, pp. 49–66.

Wilmot, John (Earl of Rochester). "A Ramble in St. James's Park." Wilmot, *Works*, pp. 76–80.

———. "Satyr." Wilmot, *Works*, pp. 85–86.

———. *Sodom and Gomorah*. Wilmot, *Works*, pp. 302–36.

———. *The Works of John Wilmot, Earl of Rochester*. Edited by Harold Love, Oxford UP, 1999.

Wycherley, William. *The Country Wife*. Edited by James Ogden, 2nd ed., Bloomsbury, 2014.

Part III

Historical, Political, and Cultural Contexts

Fredric V. Bogel

Satire and Materialism in the Long Eighteenth Century

There is a significant relationship between the materialist tropes central to the satire of the eighteenth century and the philosophical materialism of the latter part of that century. It appears overtly in works by philosophical writers like Julien Offray de La Mettrie but also, more obliquely, in largely non-satiric works like Henry Mackenzie's *The Man of Feeling*, Laurence Sterne's *A Sentimental Journey*, and Denis Diderot's *Paradoxe sur le Comédien* (*The Paradox of Acting*) and those by writers as varied as Samuel Johnson, Edmund Burke, and John Cleland. To explore this relationship in the classroom is to uncover a significant connection between two phenomena often assumed to be unrelated except by contrast, since the materialist figures in Augustan satire are routinely construed as affirming an antimaterialist position. It is also to demonstrate a link between formal analysis and the historicizing perspective that has only recently begun to be seen as anything other than formalism's mortal enemy. An undergraduate course on satire or eighteenth-century literature, or a unit of such a course, can thus serve as an occasion to analyze the formal and thematic procedures of early eighteenth-century satire, to discover connections between satire and both philosophical and literary texts from the later eighteenth century, and to study the features and "moves" of two different interpretive methods—formalism and historicism—as well as the potentially fruitful links between them.

It has long been recognized that a metaphorics of the mechanical and the material plays a large role in the mocking rhetoric of Restoration and eighteenth-century satire. Matthew Prior's "A Simile" and "An Epitaph," John Dryden's *Mac Flecknoe*, Jonathan Swift's satiric poems and prose ("Phyllis; or, The Progress of Love," "The Mechanical Operation of the Spirit," *A Tale of a Tub*), Alexander Pope's *The Dunciad* and the Scriblerian *Peri Bathous*—these are just a few of the numerous texts that enlist a satiric rhetoric of materialism, mechanism, insensibility, formulaic inanity, and deathly repetition. Here, for example, is the pedantic scholiast Aristarchus, in *The Dunciad*, describing the labor of his fellow pedants and himself to the goddess Dulness:

> For thee we dim the eyes, and stuff the head
> With all such reading as was never read:
> For thee explain a thing till all men doubt it,
> And write about it, Goddess, and about it. (4.250–53)

The "material" these scholars teach their students—former persons now reduced to eyes and a single, generic "head"—is treated as mere matter ("stuff the head"); the texts studied are collections of letters and words, not meanings; the method of instruction is unvaried and ineffective (the passage is written in the "perpetual present tense" or "present tense habitual"); and the commentary these pedants produce circles its object ("about") without ever reaching it. The pedagogic goal? "With the same Cement, ever sure to bind, / We bring to one dead level ev'ry mind" (4.265–66).

For such writers, bad poets and other satiric objects are not just dim, talentless, or un-self-aware. They are like nonhuman creatures or material things. In "A Simile," although Prior's squirrel is confined in its wheel, "The foolish creature thinks he climbs" (line 10). The inane poets whom Prior demeaningly compares to the squirrel are

> Still dancing in an airy round,
> Still pleas'd with their own verses' sound;
> Brought back, how fast soe'er they go,
> Always aspiring, always low. (lines 17–20)

Mechanical, unchanging ("still"), vacant ("airy"), indistinguishable from one another, narcissistically self-absorbed but un-self-knowing, and attentive to sound rather than sense, they sharply contrast with the satiric speaker who condemns them to mechanicity and to the perpetual reenactment of failure.

Here is Flecknoe, from Dryden's great satire, praising his only proper successor:

> But Shadwell's genuine night admits no ray,
> His rising fogs prevail upon the day:
> Besides his goodly fabric fills the eye,
> And seems design'd for thoughtless majesty:
> Thoughtless as monarch oaks, that shade the plain,
> And, spread in solemn state, supinely reign. (lines 23–28)

Shadwell is a figure of utter darkness, of foggy obscurity, visually compelling only as a material building or edifice ("fabric"), without thought, treelike, and reigning "supinely"—physically inert but also passively indifferent in attitude. Since Flecknoe views Shadwell as virtually indistinguishable from himself, moreover, both are also interchangeable, nonindividual things—like those generic "monarch oaks."

Such poets and their poems are not articulators of beauty, sublimity, or meaningfulness but spiders spinning webs, empty barrels, streams of running lead, collections of mere paper, bodily glands and their secretions—or worse: a certain unproductive hack, in Pope's *Epistle to Dr. Arbuthnot* "strains, from hard-bound brains, eight lines a year" (line 182). Similarly, the religiously wayward are not just unorthodox or outright unbelievers but crackpots for whom religious inspiration is displaced by mere air or wind (Swift's Aeolists) and who therefore "affirm the gift of belching to be the noblest act of a rational creature" (Swift 153). In the realm of human character, there is the seemingly irresistible rigidity and invariability of behavior produced by what Pope, in *Essay on Man II*, "To Cobham," and "To a Lady," terms "The Ruling Passion." The reduction to materiality and mechanicity may be the master trope of Restoration and Augustan satire.

That satiric rhetoric is commonly understood to exist in secure and unproblematic opposition to such writers' characteristic language of approval: a discourse registering originality, spontaneity, intellectual penetration, volition, fecundity, even the "amazing invention" and "unequal'd Fire and Rapture" that Pope attributes to Homer (440). In short, and in several senses of the word, the writers and writings whom these satirists approve display "spirit." It is a contest of spirit and intellect versus matter, original invention versus deathly conventionality, etc. Yet this opposition holds within itself a complicated and problematic linkage between volitional authenticity and mechanistic performance—a linkage that comes into focus later in the century and, perhaps surprisingly, in some non-satiric texts that have been understood as unproblematic celebrations of affective spontaneity and exquisite sensibility, of moments "[w]hen the heart flies out before the understanding" (Sterne 28).

In these later texts, the discourse of earlier eighteenth-century satire (convention, materialism, mechanicity, artifice, performativity) pervades non-satiric representations of human agency, the affective life, volition, aesthetic experience, bodily sensation, and more. Persons of "spirit" seem surprisingly to be persons of mechanism and materiality as well. This discursive contamination fundamentally complicates Enlightenment notions of innovation, improvisation, immediacy of emotion, and freedom of volition. Some later eighteenth-century texts seem indeed to rely upon a sharp—a quasi-Augustan—opposition between terms like *sensibility* and *insensibility*, *matter* and *spirit*, and so on. Nonetheless, in other writings of this period, such simple oppositions are troubled or put in question, for an apparently simple celebration of spontaneity, spirit, and affective energy is overlaid by a materialist vocabulary suggesting the mechanicity of that which we most value as nonmechanistic: sympathy, impulse, tenderness, susceptibility—indeed, sensation and emotion.

Take the moment in Mackenzie's *Man of Feeling* when the title character, Harley, wonders whether he should offer money to a fortune-telling beggar who makes his living by inventing flattering fortunes for those he encounters:

> Harley had drawn a shilling from his pocket; but virtue bade him consider on whom he was going to bestow it.—Virtue held back his arm:—but a milder form, a younger sister of virtue's, not so severe as virtue, nor so serious as pity, smiled upon him: His fingers lost their compression;—nor did virtue offer to catch the money as it fell. It had no sooner reached the ground than the watchful cur (a trick he had been taught) snapped it up; and . . . delivered it immediately into the hands of his master. (18)

The scene is a perfect example of the mystifications of agency this text so often presents, not least because its central action is determined by the smile of a figure who is defined only negatively ("not so severe as virtue, nor so serious as pity") and who remains mysterious and unnamed. Indeed, the fact that virtue and her sister are personified, and thus individuals distinct from Harley, already moves the locus of decision making from his person to an external duo of agents both physically and emotionally effectual. The characteristic physicalizing of moral and affective agency appears not just in Harley's arm being "held back" but also in the oddly mechanical phrase "His fingers lost their compression." Does that phrase denote a decision, an instance of charitable giving, an act produced by a moral agent? Or does it name a physical and mechanical movement originating solely in the fingers and their "compression"? It hardly seems an accident that the scene closes with another quasi-mechanical performance when the dog performs "a trick he had been taught." Indeed, Mackenzie's novel offers numerous examples of compromised agency and mechanized sentiment that create an uncertainty about the spontaneous and the performative, the volitional and the mechanized—an uncertainty central to the novel's curiously problematic depiction and redefinition of sensibility (Bogel, "Personated Passion" 172).

Similarly, when Yorick, the narrator-protagonist of Sterne's *A Sentimental Journey*, suddenly becomes indisputably aware of the operations of his own soul, the experience of his immaterial being is so overwhelming, he says, that it "would have confounded the most *physical précieuse* in France: with all her materialism, she could scarce have called me a machine." Yet, startlingly, the evidence he offers is patently physicalist. "I felt every vessel in my frame dilate,—the arteries beat all cheerily together, and every power which sustained life, performed it with . . . little friction" (12). If his very being would at that moment confute Continental materialism, why depict that being as a matter—pun intended—of vessels in his "frame" dilating, of arteries at once material ("beat") and personified ("cheerily"), and of a relative absence of "friction"?

These are not singular instances. Think of the predictable, typical, and mechanized life narratives in Johnson's "The Vanity of Human Wishes." Supplicants for preferment, wealth, or fame—secular and religious figures of towering ambition—fatally enact the rise and fall of Fortune's wheel that the poem's narrator catches in a seemingly deterministic quartet of verbs: "They mount, they shine, evaporate, and fall" (line 76). Not to mention the same author's "The Vision of Theodore," in which human lives are powerfully directed by creatures called "habits" whose mechanical and mechanizing force threatens individual volition at nearly every point. Such ambiguity of identity reaches one limit in the fascinating it-narratives that Mark Blackwell has explored: narratives whose protagonists (and sometimes narrators) are at once instances of seemingly human sensibility and also, undeniably, animals or even inert things—physical objects. For example, *The History of a Pin, as Related by Itself* is an autobiographical narrative told by a pin that seems at once person and object. But a number of this narrator's claims seem to illuminate not just its problematic status but also the tendency of human beings to display a comparably divided nature in their own lives. One character is described as possessing only "that sort of artificial good breeding that is put on like a best cap or gown, only upon particular occasions," in contrast to "that fascinating civility which arises spontaneously from the heart, and which no external circumstance can alter" (Andrews 41). Shortly after, the same character is said to be "as destitute of mind as a painted doll in a toy-shop window" (42–43). At moments like these, the ontological straddling enacted by a fancifully personified object is also an emblem of the real human oscillation between artifice and spontaneity, behavior as mere habiliment or habit and behavior as expression of the "heart."

We can turn from British novels and other narratives to France and to a different discursive mode altogether, a theory of acting, in dialogue form: Diderot's *Paradoxe sur le Comédien*. Diderot's text focuses the doubleness we have been exploring on questions of the stage and on the power of stage acting to move an audience emotionally—a situation already essentially problematized by the inescapable fact that the character portrayed is never identical with the actor. More startling than this ontological fact about stage drama is Diderot's advice about how an actor should convey emotion on the stage. The player is, ideally, to feel *no* emotion and instead to repeat coolly, at each performance, gestures and tones that are "planned," and thus repeatable, night after night—gestures, tones, paces, and rhythms that are part of a fixed "*system* of declamation" (15). Indeed, "He who comes out from the wing without having his whole scheme of acting in his head, his whole part marked out, will all his life play the part of a beginner" (64). The actor must have "judgment" but also "no sensibility," for "his talent depends not, as you think, upon feeling, but upon rendering so exactly the *outward signs* of feeling" that the spectator will "fall into the trap" (7). Within the actor there must be "an unmoved and disinterested onlooker"—or, as James Boswell differently inflects this idea in his three-part essay "On the Profession of a Player," "The feelings and passions of the character which he represents must take full possession as it were of the *antechamber* of his mind, while his own character remains in the *innermost recess*" (18). This detachment will allow the actor to discover the most effective tones, gestures, pace, and more for each role and to be "one and the same at all performances" (9).

The bizarre performativity, even mechanicity, of this notion bears even more directly on the status of human emotion and expression when Boswell extends the theory from the stage to social theater, the performing of everyday life. He first instances "the barrister," who is obliged to "enter warmly into the cause of his client" even though he may not believe what he is saying and may not even "wish to prevail" (18). But Boswell goes beyond this example, which is both an instance from real life and yet a kind of legally and socially sanctioned performance (compare the conscious and conventionally accepted artifice of the "adversary system"). "In the intercourse of life," says Boswell, situations require certain "appearances," and we "insensibly" allow ourselves to "adopt feelings suitable to every occasion" (19). Diderot too at times moves from the theater to "the great play, the play of the world" (14). These theories of acting then are also images of a human nature irreducibly split between the authentic and the performative, sensibility and physicality, feeling and gesture. One thinks of the British comedy duo Flanders and Swann's witty yet rhetorically profound line: "Always be sincere, whether you mean it or not."

These two phenomena, the materialist tropes of Augustan satire and the ambiguously volitional/mechanical discourses of the later period, are rarely linked—historically, thematically, or formally. But I think they are intimately, if somewhat obscurely, connected. Seen retrospectively, as part of the literary-historical narrative of the long eighteenth century, those early satiric tropes acquire an additional meaning and valence: much as in the structure of zeugma, a single and seemingly univocal verb—here, *stain*—acquires an additional sense from the words that follow it: "Or stain her honor, or her new brocade" (Pope, *The Rape of the Lock* 2.107). In light of the contesting discourses we have been exploring in Mackenzie, Sterne, Diderot, and others, the materialist metaphorics that pervade the earlier period's satire—in addition to being the satiric weapons they have rightly been taken to be—are part of a larger questioning of, even fascination with, a newly sensed uncertainty about the boundary between the spiritual and the material, thought and thing.

Here is where a revisionist reading of satire connects with the present argument. In this reading, the satirist–satiric object relation involves not difference *tout court* but a complex play of similarity and difference, identification and repudiation, so that satirists and readers are both connected to and distanced from the objects of satire. Similarly, the Augustans' use of materialist tropes may function symbolically as an instance of pure otherness—a trait of only the satirized deviants—but also represent a threat potentially continuous with the satirists' allegedly nonmechanistic values and selves. Indeed, those tropes may represent an expulsion to the realm of otherness of traits and views and practices that the satirists both entertain and prophylactically exile. Nor is this a terribly counterintuitive notion. Is it possible to write 1,754 lines of largely closed, balanced, and nonhypermetric heroic couplets attacking mindlessness and mechanicity (the 1743 *Dunciad*) without worrying about whether one may be reenacting exactly what one is satirizing? Consequently, we can recontextualize those satiric techniques and tropes, seeing them not just as witty investments in a traditional opposition between the spiritual and the physical but simultaneously as a tacit, even partly unconscious, broaching of larger questions about human behavior that do not make an overt appearance until the later eighteenth century. The energetic deployment of materialist tropes in satire, while partly relying on and reinforcing the cultural and symbolic oppositions already referred to, simultaneously expresses an anxiety about the threat of actual materialist thought—perhaps even an apotropaic resistance to that threat, at once invoking it and warding it off.

This attempt at literary-historical revisionism has been influenced by ideas of historical change articulated by Michael McKeon in his splendid essay "Cultural Crisis and Dialectical Method: Destabilizing Augustan Literature." One quotation from that essay indicates the process by which the materialist tropes of the early satires, and their confident and insistent reinforcement of the spiritual/material opposition, hold within themselves a counter-spirit that is both threatened and fascinated by the overt materialist thought of the later period: "What looks superficially like a revival of traditional forms, categories, or activities," says McKeon, "may better be understood as an unstable compound whose residual ties to past practices cannot conceal its distinctly innovative character." Such an "affirmation of tradition and stability is likely to be most insistent precisely at those moments when tradition and stability are most thought to be endangered." At such moments, he contends, "the symbolic enactment—through language and behavior—of a system of order signifies not order but crisis, implying through the very invocation of stability an effort to rectify a felt condition of instability" (46).

We could say then that the symbolic enactment of the volitional/mechanistic distinction in Augustan satire is a wishful, even a "magical," effort to resist and deny the looming specter of the mechanistic understanding of human thought, feeling, and behavior. Part of that specter materializes (forgive the pun) at mid-century in La Mettrie's rejection/revision of Cartesian dualism, a revision in which the entirety of a human being is understood to be material and mechanistic, and in which Descartes' "soul" is replaced—entirely adequately, in the author's view—by what La Mettrie terms the *organization* (somewhat confusingly translated as "organism") of the body's parts. This organization is internal and integral to the physical body and entirely nonspiritual—though the abstractness and immateriality of *organization*, in contrast to the corporeal-material entities being organized, does allow La Mettrie to mime the soul/body dualism in another, nonspiritual key.

Two quotations show the radical rejection of Descartes's dualism that La Mettrie performs and the scope of the threat that *L'Homme Machine* and similar materialist texts posed to traditional oppositions between soul and body, mind and matter. The first affirms the adequacy of the principle of organization to account for human behavior and being: "But since all the faculties of the soul depend to such a degree on the proper organization of the brain and of the whole body, that apparently they *are* but this organization itself, the soul is clearly an enlightened machine" (128, emphasis added). The second poses the challenge in its most direct form: "The soul is therefore but an empty word, of which no one has any idea, and which an enlightened man should use only to signify the part in us that thinks" (128).

A philosophic discourse like this completes the arc from materialist tropes in Augustan satire, through ambiguous representations of human being and activity in mid- and later eighteenth-century non-satiric texts, to the full-blown materialist thought of La Mettrie, d'Holbach, and others.

Such explorations might form part of a classroom survey of eighteenth-century literature, a course on literature and philosophy in the period, or a more highly focused investigation of materialism in eighteenth-century literature and philosophy. These courses could encourage familiarity with a range of eighteenth-century texts and concepts and help students confront several problems that the teaching of eighteenth-century literature frequently underplays.

First, the distinction between the early and later eighteenth century is often presented as overly sharp. Northrop Frye's "Towards Defining an Age of Sensibility" helpfully discouraged the view that the latter part of the eighteenth century was a "pre-Romantic" era waiting to be fulfilled by the later arrival of full-blown Romanticism. Instead, Frye laid out a variety of contrasts differentiating early and later eighteenth-century writing, such as literature of product versus literature of process and metaphor as "condensed simile" versus metaphor as ideal assertion of identity: "two images . . . identified within the mind of the creating poet" (151). Frye's subtle distinction between two literary modes rather than between rules and freedom or repression and emotionality nonetheless works to strengthen the idea of a sharp divide between the two halves of the century.

Second, a similar exaggeration of difference informs traditional understandings of the relationship between satirist and satiric object in the Augustan period and elsewhere. In the standard view, satirist and object are entirely distinct, and readers are expected to identify themselves with the satirist and repudiate the satiric object with a clarity resembling the satirist's own. I have argued, however, that

> [s]atire does not simply register a prior difference between satirist and satiric object . . . ; instead, satire works to produce a difference between two figures whom the satirist—who is usually one of these figures—perceives to be insufficiently differentiated. Satire, then, is a rhetorical means to the production of difference in the face of a potentially compromising similarity, not the articulation of differences already in place. (Bogel, *Difference* 42)

In this view, the satirist's relation to the satiric object is a play of similarity and difference, identification and repudiation, that complicates and deepens our understanding of the dynamic of satire. Such a revisionist notion has consequences for our understanding of the materialist tropes Augustan satirists deploy as part of their satiric rhetoric and for our understanding of satiric texts in periods other than the eighteenth century and national literatures other than English.

Two further curricular benefits to a focus on satire and materialism are the opportunity to heal the breach between the teaching of literature and the teaching of philosophy, and thereby (in this case) enrich students' understanding of the complex cultural and historical moment called the Enlightenment, and the opportunity to explore in classroom discussion and essay writing the methodological differences between—and the intellectual benefits of combining—the rhetorical/textual focus of formalist analysis and the historical, political, and cultural concerns of historicist investigation. Instructors who model and encourage such methodological awareness and critical practice can strengthen their students' competence and sophistication in a variety of courses and disciplines.

Works Cited

Andrews, Eliza (Miss Smythies of Colchester). *The History of a Pin, as Related by Itself.* Dublin, 1799. *Google Play*, play.google.com/books/reader?id=Fj1WAAAAcAAJ&printsec=frontcover&output=reader&hl=en&pg=GBS.PP2.

Blackwell, Mark, editor. *The Secret Life of Things: Animals, Objects, and It-Narratives in Eighteenth-Century England.* Bucknell UP, 2007.

Bogel, Fredric V. *The Difference Satire Makes: Rhetoric and Reading from Jonson to Byron.* Cornell UP, 2012.

———. "'A Personated Passion': Sentiment, Performance and Mechanism in Mackenzie's *The Man of Feeling.*" *The Languages of Performance in British Romanticism*, edited by Lilla Maria Crisafulli and Cecilia Pietropoli, Peter Lang, 2008, pp. 161–83.

Boswell, James. *On the Profession of a Player.* Mathews and Marrot, 1929.

Diderot, Denis. *The Paradox of Acting.* The Paradox of Acting *and* Masks or Faces, translated by Walter Herries Pollock, Hill and Wang, 1957.

Dryden, John. *Mac Flecknoe. The Norton Anthology of Poetry*, edited by Margaret Ferguson et al., shorter 4th ed., Norton, 1997, pp. 280–86.

Flanders, Michael, and Donald Swann. "*The Reluctant Cannibal* Lyrics." *Flash Lyrics*, www.flashlyrics.com/lyrics/flanders-and-swann/the-reluctant-cannibal-32. Accessed 15 May 2018.

Frye, Northrop. "Towards Defining an Age of Sensibility." *ELH*, vol. 23, no. 2, June 1956, pp. 144–52.

Johnson, Samuel. "The Vanity of Human Wishes." *The Complete English Poems*, edited by J. D. Fleeman, Penguin, 1971, pp. 83–92.

———. "The Vision of Theodore, the Hermit of Teneriffe, Found in His Cell." *Rasselas and Other Tales*, edited by Gwin J. Kolb, Yale UP, 1990, pp. 195–212.

La Mettrie, Julien Offray de. *Man a Machine.* Translated by Mary Whiton Calkins, edited by Gertrude Carman Bussey, Open Court, 1912.

Mackenzie, Henry. *The Man of Feeling.* Edited by Brian Vickers, Oxford UP, 1967.

McKeon, Michael. "Cultural Crisis and Dialectical Method: Destabilizing Augustan Literature." *The Profession of Eighteenth-Century Literature: Reflections on an Institution*, edited by Leo Damrosch, U of Wisconsin P, 1992, pp. 42–61.

Pope, Alexander. *Poetry and Prose of Alexander Pope.* Edited by Aubrey Williams, Houghton Mifflin, 1969.

Prior, Matthew. "A Simile." 1707. *Representative Poetry Online*, tspace.library.utoronto.ca/html/1807/4350/poem1667.html.

Sterne, Laurence. *A Sentimental Journey through France and Italy by Mr. Yorick.* Edited by Paul Goring, Penguin, 2005.

Swift, Jonathan. *A Tale of a Tub: To Which Is Added "The Battle of the Books" and "The Mechanical Operation of the Spirit."* Edited by A. C. Guthkelch and D. Nichol Smith, 2nd ed., Clarendon Press, 1958.

Kirk Combe

Satire and Modern Power

I regularly teach an upper-level undergraduate seminar titled Satire in Theory and Practice. The generic course title in our English major is Studies in Late Seventeenth- and Eighteenth-Century British Literature. The enrollment limit is eighteen. My school, Denison University in Ohio, is not a university at all but rather a small liberal arts college that draws its two thousand students from the United States and abroad. Our students are well prepared, but they are certainly not well versed in literary history or cultural theory. Normally they come to my course either out of a vague interest in "satire" or through force vis-à-vis major requirements combined with scheduling constraints. No matter how they arrive in my class, invariably students know next to nothing about the history or the intricacy of the genre, let alone the early modern historical period. My broad pedagogical approach to teaching these students is twofold: 1) I involve them in the close study of satiric theory as a way to understand satiric practice; and 2) I do not restrict the satire we study to works from seventeenth- and eighteenth-century British literature. In order to make satire relevant to student experiences, we examine a good deal of twentieth- and twenty-first-century satire, particularly in film, cable television, and new media. I also take them backward in time, considering a bit of the anthropological origins of satire and the all-important Roman developments in the genre, as well as having them read some works by Horace and Juvenal. In a way, my course spans satiric theory and practice from Archilochus to Stephen Colbert.

Even more significant to my teaching of satire, however, is that I teach satiric theory not merely as a matter of comprehending features of a literary genre, but how that literary genre functions in the larger culture. Specifically, my class explores how, during the seventeenth century in England, satiric works based on the Roman model of formal verse satire came to operate as instruments of political discourse within the emerging modern state; moreover, since the seventeenth century, one of the primary uses of British and American satire has been for modern political commentary. By the modern state, I mean how Michel Foucault has theorized that political entity to be a system of differentiations wherein a powerful minority, through various instrumental modes, forms of institutions, and degrees of rationalization, is able to act upon the actions of the majority of the population. Such disciplinary power creates a regime of "truth"—a dominant and sanctioned worldview—that is a condition for the formation and development of capitalism. In the modern era, much satire has come to serve as an instrument to challenge the subject formation of what Foucault perceives as carceral discipline. Some of the most compelling modern satires display the capacity to separate "truth" from the power creating it.

What is more, I combine this cultural emphasis with the pedagogical approach of problem-posing teaching in the mode of Paulo Freire. That is, I present students with a range of materials—satiric theories, cultural theories, historical contextualization, scholarly examinations of satire, a variety of satiric texts—and ask them to formulate, express, and defend their own informed critical opinions about satire. Students should be empowered by being taught critical theory, and the study of satire in particular demands having nothing to do with the vestiges of New Criticism or the outdated pursuit of area coverage by English departments (see Graff). Equally, the effective instruction of cultural studies can have no truck with the oppressive tactics of what Freire terms *banking-style teaching*. That's why my approach to satire, both as a teacher and as a scholar, is as a cultural materialist wherein the theories of Foucault on modern power figure prominently.

The first part of this essay describes how students go about theorizing satire by their formulating a set of guidelines for recognizing and analyzing satiric works. Next, I explain my strategies for bringing the complex cultural theories of Foucault to life for students. Finally, I offer brief examples of early modern and contemporary satires read in class through the combined lenses of genre and modern power. I've found that this pedagogical approach to satire not only elucidates effectively the form, but it fulfills well many of my most important goals as a teacher: demonstrating to students how a literary genre can shift and adapt to its larger cultural context; showing students how imaginative works—not just satire—are never timeless, frozen bits of "universal" beauty but instead participate in subject formation within a power discourse; making a case to students that the early modern world continues to shape our own and thus deserves study. Investigating satire in this way also helps students develop into critically astute, politically aware, culturally literate citizens—an aim that should be primary in college education but, in this age of the neoliberal arts (see Deresiewicz), all too often takes a decided backseat.

Guidelines for Satiric Analysis

We begin the semester with a unit on satiric history and theory. Historical readings include the early pages of Robert C. Elliott's *The Power of Satire*, Kirk Freudenburg's excellent introduction to Roman satire, and segments from John Dryden's *A Discourse Concerning the Original and Progress of Satire* (1693). These works set the stage nicely for the study of early modern satire. With regard to satiric theory, there are of course a great number of readings from which to choose. I try not to overload students with satiric theory at the outset of the course. In their research later in the semester, I can recommend additional theorists for them to read. To start, I supply them with something of a post–New Criticism chronicle of theoretical takes on the genre. These are Leonard Feinberg's essay from the 1960s, Don Nilsen's essay from the 1980s, Brian Connery and my retrospective on satire from the 1990s, and portions of Ashley Marshall's recent study of early modern English satire.

From this overview, we construct as a class a handout titled "Guidelines for Satiric Analysis." This handout will aid students of satiric works during the rest of the semester, and it gets augmented as we go. From specific satiric theorists, students from my class in the fall of 2015 assembled some characteristics of satire. From Feinberg, they learned that satire always criticizes, always distorts, and always entertains. From Nilsen, they learned the four necessary conditions for satire (grounding in reality, distortion, negative tone, a posture of attack) and three strongly correlative conditions (irony, social bonding, and humor). They also noted Rosenheim's oft-quoted statement that satire is an "attack by means of a manifest fiction upon discernible historical particulars" (31). Appropriate questions, therefore, to ask of a satire include the following: Who or what, exactly, is being attacked? What kind of obvious fabrication—often meaning the manipulation of an established genre or cultural practice—is being used in the attack? Which historical particulars, precisely, are being brought into play, and exactly how visible are those local concerns?

From all of our background readings, students drew ideas to formulate three general features of satire. First, satire is a polemic: a passionate argument against something and, thus, in favor of something else; a combination of *laus et vituperatio* (praise and blame). Negative behaviors being condemned are highlighted and predominant, and positive behaviors being recommended are sometimes clear, implied, or even indistinct. It is an exploration of important cultural issues of the day, be it social (e.g., religion, class, gender, race, literary matters, tastes and fashions, etc.), philosophical (e.g., ethical conduct, nature of the "good," human perception, etc.), or political (e.g., the best form of government, factional wrangling, truth and power, etc.), though often these types of issues are in combination.

Second, satiric persona is a key element: What kind of narrator is the satirist presenting to us and why? That is, what rhetorical and polemical functions does that narrator serve? For example, the Horatian *vir bonus* (the good, honest man), the Juvenalian *vir iratus* (the irate, indignant man), the parodic narrator (pretending to be someone or something else), the self-damning narrator (a trap for the reader), the unreliable narrator (sometimes reasonable, sometimes ludicrous), or any combination of these and other types.

Third, satiric form needs to be evaluated: what structure or manner of communicating does the satirist construct and why? For example, the thesis-exempla satire is fundamentally an essay with a main point followed by supporting argumentation and a loose series of examples. The situational satire is a semidramatic story line presented through various scenes, characters, and voices (such as an adversarius). Some satire is a mixture of both thesis-exempla and situational elements. Menippean satire, a longer prose work usually condemning the dominant orthodoxy of the day, often involves fantastical settings and situations—utopias, dystopias, incredible journeys, etc. Satire can also invade another genre or form—personal letter, philosophical dialogue, newspaper editorial, scientific article, film documentary, musical, television news program, etc.

Along with investigating polemic, persona, and form, I stress to students how the reader of satire must be a crucial consideration. Satire generates a particularly concerted transactive reader-response dynamic. That is, if text + reader = meaning, then satirists are especially attuned to precipitating an exact kind of partnership with their contemporary readership. As much critical attention needs to be paid to the satiric narratee as to the satiric narrator. Questions to be deliberated include the following: Precisely who is the contemporary audience for a given satire? Exactly how is that current-day reader being manipulated into becoming the ideal reader of a piece—that is, to fall into complete agreement with the satirist? Is the reader being bullied or cajoled, having heartstrings tugged on, collective fears tapped into, empathy created, outrage fomented, shame provoked, or pride stimulated? Is the satirist preaching to a choir or making a broader appeal to the society? Has the satirist ventured into the lion's den of the oppositional camp? Who is listening has everything to do with how a satirist embeds a text with things for that reader to do. Obviously, with these readerly issues comes the all-important historical contextualization of each piece of satire we consider in the course.

Another vital component to consider when recognizing and analyzing satiric works is that satire is a genre of power. In the Western tradition, satire very much tends to be works created by educated urban men of means—that is, the dominant social group. Thus satire can be seen as a patriarchal genre, one produced by those participating in the hegemonic masculinity of the day. Is satire then merely infighting among the elite? Satire also tends to be located in the major city of its day: Athens, Rome, Paris, London, New York. While such major urban centers obviously blend together a diverse population, they are nonetheless the focal points of political, economic, and cultural power. Given this privileged backdrop for satire, some interesting questions emerge regarding the form. Where do women fit in the satiric game—aside from being its constant targets? Where do nonwhite, non-European peoples fit in? What about lower-class voices? Can satire be an instrument of social justice? Or is satire an instrument of social disciplining and control? As you can see, when raising these issues and asking these questions, my students enter the ambit of cultural power and the theories of Foucault.

Foucault's Greatest Hits

Reading Foucault can be confusing and intimidating at first for undergraduates. With some untangling of his ideas, though, students soon acquire a number of useful theories for textual and cultural analysis. They readily see panoptic discipline at work in their own lives. (They've all been subjected in modern schooling.) The study of satire also presents them with vivid exposés of power discourse as well as striking examples of genealogy at work. (They've all seen Colbert, Jon Stewart, and John Oliver at work.) While there is much to choose from in the writings of Foucault, I've found that three works particularly suit my purposes. These are *Discipline and Punish*, "Truth and Power," and "The Subject and Power." From these works I highlight certain ideas that pertain well to the analysis of early modern and modern satire. For example, from *Discipline and Punish*: how the main effect of the panopticon on the prisoner is a permanent visibility that assures the automatic functioning of power (201–02); how the early modern transition from feudal monarchal spectacle to modern panoptic surveillance featured a new conception of power as a set of actions upon other actions (208–09); and how feudal power sought to form a single great cultural body, but modern power seeks to fabricate particular kinds of individuals that contribute to the productivity of the regulated state (216–17). All of these phenomena become distinct when students compare the feudal and monarchal intimidation taking place in Dryden's *Absalom and Achitophel* (1681) to the carceral control enacted by the modern state in, say, Terry Gilliam's film *Brazil* (1985). Similarly, from "Truth and Power," I draw the following key points: that whereas feudal power was a repressive power that said no, modern power is a productive power that produces goods, induces pleasure, forms knowledge, and constructs discourse (307, 311); that modern power is a form of warlike domination by the hegemonic group in a society and thus "[p]eace would then be a form of war, and the State a means of waging it" (310); and, quite importantly, that resisting modern power requires working to detach the hegemonic power from the "truth" it creates (317–18). Read as anti-Whig satire and a reaction against the emerging modern state, Jonathan Swift's *Gulliver's Travels* (1726) demonstrates vigorously all of these cultural occurrences.

Although an especially dense and daunting piece, "The Subject and Power" repays study because of its focus on the relationship between the individual and the modern state. Students glean a number of instrumental concepts to bring to their investigations of satire. For example, Foucault discusses the ways people resist being made subject to the modern state. These struggles generally are of three kinds: 1) against forms of domination, such as ethnic, social, and religious; 2) against forms of exploitation by the rich, which separate individuals from what they produce; 3) against that which ties the individual to forms of subjectivity and submission to authority (130). Both Swift's "A Modest Proposal" (1729) and Spike Lee's *Bamboozled* (2000) can be read as satires embodying ethnic and economic resistance to the hegemonic culture. With regard to opposing imposed identity positions, Aphra Behn's "The Disappointment" (1680), Mary Astell's *Some Reflections upon Marriage* (1700), and Lady Mary Wortley Montagu's "The Reasons That Induced Dr. Swift to Write a Poem Called 'The Lady's Dressing Room'" (1734) can be seen as early modern women using satire to contest gender bigotry. Students examine whether, currently, Amy Schumer engages in a similar satiric struggle. Perhaps most important, Foucault asserts that while power is an indispensable feature of society, any given manifestation of it should not be taken fatalistically. Modern hegemony is always under challenge and thereby subject to change. For this reason, Foucault advises us not to pursue "universal philosophy" but to inspect instead the historical here and now—that is, how the current hegemonic discourse came into power and what can be done to thwart its oppressive disciplining ("Subject" 134). Whether defending or attacking the status quo, modern satire is a clear-cut participant in this cultural battle.

Early Modern and Modern Satire

Through these perspectives of genre and modern power, students explore the workings and the impacts of satire since the seventeenth century. In Dryden, Swift, and Pope, they can see literary power brokers defending against modern innovations. In Andrew Marvell and Rochester, they witness republicanism on the rise. The satires of Rochester in particular serve as excellent case studies for a new mode of satire in the emergent modern state. Using both textual and embodied satire, *Alexander Bendo's Brochure* (1676) exposes the political smoke and mirrors of Charles II's regime of truth (see Combe). Students readily appreciate how Colbert, albeit in a far more technologically advanced way, uses the same techniques to expose the machinations of modern power when he takes on, for example, the shady political dealings behind the super PAC (see "Colbert PAC"). In a manner similar to Nietzsche's scrutiny of social convention, Rochester's "A Satire against Reason and Mankind" (c. 1675) strips raw the power constructs of his day, asserting that people structure their lives upon ignorance, fear, vanity, and lies. Moreover, a hegemonic group, what Rochester calls "the pretending part of the proud world," runs this pathetic show to its own advantage. Being "swollen with selfish vanity," these political, religious, and cultural elites "devise / False freedoms, holy cheats, and formal lies, / Over their fellow slaves to tyrannize" (176–78). Colbert encapsulates these same power moves in his crowning satiric creation: the concept of "truthiness." Equally, when Stewart signs off as host of *The Daily Show*, he warns viewers always to be on the lookout for this identical brand of modern bullshit.

To involve students in current popular modes of satiric expression (fake news programs, mockumentaries, viral videos, and performance satire of various kinds), I use Amber Day's excellent study *Satire and Dissent.* Now, however, when students watch Colbert eviscerate President George W. Bush at the 2006 White House Correspondents' Association Dinner, they've seen this kind of factional wrangling before in the paper scuffles of Tory vs. Whig. Dryden vilifying Shaftesbury, Marvell unmasking Charles II, Swift incriminating Walpole, and Pope duncifying George II all concern the clash of modern political parties. In this fertile critical atmosphere, students bring fresh satiric interpretations to the table all the time. One group surprisingly presented James McTeigue's film *V for Vendetta* (2005) to the class for satiric analysis. In the character of V, the presenters saw a satirist figure, similar to a Rochesterian or Swiftian narrator, inviting fellow citizens to join him in a historical and political assessment of their oppressive here and now. These students made a solid case for how, as a political satire, *V for Vendetta* accomplished the same for its contemporary moviegoers. That is, the film invited American audiences to undertake a similar discourse analysis of conservative vs. progressive worldviews before the 2008 presidential election. Boom goes the Foucauldian-Freirean dynamite. In my teaching experience, exploring satire as a playground of signification and modern power relations is a rewarding way to introduce, to open up, and to make relevant this complex genre to students.

Works Cited

Colbert, Stephen, creator. "Colbert PAC—Trevor Potter." *The Colbert Report*, season 7, episode 43, Comedy Central, 30 Mar. 2011.

———, creator. "Truthiness." *The Colbert Report*, season 1, episode 1, Comedy Central, 17 Oct. 2005.

———, performer. "2006 White House Correspondents' Dinner." *C-SPAN*, www.c-span.org/video/?192243-1/2006-white-house-correspondents-dinner.

Combe, Kirk. "Making Monkeys of Important Men: Performance Satire and Rochester's *Alexander Bendo's Brochure*." *Journal for Early Modern Cultural Studies*, vol. 12, no. 2, Spring 2012, pp. 54–76.
Connery, Brian A., and Kirk Combe. "Theorizing Satire: A Retrospective and Introduction." *Theorizing Satire: Essays in Literary Criticism*, edited by Brian A. Connery and Kirk Combe, St. Martin's Press, 1995, pp. 1–14.
Day, Amber. *Satire and Dissent: Interventions in Contemporary Political Debate*. Indiana UP, 2011.
Deresiewicz, William. "The Neoliberal Arts: How College Sold Its Soul to the Market." *Harper's Magazine*, Sept. 2015, pp. 25–32.
Elliott, Robert C. *The Power of Satire: Magic, Ritual, Art*. Princeton UP, 1960.
Feinberg, Leonard. "Satire: The Inadequacy of Recent Definitions." *Genre*, vol. 1, 1968, pp. 31–37.
Foucault, Michel. *Discipline and Punish: The Birth of the Prison*. Translated by Alan Sheridan, 2nd ed., Vintage Books, 1995.
———. "The Subject and Power." Rabinow and Rose, pp. 126–44.
———. "Truth and Power." Rabinow and Rose, pp. 300–18.
Freire, Paulo. *Pedagogy of the Oppressed*. Translated by Myra Bergman Ramos, Continuum, 1986.
Freudenburg, Kirk. "Introduction: Roman Satire." *The Cambridge Companion to Roman Satire*, edited by Freudenburg, Cambridge UP, 2005, pp. 1–30.
Graff, Gerald. "Taking Cover in Coverage." *Profession*, 2012, pp. 109–18.
Marshall, Ashley. *The Practice of Satire in England, 1658–1770*. Johns Hopkins UP, 2013.
Nilsen, Don L. F. "Satire—The Necessary and Sufficient Conditions—Some Preliminary Observations." *Studies in Contemporary Satire*, vol. 15, 1988, pp. 1–10.
Rabinow, Paul, and Nikolas Rose, editors. *The Essential Foucault: Selections from Essential Works of Foucault, 1954–1984*. The New Press, 2003.
Rosenheim, Edward. *Swift and the Satirist's Art*. U of Chicago P, 1963.
Stewart, Jon. "Jon Stewart's Final Episode." *The Daily Show*, season 20, episode 142, Comedy Central, 6 Aug. 2015.
Wilmot, John (Earl of Rochester). "A Satire against Reason and Mankind." *The Norton Anthology of English Literature: The Restoration and the Eighteenth Century*, edited by James Noggle and Lawrence Lipking, vol. C, 9th ed., Norton, 2012, pp. 2301–07.

Adam Rounce

Satire on Scholarship in the Eighteenth Century

A quandary familiar to teachers of satire at any level of education is the amount of information that students require to understand, let alone explicate, texts that deliberately mock, ridicule, criticize, and lampoon aspects of their particular world. The appeal of satire may be general, but the details of its argument still need to be understood by students; otherwise the effect is like explaining the punch line of a joke at which people feel obliged to laugh. The teaching of satire necessitates student understanding of a context that, in its potential immensity, can overwhelm the satire itself, in terms of what students need to know, and the time and resources available to them. This holds as true for reading (and teaching) Juvenal or Jane Austen, Mark Twain or William Gaddis.

This problem is especially acute for teachers of satire in English literature from 1660 to 1780, its most prominent period as a literary and especially poetic mode. In works of this period, the degree of contextual knowledge that students require to negotiate the primary and implicit meanings of texts and to participate in a discussion of satiric forms often seems insurmountable. Without such knowledge, debates around satiric texts can turn into reductive summarizing from teachers (of the "Bentley was an enemy of Pope and Swift" variety) or a tautologous mangling of any satiric effect or charge made in the primary text ("Dryden thought Zimri/Buckingham was superficial and opinionated"). There is no obvious way around the problem: the teaching of key satiric works requires a frame of historical, political, and social reference, and when this is absent, the very aspects central to great satire—local but also timeless relevance, biting wit, the specific but also universal contexts of human vanity and folly—are often obscured or negated altogether.

An example is Pope's put-down in *An Epistle to Arbuthnot* of his critical enemies:

> Did some more sober Critic come abroad?
> If wrong, I smil'd; if right, I kiss'd the rod.
> Pains, reading, study, are their just pretence,
> And all they want is spirit, taste, and sense. (603)

The level of precision here, the exquisite symmetry between the qualities that his foolish critics aspire toward ("Pains, reading, study") and what they lack ("spirit, taste, and sense"), extended even to the oral dimension (each description has five syllables and attendant stresses), makes this a perfect case of how an apparent parallel turns into a satiric antithesis, and I have often used it to introduce basic features of couplet poetics and their relation with satire. Although useful as a poetic illustration, the satiric content is harder for students to grasp: undergraduates cannot be expected to be familiar with Richard Bentley or Lewis Theobald, these pedants who lack taste and judgment. Simply glossing "slashing Bentley" and "piddling Tibbald" with a brief summary of classical or Shakespearean editing of the period only partly alleviates the problem, revealing a little of the intended effect of the passage, but leaving unclear the reasons behind Pope's contempt for "each Wight who reads not," or indeed what such partial or misguided reading means and why it differs from his own practice.

One solution to these problems is for teachers to introduce satire through a range of texts that are affiliated with the canonical, as these provide students with an immediate and easily realizable context through their very rationale. This involves a more intense focus on Pope's general target in the passage above, namely editorial excess, given that one of the most significant strands of satire after 1660 is related to the book, especially the scholarly edition. Therefore, to use examples of the works associated with Bentley, Theobald, William Warburton, and other similar figures is to offer satires on and around scholarly editions (particularly of Milton and Shakespeare) as an accessible way of introducing central satiric questions through the lens of familiar texts, albeit somewhat eccentrically edited. The advantage of this approach is that footnotes on *Paradise Lost* or *Macbeth* (or whichever of Shakespeare's plays are most germane or known to students) do not require additional contextual knowledge for undergraduate or master's-level students and also allows students to interact with works from which they may have previously felt distanced, to participate in different textual and interpretative choices, and to consider the significance of such satiric debates far beyond their immediate range and effect.

Bentley's notorious 1732 edition of *Paradise Lost* is a good introduction for students to the satiric consequences of eighteenth-century scholarship. It encompasses excesses of conjectural emendation (an alien but crucial concept to readers who might assume that the text on the page was timeless and sacrosanct) and a decadent application of sound scholarly principles; above all, Bentley's approach has a literal quality both in its interpretations and its rationale, which is attractive in its willfulness, almost to the point of being a scholarly self-parody.

The following descriptions of teaching practice were designed around two-hour seminars for third-year undergraduate students (finalists, in the United Kingdom) numbering between ten and twenty-five. As an opening example, I present students with parts of Bentley's prefatory remarks, where he explains what he is doing (offering emendations to *Paradise Lost* based on his theory of faulty and malicious copying and transmission by lazy or mendacious secretaries, editors, and printers), to encourage them to consider the workings of editorial principles, howsoever bizarre. I also give them printed pages of Bentley's most unusual suggested emendations, as the textual interventions and argumentative footnotes form a marked contrast with the more sober modern editions of poets that students normally use.

I have found that students, bewildered by erstwhile more abstract discussions of philology and the importance of textual study, are far more open to Bentley's detective-story narrative in his preface, where the supposed errors of transmission "are not to be charg'd upon the Poet, but on the Amanuensis," not to forget "the Friend or Acquaintance, whoever he was, to whom *Milton* committed his Copy and the Overseeing of the Press," but who "did so vilely execute that Trust, that *Paradise* under his Ignorance and Audaciousness may be said to be *twice lost*" (sig. Ar). They are intrigued by the elaborate framework created to basically justify where Bentley does not like Milton's choice of words and entertained by the almost absurd re-creations of the supposed crimes against the text.

It can be useful for a teacher to ask students to consider whether such excess of interpretation and overstepping of editorial involvement can ever be justified, and if not, why not? It is valuable at this point to discuss why Bentley's more well-known interventions seem to end in bathos. The most famous of these, the suggestion of "No light but rather a transpicuous Gloom" instead of "No light but rather darkness visible," is often used as a test case for the understanding of metaphor in poetry. I have found that Bentley's summary of the original as "a flat Contradiction. *Darkness visible* will not serve to *discover Sights of Woe* through it, but to cover and hide them" (4) always seems risible to students. On reflection, they often decide that it is not flexible enough in its understanding of metaphor, whereas an oxymoron like "darkness visible" is more powerful because it challenges us to conceive of what hell seems like. Moreover, their poetic understanding leads them to conclude that Bentley replaces Miltonic grandeur with vulgar literalism to no real end (an illustration of the sort of solipsistic vandalism that Pope implied by "slashing Bentley"). The barbs in the pamphlets written against Bentley are less subtle, but they do show how literary culture in the period rarely existed in a vacuum and instead generated a satiric response in proportion to its own lofty ambitions: "If there were really any Darkness in this Passage, I am sure the Doctor has not rendred it visible by his Note upon it" (*Milton Restor'd* 26). Students enjoy such witty put-downs, and their sense of engagement with Milton's poem and its reception is greatly enhanced. Students introduced to Bentley's *Paradise Lost* and some of the satire it produced understand, therefore, something of the disdain of Pope and Swift toward their scholarly enemies and are better placed to recognize the layering of that contempt in the apparatus of *The Dunciad Variorum* and *A Tale of a Tub*, among other works.

A companion to Bentley with regard to the amount of satirical energy produced is Pope's executor William Warburton's 1747 edition of Shakespeare's works, renowned for its interventions into the text and egocentric annotations. Warburton's Shakespeare is an ideal tool for introducing satire around scholarship to students, as the tone of his explanations is a useful example of scholarly excess. Warburton's humble aim was in "restoring the Poet's genuine Text; but in those Places only where it labours with inextricable Nonsense. In which, how much soever I may have given Scope to critical Conjecture, where the old Copies failed me, I have indulged nothing to Fancy or Imagination; but have religiously observed the severe Canons of literal Criticism" (1: xiv). It is useful for teachers to ask students to think of any potential self-contradiction here, since Warburton is both handmaiden to these supposed "severe" critical "canons," while at the same time giving "scope" to conjecture. In short, as can be easily demonstrated, Warburton did what he liked, justifying his interventions with lengthy, often hectoring footnotes at the expense of previous editors. In a seminar, these footnotes raise valuable questions about what readers, critics, and editors do when they interpret a text and what sort of limits can or should be placed around our interpretations.

Of the many mockeries of Warburton, a striking one to introduce is by the satirist Charles Churchill, who wrote his "Dedication to the Sermons" as a mock panegyric, saluting Warburton's editorial genius through ironic supposed praise in ways that draw upon Pope's *Epistle to Arbuthnot*:

> His judgment teach me, from the critic school,
> How not to err, and how to err by rule;
> Instruct me, mingle profit with delight,
> Where Pope was wrong, where Shakspeare was not right;
> Where they are justly praised, and where, through whim,
> How little's due to them, how much to him. (84–85)

I ask students to discuss the implications of Churchill's charge, that the scholar could be seen as absorbing the creative impulse behind (and taking credit for) the writers upon which they worked. The writings of a Pope or Shakespeare become a mere platform to display the editor's own learning and supposedly profound insights. This is followed by an extended look at the Shakespeare edition to illustrate this point. Warburton's style combined high-handedness with misplaced and often redundant pedantry. I prepare various examples for students to consider individually or in groups, which they then present to the class after time for reflection. These involve specific types of questionable editorial intervention.

For example, students consider how Macbeth's despairing description of sleep as the "death of each day's life" produces the following criticism from Warburton:

> I make no question but *Shakespear* wrote,
> The birth of each day's life,
> The true characteristic of sleep, which repairs the decays of labour, and assists that returning vigour which supplies the next day's activity. The Player-Editors seem to have corrupted it for the sake of a silly gingle between life and death. (6: 361)

Students recognized that the tone of Warburton's ad hominem criticism of John Heminge and Henry Condell, compilers of the First Folio, for their supposed "silly" emendation is a problem, as is his imposition of a literalism that has no basis in any textual history (the strange claim that sleep is restorative, so should be associated with birth, even though death is understandably more resonant for the blood-soaked Macbeth). The principle of restoring the corrupted text is, as with Bentley, an excuse for misplaced creativity.

Warburton was learned and not always wrong, and student awareness of the wider problems of editing, beyond a few perverse examples, can be enhanced by those cases where Warburton's mudslinging against his predecessors was justified. Sir Thomas Hanmer's alteration in *Macbeth*, where "To know my deed, 'twere best not know myself" becomes "*To* unknow *my deed*," is seized upon by Warburton with glee; it is a crude attempt to summarize Macbeth's meaning that ends up offering its exact opposite, replacing the implication of understanding the deed with forgetting. Yet Warburton's description of Hanmer's "perceiving neither the sense, nor the pertinency of the answer," reflects perfectly the acidic and unforgiving tone of his editing, which would ensure his satiric downfall (6: 361–62). In classes, the students agreed that Hanmer's emendation is a distortion of the lines' meaning but found Warburton's contempt gratuitous.

At this point, it is helpful to introduce students to examples from Thomas Edwards's irreverent popular satire *The Canons of Criticism* (1748, and expanded in the many subsequent editions), which was given its title and impetus by Warburton's own grandiloquence. All Edwards did, in many instances, was list Warburton's follies according to different categories of errors (a parody of the supposedly "severe canons" of criticism). The result is a sparkling and often brilliant pricking of pomposity and editorial excess, especially useful for challenging initial student assumptions about an editorial apparatus being definite and above criticism.

The value of Edwards's critique can be understood by asking students to consider what makes his satire so effective. One answer involves the different layers of irony applied to Warburton's commentary. There is, of course, the straightforward and rather facetious pointing out of error. A striking example is in *Julius Caesar*, where Cassius's "And, in their steads, do *ravens*, crows, and kites / Fly o'er our heads" (5.1.84–85) does not cry out for emendation, but Warburton finds a way: "A raven and a crow is the same bird of prey: the first name taken from its nature; the other from it's [sic] voice. We should therefore read ravenous crows and kites" (Edwards 36). Edwards tries not to sound too incredulous, and students appreciate the sarcasm: "Though Mr. Warburton cannot find it in the Dictionaries, yet every crow-keeper in the country will tell him there is as real a difference between a raven and a crow, as there is between a crow and a rook, or a rook and a jack-daw." It is worth asking how the satiric tone works here and whether Edwards, pointing out the bizarre error, also hints at the strange need to rewrite the text, which suggests a process of overinterpretation—it cannot be allowed to stand in its simplicity, so "ravens" must become "ravenous."

In my experience, students find that Warburton's editorial method is ultimately self-serving, an excuse for latent critical analysis, where the meaning of the text cannot be allowed to settle; to put it bluntly, it's more about him than Shakespeare. Even when every apparent textual detail is established, his interventions have to inexhaustibly continue. The oppressive annotation that results, along with Edwards's barbs and rejoinders, asks students important questions about how we read and why, and they welcome the opportunity to explore cases where criticism becomes counterproductive and debilitating and the cumulative effect of analysis is to negate its supposed job of bringing clarity and insight.

The not-uncommon editorial tendency to rewrite the text is accompanied by Warburton's more unusual trait, a tendency to offer as fact information impossible for any reader to glean without supernatural means. The funniest case, a boon to any teacher wanting to demonstrate where critical authority overleaps itself, is from *Cymbeline*, as Edwards describes:

> ere I could
> Give him that parting kiss which I had set
> Betwixt two charming words, comes in my father [1.4.33–35]
>
> Mr. Warburton in his note on this passage has had the felicity to discover, what were the two charming words, between which Imogen would have set her parting kiss; which Shakespeare probably never thought to. He says "without question by these two charming words, she would be understood to mean
> ADIEV, POSTHVMVS.
> The one religion made so; and the other love." (51)

It is unusual, to say the least, to try to surmise what such words might be; Warburton alone, perhaps (anticipating in ghostly fashion the ceaseless assumptions and conspiracies of the anti-Stratfordians), could have the confidence to proclaim what they are "without question." As Edwards remarks, replete with dripping sarcasm,

> Imogen must have understood the etymology of our language very exactly, to find out so much religion in the word *adieu*, which we use

> commonly, without fixing any such idea to it; as when we say, that such a man has *bid adieu* to all religion. And on the other side, she must have understood the language of love very little, if she could find no tenderer an expression of it, than the name, by which every body else called her husband. (51)

In a seminar, students tend to side with Edwards, finding it remarkable that an editor could pretend to know such a commonplace and insignificant detail: of what value is it that Imogen uses her husband's name (Posthumous) when saying farewell, and why should the (as one student pointed out, looking it up online) literal but hardly everyday meaning of *adieu* be alongside it, in order to show Imogen venerating both love and religion? The general reaction was that Warburton was perverse, having the chutzpah to assume to know more than Shakespeare did about his own text but coming up with a bold claim that actually reveals nothing.

As Edwards says, Shakespeare "probably never thought to" care about the two words that Imogen might have said had her father not walked in the door; Warburton's need to seek them out is one of the many reasons his edition is a gift to satirists, a compendium of critical prejudices, and a great introduction to arguments around eighteenth-century literary scholarship. Looking at it, and satires like Edwards's, compels students to question what constitutes the text of a Shakespeare play and what makes the words of it appropriate, well chosen, or exact. In "Canon XX," Edwards chides Warburton's absence of poetic register in his attempts to show his "*universal learning*" by minutely and pedantically tracing the source of every metaphor, such as "prayers from *preserved* souls / From *fasting* maids," where "[t]he metaphor is taken from fruits preserv'd in sugar." Edwards points out this is not literal enough and inserts a cod-Warburtonian emendation: "In order to continue the metaphor, we should alter *fasting* maids to *pickled* maids" (53). Students were alert here to the unpoetic register of "*pickled*": parody is a devastating form of satire, exposing both Warburton's stating of the obvious and his erstwhile failure to tell the difference between a poetic vehicle of meaning and its literal representation. Such examples allow students to judge what precisely they find to be poetic or literary through comparison with (apparently) less-well-formulated figures and images.

Warburton's version of Shakespeare and its satiric aftermath raise substantial critical questions for students. The consequence of an editorial theory that is allowed to reshape the text according to its own understanding of what it should mean is in some ways not so much an ideal version as a critical rewriting of it. Discussing this explains more fully to undergraduate readers what Pope, Churchill, Swift, and other satirists meant when lampooning the "modern" tendency to take over, without sufficient taste or judgment, those works they were ostensibly celebrating. A teacher can also suggest that such editorial theories anticipate the more recent poststructuralist and postmodern approaches, where the text means to some extent what the reader thinks it means. *Paradise Lost* and Shakespeare are rewritten by Bentley and Warburton in their historical moment, and these versions and the satiric responses to them challenge the idea that the text is a remote and perfectly unchanging Grecian urn, being instead something socially received and consumed and possibly fashioned into a new meaning by every reader.

In my experience, students (and indeed their teachers) can find the implications of this outlandish to some degree, but the oddities of eighteenth-century scholarship make both it and its satires an excellent way of developing such questions, encouraging classroom discussions of the purpose of literature and the ownership of meaning—whether it belongs to author, editor, or reader—and offering a way of extending the teaching of satire from a notionally self-contained area of referents, context, and social and historical critique to a wider examination of the very purpose of interpretation and literary criticism. On one level, works like those discussed here are an entertaining introduction to the substance of eighteenth-century arguments about scholarship, taste and aesthetics, and cultural history; on another, to engage with them fully is to compel students to think about how we read and interpret and why, about what is valued in literature and whether that value is operative across centuries.

Note

I am grateful to the following students for testing some of the editorial examples discussed here: Johnny Cammish, Charlotte Coomber, Lucia Dove, James Gable, Kay Henderson, Jodie Marley, Jack Pedder, Florence Ross, and Katherine Taylor.

Works Cited

Bentley, Richard, editor. *Paradise Lost. A New Edition*. By John Milton, London, 1732.

Churchill, Charles. *Selected Poems*. Edited by Adam Rounce, Trent Editions, 2003.

Edwards, Thomas. *The Canons of Criticism, and Glossary*. London, 1748.

Milton Restor'd and Bentley Depos'd. London, 1732.
Pope, Alexander. *The Poems of Alexander Pope.* Edited by John Butt, Methuen, 1963.
Warburton, William, editor. *The Works of William Shakespeare.* London, 1747. 8 vols.

Matthew Stratton

Form, Norm, and Gender in the 1920s: Dorothy Parker and Anita Loos

Anyone raised on a steady diet of *The Daily Show* and *The Simpsons* is a comfortable interpreter of satire, but satire's pervasive influence on recent popular culture has not necessarily made it easier to teach. Some of the key challenges of a literature classroom, of course, are enabling students to recognize their own varying levels of expertise in navigating the cultures and conversations of daily life, giving them a technical vocabulary to reflect upon their own interpretive processes while joining a larger critical conversation, and connecting those habitual abilities with the experience of reading decreasingly familiar literary forms. Whatever the class, my broader pedagogical goals are often the same: to trace multiple permutations of literary history, to situate texts simultaneously in their historical context and in current perspective, and to connect aesthetic pleasure and displeasure with the ideological forms that persist in our lives. In my own teaching life, satire turns out to be perhaps the most rewarding path for accomplishing all of these goals, perhaps never more so than when the conversation centers on the inextricable connections among gender, power, and the fraught process of identifying the stable object of a seemingly simple feminist satire.

Whether I'm introducing students to Horace by way of Wilfred Owen or to the ethical force of postmodern fiction by way of Ishmael Reed, I start conversations about satire by projecting a story from the news and declaiming how offended I am—or how gratified I am, depending upon the day and how deep my Socratic reservoir is running—by something I just learned. So, for example, I might strike up a loud conversation with someone in the front row about a noteworthy news item like "Maybelline Introduces Line of Injectable Makeup to Enhance Appearance of Internal Organs" from *The Onion*: "'With our new injectable makeup options, women can finally have the type of flawless, gorgeous-looking digestive and cardiopulmonary systems they've always wanted,' said Maybelline spokesperson Diane Moss, adding that women will soon be able to use a 10cc Maybelline syringe to apply their new set of cosmetics, which currently includes a 'bold and flirty' line of lung shadow." With either visible outrage or enthusiastic interest in the wonders of modern progress, I'll continue: Can you believe that a newspaper would endorse a product like this? This is a horrific/wonderful development! Should *I* buy this stuff as I fight off the depredations of middle age? Should you?

If there are students whose inability to recognize the satire matches my profession of ignorance, they have yet to announce themselves. Students do announce that this story is not to be taken literally; that because of the apparent generic familiarity of the newspaper format, I have made a mistake in believing that the newspaper endorses this product; that, despite the existence of a real cosmetics company with this name, no such product actually exists. The next step is demanding that they not only defend their positions but also teach *me* to recognize the figurative work of seemingly literal prose, as well as articulate what exactly is being ridiculed. In the space of five energetic minutes spurred by a few straightforward questions—chiefly variations on "How can you tell that's what it means?" explicitly introducing social and cultural context into textual close reading—we arrive at a pointed conclusion: that what is ridiculed is neither the existence of organ makeup nor a newspaper that is promoting a product when it should be objectively informing readers about important political events of the day. Rather, what is attacked is the grotesquely misogynist set of cultural expectations about the performance of beauty as it is indexed, advertised, and aggressively sold as a dominant version of femininity. This last, salient point is made all the more effectively by virtue of the fact that students themselves articulate it, often more convincingly and eloquently than I could impress upon them in a lecture. If Socratic performance isn't your thing, the approach succeeds as a writing exercise before class, especially in the form of a "translation" exercise. Instead of translating one national language into another, invite students to translate a particular "literal" sentence or passage from the satire into the figurative, targeted meaning, then open class by asking them to share their translation process.

The interpretive work for decoding satire as a mode and genre is thus already well under way before the class seems to have started, a tactic I have used for the past several years to introduce my undergraduates at the University of California at Davis to Anita Loos's *Gentlemen Prefer Blondes* (1925). This novel employs a misogynist gender norm to provide both a structuring principle of the text and the object of the author's satire, and the book does so in a way that readers are tempted to read it as endorsing the very norms that Loos satirically stabs. Identifying the object of the novel's satire allows undergraduates to see how social norms and literary interpretation are inextricably connected; when they articulate how irony and satire simultaneously rely upon and disrupt conventional expectations about gender and genre, they also confront ways in which their own assumptions come under attack.

Recent iterations of the syllabus for the upper-division course in which I teach this novel (The American Novel after 1900) trace an American literary history running roughly from Willa Cather's *O Pioneers!* (1913) to Rachel Kushner's *The Flamethrowers* (2013). I often introduce those novels through other literary genres to focus attention on the craft of close reading while framing the thematic, historical, and formal concerns of the novels to come. When students encounter Loos's masterpiece, for example, they have just read *O Pioneers!* alongside Walt Whitman's "Pioneers! O Pioneers!" As we move to Loos, I follow our reading of *The Onion* headline as epigram with a brief definition of satire courtesy of M. H. Abrams and Dorothy Parker's "A Certain Lady" (1926). The poem serves as a preface to the novel's tactic of ironizing seemingly straightforward language within a recognizable cultural discourse in order to satirize restrictive assumptions about gender. Attending to the specific work of irony in the poem impresses upon students the need to be attentive re-readers of all kinds of literary texts, to be alert to the ludic ways in which the meaning of lines changes as the poem unfolds, and to identify moments when lambent irony transforms into what Northrop Frye called the "militant irony" of satire (223).

The first part of Parker's poem seems to detail the disappointed longing of a speaker who performs her modern feminine duties by knowingly indulging and seemingly enjoying her lover's tales of sexual exploits:

> Oh, I can smile for you, and tilt my head,
> And drink your rushing words with eager lips,
> And paint my mouth for you a fragrant red,
> And trace your brows with tutored finger-tips.
> When you rehearse your list of loves to me,
> Oh, I can laugh and marvel, rapturous-eyed.
> And you laugh back, nor can you ever see
> The thousand little deaths my heart has died.

Getting students to slow down might be the single most important precondition for teaching close reading; with the aim of inductively establishing a set of social norms that make the poem coherently signify, the interpretive task expands into translating individual words through and within a poetic form until what seems to be a conservative affirmation of gendered norms is revealed to be a feminist transvaluation of those norms. For example, as students will quickly point out when asked to choose single words with at least two distinct meanings, the poem suggests how a "death" can be both literally physical but more obviously figurative and emotional. After reading *The Onion* piece on cosmetics, everyone is suspicious about the fact that the speaker's body ("finger-tips") and mind have been explicitly "tutored" to "paint" her mouth and deliver caresses. When approached through the question of just who has taught the speaker to act in this way, the most seemingly private, intimate moments of lyric are legible as a publicly staged theatrical performance for the pleasure of a lover who can see and smell colors but is blind to more essential transformations: the addressee doesn't so much relate his adventures as theatrically "rehearse" them, and the speaker makes him "believe, so well I know my part," that she enjoys rather than suffers through nonmonogamy.

When prompted to describe the first part of the poem's meaning, students often read the first twelve lines as essentially reinforcing what they think they know about literary history: that even—or especially—modern women silently suffer the fallout of a sexual revolution that leaves them pleasing but not pleased, liberated but secretly pining for the comforts of monogamy, bound by singular desire to a partner who will "never know" the "straining things within my heart." Yet, as the second half of the poem describes the "tales of fresh adventurings" regaled as poetic "sagas of your late delights," the students' expectations (already destabilized by the word *satire* in the air) are completely upended:

> And when, in search of novelty, you stray,
> Oh, I can kiss you blithely as you go. . . .
> And what goes on, my love, while you're away,
> You'll never know.

The work that they have done to "translate" a series of seemingly denotative but actually ironic claims in the faux advertisement now doubles down when the meaning of "You'll never know" is reversed and revalued as a kind of formal equality in action.

After reading the poem aloud, students are asked to identify its formal features. With some prompting, they see how what first appears to be a twenty-four-line lyric in rhyming iambic pentameter can also be read as a brilliant riff on the double English sonnet: two twelve-line stanzas with familiar rhyme and meter, but both stanzas about a couple conspicuously lacking the concluding heroic or commentary couplet. Depending upon the course the conversation takes, I might even talk a bit about the sonnet in particular, invoking formal arguments by people like Phillis Levin, who claims that "by virtue of its infrastructure the sonnet is asymmetrical. . . . Being dialectical, the sonnet is divided by nature: its patterns of division multiply perspective and meaning" (xxxviii). Walking slowly through the sonnet form also gives students who may be less comfortable with satire an opportunity to rehearse their own prior experience with different literary forms and to connect the poetic asymmetry with the dialectical power relations between speaker and addressee.

As the conversation continues, I will often project subsidiary *OED* definitions of *certain* to emphasize that the speaker is not only a "particular" lady but also a lady who is "wholly trustworthy or reliable." This further expands the conversation about verbal and situational irony and about unequally gendered expectations about sexual fidelity, and it emphasizes how the poem's use of irony and poetic form undermines any argument that the poetic speaker or novelistic narrator would find a monogamous coupling to be either particularly desirable or remotely heroic. Once again, the literary codes that echo with gendered social norms such as fidelity, privacy, and domesticity can no longer be claimed as natural and instead fall under the rubric of social, theatrical performance, the unequal power structure of which is now ridiculed as highly conventional. When students further need to define *lady* and distinguish it from thesaurus synonyms—*woman*, *girl*, *female*—we arrive at the perfect segue into discussing how Loos stages the comedic, satirical emergence of her narrator's public literary performance as a feminist political statement about physical and economic satisfaction outside the bonds of matrimony.

The class-ridden tension between public and private expectations is delineated in the move from Parker's "Lady" to Loos's subtitle—*The Illuminating Diary of a Professional Lady*—when I ask if anyone has ever kept a diary and whether that was primarily a public or private document. Directly asking "So you'd be fine with your mother or little brother reading your diary then?" gets us right into the presumed intimate privacy of the diary genre, so we next arrive at Lorelei's entry for April 1: "I am taking special pains with my diary from now on as I am really writing it for Gerry" (15). The narrator, Lorelei Lee, is most immediately known for her grammatical mishaps, misspellings, and uncouth materialism, and one expects a few students to denounce her as ignorant, greedy, vapid, and insufficiently attuned to the expectations of sexual self-control. But with the specters of feminist irony and satire already hanging in the air, we are forced to consider that the first chapter of this novelized diary is asking us to suspect that the "April fool" is not Lorelei but anyone who shares Gerry's ignorant insistence on Lorelei's need for "improvement."

To give one brief example, students are invariably struck by the protagonist's most famous line: at a key moment, Lorelei concludes, "So I really think that American gentlemen are the best after all, because kissing your hand may make you feel very very good but a diamond and safire bracelet lasts forever" (75). Even after the warning signs of the Parker poem, the book's subtitle, and the subtle generic alerts of the first chapter, some students will invoke this line as irrefutable evidence that the novel's protagonist is an irritatingly ignorant materialist who is subject to authorial censure because of her moral and grammatical bankruptcy. Yet there are more students who are willing to defend Lorelei's performed ignorance as evidence that she has so deeply mastered misogynist cultural discourses that she is able to harness "riskay stories" (15) for her own economic sustenance and affective pleasure. As Marilyn Monroe proclaims in the most famous musical number from Howard Hawks's 1953 film *Gentlemen Prefer Blondes* (with writing credit shared by Loos herself), "A kiss may be grand, but it won't pay the rental on your humble flat / Or help you at the automat."

Some historical context is inevitably required for those who don't immediately associate "automat" with food or who don't immediately recognize the narrator's name as a gendered trope from German Romanticism with its own mythic backstory. Because Lorelei has recounted that "it was Judge Hibbard who really gave me my name because he did not like the name I had because he said a girl ought to have a name that ought to express her personality" (33), it's important to mention that the 1920s saw the founding of the Lucy Stone League, whose motto asserted that "My name is my identity and must not be lost" and who fought for women to keep and use their own name after marriage. Many students will bring in a bit of Marx and Engels to remark upon the commodity fetishism required to understand how a diamond might be anyone's, but most particularly a "girl's," best friend. Often students will point out that the novel was written in the decade that saw some American women emerge into the political public sphere via supposedly universal suffrage, and I point out that institutional racism fundamentally excluded many nonwhite women from the achievement of the Nineteenth Amendment.

As we move from the definition of satire to particular examples from pop culture, poetry, and Loos's novel, I delineate how the literary history of satire has not been conventionally equitable in its treatment of men and women and how since Juvenal's *Satire VI* misogyny has been more than just a frequent characteristic of the genre. As one scholar notes, "The virtual absence of women as satirists before the twentieth century . . . seems an instance of the historical exclusion of women from authorship, from public activity, and from controversy," which has made "satire more-or-less a masculine genre" (Knight 7–8, 6). Indeed, the notion that both the content and the authorship of satire depend upon a conservatively gendered relationship between literary and social norms extends well into modernity; witness a 1913 protégé of Ambrose Bierce, who attributed what he called "The Death of Satire" directly to "feminine minds, which, exercising more and more power, at last establish emasculated standards and erect a tyranny of taste in accordance with them" (Scheffauer 82).

When Lorelei ends up in a chaste, profitable marriage with an enjoyable lover on the side, the novel connects and then divorces the financial economics of marriage from the misogynist hypocrisy of a sexual economy where "a gentlemen never pays for [a reputation for sexual promiscuity], but a girl always pays" (41). Finally, after navigating the novel's tricky equipoise of rhetorical affirmations and negations of lopsided sexual norms, we recognize that Lorelei is not a gold digger but an investor who has mastered the strategies needed to profit from limited and limiting discourses about women. To deny the novel's satire is to endorse the most egregiously misogynist assumptions that the novel has been consistently attacking. Students recognize not only the specific gender ideologies at work in Parker and Loos but also how authors can repurpose satire's conservative gender norms to serve a literary and political feminism that demands both economic and sexual equality. Ultimately, challenging undergraduate students to explain how they are able to identify the object or target of a satire allows them to recognize their own interpretations of literary and social texts and thus to slow down and attend to the ideological foundations of habitual reading.

Works Cited

Frye, Northrop. *Anatomy of Criticism: Four Essays.* Princeton UP, 1957.

Knight, Charles A. *The Literature of Satire.* Cambridge UP, 2004.

Levin, Phillis, editor. *The Penguin Book of the Sonnet: Five Hundred Years of a Classic Tradition in English.* Penguin, 2001.

Loos, Anita. *Gentlemen Prefer Blondes.* 1925. Liveright, 1998.

"Maybelline Introduces Line of Injectable Makeup to Enhance Appearance of Internal Organs." *The Onion*, 23 Apr. 2015, www.theonion.com/maybelline-introduces-line-of-injectable-makeup-to-enha-1819577723.

Parker, Dorothy. "A Certain Lady." *The Collected Poetry of Dorothy Parker*, Random House, 1944, p. 75.

Scheffauer, Herman. "The Death of Satire." *The Living Age*, 12 July 1913, pp. 82–90.

John Clement Ball

Postcolonial Satire

Modal satire appears frequently in postcolonial fiction,[1] but in postsecondary classrooms its combination of referentiality and distortion—its deliberate misrepresentation of people, events, or sociopolitical conditions that may not be familiar in the first place—can make satire confusing and politically touchy to students trained to be respectful of others and of unfamiliar cultures. Indeed, satire's very modus operandi can seem antithetical to a postcolonial sensibility: its apparent reliance on binary hierarchical models of norm and deviation, or ideal and actual, can readily be seen to resemble and even reinforce the condescending colonialist and racist discourses that postcolonial authors and critics oppose. As a form of "othering"—of symbolic or representational violence—satire must be handled with care. Its mocking, nose-thumbing, aggressive ways can make it explosive and offensive; its indirection and instability can blur its intentions, move its targets, indict broadly, and do much collateral damage. Students, like any readers, can be turned off by the satirist's accusatory ways and eschewal of fair representation, which can shade into essentialism and stereotypes. Nonetheless, as a form of playful opposition and corrective resistance that holds the powerful and dangerous to account, and with its pleasures of laughter, moral-high-ground-claiming judgment, and immersion in alternative worlds, among others, satire can be very appealing. Many undergraduates' attraction to strongly held political and ethical positions—not to mention clear-cut textual interpretations—can be satisfied by satire's dualistic writing of wrongs.

As much as that of John Donne or Jonathan Swift, postcolonial satire requires careful historicizing, both of the referential world the fiction invokes and the authorial ethos or cultural moment that informs its satiric gestures. Beyond mediating the unfamiliar, such contextualizing may be necessary even to identify a work or passage *as* satire; discussion of the who, what, why, and how of the satiric representation, the attitudes and intents that inform it, and the effects and affects it generates is best undertaken on a referential footing. Sometimes sociohistorical context is provided by the text itself in ways that offset and frame its satiric elements. For instance, reading Chinua Achebe's *Things Fall Apart* (1958)—a much-taught historical novel that gives many their first encounter with African literature and with Britain's imperial incursions—students readily note the narrator's changed tone in the famously satiric final paragraph of this otherwise realist, tragic narrative.[2] Whether they see that paragraph as satiric, ironic, or simply oppositional, they typically find satisfaction and a sense of justice in Achebe's rhetorical diminishment of the District Commissioner and the palpably deficient colonialist discourse with which he would reduce the expansive, empathetic story of Okonkwo that they have just read to his own "reasonable paragraph" (187). The target here, after all, is an English administrator and the arrogant ignorance with which this fictitious but representative character would presume to understand and sufficiently render (but actually simplify and objectify) a complex society. Achebe's critique fits politically with postcolonialism's well-known "Empire Writes Back" framework (Ashcroft), and the novel's fulsome narrative enables the satire to pop out as a seemingly just, tit-for-tat diminishment of one reductive paragraph through another.

Teaching *Things Fall Apart* involves outlining aspects of nineteenth-century Igbo life and the history of European involvement in Africa, so students arrive at the end of Achebe's novel—or at least classes on it—aware of how much more they know than the District Commissioner does about Okonkwo's complex, sophisticated society. (One hopes they are also aware of how much more there is to learn.) I always devote my last class to a group discussion of the final paragraph. What is it doing there? What effect does it have? As they share ideas and respond to further prompts, students can begin to see how much satiric representation shares with the very all-knowing, immobilizing, dehistoricizing, silencing colonialist discourse that it is, in this instance, critiquing. Students may feel this correspondence is perfectly apt, or they may then be less delighted by the jarring shift of register. The issues opened up—epistemological, political, mimetic, stylistic—can be extended to other satirized English characters that, like the District Commissioner, stand out like sore thumbs from the dominant narrative mode and sensibility of the historical novels in which they appear.[3] But even through this short passage, some foundational aspects of satiric representation and of postcolonial theory can be taught in tandem.

Achebe's satiric exclamation mark can also serve as a starting point for discussion of novels that are more fully permeated and transformed by satire—and therefore less stable and less straightforwardly "postcolonial" in their politics. In Sam Selvon's carnivalesque comedy *Moses Ascending* (1975), narrator Moses, a longtime Caribbean immigrant to London, offers an early set piece that purports to celebrate black residents' superior employment conditions: waking up before everyone else, the black worker "does not know how privileged he is to be in charge of the city whilst the rest of Brit'n is still abed"; "He holds the keys of the city, and he will unlock the doors and tidy the papers on the desk, flush the loo, straighten the chairs, hoover the carpet" (5, 6). Through ironic indirection and reversal, Selvon's tongue-in-cheek satire can expect readerly completion and recognition of its target: white Britain's consignment of black labor to lowly duties and shift work. In case anyone takes literally Moses's claim that the black worker is "Chief Executive of London Transport and British Railways, . . . Superintendent of all the hospitals" (6), he clarifies by mock-lamenting, "Oh, the ingratitude, the unreasonableness of those who only see one side of the coin, and complain that he is given only the menial tasks to perform!" (7). The simple postcoloniality—and, for most students, reasonableness—of this amusing critique of white privilege is not typical, however: the rest of the novel will likely unsettle some readers with Moses's vulgarity and unreconstructed sexism (against black and white women) and racism (against South Asians). His scattershot caricatures of Caribbean and American black power radicals, Asian human traffickers, and a white British bandwagon-joining opportunist, not to mention Moses's own buffoonish, self-satirizing qualities, not only risk offending but raise more questions than they answer about Selvon's satiric intents and effects. What is his target? What are his politics? Which if any of Moses's views does Selvon endorse? Where do readers position themselves vis-à-vis

Moses and his/Selvon's multifarious satiric forays? Is there a normative, stable stance to be found? If we attend to the also-evident satire of more "universal" human foibles (e.g., hypocrisy, venality, pride), are we ameliorating uncomfortable racial politics or simply avoiding them?[4]

The answers may, paradoxically, be the questions themselves and the fact that so many are prompted so readily. Theoretical studies from the 1990s and 2000s challenge old notions of satire as a stable, bipolar form that identifies, defines, and polices difference *as* difference: that author-subject castigates victim-object and invites readerly recognition of its defective otherness, based on shared standards and norms, through the inventive, engaging techniques of satiric representation. Dustin Griffin, notably, departs from what he sees as an ossified critical consensus from the 1960s, proposing instead that "satirists characteristically regard their targets with an attitude more complex than simple rejection" (64). Aiming to reorient critical understanding of satire from calculated ends to experimental means, Griffin argues that satire is more open-ended and exploratory than traditionally understood; therefore, "[w]e need to supplement the old rhetoric of persuasion with a rhetoric of inquiry and provocation" (64). Satire, in this view, is more about discovering and questioning than judging and accusing. For Frank Palmeri, likewise, satire "counterpoises multiple frames of understanding without assenting to the authority of any single perspective" (3); and for Fredric Bogel, "reading satire is not so much about finding a position we can plug ourselves into as about exploring the complexity of a particular moral position" (62). Given postcolonial theorists' simultaneous moves to complicate their views of colonial power and postcolonial resistance beyond dualistic models—through recognition of the dynamic, relational, and mutual aspects of (de)colonized identities and the multivalent energies and agendas of postcolonial texts—such ways of rethinking satire can liberate scholars, instructors, and students in ways beneficial to the understanding of satire and of postcolonial fiction. If, as Salman Rushdie writes, the novel is the genre that "tells us there are no answers; or, rather, . . . that answers are easier to come by, and less reliable, than questions" (*Imaginary Homelands* 423), teaching satire as a mode of exploratory inquiry rather than a sure-footed answer—as a process of responding rather than the product of a response—can make it more palatable, more interesting, and more complex.

Selvon's loose deployment of a reversed allegory of *Robinson Crusoe*—Moses as new black landlord employing Bob, a white "man Friday" (4)—offers one foothold for interpretation, and many students like the security such footholds provide. But the intertext doesn't clearly ground or explain the book's unruly satiric energies. This happens often when satire joins forces with allegory, even in texts where these modes are more fully sustained and intrinsic to textual meaning. Rushdie's most consistently satiric novel, *Shame* (1983), allegorizes Pakistan's ruling elite of the 1970s and seems to offer a stable satiric thrust: main characters have clear real-life counterparts, and it is the clown-like Zia and Bhutto equivalents who are most responsible for the various ills—neocolonialism, oppression of women, infantilizing neglect of the body politic—that line up in the satirist's sights. The women in question, however, are elite women oppressed by fathers and husbands; the ordinary women and men who compose that neglected body politic are invisible. Indeed, by narrowing its field of vision so much that it leaves out the very people who suffer most from its tyrants, *Shame* invites discussion of class, resistance, and whether this entire novel, like Achebe's final paragraph, should be admired or interrogated for enacting the exclusive, blinkered vision it critiques.[5] Nonetheless, as it channels its satiric energies through female members of the ruling families—Rani, Bilquìs, Arjumand, the Shakil sisters, and, most powerfully, Sufiya, the victim-turned-victimizer monster figure who embodies an extreme satiric spirit of humiliation-cum-annihilation—*Shame* invites further discussion of gender in this most male-identified of genres and male-dominated of societies. Rushdie's fantastical dark fairy tale can further prompt students to discover satire's compatibility with the inherent instability of the monstrous and grotesque.[6]

Bernardine Evaristo's *Blonde Roots* (2008) similarly offers a seemingly clear allegorical hook: like Selvon's *Moses Ascending*, it presents itself as a racial role-reversal allegory, with transatlantic slavery reimagined as a history of "blak" masters enslaving and transporting "whytes" to overseas plantations in the "West Japanese Islands." With its humorous mash-up of historical and twenty-first-century referents, its blend of genres (speculative fiction, slave narrative, antiabolitionist tract), and its topsy-turvy geography (recognizably shaped but rearranged continents Europa, Aphrika, and Amarika), *Blonde Roots*'s galvanizing counterfactual question (what if?) prompts an inquiry not only into the physical, psychological, and emotional experience of slavery (the usual stuff of slave narratives) but also into racialized thinking writ large.

It does so, however, in a discomfiting and destabilizing environment. When traditional referents for racism and slavery are upended, even the most overt instances of satire get complicated. Book 2 of Evaristo's narrative consists of an outrageously self-justifying publication by Chief Kaga Konata Katamba, a.k.a. Bwana, the blak master of whyte slave Doris, protagonist and narrator of books 1 and 3. After a parodically eighteenth-century-style title page, Bwana's Menippean entries in "*The Flame*" expose how effortlessly and arbitrarily racial/cultural otherness can be constructed and denigrated. He ruminates complacently on the superiority of "the capacious skull of the Negroid" and the brain it encases over those of the "Caucasoinid" (119, 121), on whytes' inability to suffer from "physical 'pain'" (120), and on slavery as a "Mission of Liberation" in which "Europane slaves have been saved from the most horrendous deaths, punishments, morally reprehensible indulgences and serfdom, whilst being given the opportunity to adopt the manners and customs of civilised men" (121). Bwana is clearly a butt of satire, but what does he represent exactly? Is there a stable target and a clear intention underlying this outsized creation? Students will readily identify *The Flame* as an exemplar of the sort of racist and colonialist discourses that justified transatlantic slavery, reoriented around a blak-is-best normativity. But does Evaristo's satire point firmly to the past, or does it have present-day relevance (since there is arguably little point in satirizing discourses that no longer hold sway)? Put another way, does Bwana's text parodically critique European proslavery and antiabolitionist discourses specifically, or does its upside-down racist logic universalize those discourses—even, thereby, exonerating Europeans and implicating Africans—by showing how alarmingly easily racist discourses might be transferred to and replicated by their original victims—or any other group with the intent and wherewithal to subordinate? If the normative position the novel asks readers to share is that slavery and racism demean both sides of the encounter, and if for all its dehistoricizing play the text rests on that foundation and conveys that message, is it saying anything new or just colorizing old ideas? Is the novel (including Doris's less wholly satiric narrative) more rewarding if we see it not as targeted attack but as exploratory, playful inquiry into the ways discursive constructions of difference manifested themselves in slavery and continue their seductive, disruptive ways?

Asking such questions (less rhetorically in the classroom than in summary form here) about the novel's unmooring of well-known frameworks can lead to lively class debates. Two term papers in my 2010 honors seminar on postcolonial fiction enthusiastically took on *Blonde Roots*'s multivalent complexities and engaged in sophisticated ways with its satire. For Rachael Wyatt, "Though many critics have described the novel as satiric, it does not have the conventional thrust of a satire. In looking at the novel as a whole, the reader expects to find some target: perhaps the novel critiques modern assumptions about slavery, our own comfortable dominant narratives or the prejudices and cultural artefacts that remain in the wake of slavery." Attending as much to the novel's postmodern as satiric elements and to its defamiliarizing play with consumer culture as with slavery, Wyatt concluded that "the distance imposed by a combination of parody, pastiche and comic translation keeps the novel from having an overriding ethical or moral agenda." Ashlee Joyce, acknowledging reviewers' complaints that *Blonde Roots* lacks new perspectives on slavery, argued,

> Evaristo does not seek to establish new perspectives as much as she seeks to reinvent old ones. She achieves this reinvention . . . by parodying the conventional slave narrative through ironic inversion, and manipulating the language that surrounds popular ideologies established by the slave narrative. . . . In doing so Evaristo satirises the process by which these arbitrary ideologies become established by the dominant social order, and ultimately subverts them.

Joyce commends the novel's lack of closure, concluding that it

> transcend[s] race in order to broaden readers' perception of slavery from that of a phenomenon only victimizing blacks, to that of a shared experience of the process by which arbitrary social norms are imposed. Evaristo does not seek to impose new conclusions to the slave narrative, but to open up channels of discussion that were previously thought to be closed. To be prescriptive would be to limit the very channels *Blonde Roots* succeeds in opening.

For both students, satire is but one of several modes worth interrogating in the novel, and to the degree that it is a defining one, it is so in the exploratory, open-ended way Griffin advocates more than the norm-driven, attack-oriented way of older models.

Satire's instability, indirection, and resistance to closure and singular meaning can make it a useful springboard to broader hermeneutic questions about contemporary fiction, satiric or not. And satire's fondness for irony can prompt discussion of how what Linda Hutcheon calls "discursive communities" form (or fail to form) among the culturally and geographically disparate, dispersed readers and writers of postcolonial fiction in particular (91). In today's universities, particularly those whose multicultural student bodies begin to resemble that diffuse global audience, reading postcolonial fiction for its variously dualistic and multivalent satiric forays can generate bracing debates about the perils of (mis)representation, the ethics of judgment, the politics of race, and the mutuality and mutability of literary meaning.

Notes

1. Satire—a notorious borrower and/or infiltrator of other genres—also appears in postcolonial poetry (e.g., Derek Walcott, Louise Bennett-Coverley) and drama (Wole Soyinka). However, the emphasis in this essay, as with most research and teaching of literature from former British colonies, is on fiction.

2. For an analysis of this paragraph as satire, see Ball, pp. 86–90.

3. See, for instance, discrete chapters involving the characters Winterbottom and Clarke in Achebe's *Arrow of God*, Browning and Smith in Yvonne Vera's *Nehanda*, or Mr. Slime in George Lamming's *In the Castle of My Skin*.

4. Postcolonial scholarship often eschews "universals" in favor of historical and cultural particulars since the former can erase differences through presumptively humanist and Eurocentric concerns.

5. See Ahmad, pp. 137–39; Ball, pp. 136–37.

6. I teach *Shame* frequently in a course called Monsters and the Grotesque in Literature.

Works Cited

Achebe, Chinua. *Things Fall Apart.* 1958. Heinemann, 1965.
Ahmad, Aijaz. *In Theory: Nations, Classes, Literatures.* Verso, 1992.
Ashcroft, Bill, et al. *The Empire Writes Back: Theory and Practice in Post-colonial Literatures.* Routledge, 1989.
Ball, John Clement. *Satire and the Postcolonial Novel: V. S. Naipaul, Chinua Achebe, Salman Rushdie.* Routledge, 2003.
Bogel, Fredric V. *The Difference Satire Makes: Rhetoric and Reading from Jonson to Byron.* Cornell UP, 2001.
Evaristo, Bernardine. 2008. *Blonde Roots.* Penguin, 2009.
Griffin, Dustin. *Satire: A Critical Reintroduction.* UP of Kentucky, 1994.
Hutcheon, Linda. *Irony's Edge: The Theory and Politics of Irony.* Routledge, 1994.
Palmeri, Frank. *Satire in Narrative: Petronius, Swift, Gibbon, Melville, and Pynchon.* U of Texas P, 1990.
Rushdie, Salman. *Imaginary Homelands: Essays and Criticism 1981–1991.* Granta, 1991.
———. *Shame.* 1983. Vintage, 1997.
Selvon, Sam. *Moses Ascending.* 1975. Heinemann, 1984.

Part IV

Visual Satire

Michael J. Conlon

The Eye and the Text

As for pure satire—there the eye is supreme.

—Wyndham Lewis

In the interest of teaching students the visual character and concerns of satire, I propose an approach that covers three related topics: the rhetorical and visual components of satire; the uses of caricature and the grotesque in satire; the double embrace and suspicion of the visual by satirists from the eighteenth century to the present. From a pedagogical perspective, this approach presumes that students will bring to their study some experience reading satire and more experience viewing it, whether through television, the internet, comics, or movies. This may be an opportunity, therefore, for them to question and reflect on how satiric texts and images mix and interact.

Talking to the Eye

By most accounts, the art of satire owes much to the classical writings on rhetoric and to what Jens E. Kjeldsen calls "talking to the eye" (133). From "rhetoric came the ideal of vivacious imagery, of enargia, of visual palpability and lifelikeness" (Hagstrum 174). Giving evidence in an argument meant creating a picture of the subject (the Latin *evidentia* comes from the verb *videre*, "to see"). And the importance of "talking to the eye" was not lost on the great classical satirists Horace and Juvenal or on the poets and novelists of eighteenth-century England, the so-called age of satire. "The central project of [early modern] satire," Katherine Mannheimer reminds us, "was to perform a kind of visual pedagogy on the reader—by [not only] engaging the reader's visual imagination, but also controlling the reader's actual and immediate acts of looking and seeing" (1). She goes on to show how Alexander Pope's *An Epistle to Dr. Arbuthnot* (1735) perfectly captures the convergence of the verbal and the visual. When Arbuthnot cautions Pope to refrain from attacking the profligate courtier Lord John Hervey, Pope responds with his portrait of Hervey as Sporus (lines 305–30), a "creature" of specious appeal: a "bug with gilded wings" and "painted child of dirt," with a "Cherub's face, a Reptile all the rest," and, finally, "Beauty that shocks you." Here it's helpful to pause and read Margaret Atherton's essay "How to Write the History of Vision." Her reading of George Berkeley's *Essay towards a New Theory of Vision* (1709) explains how Pope, Jonathan Swift, and their circle understood the idea of the "educated eye."

Satirists also used the typography and visual features of their texts, playing against their readers' expectations about how a book or poem should "look." Swift's *A Tale of a Tub* (1704), Pope's *The Dunciad* (1743), Laurence Sterne's *The Life and Opinions of Tristram Shandy* (1759–67), Edwin Abbott's story of a two-dimensional universe called *Flatland* (1884), the poems of E. E. Cummings, and more recently the poetry and prose of Ishmael Reed offer striking examples of satirists controlling how readers see the text as they read it. William Makepeace Thackeray not only called his most esteemed satiric novel *Vanity Fair* (1847–48) but also added the subtitle *Pen and Pencil Sketches of English Society* and executed those sketches himself in order to catch the reader's eye and provide a visual counterpoint to the narrator's description of events and characters.

Ekphrasis, the verbal representation of a visual representation, in both verse and prose, puts in sharp relief for students how satirists use the visual arts to "disturb" the reader and provoke a response. James A. W. Heffernan makes the point in his rich study of ekphrasis, *Museum of Words* (1993): "To represent a painting or sculpted figure in words is to evoke its power—the power to fix, excite, amaze, entrance, disturb, or intimidate the viewer—even as language strives to keep that power under control" (7). All of this happens in striking fashion in the British writer Blake Morrison's dramatic monologue "Teeth," published in an anthology of ekphrases titled *With a Poet's Eye* (1986). A wealthy businessman and art collector, showing off his home to an associate, pauses before "his Francis Bacon":

> And here—come closer—framed so you can
> See yourself in it, my Francis Bacon,
> Early, yes, but far from an apprentice piece
> So the experts reassure me. . . . (lines 1–4)

The poem's occasion and words recall the first words of the duke to the envoy in Robert Browning's "My Last Duchess" (1842): "That's my last Duchess painted on the wall, / Looking as if she were still alive" (lines 1–2). Indeed, as Morrison's monologue unfolds, traces of content from Browning's show through and form a palimpsest: both speakers covet their art objects; both have fought with wives, who then met their deaths under questionable circumstances; both are possessive and jealous; and both relish their power over people and their art collections. In the last stanza of "Teeth," the speaker, anxious to talk business, dismisses the subject of Bacon's portrait, a screaming pope inspired by Diego Velázquez's portrait of Pope Innocent X from around 1650 (fig. 1):

> But notice, as you pass, how the steady
> Eyes of that Pope seem to accuse and track
> Us, as if we'd personally stretched him on that rack.
> Just an artist's trick, friend—no need to get
> Jumpy. We'll see that bastard roasting yet. (lines 60–64)

The words allude to the grimacing figure of Bacon's pope—by all accounts an image of power made vulnerable. The pope's eyes burn through the boastful words of the businessman just as the duchess's smile in Fra Pandolf's painting subverts and prevails over the lecture the duke has given the envoy on what he expects from his next wife.[1]

My last example of the satirist's "talking to the eye" is Nathanael West's *The Day of the Locust* (1939), in John Hollander's phrasing a "notional ekphrasis," or the representation of an imaginary work of art (209). The events of the novel loop through descriptions of the protagonist Tod Hackett's painting *The Burning of Los Angeles*, inspired by the Italian masters of caricature and the grotesque. West uses the artist's eye to penetrate the specious character of Hollywood. The houses Tod sees on the slopes

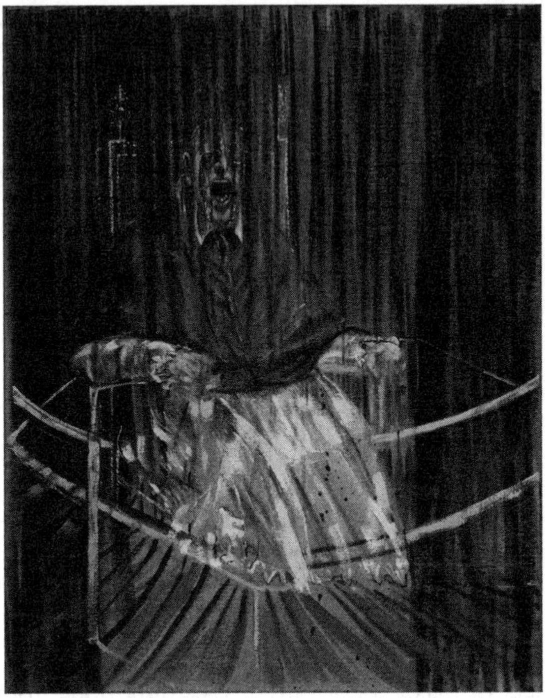

Figure 1. Francis Bacon, *Study after Velázquez's Portrait of Pope Innocent X*. After 1953. © Des Moines Art Center.

of the canyon are so many facades made to look like something else, and the metaphor of the "false front" extends to the people. They are not what they appear to be: "The fat lady in the yachting cap was going shopping, not boating; the man in the Norfolk Jacket and Tyrolean hat was returning, not from a mountain, but an insurance office; and the girl in slacks and sneaks with a bandanna around her head had just left a switchboard, not a tennis court" (22).

Caricature and the Grotesque

Satirists have habitually learned and borrowed from the visual arts of caricature and the grotesque. The word *caricature*, introduced by the Italian painter Annibale Carracci (1560–1609), comes from the Italian word caricare, meaning "to load," "to charge," or exaggerate a portrait in order to capture a person's true character. Satiric caricatures in the eighteenth century, Mark Hallett points out, "consistently engaged with texts" like George Bickham's 1743 caricature of Sir Robert Walpole (9). Bickham included revised lines from the October 1743 reissue of Pope's *The Dunciad.* He shows Walpole's large head collapsing into a yawn and linking the "great" man's spent and corrupt ministry to the reign of the goddess Dulness over the nation (fig. 2).

Caricature, Ernst Kris writes, is "a deliberate transformation of features in which faults and weaknesses of the victim are exaggerated and brought to light" (189). Henry Fielding's Parson Trulliber, the keeper of hogs in *Joseph Andrews* (1742), is, in both character and appearance, a hog and figure of gluttony (141–46). Trulliber's porcine traits remind us that from its earliest examples, caricature plays with the transformation of humans into animals, an art Francis Grose promotes in his *Rules for Drawing Caricature* (1788). The transformation of human to beast "play[s] upon an anxiety . . . that our moral condition as beasts may begin to show itself in our bodies" (Sherry 59), and we have a memorable example in Eugène Ionesco's satire on mass movements in his play *Rhinoceros* (1959).

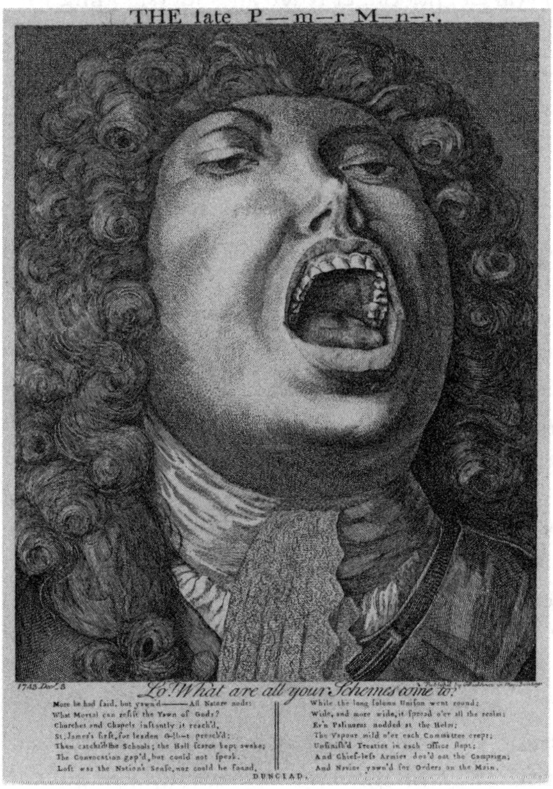

Figure 2. George Bickham the Younger, *The Late Prime Minister.* 1743. © The Trustees of the British Museum.

Ionesco's play brings into sharp relief the dialectic of word and image. Humanity begins with speech, which gradually dies as the French villagers transform into beasts. When the first rhinoceros appears on the main street of the village, speech quickly descends into strings of platitudes, exclamations, and bits of fractured logic: "A Rhinoceros!" "Well, I'll be . . ." "Well, of all things!" (9–10). An old man concedes to a man called the Logician that his dog must be a cat, and patrons of a café argue over the number of horns on the rhinoceros. Rational conversation turns to prattle, and an overbearing, self-absorbed patron named Jean berates his companion, Berenger, over his appearance: "I feel ashamed to be your friend" (6). Jean's eventual transformation into a rhinoceros, together with everyone in the village except Berenger, captures the dynamic of mass movements. People lose their voices, eyes, and minds. The menacing beasts suddenly look beautiful to the villagers, and Ionesco's caricature of Jean as a rhinoceros strikes the audience as nothing less than an extension of his character. When "people no longer share your opinion," Ionesco explains in *Notes and Counter Notes*, "when you can no longer reach an understanding with them, you have the impression you are trying to get through to monsters. . . . They would kill you without a qualm if you did not think as they do. And in the last quarter of this century history has given us clear proof that people transformed in this way are not just like, but truly become rhinoceroses" (205).

Ionesco's monsters bring us to the grotesque, and by definition, Northrop Frye insists, "satire demands at least a token fantasy . . . which the reader recognizes as grotesque" (224). The complicated history of the word, which originally meant "grotto-like" and referred to certain kinds of fanciful, harmless decorations, should give students pause and time to consider the challenges of defining terms that accumulate contradictory meanings over time. Wolfgang Kayser's *The Grotesque in Art and Literature* (1957) is the classic study of the subject, but M. M. Bakhtin offers a different, even liberating view of the grotesque in *Rabelais and His World* (1965). Satire approaches the grotesque, in Geoffrey Harpham's phrase, as a "species of confusion" (xxi). Flannery O'Connor's *Wise Blood* (1952) uses this sense of the grotesque and its metaphors of deformation to alienate her reader from what she perceives as fundamentalist perversions of Christianity. *Wise Blood* opens to us like the panels of a triptych, showing the stages of Hazel Mote's unsuccessful attempt to fight off any belief in Christ and the redemption by creating and preaching the benefits of his "Church Without Christ" (71). Images that mix humans and animals drive the satire and evoke in the reader a sense of alienation, a strategy, Susan Edmunds suggests, O'Connor takes from Bertolt Brecht (185). "A representation that alienates," Brecht explains, allows us to recognize its subject but at the same time makes it seem unfamiliar. We see the subject afresh "with an astonished eye" (144).

The Madness of Vision

While satirists frequently deploy the visual, they also deplore what Maurice Merleau-Ponty called, in his posthumously published book *The Visible and Invisible* (1968), "the madness in vision" (75). The book reflects the modern and postmodern interrogation of the visual that began in earnest with Friedrich Nietzsche (1844–1900) and Henri Bergson (1859–1941) in the fin de siècle but goes back to suspicions of the visual in the eighteenth century in the satires of Pope, Swift, and their circle. *Gulliver's Travels* (1726) repeatedly conveys Swift's skepticism over the empiricists' faith in direct observation and highlights Gulliver's moments of disorientation and misjudgments of distance and size. Swift finds much that fools the eye, and Gulliver's unreliable sight reflects his limited insight. Like all of us, he never completely and accurately sees himself or fully knows himself, remaining to the end dependent on either mediating devices or the eyes of others.

Martin Jay points out that in the modern critique of ocularcentrism the "visual was still the privileged sense, but what that privilege produced in the modern world was damned as almost entirely pernicious" (384). This included the way looking could lead to idolatry, voyeurism, the more disturbing effects of the gaze, and the uses of surveillance and spectacle by the state.

The pernicious uses of surveillance singled out by Michel Foucault occur in a number of modern dystopias, among them Yevgeny Zamyatin's *We* (1924) and Margaret Atwood's *The Handmaid's Tale* (1985). *We*, written in 1920–21, consists of the journal entries of D-503, the principal designer of the Integral, a rocket that the One State will send "soar[ing] into cosmic space," the government's ultimate goal being the "subjugat[ion of] the unknown beings of other planets, who may still be living in the primitive condition of freedom, to the beneficent yoke of reason" (1). The Numbers of One State "live behind . . . transparent walls that seem woven of gleaming air—[they] are always visible, always washed in light. [They] have nothing to conceal from one another [and] this makes much easier the difficult and nobel task of the Guardians" (19). Zamyatin also connects the coercive use of surveillance to the spatialization of time, achieved in the One State by applying Frederick Winslow Taylor's principles of time management—another form of scrutiny—to the lives of workers.

In Atwood's Republic of Gilead, the dystopian theocracy of *The Handmaid's Tale*, orthodoxy is maintained by an agency of the state called the Eyes. The acts of looking, gazing, and spying connect politics and sex in Gilead, where declining births have led the authorities to designate and control handmaids, who are valued for their viable ovaries. When the handmaid and narrator, Offred, goes for a walk, wearing a full-length red dress, red gloves, and a cap with white wings "to keep us from seeing," a Guardian asks to see her pass. He bends his head "to try to get a look at my face. I raise my head a little, to help him, and he sees my eyes and I see his, and he blushes" (21). She is tempted to put her hand on his face, but he turns away. She calls it a "small defiance of rule" and imagines visiting him in the night and showing herself to him. This image is followed by the appearance of the Eyes in a "black painted van, with the winged Eye in white on the side. The windows of the van are dark-tinted, and the men in the front seats wear dark glasses: a double obscurity" (21–22). Both the image of the van and Offred's encounter with the Guardian capture the state's control over and surveillance of sexuality.

Two important critiques of the visual, Guy Debord's *Society of the Spectacle* (1967) and Jean Baudrillard's *Simulacra and Simulation* (1981), provide a context for reading Don DeLillo's novel *White Noise* (1985), a satiric novel about the Gladney family, which in several ways takes Martin Heidegger's idea of the "world as picture" as its premise. An early episode, and the subject of much comment, provides a benchmark for the themes of simulation and spectacle that thread the novel. Jack Gladney's friend Murray takes him to see "the most photographed barn in America." They stand at a distance and watch the photographers, and Murray tells Jack that "[n]o one sees the barn." They are there to sustain a "collective perception" of it. They are "taking pictures of taking pictures," and whatever the barn was before it was photographed no longer exists (12–13). The Gladney family lives in the "world as picture," bewitched by the lure of spectacle and captivated by anything that is mediated and simulated on television or in film or the tabloids. In addition to the writings of Debord and Baudrillard, students will find a rich and illuminating context for *White Noise* in Walker Percy's essay "The Loss of the Creature," a meditation on the increasing difficulty to get beyond the preformed, mediated, and prepackaged to see "the Thing itself" (47).

The three topics—talking to the eye in satire; caricature and the grotesque; the satirist's dual embrace and suspicion of the visual—do not, of course, exhaust the subject. Visual studies and the so-called pictorial turn have inspired a huge number of articles, books, and journals devoted to the relationship between image and word (Mitchell 11–34). In the case of satire, students have much to learn from its optical devices, images, mirrors, glasses, spectacles, scopes, and tableaux, but a full review of the subject is beyond the limits of this essay. By way of closure, however, I encourage students to consider my three topics in the context of Norman Daly's exhibition entitled *The Civilization of Llhuros: An Exhibition of Artifacts from Recent Excavations of Vanibo, Houndee, Draikum and Other Sites* (1972). The exhibition is an elaborate parody consisting of some 150 carefully referenced artifacts. Think of Gulliver upon his return from Lilliput or Brobdingnag presenting his "Collection of Rarities" in an exhibit at the Royal Society. Some Llhuroscian artifacts are grotesque, others are ludicrous, but the the exhibition as a whole draws the spectator into a kind of "charade" or visual riddle, and its satire on contemporary civilization astonishes the eye.

Note

1. Tamar Yacobi comments at length on the poem's allusions to Browning's "My Last Duchess" in "Ekphrastic Double Exposure."

Works Cited

Atherton, Margaret. "How to Write the History of Vision: Understanding the Relationship between Berkeley and Descartes." *Sites of Vision: The Discursive Construction of Sight in the History of Philosophy*, edited by David Michael Levin, MIT P, 1993, pp. 139–65.

Atwood, Margaret. *The Handmaid's Tale*. Anchor Books, 1986.

Bakhtin, M. M. *Rabelais and His World*. Translated by Helene Iswolsky, Indiana UP, 1984.

Baudrillard, Jean. *Simulacra and Simulation*. Translated by Sheila Faria Glaser, U of Michigan P, 1994.

Brecht, Bertolt. *Brecht on Theatre: The Development of an Aesthetic*. Edited and translated by John Willett, Hill and Wang, 1992.

Browning, Robert. "My Last Duchess." *Selected Poetry*, Random House, 1951, pp. 51–53.

Daly, Norman. *The Civilization of Llhuros: An Exhibition of Artifacts from Recent Excavations of Vanibo, Houndee, Draikum and Other Sites*. 1972. Civilization of Llhuros, civilizationofllhuros.org.

Debord, Guy. *Society of the Spectacle.* Translated by Ken Knabb, Rebel Press, 2005.

DeLillo, Don. *White Noise.* Penguin, 1986.

Edmunds, Susan. *Grotesque Relations: Modernist Domestic Fiction and the U.S. Welfare State.* Oxford UP, 2008.

Fielding, Henry. *Joseph Andrews.* Edited by Douglas Brooks-Davies, Oxford UP, 1999.

Frye, Northrop. *Anatomy of Criticism: Four Essays.* Princeton UP, 1957.

Grose, Francis. *Rules for Drawing Caricature: With an Essay on Comic Painting.* London, 1788.

Hagstrum, Jean H. "Verbal and Visual Caricature in the Age of Dryden, Swift, and Pope." *England in the Restoration and Early Eighteenth Century: Essays on Culture and Society*, edited by H. T. Swedenberg, Jr., U of California P, 1972, pp. 173–95.

Hallett, Mark. *The Spectacle of Difference: Graphic Satire in the Age of Hogarth.* Yale UP, 1999.

Harpham, Geoffrey Galt. *On the Grotesque: Strategies of Contradiction in Art and Literature.* Princeton UP, 1982.

Heffernan, James A. W. *Museum of Words: The Poetics of Ekphrasis from Homer to Ashbery.* U of Chicago P, 1993.

Hollander, John. "The Poetics of Ekphrasis." *Word and Image*, vol. 4, no. 1, 1988, pp. 209–19.

Ionesco, Eugène. *Notes and Counter Notes: Writings on the Theatre.* Translated by Donald Watson, Grove, 1964.

———. Rhinoceros *and Other Plays.* Translated by Derek Prouse, Grove, 1960.

Jay, Martin. *Downcast Eyes: The Denigration of Vision in Twentieth-Century French Thought.* U of California P, 1994.

Kayser, Wolfgang. *The Grotesque in Art and Literature.* Translated by Ulrich Weisstein, McGraw-Hill, 1966.

Kjeldsen, Jens E. "Talking to the Eye: Visuality in Ancient Rhetoric." *Word and Image*, vol. 19, no. 3, 2003, pp. 133–37.

Kris, Ernst. *Psychoanalytic Explorations in Art.* Schocken Books, 1964.

Mannheimer, Katherine. *Print, Visuality, and Gender in Eighteenth-Century Satire: "The Scope in Ev'ry Page."* Routledge, 2011.

Merleau-Ponty, Maurice. *The Visible and Invisible.* Edited by Claude Lefort, translated by Alphonso Lingis, Northwestern UP, 1968.

Mitchell, W. J. T. *Picture Theory: Essays on Verbal and Visual Representation.* U of Chicago P, 1994.

Morrison, Blake. "Teeth." *With a Poet's Eye: A Tate Gallery Anthology*, edited by Pat Adams, 2nd ed., Tate Gallery, 1993, pp. 128–30.

O'Connor, Flannery. *Wise Blood. Collected Works*, edited by Sally Fitzgerald, Library of America, 1988, pp. 3–131.

Percy, Walker. "The Loss of the Creature." *The Message in the Bottle: How Queer Man Is, How Queer Language Is, and What One Has to Do with the Other*, by Percy, Farrar, Straus and Giroux, 1980, pp. 46–63.

Pope, Alexander. *An Epistle to Dr. Arbuthnot. Poetry and Prose of Alexander Pope*, edited by Aubrey L. Williams, Houghton Mifflin, 1969, pp. 197–211.

Sherry, James. "Four Modes of Caricature: Reflections upon a Genre." *Bulletin of Research in the Humanities*, vol. 1, 1986–87, pp. 29–62.
Swift, Jonathan. *Gulliver's Travels*. Edited by Claude Rawson, Oxford UP, 2005.
West, Nathanael. *The Day of the Locust*. Signet, 1983.
Yacobi, Tamar. "Ekphrastic Double Exposure: Blake Morrison, Francis Bacon, Robert Browning, and Fra Pandolf as Four-in-One." *On Verbal/Visual Representation*, edited by Martin Heusser et al., Rodopi, 2005, pp. 219–27.
Zamyatin, Yevgeny. *We*. Translated by Mirra Ginsburg, Avon Books, 1987.

Frank Palmeri

Narrative and Graphic Satire in Nineteenth-Century England

My upper-division course on fictional and visual satire in nineteenth-century Britain focuses on a time when satire undergoes a transition in the forms it assumes. From the mid-1840s to the late 1880s, in both print and visual culture in Britain, satire ceases to figure as the primary form, even though there was little or no state censorship to suppress satiric criticism of policies and institutions. However, in these decades, as Guinevere Griest shows in *Mudie's Circulating Library and the Victorian Novel*, the circulating libraries exerted a nearly monopolistic control of novelistic content; readers' reports singled out elements that would violate Mudie's standard for decency—material should be fit for young girls' eyes. In such circumstances, most authors and artists evaded censorship by self-censoring; they avoided deviations from middle-class decorum in relation to both sexual and radical political matter.

In this period, narrative is dominated by the realistic novel of Charles Dickens, George Eliot, Elizabeth Gaskell, and Anthony Trollope and by the sensation novel of Mary Elizabeth Braddon, Wilkie Collins, and Ouida. Satire appears in long narratives only in fugitive and episodic ways—for example, in the caricatured figures and subplots of Dickens's novels—almost always subordinated to a larger comic, tragic, or gothic design. William Makepeace Thackeray's *Vanity Fair* (1847–48) constitutes almost the last instance of a thoroughly satiric narrative for about forty years, Trollope's *The Way We Live Now* (1875) being a comparable exception later in the period. In graphic art, the fierce political satire of James Gillray and George Cruikshank from the 1790s to the early 1820s fades away in the 1830s, with only a brief return to strong satiric form in the early years of *Punch* from 1842 to 1845; the radical graphic satire of Charles Jameson Grant also continues just into the 1840s. But graphic satire from the late 1840s to the late 1880s is confined almost entirely to comic periodicals such as *Punch*, *Judy*, and *Fun*, which provided only mild social satire and did not stray far from the middle of the political spectrum, aside from the exceptions of the short-lived periodical *Tomahawk* (1867–70) and the first few years of *The Graphic* from 1869 to 1873.

It might seem then that the course addresses the difficult task of studying a phenomenon that is *not* present, discerning the operations of a genre that is not at work in the period. In fact, the course examines the ways that the energies of satiric form were diverted into other forms. Although courses on genres, including satire, would usually focus on periods when they are prominent, it is also worth attending to periods, like that between 1850 and 1890 in England, when satiric energies have been hidden, suppressed, or displaced. Parallels in American history raise the same question: in the United States, a time of effervescent satiric productivity from 1960 to 1980 was bracketed by two twenty-year periods when satiric dissent became the exception rather than the rule.

In the fifty years before Victoria assumed the throne in 1837, political satire flourished, both in verbal and visual forms, despite government efforts to control speech and expression through various means, including the Treason Trials of 1794–95 and the Gagging Bills of 1820. This strong satiric activity peaked in the mid- and late 1790s and again in the years around 1820. In order to establish a baseline or point of reference and comparison at the beginning of the course, we read two strongly satiric works from this latter period: Byron's *Don Juan* (cantos 1–3 [1819–20]) and Thomas Love Peacock's *Nightmare Abbey* (1818). Both of these works satirize the Romantic poets, even though Byron was arguably a Romantic himself and Peacock was a friend of Byron, Shelley, and the others whom he mocked. In addition, Byron satirizes through parody the conventions of epic—"I want a hero" (1.1)—and the concluding couplets of his stanzas typically demystify, lower, or expose pretense, hypocrisy, or claims of high-minded triumph over the material and physical. Both works are open-ended; both maintain ideological and philosophical oppositions unresolved. Both frustrate processes of identification by readers with characters, introducing instead a pervasive irony, epitomized by the labile narrator's voice in Byron's poem. Neither subscribes to a narrative of progress: both envision the persistent reign of the corrupt and the silly.

Cruikshank's satiric images from the years around 1820 provide near analogs of the verbal satire of Byron and Peacock—in particular the pamphlets he produced in collaboration with William Hone from 1818 to 1821, especially *The Political House That Jack Built* (1819). In these brilliant satires, Hone parodied children's rhymes, while in the accompanying illustrations, Cruikshank employed a simple, even crude style to caricature government ministers, bishops, and other officials, not excepting the prince regent. At the end of *Political House*, Cruikshank represents a printing press as the "Thing" that can expose the malfeasance and corruption of government and church.[1] But after the Six Acts, or Gagging Bills, were passed in 1820, he depicts a "Free Born Englishman" in rags, his lips shut by a huge padlock, arms and legs in irons, a sword of justice twisted and broken at his feet, and an ax labeled the "Law of Libel" whole and sharp beside it.[2]

At this point, perhaps two and a half weeks into the semester, one must decide whether to include a Victorian novel with satiric elements. Two of Dickens's novels, *Oliver Twist* (1838) and *Hard Times* (1854), present good and usable choices here. In both works, a sharp but one-sided satiric critique gives way to other concerns and genres. In the earlier novel, after the satire of the Poor Law of 1834 and of the fatuous workhouse administrator Bumble, the narrative works through the conventions of a Newgate novel and a thriller to restore Oliver to his rightful status as a middle-class boy. In *Hard Times*, after the strong but again one-directional satire of vulgar utilitarian thought and pedagogy, the novel traces the tragic consequences of Gradgrind's philosophy in the lives of his two children and the alternate comic vision of the circus people who cultivate the life of the imagination. Both narratives are predominantly comic, generic hybrids, with elements of melodrama, crime, suspense, and satire contributing to the overarching form. But they are not predominantly open-ended, double-voiced, or parodic satires.

Whether or not one has included a novel such as these two by Dickens, the course can now turn to the major work of the term, the paths by which satire played a substantive role in shaping narrative forms outside the novel. Of these forms, three of the most important were children's literature, science fiction, and utopian/dystopian fiction. Four works published between 1865 and 1875 demonstrate the availability and usefulness of these forms for satiric purposes: Lewis Carroll's *Alice's Adventures in Wonderland* (1865) and *Through the Looking-Glass* (1871), Edward Bulwer-Lytton's *The Coming Race* (1871), and Samuel Butler's *Erewhon* (1872).

In the worlds Alice encounters in her adventures, plays on words and puns abound, leading conversations in unforeseen and unconventional directions. Peculiar forms of reasoning often derail expectations, being either excessively, strictly logical (but nonsensical) or almost entirely illogical. But amid the welter of literal interpretations and bewildering inferences, certain constants emerge. Chief among these recurring features: the other characters, whether playing cards, chess pieces, or unusual animals, are almost always correcting, reprimanding, or even threatening Alice. When the Duchess hears Alice say that the world revolves on its axis, that reminds her: "Talking of axes," she pronounces, "chop off her head!" (62). The modes of meaning-making among adults and authorities in these worlds are opaque and disorienting to the child Alice. In another disconcerting pattern, one law that continues in force is the law of the stronger: at the end of "The Walrus and the Carpenter," none of the little oysters responds to the Carpenter's final question, "And this was scarcely odd, because / They'd eaten every one" (166). The *Alice* books, in other words, satirize the social and political order of the adult world, the nonsense that passes for sense, and the illogicality of strict logic. Carroll's satire is consistently skeptical, antididactic, and covertly political.

Butler's satire in *Erewhon* works in a similar way. The strange society the narrator discovers seems at first to present an upside-down or backward world. But on reflection we may recognize that Anglo-American society also treats some crimes as evidence of sickness, or at least an illness of the mind, that warrants treatment rather than punishment. Much more disturbing, we may also realize that our society, like Butler's, may treat misfortune or sickness—accidents of birth, not determined by character—as crimes for which the poor and unfortunate continue to be punished unjustly throughout their lives. In addition, our schools may also be colleges of unreason, and perhaps our most advanced machines threaten to become our masters, rather than our servants, just as the Erewhonians believed. But then Butler's narrator steps back and declines to draw these implications, making a case instead against the extremism or fanaticism of strict logic and for the need to accept illogic in human affairs. He sees through the hypocrisy, inconsistency, cruelty, and inequity of his society but decides to accept its moral emptiness as necessary and not to press his critique. Still, his narrative radically undermines Victorian belief in the inevitability of material progress and moral growth.

By parallel means, Bulwer-Lytton arrives at a similar conclusion in *The Coming Race*. The society this narrator discovers within the earth is incredibly advanced: its inhabitants practice mental telepathy and control an apparently infinite source of electrical energy—vril—that lights their world, brings them health and vitality, and powers their laser-like hand weapons. Having overpowered their neighbors and solved all their internal problems, the Vril-ya live a peaceful utopian existence enjoying material plenty and aesthetic beauty. However, when the narrator becomes the object of desire of a young woman who is one of the most powerful, knowledgeable, and accomplished of the Vril-ya, he flees, terrified that he will be consumed by fire in her embraces, as Semele was when visited by Zeus. He returns to the upper world with the warning that the technologically superior Vril-ya will soon be coming to conquer it. The narrative implies both a fascination with and a deep fear of strong women and unlimited material progress, even though confidence in a beneficial and inevitable progress constituted a prime article of belief in dominant upper-middle-class Victorian society.

Graphic satire of the period reveals similar developments and displacements, although the images generally do not have as sharp a satiric bite as the fiction. For example, George du Maurier, one of the illustrators for *Punch*, helped turn that periodical away from a concern with social justice that marked its first five years toward comic, gently ironic portrayals of the fashionable upper middle class and its foibles and silliness. But in the 1860s and 1870s, he also worked with images that include fantastic, almost utopian elements of science fiction, as well as prints that adopt a child's perspective. His cartoons envisage advanced technologies such as videophones and the recording of musical performances and their storage in bottles, like wine, presenting such utopian ideas without much anxiety. On the other hand, some of the images produced from a child's point of view take the form of nightmares, communicating, like the *Alice* books, a sense of the threatening disorientation that the logic of the adult world produces in the young person.

One other form of representation contributed to the eventual return of satire in the 1890s: the representation of working-class men, women, and children outside of previously prevailing comic and sentimental modes, both in verbal and visual forms. An early precursor of this development, Luke

Fildes's famous "Houseless and Hungry," which appeared in the first issue of *The Graphic* in December 1869, depicts a line of workingmen, women, and children waiting in the cold for a place to sleep for the night.[3]

The science fiction of Jules Verne, which contains strong satire of the British empire, was for that reason heavily censored when it was translated into English. However, the publication of H. G. Wells's first science fiction, *The Time Machine* (1895), marks the 1890s as the decade when satire returned as a powerful, radical form in England. As the tale develops a view of the future based on evolutionary trends in labor, it becomes clear that the relations between the two anthropoid species that have developed eight hundred thousand years in the future reverse the progressive view of evolution. The small, soft, androgynous descendants of the Victorian owners of capital have become the source of meat for the fierce albino denizens of the future underworld—descendants of the Victorians workers—who continue to labor on machines that produce goods for their upper-class cattle. In his science-fictional extrapolation into the distant future, Wells's vision of Victorian owners and workers evolving into new species radically satirizes not only contemporaneous means of production but also the social Darwinist argument that evolution leads inevitably to the progressive improvement of the species.

Wells's science fiction does not constitute the only strong, radical satire from the 1890s to make use of genres that served as vehicles for more covert satire from mid-century on. In William Morris's *News from Nowhere* (1890), the satire of ugly and unjust industrial England emerges clearly, but mostly indirectly, by contrast with the utopian, anarchic future condition of England as Nowhere. Still, a few satiric details stand out, such as the conversion of the old Parliament buildings into giant barns for the storage of manure.

Oscar Wilde's fairy tales provide an equally striking instance of the return of strong, radical satire. For example, in "The Happy Prince" and "The Nightingale and the Rose," self-sacrificing love and aid for the poor lead to the deaths of birds that are misunderstood and unappreciated by a shallow, vain, hypocritical society, yet the tales accept such deaths unsentimentally as the way of the world. In addition, Wilde's dialogue/essay "The Decay of Lying" illustrates the importance of paradox in the emerging modernist paradigm. Indeed, after the 1890s, almost all satire is bound up with irony, even if not all irony is satiric.

A class on the return of strong visual political satire in the 1890s can examine some of Phil May's sharp, simple, but effective images of the urban poor—many of which appeared in *Punch*, thus bringing that serial full circle, back to its radical first years—along with some of F. C. Gould's satires of political events, which were the first political cartoons to appear regularly in a daily newspaper, the *Westminster Gazette*.[4]

Tracing the retreat, displacement, and reemergence of radical satire in the second half of the nineteenth century is not the same as addressing the reasons for such a cycle. At some point in the second half of the term, I direct attention to the effectiveness of the circulating libraries in restricting publication, by having the class read a chapter from Griest's *Mudie's Circulating Library*. We also consider the growth and waning of belief in the inevitability of progress during this half century, as well as the resurgence of the labor movement and the rise of socialist thought and activity in the 1880s. I try not to pursue a monocausal explanation of the retreat and return of radical narrative and graphic satire but to consider multiple conditions that made possible this episode in the history of the genre—and perhaps others, for example in the twentieth century.

Notes

1. Cruikshank and Hone's collaborations of 1819–21, including *The Political House That Jack Built*, have been reprinted in Rickword's *Radical Squibs and Loyal Ripostes*.

2. The possibility that legal efforts at censorship produce strong satire in response deserves being considered in the course.

3. Fildes later reworked this image into a large oil painting that became one of the early icons of social realism: see Korda.

4. Numerous interconnections link these forms: works of fantastic children's literature, such as Charles Kingsley's *The Water-Babies* (1863), helped prepare the way for a return of satire in Wells's science fiction of the 1890s. Similarly, in graphic forms, satiric energies that found an outlet in science fiction fantasies by Cruikshank (in *The Comic Almanack* [1835–53]) as well as by du Maurier prepared the way for depictions of street scenes of the poor, especially children, by Phil May around 1890 and the appearance of the first regular political cartoonists in newspapers of the 1890s. It is worth noting that not only are the narrative works for this course all in print but the graphic works too are widely available either in electronic form or on paper, many libraries possessing nearly complete runs of *Punch*, for example.

Works Cited

Bulwer-Lytton, Edward. *The Coming Race*. Edited by Peter W. Sinnema, Broadview Press, 2008.

Butler, Samuel. *Erewhon*. 1872. Edited by Peter Mudford, Penguin, 1985.

Byron, Lord (George Gordon). *The Major Works*. Edited by Jerome J. McGann, Oxford UP, 2008.
Carroll, Lewis. *Alice's Adventures in Wonderland*; *Through the Looking-Glass*. Signet Classic, 2000.
Griest, Guinevere L. *Mudie's Circulating Library and the Victorian Novel*. Indiana UP, 1970.
Korda, Andrea. *Printing and Painting the News in Victorian London:* The Graphic *and Social Realism, 1869–1891*. Ashgate, 2015.
Peacock, Thomas Love. *Nightmare Abbey*; *Crotchet Castle*. Edited by Raymond Wright, Penguin, 1986.
Rickword, Edgell, editor. *Radical Squibs and Loyal Ripostes: Satirical Pamphlets of the Regency Period, 1819–1821*. Barnes and Noble, 1971.
Wells, H. G. *The Time Machine*. Bantam, 2003.
Wilde, Oscar. *The Works of Oscar Wilde*. Walter J. Black, 1927.

Kerry Soper

Twentieth-Century Comic Strip Satire

At first glance, the mainstream comics page in twentieth-century American newspapers seems like an unpromising field for studying satire in a traditional, literary sense for several reasons: there were only a handful of strips in that century-long history that featured topical, politically engaged satire; a variety of commercial pressures and institutional filters often prevented cartoonists from engaging in cultural criticism or from exploring darker, Juvenalian tones in their comedy; and the lowbrow status of the medium prevented critics and academics from taking it seriously until recent decades. Upon closer examination, however, the accessibility of the medium gives students an inviting and familiar focus for exploring a variety of theoretical and practical issues related to how satire is created, distributed, and interpreted in contemporary society. In particular, an exploration of this medium allows one to study satire in both an expansive sense (including rowdy visual/verbal genres that thrived in twentieth-century entertainment media) and within a broad cultural context (considering how institutions, technology, and economics shape the meanings and uses of subversive comedy).

This brief essay lays out some of the key issues, concepts, and theoretical frames for studying satire in this medium. First, I describe ways to address visual/verbal and aesthetic qualities of the form. Second, I outline some of the most useful frames for studying comic strips that were explicitly topical and politically engaged in their satire (e.g., Al Capp's *Li'l Abner*, Walt Kelly's *Pogo*, Garry Trudeau's *Doonesbury*, Berke Breathed's *Bloom County*, Nicole Hollander's *Sylvia*, and Aaron McGruder's *The Boondocks*). In particular, I focus on methodologies that address the economic pressures and institutional filtering that shaped the medium and determined (sometimes delimiting and other times enabling) the kinds of satire it could feature. Third, I suggest ways for discussing comic strips that could be considered satiric within an expanded conception of the genre, including carnivalesque, cosmic, and deconstructive modes. That expanded umbrella allows one to study productively a variety of vivid and sometimes rowdy comedic works: *Hogan's Alley* (Richard Outcault), *Mutt and Jeff* (Bud Fisher), *Happy Hooligan* (Frederick Burr Opper), *Bringing Up Father* (George McManus), *Krazy Kat* (George Herriman), *Popeye* (E. C. Segar), *Peanuts* (Charles Schulz), *Zippy the Pinhead* (Bill Griffiths), *The Far Side* (Gary Larson), *For Better or for Worse* (Lynn Johnston), *Calvin and Hobbes* (Bill Watterson), *Dilbert* (Scott Adams), *Get Fuzzy* (Darby Conley), *Cul de Sac* (Richard Thompson), and *Pearls before Swine* (Stephan Pastis).

To begin, the meanings and uses of comic strip satire are best studied with a clear understanding of the visual/verbal workings of the medium and the underappreciated power of distilled cartoon imagery. Scott McCloud's now-classic text *Understanding Comics* offers a great entry into these issues; students appreciate the text's clarity, humor, and lucid illustrations of key concepts. Two ideas from this text in particular—the notion of "amplification through simplification" and "reader identification with distilled cartoon faces/forms"—are helpful in assessing degrees of sympathy and contempt in various strips' satiric treatment of their targets (30, 36).

The notion of amplification through simplification suggests that cartoon satire is especially effective at distilling targets down to iconic caricatures and types. That visual shorthand has a potency that can be used for politically progressive purposes by some artists and in reactionary or punitive ways by others. For example, one can investigate the ethics of visual stereotyping in comics: on the one hand, this practice is perhaps justified when the target is a public figure and the physical exaggerations in the cartoon serve as metaphors for abstract moral failings such as greed or vanity—a criteria articulated by Jonathan Swift in the eighteenth century

Figure 1. Walt Kelly, "The Constitution." *Pogo*, 7 May 1953.

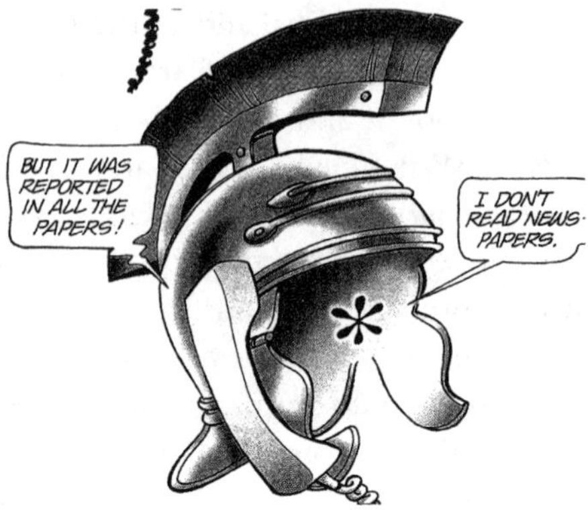

Figure 2. Garry Trudeau, "I Don't Read the Newspapers." *Doonesbury*, 2004.

(529). Walt Kelly's caricature of Senator Joseph McCarthy as a menacing, beady-eyed, heavily bearded bobcat in *Pogo* works as a good example of this practice (fig. 1). One could also consider the effectiveness/fairness of Garry Trudeau distilling public figures to vivid icons (a floating waffle for Bill Clinton or an asterisk inside a Roman military helmet for George W. Bush [fig. 2]).

On the other hand, distilled caricatures can sometimes unfairly scapegoat marginalized social groups, reinforcing racist and classist hierarchies as they visually amplify anxious lies about ethnic "others" (Bhabha 66). In still other cases, nevertheless, ethnic characters might appear like racist types on the surface (wearing a reductive mask assigned by a dominant culture) but actually behave in sympathetic and intelligent ways—effectively embodying a trickster figure or wise fool (as in *Bringing Up Father* [fig. 3]). To help tease out these nuances, one can chart the shifting meanings and uses of

Figure 3. George McManus, "You've succeeded . . ." *Bringing Up Father*, 1921.

stereotypes—ranging from denigration to sympathetic identification—by considering shifting factors such as historic moment, creator, and target audience (Soper 257).

Figure 4. Charles Schulz, "Everything I Do Makes Me Feel Guilty . . ." *Peanuts,* 1969.

McCloud's second concept—reader identification with/through distilled cartoon character faces and forms—allows one to assess how differing aesthetic approaches (cute distillation vs. more detailed, realistic caricaturing, for example) reinforce different satiric tones or meanings for the reader. To elaborate, the simplicity of the aesthetics in a strip like *Peanuts* might lead a casual observer to assume that its characters and comedy are also simplistic. Charles Schulz's cutely distilled drawing style, however, belied the rich emotional complexity and dark themes of the *Peanuts* world, and the innocent openness of Charlie Brown's face—a round circle containing two widely spaced dots for eyes, a button nose, and a minimalistic mark for a mouth—allowed engaged readers to project themselves more readily into his existential musings (fig. 4). McCloud convincingly suggests, moreover, that the simpler the face of a cartoon character, the greater the potential for identifying with—or projecting one's self emotionally into—his or her psychological world. This concept explains why the detailed caricatures of villainous (and often ethnically coded) types in a strip like *Dick Tracy* were likely to evoke contempt rather than sympathetic identification (fig. 5), or it could illuminate how the simple practice of hiding a character's pupils behind opaque glasses or a slashed brow (as in Gary Larson's *The Far Side*) prodded readers to experience feelings of schadenfreude

Figure 5. Chester Gould, "They've Got Stud!" *Dick Tracy,* 1938.

Figure 6. Gary Larson, "Free the Mayonnaise Jar Seven." *The Far Side*, 12 April 1990.

rather than a gentler sense of sympathetic identification (fig. 6).

Shifting from aesthetics to economics and institutions provides a clear understanding of the pressures faced by a cartoonist creating topical satire or other brands of challenging comedy. Like popular film, comics were initially considered a lowbrow medium for immigrant and working-class audiences in the decades straddling the turn of the twentieth century. In light of those humble origins—and with the help of Walter Benjamin's seminal essay "The Work of Art in the Age of Mechanical Reproduction"—one could argue that the cheapness and ubiquity of the medium gave it the potential to be an especially democratic vehicle for satire that could also feature subversive voices from the margins of society. Some of that irreverent, dialogical potential, in fact, was achieved in early carnivalesque strips like *Hogan's Alley*, *Mutt and Jeff*, *Bringing Up Father*, and *Popeye.*

As with popular film, nevertheless, comic strips were so widely loved (and potentially lucrative) that publishers and editors conspired to "clean up" and standardize the medium to appease national brand advertisers, cultural guardians, and the most reactionary readers. The result was a gradual process of gentrification from the mid-1910s onward by syndicates and newspaper publishers that established a number of practices that delimited the variety of voices and satiric tones that could thrive on the mainstream page. Those conventions included the introduction of strict genre categories and conventions; the filtering or censoring of subject matter that was offensive or challenging (including controversial satire); the favoring of cute, merchandisable characters over more rough-edged aesthetics and content; and the use of draconian contracts that limited an artist's rights and freedoms (including copyright ownership, control of merchandising decisions, the taking of sabbaticals or retirement, and final say over content).

In light of those oppressive practices, one could be tempted to adopt the perspective of an old-fashioned Frankfurt school scholar and see the medium as another victim of capitalistic culture industries that thoroughly flatten authentic art and challenging comedy. A more generous and nuanced view of the resilience of satirically minded cartoonists and intelligent audiences (and the occasional forward-thinking syndicate editor) reveals a different story, however. Indeed, despite the generally artist-*unfriendly* practices of syndicate and newspaper industries, a number of cartoonists working within this supremely "family-friendly" (read: inoffensive, non-satiric) medium found ways to create potent, politically engaged satire and to connect with readers eager to enjoy, and advocate for, brands of challenging comedy.

To understand how cartooning satirists survived and often thrived on the mainstream comics page, one can borrow a modified concept of the auteur theory from cinema studies as a starting point. The articulation of this theory in the 1960s by French critics was an effort to celebrate studio-system-era film directors who were able to create a distinctive and sometimes challenging body of work despite the restrictive conditions within which they worked (rigid contracts, strict genre rules, institutional practices that favored commerce over art, censorship, etc.). For example, satirically minded directors like Charlie Chaplin, Orson Welles, Preston Sturges, and Billy Wilder were able to create provocative films during these mid-century decades by negotiating artist-friendly contracts, cleverly evading the most draconian efforts to censor or flatten their work, and then protecting their clout to varying degrees as they achieved popular success.

The auteur theory has some inherent flaws, of course; for example, it over-celebrates the contributions of one figure (the "cult of the director") in a medium that requires a great deal of collaboration. The general idea at its core, nevertheless—that some popular creators were able to achieve an unusual degree of clout and independence in the midst of intense commercial and institutional pressures—works well in approaching comic strip satirists. Kelly and Trudeau, for example, were able to defy industry conventions by negotiating contracts that gave them copyright ownership of their work and control over merchandising decisions. That foundation of artistic independence affected other aspects of their work as well, enabling them to take sabbaticals, openly critique industry practices, and include pointed cultural criticism in their comedy. At the same time, their iconoclasm could sometimes put them in conflict with editors and reactionary readers who were offended by the topicality and perceived partisan quality of their satire in a supposedly politics-free medium. There were periodic campaigns, in fact, to censor their work, move it to the editorial page, or excise it from a particular newspaper altogether. Those efforts invariably failed, nevertheless, since the grassroots support of avid readers protected these cartooning auteurs from any kind of permanent cancellation or long-term censorship.

The layeredness of comic strip satire can also be studied and discussed by combining the auteur theory with a neo-Marxist framing of the commercial pressures and cultural negotiations faced by independent-minded artists. For example, one could study the careers of these cartoonists in light of Antonio Gramsci's conception of how negotiations play out and compromises are made between culture industries and satirically minded artists (Bennett xix). On the one side, by incorporating a subversive artist/text into a mainstream medium, the dominant culture benefits from the monies that can be generated by a genuinely popular cultural product while still maintaining hegemony as it tolerates (and, to a degree, corrals) social/political dissent. On the other side, a cartooning satirist can greatly amplify his or her reach (and, in the long run, even change the dominant culture in progressive ways from within) by ceding to some of the editing, censoring, and shaping exerted by a popular culture industry (as represented by syndicates and newspaper editors). As illustrations of these dynamics, we can look at Kelly and Trudeau again: in order to achieve and maintain the clout that came with mainstream popularity, they could not always behave like incorrigible rebels or allow their satire to wax too dark and misanthropic; they often had to "pander" to mainstream audiences and make some concessions to industry practices and pressures. In Kelly's case, this meant behaving like a stand-up comedian in public, hobnobbing with newspaper editors, and coding his satiric attacks into an accessible animal allegory with Disneyesque aesthetics, generous wordplay, and physical slapstick (fig. 7). Trudeau created endearing characters

Figure 7. Walt Kelly, "Poisoning Is Too Good . . ." *Pogo*, 7 June 1953. © Okefenokee Glee & Perloo, Inc. Used by permission (permissions@pogocomics.com).

that aged in real time, took advantage of new digital means of audience building, and connected with editors, critics, and audiences in empathetic ways (particularly when creating satire about the lives of American soldiers involved in military efforts that Trudeau did not support [fig. 8]).

One could also profitably compare the career arcs and popular impact of "incorporated" artists, such as Trudeau and Kelly, with more genuinely counter-discursive satirists who either refused or were not required to make the kinds of concessions that would have garnered them higher levels of syndication or popularity. Consider the following examples:

George Herriman, in *Krazy Kat*, was free to engage in surrealistic art, cosmic satire, and deconstructive wordplay because his publisher, William Randolph Hearst, exempted him from typical commercial pressures, promising to syndicate his work no matter how low his numbers fell.

Nicole Hollander, the creator of *Sylvia*, self-syndicated her work, using her artistic independence to attract a cult following that appreciated her acerbically feminist brand of satire.

In the 1960s R. Crumb saw the limitations of the mainstream comics page and opted to work in the wholly uncensored field of underground "commix"; that freedom from institutional meddling allowed him to create sharp and sometimes brilliant satire but also resulted in his work derailing at times into gratuitous vulgarities, fetishistic obsessions, and misanthropic hang-ups.

A number of cartoonists opted for the relative freedoms of big-city "alternative" weeklies in the 1980s and 1990s, catering to devoted,

Figure 8. Garry Trudeau, "Hey, New Guy!" *Doonesbury*. © 2004 G. B. Trudeau. Reprinted with permission of Andrews Mcmeel Syndication. All rights reserved.

> niche audiences with hard-edged, unapologetically partisan satire. They included Matt Groening (*Life in Hell*), Ruben Bolling (*Tom the Dancing Bug*), Lynda Barry (*Ernie Pook's Comeek*), Tom Tomorrow (*This Modern World*), Alison Bechdel (*Dykes to Watch Out For*), and Ted Rall. In a highly anomalous career trajectory, Groening's alternative brand of satire jumped from the narrow scope of big-city weeklies to *The Simpsons*, a highly popular animated television show that radically expanded the palette for mainstream satire.

Finally, one can use mainstream comic strips as a focus for exploring a variety of nontopical satiric modes. Three more expansive genres in particular—carnivalesque, cosmic, and deconstructive—allow one to explore the meanings and uses of a variety of rowdy and sometimes philosophical comic texts. To begin, M. M. Bakhtin used medieval folk festivals as a starting point for describing a type of carnivalesque, multivoiced, subversive (though often politically ambivalent) grassroots cultural experience or text that uses earthy comedy and social inversions to challenge dominant cultural ideals, hierarchies, dogmas, and identities (8, 10, 18). While Bakhtin saw rollicking, dialogical novels as the most likely inheritor of these carnivalesque tones in the twentieth century, one could argue that the lowbrow comics page—especially in its earliest ethnic, immigrant

Figure 9. Frederick Burr Opper. "Happy." *Happy Hooligan*, 1910.

oriented and themed comedy—embodied well this bottom-up democratic brand of satire. Examples of early strips in this genre include *Hogan's Alley*, *Happy Hooligan*, *Mutt and Jeff*, and *Bringing Up Father* (fig. 9). And while the most vividly carnivalesque qualities were gentrified out of the medium from the 1910s onward, one can still identify vestiges of that mode in earthy texts like *Popeye*, *Li'l Abner*, *Pogo*, *Bloom County*, *The Far Side*, *Get Fuzzy*, and *Pearls before Swine* (fig. 10).

Figure 10. Stephan Pastis, "Never Mind." *Pearls before Swine*, 2012.

Other comic strips featured cosmic satire—a mode that transcends topical attacks to expose the foibles and flaws of universal human behavior and cultural patterns. This subgenre engages in a "larger, darker, more compassionate" treatment of its targets than topical satire, and transcending the functions of punitive satire, it can communicate a profound vision of "man desperately—and unsuccessfully—trying to become what he thinks he ought to be" (Tilton 5). In twentieth-century novels like *Catch-22*, *Slaughterhouse-Five*, or *The Crying of Lot 49*, this cosmic approach overlapped with bracingly dark comedic tones: black humor, existentialism, and absurdism. In comic strips, those astringent tones thrived in deceptively cute and comedically accessible packages: the existential probings of human psychology and armchair philosophy in *Peanuts* and *Calvin and Hobbes* (fig. 11), dissections of the ethical anomie of contemporary corporate bureaucracies in *Dilbert*, and gentle but incisive reflections about suburban life and familial dynamics in *For Better or Worse* and *Cul de Sac*.

Figure 11. Bill Watterson, "Your Grandpa Takes the Funnies Pretty Seriously." *Calvin and Hobbes*, 1989.

A handful of unusually surreal and self-reflexive strips (Griffiths's *Zippy the Pinhead*, Breathed's *Bloom County*, and Herriman's *Krazy Kat*) also give the student a chance to explore the

Figure 12. George Herriman, "Krazy and Ignatz." *Krazy Kat*, 1920.

mechanisms of deconstructive satire. The comedy and aesthetics of these strips, for example, continually drew attention to their own constructedness, breaking the fourth wall in metafictive ways and playfully satirizing the conventions of the medium. At times this kind of self-aware strip can also engage in an organic brand of satiric deconstruction, subverting hierarchies of cultural value, poking fun at ideological assumptions, and reflecting "suspiciously on all ways of making meaning, including its own" (Weisenburger 1, 3, 28, 139). As an example, *Krazy Kat* is an acquired taste for many readers, but if students immerse themselves for a time in this world of shifting landscapes, ambiguous love triangles, and omnivorous wordplay, they gain an appreciation for this type of deconstructive art and comedy (fig. 12). The star of this strip, Krazy, is especially compelling; E. E. Cummings's claim that this gender-ambiguous black cat is the "one, true revolutionary protagonist" gains credence as one witnesses how Krazy's wise-fool innocence and trickster-figure wit gently demolish a variety of dogmas, gendered hierarchies, and racial divides (Cummings 7).

Works Cited

Bakhtin, M. M. *Rabelais and His World*. Indiana UP, 1984.

Benjamin, Walter. "The Work of Art in the Age of Mechanical Reproduction." *Illuminations*, edited by Hannah Arendt, translated by Harry Zohn, Schocken Books, 1968, pp. 217–52.

Bennett, Tony. "Popular Culture and 'The Turn to Gramsci.'" *Popular Culture and Social Relations*, edited by Bennett et al., Open UP, 1986, pp. xi–xix.

Bhabha, Homi K. *The Location of Culture*. Routledge / Kegan Paul, 1994.

Cummings, E. E. Introduction. *Krazy Kat*, Henry Holt, 1946, pp. 1–7.

McCloud, Scott. *Understanding Comics: The Invisible Art*. Edited by Mark Martin, HarperPerennial, 1993.

Soper, Kerry. "From Swarthy Ape to Sympathetic Everyman and Subversive Trickster: The Development of Irish Caricature in American Comic Strips between 1890 and 1920." *Journal of American Studies*, vol. 39, no. 2, Aug. 2005, pp. 257–96.

Swift, Jonathan. "Verses on the Death of Dr. Swift, D.S.P.D." *Jonathan Swift: A Critical Edition of the Major Works*, edited by Angus Ross and David Woolley, Oxford UP, 1989, pp. 514–30.

Tilton, John W. *Cosmic Satire in the Contemporary Novel.* Bucknell UP, 1977.

Weisenburger, Steven. *Fables of Subversion: Satire and the American Novel, 1930–1980.* U of Georgia P, 1995.

Matthew Henry

Animated Television Satire

The genre of animated television satire, which is today so commonplace on both network and cable television, is a fairly recent innovation, although not without precedent. The show that inaugurated the recent popularization of both animation and satire is, of course, *The Simpsons.* As the editors of *Satire TV: Politics and Comedy in the Post-Network Era* rightly note, "No single program is as important in creating the televisual space for the satire TV boom as *The Simpsons*" (Gray et al. 25). *The Simpsons* has had a profound influence on many subsequent programs, including animated shows such as *South Park*, *King of the Hill*, and *Family Guy* and political comedies such as *The Daily Show* and *The Colbert Report.* Obviously, today's crop of satirical animated comedies also have antecedents—specifically in the animation produced for television in the late 1950s and early 1960s, as well as the animation created for theatrical bills by Disney, Warner Bros., and MGM from the early 1920s through the late 1940s—and to these works they owe a significant debt. All of these materials are part of an interdisciplinary cultural studies course that I have been teaching for the past several years, designed to serve as an introduction to media studies, an examination of satirical comedy, and an exploration of contemporary America culture.

A great challenge in this course is getting students to critically examine television, which they tend to dismiss as "just entertainment" and thus without significance. Therefore, I first provide readings and exercises designed to develop students' media literacy skills. I introduce students to Stuart Hall's seminal work in media and communication studies with a short handout that distills Hall's key insights and simplifies some of his terminology. This document defines the concepts of *encoding* and *decoding*, explains the role of social positioning in the reception of mass media texts, and outlines the interpretive positions one can take, which I simply identify as *preferred*, *negotiated*, and *resistant*. Students also read Douglas Kellner's "Cultural Studies, Multiculturalism, and Media Culture," which explains how mass media "contribute to educating us about how to behave and what to think, feel, believe, fear and desire" (7). Like many people, students don't like to believe that media can shape our ideas, beliefs, and behaviors, so a useful way to begin is with the analysis of advertising, which students will at least concede has an ulterior motive. Typically I spend only a short time with such analysis, briefly reviewing examples of contemporary ads and discussing how they reveal certain cultural assumptions (e.g., about beauty standards, normative gender roles, or racial and ethnic identities) and how they exploit common ideologies (e.g., individualism, materialism, or patriotism). With this foundation, it becomes easier for students to critically assess televisual texts. To help facilitate this shift, I first have students analyze clips of older television shows, from which they have adequate critical distance. This works quite well with programs that embody outmoded ideologies (such as *Father Knows Best* and *Leave It to Beaver*, in which sexism and patriarchy are blatant) or with programs that regularly challenge dominant ideologies (e.g., *All in the Family*, *Roseanne*, and *Murphy Brown*, which are often openly political). Situation comedies such as these are templates for many animated programs, so students should be familiar with them; moreover, sitcoms are often incorporated into shows such as *The Simpsons*, *South Park*, and *Family Guy* through allusion and parody, so they are also helpful for illustrating these concepts later on.

Before getting into definitions of concepts or analyses of contemporary animated programs, I provide students with background information on the history of both theatrical and television animation and screen select examples of each. Students read Jason Mittell's "The Great Saturday Morning Exile," which concisely outlines the history of theatrical animation, the demise of the studios' animation units after the 1948 Paramount

Decision, the development of a "limited animation" style for television, and the industrial processes that led to animation being "marginalized into the kid-only Saturday morning periphery" by the end of the 1960s (34–35). A subsequent presentation featuring a selection of "classic" cartoons highlights the different styles of animation used by Disney, MGM, and Warner Bros. and familiarizes students with the work of influential animators and directors such as Ub Iwerks, William Hanna, Joseph Barbera, Tex Avery, and Chuck Jones.[1] I also show clips from *Rocky and Bullwinkle*, both to introduce Jay Ward's artwork and sophisticated humor—which *Simpsons* creator Matt Groening has cited as an influence—and to illustrate how earlier animated television programming employed irony and sarcasm for subtle critique (in this case, of Cold War politics). Last, I show clips from both *The Flintstones* and *The Jetsons*, highlighting how each incorporated popular culture through parody, thereby appealing to adults and children alike, and noting how this created a template for contemporary prime-time animated situation comedies such as *The Simpsons* and *South Park*, which employ parody as well, often in service of satire.

Because the terms *parody* and *satire* are often conflated and confused with each other, I invest a lot of time distinguishing between the two, first offering specific definitions and then showing and discussing numerous examples. *Parody* is defined for students as an artistic work that alludes to and offers a humorous imitation of another text. This must be nuanced, however, since parody has two distinct modes: one that is more playful and offers tribute (homage) to the parodied work and another that is more critical and designed to mock the referenced material. I commonly provide examples of both kinds of parody with still images and video clips from advertising, television programs, and Hollywood films. I also frequently return to the classic studio shorts shown earlier, since many of these or their styles of animation have been parodied in shows such as *The Simpsons* and *South Park*. Once students have a good feel for parody, we move on to satire. *Satire* is defined for students as an artistic work in which individual or social wrongs, flaws, faults, or vices are humorously held up for censure—using methods such as parody, irony, sarcasm, juxtaposition, and exaggeration—with the intent of raising awareness of an issue and bringing about improvement or social change. I also provide brief descriptions of Horatian and Juvenalian forms of satire, and we discuss the characteristics that distinguish one from the other.[2] To help students better understand both parody and satire, I again show a variety of examples, including clips of Tina Fey's remarkable impersonation of Sarah Palin on *Saturday Night*

Live, which she premiered in 2008 and reprised during the election cycles in 2010, 2012, and 2016. This always provokes spirited classroom debate over whether Fey's performance is mocking parody or satire—or, if satire, whether it is more Horatian or Juvenalian—which helps students further hone their interpretive skills.

The best means of getting students to understand satire is to let them grapple with examples of it. One of the finest is the animated sequence from Michael Moore's film *Bowling for Columbine*, entitled "A Brief History of the USA," which offers a scathing indictment of fearmongering in American history and culture and its connection to slavery, genocide, segregation, xenophobia, and violence against others. The satire in this clip—which is sadly just as relevant today as when it first appeared in 2002—is fast and furious, so I show it numerous times, pausing after each showing to have students analyze it in detail. On a chart that I provide, students first identify the topics being addressed; in subsequent columns, they identify what they see as targets of the satire, the methods used by the artist, and the reasons for the censure. After repeated viewings and individual reflection, we begin a full class discussion, transferring the information onto the board at the front of the room. Overall, this clip works exceedingly well at helping students to understand how satire operates and to distinguish between types of satire. It also generates valuable discussion about how we interpret and respond to media, particularly to art as overtly political as satire.[3] Equally useful as demonstrations of satire are segments of both *The Daily Show* and *The Colbert Report*. Prior to viewing clips from these, I have students read Geoffrey Baym's essay "*The Daily Show* and the Reinvention of Political Journalism," which offers a close reading of the parodic and satiric elements of *The Daily Show*, examining its strategies, techniques, and purposes, and which closes with a persuasive argument for the value of satire as a means of furthering "deliberative democracy" (118–19). To illustrate these ideas, I show students a series of "news" clips (taken from ABC, CBS, NBC, CNN, and FOX) and then parallel clips from either *The Daily Show* or *The Colbert Report* dealing with the same story or issue (and often broadcast the very next day). From these juxtapositions, students quickly see how both parody and satire are used to expose serious societal problems—in this case, bias, hypocrisy, "spin," and the general failure of mainstream news media to fully inform the citizenry.

By this point, students usually have a good understanding of how satire operates, so the remainder of the semester is given over to an examination of American culture as it is reflected in animated television satire, primarily in episodes of *The Simpsons* but also in select episodes of *King of the Hill*, *South Park*, and *Family Guy*. Collectively, these shows provide an excellent means of exploring topics such as race, class, gender, sexuality, religion, politics, education, and the environment and the problems and controversies attendant to each. At times, I have found it beneficial to compare and contrast episodes of different programs that deal with similar topics or issues. For example, I continue to use two episodes of *The Simpsons* and *South Park* addressing censorship: "Itchy & Scratchy & Marge," which deals with Marge Simpson's efforts to eliminate violence from *The Itchy & Scratchy Show*, her children's favorite cartoon, and "Death," which partly concerns the efforts of the parents of South Park to eliminate the scatological cartoon *Terrance and Phillip*, which is deemed obscene. Analyzing and discussing these episodes, which largely satirize the methods and motives of censors, leads to productive conversations about the politics of network and cable television, the ways in which "obscenity" is continually redefined, and the place of censorship in an open and democratic society. Another pairing of episodes from *The Simpsons* and *South Park* is used to address sexuality: "Homer's Phobia," which focuses on Homer Simpson's fears that his son, Bart, might be gay, and "Big Gay Al's Big Gay Boat Ride," which concerns Stan Marsh's fears that his dog, Sparky, might be gay. These—along with later episodes from both shows on the same subject matter—can generate conversations about the historical representation of LGBT people in mass media, the struggle for visibility and positive imagery, the political battle for equal rights, and the continuing problem of cultural homophobia. I have paired *The Simpsons* with *Family Guy* as well, using "Lisa the Beauty Queen" and "Mr. Griffin Goes to Washington," which tell similar stories, positioning the protagonists (Lisa Simpson and Peter Griffin) as first spokespersons for and then protestors against Big Tobacco. As these episodes were produced nearly a decade apart (1992 and 2001, respectively), they are additionally useful for generating discussions about the importance of cultural contexts—in this case, with perceptions of the Congress and government and with attitudes toward both smoking and social activism.

In addition to engaging in classroom discussions, students are also required to write critical and interpretive essays, analyzing the satirical treatment of various social and cultural issues raised by the animated programs used in the course. One assignment I provide asks students to assess how animated satires address gender. *The Simpsons* works well for this, as it regularly reflects on the complex manifestations of both femininity and feminism, particularly in episodes focused on the experiences of Marge Simpson and Lisa Simpson, such as "Lisa vs. Malibu Stacy" and "The Springfield Connection." While one could use *The Simpsons* to explore masculinity as well, episodes of *King of the Hill* provide much richer material for this inquiry. As Ethan Thompson notes, a generational struggle over the "normative" modes of masculinity—evident mainly in Hank Hill's attempts to shape his son Bobby's manhood in traditional ways—is one of the fundamental elements of *King of the Hill*'s social critique (45). Another assignment asks students to examine the complexities of race, ethnicity, and national identity in American culture. For this, I have had students analyze episodes of *The Simpsons* such as "Much Apu about Nothing," which explores attitudes toward illegal immigration; "Bart-Mangled Banner," which reflects on patriotism in a post-9/11 world; and "MyPods and Boomsticks," which pointedly addresses Islamophobia. An argumentative essay assignment focuses on the portrayal of religion in animated satires. In this case, students may select either *The Simpsons* or *South Park* for analysis; they then independently review recommended episodes and write an essay in which they argue whether the show aligns itself more with an institutional tradition or a secular perspective. For the final essay, which involves limited research, students are free to choose their own topics, although I encourage them to select ones that have not been explicitly dealt with in previous assignments, such as education or the environment, which are also primary concerns within and fodder for satire on *The Simpsons*, *South Park*, and *King of the Hill*.

Given that I teach at a community college, I focus mainly on analyzing and interpreting the media used as primary texts in the course, keeping supplemental reading materials to a minimum. Instructors teaching at a more advanced level might wish to incorporate other readings that can further challenge students' thinking or generate more classroom debate. The past decade has seen a significant increase in the amount of scholarship on political and satirical comedy, particularly animated television satire. Much of this is celebratory, praising shows such as *The Simpsons*, *South Park*, and *King of the Hill* for exposing serious problems in American culture, often from a leftist political perspective. My own work on *The Simpsons* follows in this vein, highlighting how the show engages with topics such as racism, sexism, classism, nationalism, and religious fundamentalism.[4] Animated television satire is not without its detractors, however, and a fair amount of the existing scholarship is of this type. For example, Robert Singh argues that the satire of *The Simpsons* and *South Park* is superficial and that each has proven itself "far more supportive than subversive of traditionalist America" (207). Stephen Groening similarly argues that *South Park* "approaches ideological critique" but ultimately withdraws from political action and thus fails as satire (113). And similar claims have been made about *Family Guy*, which some critics argue never rises to the level of authentic social critique and should not be mistaken for "true satire" (DeRochi 36).

Whether animated television programs such as those discussed here succeed as satire is open for debate. What they assuredly do succeed at is providing an engaging way to involve students in serious discussions of a variety of important social, political, and cultural issues. In this regard, satirical animated television shows are an excellent pedagogical tool for the college classroom.

Notes

1. Typically I show the following: *Steamboat Willie* (1928), the "Sorcerer's Apprentice" segment of *Fantasia* (1940), *Mouse in Manhattan* (1945), *Fast and Furry-ous* (1949), *The Scarlet Pumpernickel* (1950), and *What's Opera, Doc?* (1957), which feature the antics of Mickey Mouse, Tom and Jerry, Wile E. Coyote and the Road Runner, Daffy Duck, and Bugs Bunny and Elmer Fudd.

2. Traditional concepts of satire are often presumed to be incompatible with the "postmodern," a label commonly applied to many current animated programs. Instructors interested in exploring this territory should review Steven Weisenburger's discussion of degenerative satire, which "functions to subvert hierarchies of value and to reflect suspiciously on all ways of making meaning" (3). This is applicable to many animated comedies, especially *South Park*.

3. As one might imagine, not all students share Michael Moore's worldview, and every semester I have a few who get quite angry while watching this clip. While discussing it, I refer back to concepts studied earlier (i.e., encoding, decoding, and preferred and resistant readers) and allow frustrated students to explain why they take a resistant reading position, which usually eases any tensions.

4. My most recent thoughts on these topics can be found in my book The Simpsons, *Satire, and American Culture*.

Works Cited

Baym, Geoffrey. "*The Daily Show* and the Reinvention of Political Journalism." *From Cronkite to Colbert: The Evolution of Broadcast News*, Paradigm, 2010, pp. 101–21.

DeRochi, Jack. "'What Have You Learned?': Considering a New Hermeneutic of Satire in *Family Guy*." *Studies in American Humor*, vol. 3, no. 17, 2008, pp. 35–48.

Gray, Jonathan, et al., editors. *Satire TV: Politics and Comedy in the Post-Network Era*. New York UP, 2009.

Groening, Stephen. "Cynicism and Other Postideological Half Measures in *South Park.*" *Taking* South Park *Seriously*, edited by Jeffrey Andrew Weinstock, State U of New York P, 2008, pp. 113–29.

Hall, Stuart. "Encoding, Decoding." *The Cultural Studies Reader*, edited by Simon During, 3rd ed., Routledge, 1993, pp. 90–103.

Henry, Matthew A. The Simpsons, *Satire, and American Culture*. Palgrave Macmillan, 2012.

Kellner, Douglas. "Cultural Studies, Multiculturalism, and Media Culture." *Gender, Race, and Class in Media*, edited by Gail Dines and Jean M. Humez, 3rd ed., Sage, 2011, pp. 7–18.

Mittell, Jason. "The Great Saturday Morning Exile: Scheduling Cartoons on Television's Periphery in the 1960s." *Prime Time Animation: Television Animation and American Culture*, edited by Carol A. Stabile and Mark Harrison, Routledge, 2003, pp. 33–54.

Singh, Robert. "Subverting American Values? *The Simpsons, South Park*, and the Cartoon Culture War." *American Politics and Society Today*, edited by Singh, Blackwell, 2002, pp. 206–29.

Thompson, Ethan. "'I Am Not Down with That': *King of the Hill* and Sitcom Satire." *Journal of Film and Video*, vol. 61, no. 2, Summer 2009, pp. 38–51.

Weisenburger, Steven. *Fables of Subversion: Satire and the American Novel, 1930–1980*. U of Georgia P, 1995.

Amber Day

Parodic Television News and Political Engagement

Due to my own research focus in the area, I teach a course devoted exclusively to political satire. Situated in an interdisciplinary department (Literary and Cultural Studies) at a university with a historic business focus, I have the disadvantage of teaching mostly nonmajors with a wide range of previous exposure to the subject matter (from avid fans to wide-eyed neophytes who are simply fulfilling a requirement), but I have the advantage of freedom to pull widely from a variety of media forms and disciplines. We visit a few historical touchstones, reading "A Modest Proposal" and watching *Dr. Strangelove*, for instance, but we focus primarily on the here and now. This is because my main goal in the course is to use satire as a means of examining contemporary culture and political debate, from the flaws of the news media to the cultural ambivalence around entertainment and popular culture. We get there by deconstructing both the substance of contemporary satire—the conversation/critique happening within it—as well as the wider conversation *about* political satire.

Since the students are most well acquainted with the newly burgeoning genre of news parody, and given the fact that many of these programs have garnered attention because they are genuinely providing a critique that is not being articulated elsewhere in public debate, we spend a fair amount of time discussing programs like *The Daily Show*, *The Colbert Report*, *Last Week Tonight with John Oliver*, and *Full Frontal with Samantha Bee* (while also briefly surveying similar English-language programs in Canada and Great Britain). We have several units dedicated to news parody, but the shows also regularly come up in discussion of other texts (such as viral videos, satiric documentaries, activist techniques, etc.). As numerous scholars of news parody have noted, these programs teach a valuable form of media literacy (Meikle, Gray et al., Meddaugh, Day).

While news parody existed prior to this more recent explosion of programming, what was groundbreaking about a show like *The Daily Show with Jon Stewart* was that it did not simply poke fun at politicians or exaggerate the pomposity of television news anchors. Rather it provided a sustained critique of the flaws of television news and of the political discourse the industry engendered. One of the first readings that I assign to students is a segment from Geoffrey Baym's book *From Cronkite to Colbert: The Evolution of Broadcast News*, which details the industrial and stylistic shifts in television news over the decades and gives some perspective on the form. We also examine the critique being made on particular parodic news segments or in extratextual moments, like Jon Stewart's famous rant on the debate show *Crossfire* about the irresponsibility of *Crossfire* and its ilk, where he begged host Tucker Carlson to "stop hurting America" (15 Oct. 2004). Though individual targets clearly change from segment to segment and show to show, the unwavering critical through line tends to be the amplification without interrogation so common in contemporary political discourse: the existence of tightly scripted political talking points, the fact that those talking points are not deconstructed but are rather repeated ad nauseum in most televisual news, the groupthink, and the tendency toward sensationalism and spectacle. In the United States, Stewart in particular made a name for himself and forged a new genre (soon followed by Stephen Colbert) by repeatedly pulling back the curtain and asking audiences to focus on how both the news and our understanding of the issues of the day are produced.

We reflect on why there seems to be such hunger for this critique to be made and note that it is not one being articulated in most other straight (noncomedic) media. Indeed, as we discuss, the current renaissance of political satire appears to have developed to fill a void or speak to a lack in political discourse. In many ways, I use the satiric texts to help students take a step back and diagnose the ills and the quirks of contemporary culture and political discourse. Of course, that does not mean that we all see the issues in exactly the same way. Many of the students, for instance, are resistant to the idea that our entertainment media are actually "doing" something and that their popularity can be attributable to anything in addition to their funniness. But, in many ways, that tension helps feed some of our central structuring questions in the course.

A quick dive into the literature around parody, irony, and satire, particularly televisual satire, demonstrates that there are two conceptions of satire's intent and effects. On the one hand, there is a widespread assumption that humor and entertainment signal a form of trivialization and a retreat from political engagement. On the other, there is a developing body of scholarship and journalism that points to particularly impassioned examples of contemporary satire as potent forms of political commentary and engagement. This is a theoretical debate that continues to crop up throughout the course, as they are the opposing assumptions underlying so much of the writing on satire.

On the first day of class, we read two pieces on irony and cultural attitudes that set up these diametrically opposed viewpoints. The first is the opening section of Jedidiah Purdy's 1999 book *For Common Things: Irony, Trust, and Commitment in America Today*. Purdy uses *irony* to describe a lot of the cultural attitudes of the 1990s that he finds problematic, arguing that we hide within the ironic mode out of fear of being seen as silly or naive, instead demonstrating how self-aware we are. He contrasts irony with trust and hope—the belief that things can be different and that an engagement in politics can change the world for the better. In his view, irony has become a disturbing cultural dominant that encourages us all to make snide comments from the sidelines while sitting out the hard work of cultural change.

The second piece is an article in *Salon* by David Beers, which was written within weeks of the September 11 terrorist attacks in response to the commentators who had loudly announced that the event would finally bring on the death of irony in the United States. In contrast to Purdy (and those 9/11 commentators), Beers argues that most irony is about engagement, rather than disengagement, and that it employs healthy skepticism to critique policies or practices in the hopes of bettering them. In other words, it has less to do with an absence of caring than with an excess. He goes on to argue that it was then, in the wake of the attacks, that the country was most in need of irony, as it could guard against being swept up in the wave of jingoism and provide some needed critique and discussion on proposed policies and reactions. As he puts it:

> that kind of irony would wonder if in this new battle on behalf of freedom, we may rush to strip away civil liberties. That kind of irony would wonder whether this new kind of war, waged to make us safe from terrorist attacks, might plunge the world into a far more dangerous conflagration. . . . To note these ironies is to engage yourself in the grave purpose at hand and take some responsibility for helping to think it through—and that's the opposite of ironic detachment.

While the turn of the millennium might feel remote to today's undergraduates, these essays helpfully set up the two different ways that irony (and usually by extension satire and parody) gets linked to the political—either as disengaged smart-assery or engaged passion and commitment to debate. Furthermore, this conversation sets the scene for the rise of much of the ironic and satiric media that exploded in relevance and popularity shortly thereafter (precisely to note many of the ironies Beers anticipated). These warring instincts about irony, satire, and the political then returned with a vengeance in both the journalistic and scholarly writing about parodic news shows as they grew in popularity.

I have students read a sampling of articles accusing *The Daily Show* in particular of cynicism as well as those defending the program. A number of scholars have raised concerns about the show promoting cynicism and by extension apathy in the political process. Some have argued that because the program generates distrust or dissatisfaction with the news media that it will presumably lead to decreased attention to the political conversation and decreased participation in the political system. Others (myself included) have refuted these conclusions by pointing out that the appearance of cynicism is, in these studies, highly subjective. Indeed, there is far more evidence to suggest that viewers' unhappiness with the reality of the political debate is a form of engaged dissatisfaction, as these shows encourage the belief that we deserve better and that, in fact, something different is possible. As Robert Hariman puts it, rather than promoting apathy, *The Daily Show* "continually calls the audience to informed participation, civil speech, and rational argument on behalf of sound public policy" (274), functioning as an extended defense of democratic deliberation.

It should be noted that in many of the studies designed to measure whether the show breeds cynicism, there is an unspoken assumption that comedy is inherently trivializing and that irony always stands in opposition to earnestness. The beginning premise tends to be that popular culture and entertainment (particularly of the comedic variety) are easily separable from the serious world of the political public sphere (or that it should be so). However, a quick look at the contemporary landscape tells us that this is far from the case (and was never the full story in previous eras). Indeed, parodic news shows often offer more earnest and informed critique than coverage of the same issues on traditional news broadcasts or "serious" chat programs. But the anxiety around these programs is indicative of our conflicted cultural feelings about art and entertainment in general and the angst that has always surrounded boundary-crossing genres like satire.

The debate is a useful one for getting students to evaluate the academic research itself. I encourage students to find the flaws in the publications we survey—for instance, when a quantitative study designed to putatively measure a viewer reaction or change in attitude is, because of a lack of textual analysis, premised on flimsy presumptions about what the text communicates. Most important, the academic disagreement leads into a discussion about what we actually mean by media "effects" in the first place. What sorts of "effects" are we looking for? And how can they actually be measured?

When most people speak about the effects of satire, including academics, they are referring to immediate and dramatic changes in attitude. Journalists who write about satire often focus even more narrowly on how a given sketch or program will effect votes in an election. That is, it should be noted, an incredibly high bar. Indeed, if it is the metric one uses, one will likely come to the conclusion, as many classical literary theorists did, that satire has no effect at all. As Edward and Lillian Bloom lament, "even the best intended satire does not readily convert desire into action" (16). This line of thinking goes in search of a one-to-one relationship between satiric text and action, attempting to measure whether one television episode, book, or magazine article has managed to spark a quantifiable shift in voter behavior, almost inevitably deciding that it has not. The accompanying conclusion is that satire is only "entertainment," implying that it is somehow outside or in opposition to the political real world.

While this may be a tangible and accessible way to measure satire's efficacy, we discuss the ways in which it paints a narrow picture of an individual's role in a democracy (as well as a narrow vision of how we interact with art and entertainment). It implies that we are activated as citizens only intermittently, at most every couple of years immediately prior to an election, ignoring the ways in which we are always engaged with others in a civic conversation, continually and incrementally negotiating cultural understandings of issues and ideas. It would be naive to assume that the majority of us do not already have existing opinions, allegiances, and commitments or that we are so easily swayed that simply hearing a political critique wittily stated instantly moves us to shift allegiances or take immediate action. However, even seemingly intractable majority opinions do shift over time. These shifts are preceded by subtle changes in the public conversation, challenges to the dominant framing of the issues, or growing mainstream familiarity with the ideas in question. I deliberately select some contemporary theory that directly or indirectly makes the case that satire has the ability to help shift that public conversation: to push otherwise peripheral topics into the mainstream, to alter the frames we use for talking about a particular issue, or to create a rallying point for dissatisfaction around a policy. Of course, this is a far more difficult effect to measure than immediate and dramatic changes in voting patterns, but that does not make it insubstantial. I push the students to examine their own instincts on what it is that we might expect good satire to do and how we might go about assessing its effects.

Ultimately, my aim is not necessarily to convince students of anything in particular but to force them to fully dig in to the academic debate as well as the cultural conversation. The course as a whole is designed to use satire as a window into public discussion, shining a light on how it is conducted and what it says about us. While I certainly want students to come away from the class with a greater understanding of satire theory and the history of the form, I am particularly intent on them becoming stronger critical thinkers adept at reflecting on their own cultural and political landscape.

Works Cited

Baym, Geoffrey. *From Cronkite to Colbert: The Evolution of Broadcast News.* Paradigm, 2010.

Beers, David. "Irony Is Dead! Long Live Irony!" *Salon*, 25 Sept. 2001, www.salon.com/2001/09/25/irony_lives.

Bloom, Edward A., and Lillian D. Bloom. *Satire's Persuasive Voice.* Cornell UP, 1979.

Day, Amber. *Satire and Dissent: Interventions in Contemporary Political Debate.* Indiana UP, 2011.

Gray, Jonathan, et al., editors. *Satire TV: Politics and Comedy in the Post-Network Era.* New York UP, 2009.

Hariman, Robert. "In Defense of Jon Stewart." *Critical Studies in Media Communication*, vol. 24, no. 3, 2007, pp. 273–77.

Meddaugh, Priscilla Marie. "Bakhtin, Colbert, and the Center of Discourse: Is There No 'Truthiness' in Humor?" *Critical Studies in Media Communication*, vol. 27, no. 4, 2010, pp. 376–90.

Meikle, Graham. "Naming and Shaming: News Satire and Symbolic Power." *The Electronic Journal of Communication*, vol. 18, nos. 2–4, 2008, www.cios.org/www/ejc/EJCPUBLIC/018/2/01847.html.

Purdy, Jedediah. *For Common Things: Irony, Trust, and Commitment in America Today*. Knopf, 1999.

Stewart, Jon, guest. *Crossfire*. CNN, 15 Oct. 2004. *YouTube*, uploaded by Alex Felker, 16 Jan. 2006, www.youtube.com/watch?v=aFQFB5YpDZE.

Part V

Satire, Affect, and Student Response

Danielle Bobker

Satire and Offensive Humor

Does laughter always signal agreement with or approval of the words that elicited it? Why do we feel hurt or ashamed when others laugh but we don't, and vice versa? Are certain topics inherently offensive and off-limits for humor? With reference to a small archive of stand-up comedy about sexual violence as well as several key concepts in humor theory, many of my classes have explored such questions over the past five years—most recently in the winter 2018 semester, at the height of the #metoo moment. This analysis has sometimes fed into investigations of canonical literary rape jokes, such as those in Aphra Behn's comedy of manners *The Rover* and Alexander Pope's mock-epic "The Rape of the Lock." However, the approach to joke analysis that I outline here can stand on its own or frame a conversation about the provocations to laughter in any satire, setting the stage for broader inquiries into the subjectivity, sociability, and potential divisiveness of humor.

It's useful to begin by acknowledging satire's formal commitments to humorous provocation. As a rule, satirists reject the common assumptions that only trivial matters can be funny and, conversely, that important things must be treated with seriousness. In Robert Phiddian's recent definition, satire "is a rhetorical strategy (in any medium) that seeks wittily to provoke an emotional and intellectual reaction in an audience on a matter of public (or at least inter-subjective) significance" (44). Noting its pervasiveness across twenty-first-century media, Phiddian also stresses the polarized reactions that this rhetorical strategy often elicits. Wayne Booth, Linda Hutcheon, and other theorists of irony have pointed out that satirists' indirect style of communication puts extra pressure on audiences to understand what satirists mean to convey. But Phiddian encourages contemporary students of satire to balance attention to authorial intention with attention to reception: "Where satirical controversies occur, it is [the] effects of satire that matter, and not some ideal or virtuosic interpretation of the text of satire" (55). Given the wide range of views on humor about sexual violence in the culture at large these days, students are likely to have significant differences of opinion about it. Taking cues from Phiddian, my students and I explore the range of our reactions to specific instances of satirical humor, seeking to identify not the very best interpretations or most desired responses to jokes but rather the most significant points of conflict or tension among us.

It's also useful to acknowledge from the start that, because of its provocations, satirical humor provides a valuable focal point for developing skills in generous, thoughtful disagreement about sensitive topics and that making a space in which we can name, understand, and navigate differences together is indeed one of the explicit aims of the exercise. On the one hand, the success of our conversation depends on a collective willingness to temporarily suspend moral judgments of other people's sense of humor and to consider how aspects of personal identity and experience may have shaped one's own. On the other hand, wanting distance from people whose tastes clash with one's own is an impulse that will be explicitly incorporated into our analysis. I give a trigger or content warning, and I invite students to talk about their own investment in them, with reference to a recent article that summarizes some of the psychological benefits to the students of such warnings (Boysen). The emotional support for the most vulnerable people in the room that such statements provide is a very important consideration for me. Thus while I encourage each class to distinguish between the posttraumatic stress that some survivors of sexual assault experience and the awkwardness that many people feel around interpersonal conflict, I encourage students to determine how best to handle either sort of anxiety—including leaving the room if necessary—with no obligation to explain themselves. I give an overview of legal, feminist, and any relevant historical perspectives on sexual assault before the class addresses the jokes. I also share contact information for the sexual assault resource center, office of rights and responsibilities, and counseling services on my campus.

Two posts from popular feminist blogs, by Jessica Valenti and by Lindy West—both from 2012, the "Year of the Rape Joke," as *The Daily Beast* dubbed it (Romano)—provide the basic comic material for the core discussions. These posts consider the controversy that then surrounded the stand-up comedian Daniel Tosh. When Tosh announced at a show, "Rape jokes are always hilarious," a woman called out, "Actually, rape jokes are never funny." He retorted, "Hey, wouldn't it be funny if that girl got raped by, like, five guys right now?" (Romano). The woman left and tweeted about her experience, and a media frenzy ensued. Valenti and West wrote with understanding and respect for people who find jokes about sexual violence categorically not funny. West in particular reasons that sexual assault poses a special problem for comedy because it reflects the structural discrimination of women ("How"). Unlike misfortunes such as cancer that befall people at random, women are likely not only to become targets of sexual violence but also to be held responsible for it. West draws a comic analogy between patriarchal society and a place where people are regularly mangled by defective threshing machines and then blamed for their own deaths: "If you care . . . about humans not getting threshed to death, then wouldn't you rather just stick with, I don't know, your new material on barley chaff (hey, learn to drive, barley chaff!)?" Compassion about this culturally loaded form of suffering would seem, automatically and intuitively, to preclude joking about it. Yet West ultimately decides that some satire about sexual violence is worthwhile, as her own humorous approach to the topic suggests. And she and Valenti offer similar guidelines for identifying acceptable rape jokes. In Valenti's words, "what [these jokes] don't do is threaten." West's "easy shortcut" for making a good joke about sexual assault is to "not make rape victims the butt of the joke." They both give examples and links to well-known comic work that, they believe, meet this criterion.

I invite students to select a joke from Valenti's and West's lists that speaks to them in some way—they may love it, hate it, or something in between. With reference to key concepts from humor studies, students at first base their analysis of the joke on their individual reactions, then work with others who've chosen the same joke to see if and how their analyses differ, and finally bring the group's findings to the whole class for further discussion. In his philosophical inquiry into joking, Ted Cohen calls the cultural ideas and information required to understand ("get") a joke its *hermetic condition* (12). Getting a joke is a necessary but not a sufficient condition for laughing at it. The *affective condition* is Cohen's name for the feelings and beliefs required to find a joke funny (21). As with the hermetic condition, generally speaking we instantly and intuitively meet (or fail to meet) this affective condition. However, explaining how we've met it—explaining the feelings attached to laughter (or its absence)—is often a complicated interpretive task.

D. H. Monro's concise comparison of classic theories of humor aids in this explication. The flexible use of these theories can clarify the differences between senses of humor, specific jokes, and the variety of interpretations and reactions a single joke may elicit. Superiority theories of humor propose that laughter occurs when an unexpected encounter with someone or something inferior reassures us of our excellence. Incongruity theorists argue that the sense of surprise is key to our pleasure in jokes, rather than the hierarchical judgments that unexpected connections may incidentally produce. Relief theorists, most famously Freud, emphasize jokes' dreamlike capacity to trick us into considering notions that we normally repress. Under this framework, amusement stems specifically from the giddy feeling of released inhibitions.[1] We assess that overall both Valenti and West are most closely aligned with superiority theorists, since binary moral positions and win/lose power dynamics are central to their interpretations of the jokes they hate and those they like. Significantly, Monro and many others assume that, as a form, satire, typically said to bite, degrade, and shame its objects, exemplifies the superiority theory of humor in particular. But by considering other psychodynamics in our responses to satirical rape jokes, we implicitly interrogate this assumption.

Many students enjoy the stand-up performance linked to West's post in which the comedian John Mulaney narrates his dawning realization that a woman he's following through a train station late one night is not running to catch a subway but to get away from him. Students who choose to analyze Mulaney's routine tend to agree that getting the joke requires our familiarity with a dominant view of men that the comedian had initially failed to register: that men are stronger and bigger than women and full of sexual aggression. As he puts it: "Late at night, on the street, women will see me as a threat. That is funny—yeah! That is funny. It's kind of flattering in its own way, but at the same time it's weird because, like, I'm still afraid of being kidnapped." When it comes to the affective condition of Mulaney's humor, many students concur with West's explanation: "The butt of the joke is John Mulaney. The woman running away from John Mulaney is not being mocked. This is a joke about how scary it is to be a woman and how easy it is for men to be oblivious" ("How"). According to West, Mulaney's routine elicits a pleasing sense of superiority through the comic's self-deprecating representation of his own ignorance of rape culture. We sympathize with the woman's fear, which is completely reasonable under the circumstances, and laugh at and along with Mulaney for his obliviousness. Others point out, however, that the joke may be better understood through the filter of an incongruity theory of humor, since it turns on the gap between the ways that Mulaney and the woman perceive their situation. That is, we laugh at the misunderstanding between them, in which both are equally implicated, without necessarily siding with one or the other. After all, Mulaney is guilty of misunderstanding the culture of male violence, not of aggressive intentions of his own. On this view, the humor of the joke doesn't depend on locating a target but on the surprising realization that the fear of sexual violence infiltrates even the most innocuous of interactions between women and men.

A joke that tends to produce even more polarized reactions is Sarah Silverman's quip, which Valenti praises in passing, about having been sexually assaulted by her doctor: "so bittersweet for a Jewish girl." The line registers as a joke to those who know the stereotype about the cultural capital of doctors, particularly as husbands, among Jews. Those who meet this hermetic condition generally agree that the intended humor of Silverman's joke rests on the use of the word *bittersweet*, which understates the cruelty of sexual assault to a ludicrous degree. But even among the smaller group of students who find Silverman's line funny, there is significant disagreement about whose misguided perspective the word *bittersweet* encapsulates and about what Silverman asks us to make of it. For some students, the delusion at the heart of the joke belongs particularly to Silverman's Jewish-princess persona, who is essentially confessing that it is only with great reluctance that she acknowledges the categorical difference between sexual assault and the consensual sex that might lead to marriage to a mensch. For these students, the joke's humor turns on both incongruity and relief: we are laughing at the unexpected revelation of an insidious, pervasive strain of sexism that renders certain men illegible as perpetrators no matter what they actually do. For others, this is a superiority joke about the ridiculous Jewish cultural obsession with doctors and the extent to which Silverman's naive princess character has been conditioned to accept the sexist cultural values that harm her. Interestingly, those who are put off by the joke generally read it through the lens of superiority as well, finding that it reinforces victim blaming and ethnic stereotyping.

Another not infrequent response to Silverman's joke is to laugh, then almost immediately feel ashamed, fearing that it degrades women, Jews, or both. This ambivalence provides a good starting point for questioning the binary opposition of funny/offensive that has long been entangled in the assumption that serious things must be addressed in a serious tone, which complicates much satire analysis. This opposition is so deeply ingrained that "That's not funny!" is widely understood as an objection to the cruelty of an utterance intended to provoke laughter. Cohen begins to deconstruct the funny/offensive opposition by questioning the hypocrisy of this ambivalence: "Wish that there were no mean jokes. Try remaking the world so that such jokes will have no place, will not arise. But do not deny that they are funny. That denial is a pretense that will help nothing" (83–84). In Cohen's philosophy, laughter occurs only if we have already registered the perspective of a given joke. The jokes we wish to reject as cruel merely reflect cruelty already in the world. While Cohen's is a "don't blame the messenger" sort of argument, humor theory provides another point of departure for rethinking the funny/offensive binary. Under the superiority paradigm of humor, for there to be laughter, something must be degraded: this principle demands that audiences identify a butt of each joke and assess whether this object merits such treatment. However, if we don't construe laughter as inherently and necessarily demeaning, then funny and offensive are incommensurate qualifiers whose opposing terms are, respectively, not funny and inoffensive. Indeed, both the incongruity and relief theories of humor provide frameworks for hearing the crassest joke imaginable as a means of laying bare the pervasive sexual violence that we normally refuse to confront. Those who laugh at Silverman's doctor joke and then feel bad may intuitively lean toward an incongruity or relief theory of laughter but more consciously hold to a superiority theory of laughter. As the more conscious theory kicks in, they worry that their laughter has been mean-spirited. Another version of this shameful double take can occur when we suddenly intuit that others are hearing a joke through a different paradigm from our own—that we, or they, have missed the point.

The importance of context has come to the fore especially in discussions of a joke by Louis CK that West included in her post: "I'm not condoning rape, obviously—you should never rape anyone. Unless you have a reason, like if you want to fuck someone and they won't let you" (qtd. in West, "How"). Before CK confirmed allegations of his sexual misconduct in November 2017, many students were eager to analyze this line, in which an apparently self-evident prohibition is contrasted with a description of nonconsensual sex whose casual diction suggests that the speaker has in fact made a habit of justifying his own acts of criminal violence. In the past, my students and I tended to observe the potential of this joke, like many by the most commercially successful comedians, to appeal to all three kinds of humor theorists. Incongruity theorists could locate the humor specifically in the glaring contradiction in CK's perpetrator persona's statement, which turns the prohibition against sexual violence into a meaningless platitude. When viewed through the relief paradigm, the joke seemed to take this insight even further by exposing how readily language may be exploited to rationalize the harms we cause others. Superiority theorists could especially laugh at the obviously insane perpetrator persona that CK had adopted, whose irrationality it was easy to see through. As West put it, the joke "is making fun of rapists—specifically the absurd and horrific sense of entitlement that accompanies taking over someone else's body like you're hungry and it's a delicious hoagie. The point is, only a fucking psychopath would think like that, and the simplicity of the joke lays that bare."

West's explanation, in 2012, leaned on her prior knowledge of the comedian's values: "Louis CK has spent twenty years making it very publicly clear that he is on the side of making things better. . . . That's why it's easy to give him the benefit of the doubt that this joke is making fun of rapists . . ." ("How"). Previously, many students who liked the joke concurred that the humor increases to the extent that we are sure of the gap between CK's values expressed elsewhere, both onstage and off, and those given voice in this joke. In one class, we fleshed out West's position by considering relevant scholarship on comic personas. "Stand-up comedians are characters in their own narrative, of their own making," Ian Brodie observes. "The audience is expected to try to determine what is true and what is play. The comedian provides cues and clues, and will quickly try to establish how best to guide a particular audience towards the preferred interpretation. Her aim is . . . to deliver whatever will pay off with laughter . . ." (175). On this view, the joke's humor rested less on the stupidity of CK's perpetrator persona than on the pleasing pressure that the joke put on us to decide how to situate CK himself. Many of us in this camp were especially reassured by CK's aside "That's so fucked up!" near the end of the bit.

Compelled by these explorations with my classes, shortly after learning about CK's sexual misconduct I wrote an essay about how many of the joke's avenues to humor are closed down now that the pleasing ambiguity over his relation to his persona is gone (Bobker). This essay set some of the terms for my most recent classroom conversations about it, in which the vast majority of students rejected the joke altogether. In past discussions, some students had felt that in requiring us to weave back through the irony and reassure ourselves of his genuine concern over rape culture, CK had been asking too much of his audience. Now the most common basis for the joke's rejection mirrored this earlier objection. CK's sexual misconduct has made visible the rhetorical trick that was always at the heart of the joke: earlier audiences, too quickly giving him the benefit of the doubt, had actually been complicit in reinforcing rape culture. Significantly, West herself stopped defending this joke in her 2016 memoir: "I should have been harder on Louis CK, I had basically let him off on a technicality" (*Shrill* 171). West's even stronger denunciation of the entertainment industry that supported CK for so many years, in her article, "Why Men Aren't Funny," also resonated with some people. Yet it was a student outspoken about her own experience of sexual violence who insisted on the depth of CK's insights into straight white male privilege. Ironically, CK's status as an abuser underscores the urgency of the critique he was trying to offer.

Finally, discussing different reactions to satires on sexual violence also affords an opportunity to assess a second order of social feelings surrounding laughter. Cohen argues that amusement at a joke produces an intense feeling of alignment not only with the teller but also with everyone else who enjoys the joke. According to Cohen, laughing with others is gratifying proof that the hermetic and affective conditions of the joke have collectively been met: efficiently signaling a shared perspective, laughter both motivates and rewards all those involved. Laughing together, Cohen writes, "is the satisfaction of a deep human longing, the realization of a desperate hope. It is the hope that we are enough like one another to sense one another, to be able to live together" (29). Our classroom disagreements inevitably complicate this account of humor's social nature. While all laughers may appear to agree and may truly enjoy the social bonding this apparent agreement affords, in fact the nature and objects of each person's laughter may greatly differ. At the same time, the intuitive association of laughter with intimacy, however misleading it may be, does go a long way toward explaining the sense of alienation, often expressed as sadness or outrage, that accompanies the experience of not finding a popular joke funny, particularly when already vulnerable people are under attack. For me, that discovery has been one of the most valuable payoffs of these discussions. As with other kinds of aesthetic, affective, and ethical experiences, it is pointless, and possibly even counterproductive, to insist that other people agree with you about what's funny or what's offensive. But trying to clarify the grounds on which we find something funny or offensive can be engaging and bonding in another way. We lose the fantasy that humor unites us even as we compensate for that loss.

Notes

This essay is for the survivors, many of whose contributions immeasurably enriched the discussions described above.

1. For a discussion of a new, evolutionary theory of humor as play, see Morreall. For an argument about the cognitive fallacy of all theories of laughter, see Parvulescu, pp. 7–8.

Works Cited

Bobker, Danielle. "Toward a Humor-Positive Feminism: Lessons from the Sex Wars." *Los Angeles Review of Books*, 17 Dec. 2017, lareviewofbooks.org/article/toward-humor-positive-feminism-lessons-sex-wars/#!.

Booth, Wayne C. *A Rhetoric of Irony*. U of Chicago P, 1974.

Boysen, Guy. "Evidence-Based Answers to Questions about Trigger Warnings for Clinically-Based Distress: A Review for Teachers." *Scholarship of Teaching and Learning in Psychology*, vol. 3, no. 2, 2017, pp. 163–77.

Brodie, Ian. "Stand-up Comedy as a Genre of Intimacy." *Ethnologies*, vol. 30, no. 2, 2008, pp. 153–80.

CK, Louis. "Never Rape Anyone Unless You Have a Reason." *YouTube*, 9 Feb. 2017, www.youtube.com/watch?v=NfxF3uXtC5s.

Cohen, Ted. *Jokes: Philosophical Thoughts on Joking Matters*. U of Chicago P, 1999.

Hutcheon, Linda. *Irony's Edge: The Theory and Politics of Irony*. Routledge, 1994.

Monro, D. H. "Theories of Humor." *Writing and Reading across the Curriculum*, by Laurence Behrens and Leonard J. Rosen, 3rd ed., Scott Foresman, 1988, pp. 349–54.

Morreall, John. "From Lucy to 'I Love Lucy': The Evolution of Humour." *Comic Relief: A Comprehensive Philosophy of Humour*, by Morreall, Wiley-Blackwell, 2009, pp. 40–68.

Parvulescu, Anca. *Laughter: Notes on a Passion*. MIT P, 2010.

Phiddian, Robert. "Satire and the Limits of Literary Theories." *Critical Quarterly*, vol. 55, no. 3, Oct. 2011, pp. 45–58.

Romano, Tricia. "Daniel Tosh, *Two Broke Girls*, and The Oatmeal: The Year of the Rape Joke." *The Daily Beast*, 17 Dec. 2012, www.thedailybeast.com/daniel-tosh-two-broke-girls-and-the-oatmeal-the-year-of-the-rape-joke.
Valenti, Jessica. "Anatomy of a Successful Rape Joke." *The Nation*, 12 July 2012, www.thenation.com/article/anatomy-successful-rape-joke/.
West, Lindy. "How to Make a Rape Joke." *Jezebel*, 12 July 2012, jezebel.com/5925186/how-to-make-a-rape-joke.
———. *Shrill: Notes from a Loud Woman*. Hachette, 2016.
———. "Why Men Aren't Funny." 14 Nov. 2017, *The New York Times*, www.nytimes.com/2017/11/14/opinion/louis-ck-not-funny-harassment.html.

Sophia A. McClennen

The Millennial Classroom: Satire as Public Pedagogy

Stephen Colbert performed at the White House Correspondents' Association Dinner in 2006 and roasted President George W. Bush to his face. While it could be argued that satire is an inherently pedagogical mode, Colbert's speech demonstrated the increasingly important role of satire as a source of public pedagogy. Panned in the mainstream media, Colbert's speech went viral anyway and showed an entirely new way that "citizen-satirists" are not only consuming satire but also producing it.

This essay will trace features of the millennial generation that incline it toward wholly new ways of defining citizenship and political participation. And it will show how satire is an essential part of that process. Despite being derided by the mainstream media, millennials vote at a higher percentage than older generations, they perform more community service than their predecessors, and they score higher on knowledge of political issues. What is of note, though, is that they also produce an impressive amount of political satire. From Twitter hashtags like #NoBudgetNoPants to Occupy Wall Street stunts, this generation combines entertainment and fun with political commentary and social action.

But do they "get" what they are doing? Can they fully appreciate the nuances of satire and irony? Or are they just copying the professionals like Colbert and Jon Stewart?

This essay will look at one key example when professional satire intersected with millennial satire in order to suggest that the "learning" process is clearly not one-sided. By tracing Colbert's founding of his own super PAC, I will show how Colbert taught the nation key features of campaign finance. But he also learned from his millennial viewers, adapting to their insights and suggestions and going on to inspire a host of mini–super PACs run by college students.

So what do those of us who teach in traditional classrooms do with all of this? How can we support the energetic engagement of millennials while also teaching them the art of satire? How do we explain the difference between mockery and satire, between caustic irony and ethical spectacle? This essay closes with specific suggestions for ways to help productively connect the college classroom with the millennial classroom.

The Millennial Citizen

Much has been made about millennials as coddled, entitled, slacktivist whiners. Most of that hype is simply not true.[1] In fact, as generational scholar Russell Dalton points out, millennials may be the most unfairly denigrated generation in history. He explains that part of the reason for this is that millennials have a different notion of citizenship—one that drastically differs from the duty-bound notion of citizenship held by the baby boomer generation. According to Dalton, the younger generations of Xers and Ys hold to a model of "engaged citizenship": "Engaged citizenship emphasizes a more assertive role for the citizen and a broader definition of the elements of citizenship to include social concerns and the welfare of others." Thus millennials see civic engagement as more important than respect for authority: "Engaged citizenship has a broader view of social responsibility than the old norms of citizen duty." Millennials may not vote, but they volunteer and perform community service. Dalton finds that they score higher on "habits of the heart" like donating blood, contributing to charities, and signing up to be organ donors (5).

Millennials come under fire for their political participation despite the fact that their voting trends are not significantly lower than previous generations of young voters—and in some elections, such as the election of Barack Obama in 2008, the youth vote has been surprisingly high. But focusing only on voting misses the various ways that the millennial generation is engaged in the political process. Millennials are some of the most active citizens today, and yet much of their activism is shunned as slacktivism, clicktivism, or worse.

Slacktivism is the term that refers to the idea that internet activism—signing petitions online, sharing political memes, reposting content on social media sites, etc.—is not *real* activism because it doesn't require enough physical engagement to be serious. It's just too easy and therefore is more likely to create self-satisfied citizens than engaged ones, or so the argument goes. But here's the crazy thing: almost all accusations of millennial political engagement as slacktivist or selfie-driven ignores the actual research on these forms of political participation.

For instance, a 2013 Pew Research Center study of "Civic Engagement in the Digital Age" proves that social networking activists are *more* politically engaged than those who aren't on those services (Smith). Furthermore, research by the Harvard Institute of Politics shows that survey participants, especially millennials, who were actively engaged on social networking sites had higher levels of political engagement and stronger partisan identity ("Survey"). According to the Millennial Action Project, "Slacktivism—as a form of digital citizenship—is a stepping stone for deeper and stronger ties to political involvement and participation. These Harvard and Pew Research Center studies reveal a legitimate connection between political participation and social media" (Weiss).

The antimillennial hype is wrong. It fails to understand that millennials have a redefined notion of citizenship, and it fails to appreciate the ways that social media is playing a serious role in shaping political participation today. But here's the part that really gets misunderstood: satire is the core political idiom for millennials. Scholars of satire know that irony, parody, and puns open up a host of possibilities for political engagement and critical thinking. But to the outside world, these forms of communication seem like nothing more than mockery, cynicism, and snark. Thus the presence of satire in millennial political discourse can often be read as disdain, disconnection, and disrespect when it is actually functioning as political participation and active engagement.

Remy Maisel and I argue in our book on satire and politics in the twenty-first century, *Is Satire Saving Our Nation?*, that one of the core distinguishing features of political satire today is the rise of what we call the "citizen-satirist." Following on the heels of citizen journalism, citizen-satirists engage directly in the political process through satirical modes of communication. What we found fascinating was that much of this millennial satire was totally spontaneous and bypassed the need for a professional satirist to create the spark that led to citizen action. We determined there were a number of contributing factors to this development: 1) well-founded lack of public trust in mainstream news, 2) increased trust in satirical "fake" news, 3) increased ease of citizen access to the public sphere through social media platforms, and 4) increased presence of satire as a mode of political discourse.

There are numerous satirical Twitter accounts, many of which are attributed to millennials, that produce daily political commentary with major impact. And Twitter opens up the space for a range of hashtags that allow for the sort of quick, witty humor connected to satirical puns and other wordplay. Accounts like @LOLGOP with 242,000 followers and @BipartisanReport with 197,000 followers are only two examples of this sort of citizen satire. The Binders Full of Women Facebook page was launched during the actual debate when 2012 presidential candidate Mitt Romney made the comment that he had "binders full of women" as governor of Massachusetts. That page is a closed group with more than eight thousand members. These are only a handful of examples, but they serve to highlight an ongoing trend where satire is used in the public sphere to comment critically on politics. One concern directly tied to the rise of citizen satire is the downside of satire's omnipresence in contemporary political discourse. It can deflate the political potential of satire and may lead satire to lose its ironic edge. Alternatively, as I'll illustrate in the next section, active engagement in satire can provide a welcome opportunity for citizen participation in the political process.

Colbert's Super PAC Is a Civics Lesson

In Colbert's run as host of *The Colbert Report* from 2005 to 2014, he offered viewers a healthy diet of productive political satire. From his viral White House Correspondents' Association Dinner performance in 2006 to his Twitter interventions, there are countless examples of ways that Colbert's satire had major public impact. I've written about much of them in *Colbert's America: Satire and Democracy*, so I'll just briefly highlight one example here.

In 2010 a series of court decisions, most notably the Citizens United decision that allowed unlimited campaign contributions from corporations, made it legal for political donations to become more secretive and more directly controlled by corporations and the wealthy. Thus the stage was set for an unprecedented amount of corporate influence in the US elections of 2012. Both Colbert and his satirical counterpart Jon Stewart dedicated significant airtime on their shows to covering the role of big money in politics.

In one example, Colbert parodied candidate Tim Pawlenty with an ad that closed with a mention of "ColbertPAC." "PAC" is a reference to a political action committee, an instrument in US politics that is able to raise unlimited funds from corporate or individual donors to support a political cause. Not only are unlimited funds acceptable, but the funds can also be used for virtually anything. Most critics agree that super PACs are a clear example of an abuse of the democratic process.

When Colbert mocked Pawlenty's PAC, it was just a joke, but when Comedy Central asked Colbert if he actually planned to found his own PAC, he started the process of filing with the Federal Election Commission (FEC) to start his own PAC. The FEC approved Colbert's request in June 2011, and he founded Americans for a Better Tomorrow, Tomorrow, colloquially known as the Colbert Super PAC. By the end of the process, Colbert had raised over $1 million, all of which would be later donated to charity. But the real story is the way that Colbert satirized this process, educated his viewers, and encouraged them to get involved.

Colbert covered his experiences with the super PAC regularly on his show, often inviting his lawyer, former FEC chairman Trevor Potter, on air to help explain the process. One of the keys to these conversations was Colbert's on-air pundit persona. Because Colbert would speak to Potter in character, he could emulate a greedy, privileged member of the US oligarchy. He could ask "dumb" questions of Potter that helped the audience understand how an outright abuse of campaign finance had been hidden in legislative legalese.

The Colbert Super PAC financed a number of political ads, which helped viewers understand how ads can support a candidate without being financed by the candidate's campaign resources. In one example he created an ad that satirically called Romney a "serial killer," since corporations are people and Romney had a history of "killing" them off. Colbert also had fun mocking GOP strategist Karl Rove, the mastermind of super PACs, with a recurring character called Ham Rove. Later, when Colbert decided to run for president of South Carolina, he had to transfer the PAC to Stewart, a move that allowed them to mock the idea that PACs are not "coordinating" with candidates. Potter explained to Colbert that he could not be "active" in the PAC and run for office, but he could "volunteer" for it.

All of these stunts helped walk the audience through the details of campaign finance while using irony, parody, and a healthy dose of puns. Colbert had clearly moved his satire well beyond the confines of a television show by entering much more directly into the public sphere. ABC News reported, "The Stephen Colbert Super PAC is run by a comedian, but the Political Action Committee's bank account is no joke, based on federal reports filed today" (Bingham). *Politico* explained that what seemed like a parodic stunt "could have real—and potentially broad—implications in the world of campaign finance. . . . If nothing else, it could help the cause of campaign finance advocates by highlighting the ability of corporations to spend unlimited amounts to support or oppose candidates" (Vogel).

Colbert wasn't content to just teach his audience about campaign finance; he decided to try to get his audience to be social actors in the process and to do more than contribute to his PAC. So he encouraged them to create their own super PACs. Inspired by an e-mail from Howie Benefiel, a student at the University of Texas at Austin, Colbert invited college students across the nation to participate by founding their own super PACs so that he could "extend 'the reach of my political tentacles across the college campuses of America'" (Schouten and Groppe). To get his audience members going, Colbert "sold" a starter kit, for a minimum donation of $99, called the Colbert Super PAC Super Fun Pack. The idea took off, and a host of Colbert-inspired super PACs cropped up across the nation. Colbert-influenced super PACs represented 2.5 percent of all established super PACs by the time of the election (Levinthal). Interviews with a range of college students who had followed Colbert's lead proved that the process was more than just a silly game: for example, Tyler Bobik, founder of San Diegans for a Better Tomorrow, Tomorrow, stated, "I formed a super PAC to help show how super PACs are undermining the political process" (Kurp).

Colbert's satirical stunt was recognized for its role as a form of public pedagogy. Colbert taught his audience about campaign finance in a satirical and entertaining fashion. In April 2012 Colbert won a Peabody Award for his super PAC parody, which was cited as an "innovative means of teaching American viewers about the landmark court decision" (Subramanian). In June 2014 the Annenberg Public Policy Center reported that the Colbert Super PAC segments improved viewers' knowledge of PACs and

501(c)(4) campaign finance regulation more effectively than other types of news media (Rozansky).

What Next?

Colbert stepped down as host of *The Colbert Report* and moved over to *The Late Show* on CBS, but that doesn't mean the era of satire as public pedagogy is over. Since then, we have seen the rise of a number of other political satirists like John Oliver, whose HBO show *Last Week Tonight* has pioneered a new form of satire activism. His long, analytical segments often end with calls to action and regularly lead to real change, as happened with his piece on net neutrality (Wilstein). In that case, thousands of viewers crashed the Federal Communications Commission Web site, and one year later the FCC voted to keep the internet open. Coincidence?

Citing direct cause and effect in these cases is almost near impossible, but there is significant evidence to trace links among satire, political knowledge, and civic engagement. In one clear example, Colbert called on viewers to engage in the Jimmy Fallon/Stephen Colbert Project, a social issue fund-raiser, and they did. What Maisel and I have found is that satire offers a unique combination of politics, entertainment, and critical thinking. Today's satire goes well beyond cynical mockery and offers millennials engaged and fun ways to critique and challenge structures of power. For millennials, the appeal of satire is the combination of pleasure and political power. As we explain, millennials participate in a notion of citizenship that refuses to believe they have to choose between "serious" action and fun.

All the most well-known millennial-related political actions, such as Occupy Wall Street and Black Lives Matter, have used social media to advance the visibility of their cause. But the important point is that they have also often used irony, satire, and snark. Stephen Duncombe points out that one of the reasons satire, spectacle, and political action are so closely tied for millennials is because satire combines passion with politics (121). He explains that this new form of political action often depends on the fun of satire for its appeal. But he cautions that not all entertaining politics is productive; instead, he urges toward what he calls an "ethical spectacle"—a productive use of fun for progressive politics. Duncombe points out that one of the best forms of ethical spectacle is the sort of politically engaging satire he has observed from both Colbert and Occupy Wall Street.

So how do we marshal this energy in our own classrooms? One of the key ways to intersect classroom pedagogy with satire as public pedagogy is to flip the classroom and allow students to bring in their own ideas and energy. While we may be experts in the scholarly history of satire, our students often have a strong grasp of the ways that they can use visual and verbal satire to get attention. Merging those skill sets can be highly productive. Students often know what has worked, but they don't always understand the deeper reasons why. I ask students to compare examples of satire, such as the State Department's use of satire to mock ISIS recruiting ads and John Oliver's mockery of GOP advertising. They know one is funnier than the other, but humor, of course, is not the ultimate goal of good satire; it is critical thinking. They need to be encouraged to not just analyze the use of irony but also the ways that satire creates in-groups who get the joke and out-groups who are its target (McClennen, "John Oliver"). Even more valuable is to assign group projects where students are asked to creatively imagine a satirical intervention. Once they have conceptualized it, they then analyze the strengths and weaknesses of their hypothetical projects. Understanding what works, what backfires, and what might land them in jail is a useful exercise. And it's a good step toward creating the next Colbert.

Note

1. For more on this line of argument, see my "What's Wrong with Slactivism?"

Works Cited

Bingham, Amy. "Stephen Colbert's Super PAC Hauls in More Than $1 Million." *ABC News*, 31 Jan. 2012, abcnews.go.com/Politics/stephen-colberts-super-pac-hauls-in-more-than-1-million/blogEntry?id=15479366.

Dalton, Russell J. *The Good Citizen: How a Younger Generation Is Reshaping American Politics*. Sage, 2008.

Duncombe, Stephen. *Dream: Re-Imagining Progressive Politics in an Age of Fantasy*. The New Press, 2007.

"The Jimmy Fallon / Stephen Colbert Project." *DonorsChoose*, www.donorschoose.org/giving/the-jimmy-fallon-stephen-colbert-proj/157284/. Accessed 21 Mar. 2016.

Kurp, Josh. "Stephen Colbert Has Inspired Bored College Students to Begin Ironic Super PACs." *Uproxx*, 21 May 2012, uproxx.com/tv/stephen-colbert-has-inspired-bored-college-students-to-begin-ironic-super-pacs.

Levinthal, Dave. "Stephen Colbert's Super PAC Spawns Mini PACs." *Politico*, 4 May 2012, www.politico.com/story/2012/05/colbert-super-pac-spawns-mini-pacs-075942.

McClennen, Sophia A. *America According to Colbert: Satire and Public Pedagogy*. Palgrave Macmillan, 2011.

———. "John Oliver Is Smarter Than the State Department: Irony Will Not Defeat ISIS." *Salon*, 6 Oct. 2014, www.salon.com/2014/10/06/john_oliver_is_smarter_than_the_state_department_irony_will_not_defeat_isis.

———. "What's Wrong with Slactivism? Confronting the Neoliberal Assault on Millennials." *Scholactivism: Reflections on Transforming Praxis Inside and Outside the Classroom*, edited by David Downing and Joseph Ramsey. *Works and Days*, vols. 33–34, nos. 65–66, 67–68, 2016–17, pp. 373–88.

McClennen, Sophia A., and Remy M. Maisel. *Is Satire Saving Our Nation? Mockery and American Politics*. Palgrave Macmillan, 2014.

Rozansky, Michael. "Stephen Colbert's Civics Lesson: Or, How a TV Humorist Taught America about Campaign Finance." Annenberg Public Policy Center of the University of Pennsylvania, 2 June 2014, cdn.annenbergpublicpolicycenter.org/wp-content/uploads/Stephen-Colberts-Civics-Lesson-release-6-02-14.pdf.

Schouten, Fredreka, and Maureen Groppe. "Crop of College Super PACs Answers Call of Stephen Colbert." *USA Today*, 7 May 2012, usatoday30.usatoday.com/news/politics/story/2012-05-04/super-PAC-spinoff-stephen-colbert/.

Smith, Aaron. "Civic Engagement in the Digital Age." *Pew Research Center*, 25 Apr. 2013, www.pewinternet.org/2013/04/25/civic-engagement-in-the-digital-age.

Subramanian, Courtney. "Stephen Colbert's Super PAC Satire Lands Him a Peabody." *Time*, 5 Apr. 2012, newsfeed.time.com/2012/04/05/stephen-colberts-super-pac-satire-lands-him-a-peabody.

"Survey of Young Americans' Attitudes toward Politics and Public Service." Harvard University Institute of Politics, 24th ed., 29 Oct.–11 Nov. 2013, www.iop.harvard.edu/sites/default/files_new/131204_IOP_Fall2013Topline.pdf.

Vogel, Kenneth P. "Colbert at the FEC? Really." *Politico*, 15 May 2011, www.politico.com/story/2011/05/colbert-at-the-fec-really-054946.

Weiss, Emily. "The Millennial Slacktivism Debate: A Political Perspective." *Millennial Action Project*, 29 Apr. 2015, www.millennialaction.org/blog/millennials-slacktivism-politics.

Wilstein, Matt. "John Oliver Explains FCC's Net Neutrality Ruling to Confused Republicans." *Mediaite*, 2 Mar. 2015, www.mediaite.com/tv/john-oliver-explains-fccs-net-neutrality-ruling-to-confused-republicans.

Christopher Vilmar

Satires of Possessive Individualism

This essay lays out a pedagogical exercise meant to help students better understand recent satires that deal with possessive individualism. This term is not meant to introduce students to a rigorously theorized concept or category of texts.[1] Rather, it is simply a general term for a tendency nearly ubiquitous in contemporary American life: the tendency to equate and express one's individuality in one's consumer choices. And even though this essay uses Chuck Palahniuk's novel *Fight Club* (1996) to provide its examples, the insights generated with this type of reading can be adapted quite easily to teaching many recent satirical texts.[2]

Intuitively it would seem that contemporary satires—especially those of the qualities and expressions of possessive individualism in the world around us—should be more accessible to students than older, canonical satires. Yet this has not been my experience as a classroom teacher. Like everyone else, college students are still coming to terms with the world they inhabit, and it is difficult to analyze a subject that one doesn't fully understand yet. The pedagogical exercise in this essay, therefore, serves at least two purposes. One, students can use it to understand possessive individualism. Two, they can then use that understanding to read recent satires with a degree of critical distance and to assess the specific criticisms that those satires make on the world around them.

Every spring I teach a satire course aimed primarily at nonmajors fulfilling general education requirements. I always begin with a definition of satire by Edward Rosenheim: "an attack by means of a manifest fiction upon discernible historical particulars" (33). As teachers of satire we have already encountered various revisions of this definition by later criticism.[3] Yet it remains a serviceable starting point for undergraduates, because it forces them to ask, What is being attacked in this satire, and by what artistic devices or means? Contemporary works of satire often elude the best efforts of my students with regard to identifying either the target of the satire or the formal qualities of the work; they make mistakes that they easily avoid when reading older satires simply by virtue of the study required to understand historical contexts and the formal qualities of art from another period. Many students reading *Fight Club*, for instance, will sum up the text in the terms of a platitude ("don't be too materialistic, because it isn't very satisfying"). Others will uncritically admire the troubling antihero Tyler Durden. Responses like these are not based on clear knowledge of Rosenheim's historical particulars or the artistic means of the text (e.g., the insidious conformism required by corporate culture, or the way Tyler's hip rebellion reproduces the worst aspects of that culture even as he tries to dismantle it).

And even though I insist to my students that historical context is indispensable, I remember that I was not attracted to satire because of history. Rather, it was the feeling I had that Jonathan Swift's outrage was undimmed by time and his formal critique of eighteenth-century English could be easily directed, with minimal loss in the transfer, to the world around me. And the same thing happens with my students, who often fail to note that time has passed since Palahniuk published his novel attacking very specific phenomena in 1990s America. They read its satirical critique in ways quite like they read the attacks of Thomas More's *Utopia* (1516), another perennial assignment on my syllabus. When we read book 1 of *Utopia*, I explain to my students the basic economic realities of sixteenth-century English wool production. But my students typically do not apply the attack on private property in book 2 to enclosing landlords and desperate sheepherders. Rather, they extrapolate that attack to the rapacious elites and exploited workers of today. They make similar temporal transpositions reading Samuel Johnson's *Rasselas* or Voltaire's *Candide* (both

1759). Johnson satirizes wealthy but vapid young men in one chapter, and Voltaire snipes at the Catholic Church throughout his text. But my students typically connect these dated broadsides with more recent targets. The relative currency of *Fight Club* only makes these kinds of connections and transpositions that much easier. The problem is not that its satire is too distant but that it is too close. Any recent satire of possessive individualism challenges views that many students hold dear—views that have quite possibly gone unexamined before entering college. The pedagogical exercise in this chapter is meant to help students identify both the ways that possessive individualism shapes the present and the specific attacks that a given satire makes on the ubiquity of the idea—and therefore, however obliquely, to consider the ways that a given satire can shape pragmatic action with regard to ideological concerns.

When students read satires of possessive individualism, the immediacy of the text and one's responses to it create problems more easily sidestepped when studying historical satires. In *Fight Club* the narrator's[4] Audi and condo full of Swedish furniture do not require explanation as Horace's Sabine farm does. And the mere fact of correlating Horace's wealth with analogous recent signifiers creates a kind of critical analysis. Many students simply cannot imagine owning an Audi or a luxury condo as an implicit criticism of corporate materialism; after all, more students attend college to pursue these kinds of rewards than to engage in the long delays of gratification in pursuing learning for its own sake. Reading these satires through ideological lenses that fail to distinguish possessive individualism is therefore a kind of piecemeal reading. It produces a chuckle when the satire concurs with existing views but ignores the more serious challenge of its full critique. Such piecemeal readings prevent students from gauging the extent to which a satire might undermine their existing ideology, largely because ideologies resist self-examination in order to maintain their own strength.

Because students cannot identify, much less analyze, the satirical attacks in *Fight Club*—historically or formally—this pedagogical exercise begins with an attempt to help students over this impasse. I introduce them, all too briefly, to the work of two influential recent thinkers on identity. I then use the theoretical specificity provided by those thinkers to help students assume a more critical distance toward possessive individualism, so they can begin to appreciate the extent of the deliberate and searching critiques on that concept by satirists.

Pierre Bourdieu's *Distinction* (1979) and Charles Taylor's *Sources of the Self* (1989) advance disparate theories about the way modern people decide their consumptive preferences and construct identities from different patterns of consumption. Though both of these thinkers examine the intersection of ideology and personal identity, they offer two very distinct ways of describing and analyzing the self. Such theorizing is germane to *Fight Club*, at the center of which is a crisis of identity. The narrator, Joe, creates an alternate personality in Tyler Durden as a response to feelings of powerlessness and anxiety; that crisis is mirrored in the experience of the members of Fight Club and later Project Mayhem, who feel that following Tyler's rules liberates them from those feelings. This pedagogical exercise has provided students with more nuanced concepts and terms to apply to the idea of identity, wherewith they can move past their initially naive rejection or identification with the text to discuss its implications in greater analytical detail.

I begin with an introductory lecture to my students on the work of Taylor for two reasons. First, *Sources of the Self* traces the historical evolution of the modern concept of individuality, most particularly the supreme importance given to the idea that individuals ought to be genuine and authentic. Second, Tyler initially seems to offer Joe an escape from the constraints of corporate life into precisely Taylor's terms: a more authentic existence. Taylor therefore provides us with an introduction to the assumptions in our ideology of the self—and a way to see that the barbed vision of *Fight Club* may not chronicle an escape to conditions making that kind of self possible so much as it attacks the very assumptions of that self.

It is not possible in one paragraph or one lecture to summarize the argument of *Sources of the Self*. The book draws on a dizzying array of humanistic disciplines over the course of its lengthy argument. Yet a cursory summary serves the purposes of this pedagogical exercise. Taylor describes the modern self as the product of three categories: "first, modern inwardness, the sense of ourselves as beings with inner depths, and the connected notion that we are 'selves'; second, the affirmation of ordinary life which develops from the early modern period; third, the expressivist notion of nature as an inner moral source" (x). The first implies self-examination and self-interpretation as a method of disentangling the self from anything that diminishes its freedom. The second requires selves to be individual and authentic; mimicry simply will not serve as a distinguishing marker. The third, which is perhaps most difficult for students, implies a rejection of scientific rationality and modern alienation as the self reconnects emotionally with nature.[5]

Taylor identifies those qualities that are implicit in our assumptions about the self, and examples of these qualities appear throughout the text of *Fight Club.* Some students read the first half of *Fight Club* as the escape of Joe from the exhaustive conformity demanded by his career working for a major automotive corporation. But with Taylor in mind, such episodes begin to seem more like the fulfillment of a workday daydream than a genuine alternative. When Joe first "meets" Tyler on a beach, several of Taylor's qualities appear at once. Joe is on another in an endless string of business trips, and he falls asleep on a beach only to awake to find Tyler sitting next to him, "pulling driftwood logs out of the surf" to create "the shadow of a giant hand" that is "perfect for one minute, and for one perfect minute Tyler had sat in the palm of a perfection he'd created himself" (32–33). Before meeting Tyler, Joe displays ample evidence of resentment toward the restrictions of affluent corporate life. But in this scene he admires the freedom with which Tyler creates a thing, however evanescent, that expresses his individual connection with nature and is therefore meaningful in ways that the duplicated forms that proliferate as the result of his corporate work can never be. And Marla, like Tyler, has escaped from the grind of gainful productivity. She lives in poverty in a squalid motel room, and Joe looks on in wonder as she preens around his kitchen in a thrift store dress proclaiming her love for similarly ephemeral things: "all the things that people love intensely and then dump an hour or a day after" (67). Joe admires the contrast between those idiosyncratic preferences and his button-down conformity, prompting a line repeated often in both book and film: "If I could wake up in a different place, at a different time, could I wake up as a different person?" (33). In spite of the real differences between his relationships with Tyler and Marla, for Joe both of them represent an ideal of inner coherence and authenticity far removed from the narrator's alienation and anxiety. These two qualities stem from his timid compliance with the expectations of his career and social class.

Tyler especially seems, at least at first glance, to have slipped free from the ideological constraints that white-collar employment places on the singular self. He is relaxed and cool, creative and introspective. These qualities—in fact his very being—seem to manifest the authentic self of Taylor's theory, and this explains his charisma both within the text to other characters and without to us as readers. At the catering gig he tells his blue-collar coworkers, "So, tell the banquet manager. Get me fired. I'm not married to this chickenshit job" (83). Eschewing "marriage" (to work and to women like Marla) makes explicit his radical disengagement from anything that diminishes his freedom: an important qualification for Taylor's authentic self. Tyler also takes on the role of prankster in this scene, a kind of Robin Hood who defends ordinary life against the abuses of the wealthy people that life serves. By encouraging coworkers to "stop treading water and do something with our lives" (83) and chortling to Joe that such pranks "are more fun as a shared activity" (84), Tyler attempts to move others toward this position of seemingly greater freedom and authenticity.

Tyler not only abets Joe in founding the insistently physical and bodily activities of Fight Club and Project Mayhem, but he also acts as a kind of spiritual guide to greater autonomy. When Joe goes in to work battered from Fight Club, he says, "It really pissed me off that I'd become this totally centered Zen Master and nobody had noticed. . . . I get totally ZEN right in everyone's hostile little FACE" (63). But when Joe informs Tyler, "I'm enlightened now. You know, only Buddha-style behavior," Tyler quips, "Sticking feathers up your butt does not make you a chicken" (69). The clever jibe only underscores that this claim is "premature enlightenment" (70). Tyler urges Joe to abandon corporate values altogether and embrace ongoing self-examination—both of which, according to Taylor, are aspects of an evolved selfhood. The importance of this spiritual quest becomes negatively manifest when the narrator, speaking over the phone to a detective about the destruction of his condo, denies that he sabotaged the place with explosives: "I loved my life. I loved that condo. . . . That was my whole life. Everything, the lamps, the chairs, the rugs were me. The dishes in the cabinets were me. The plants were me. The television was me. It was me that blew up" (110–11). The narrator's earlier confession—"It took my whole life to buy this stuff" (44)—becomes ironic in an entirely new register after this conversation. Where Joe once sought an identity measured by his material possessions, his ironic reference to that fact indicates that he now follows Tyler. And yet the mere act of *following* is precisely not one of the characteristics of Taylor's selfhood, and that Joe does not become inner-directed according to Taylor's definition simply underscores how little he has achieved with regard to self-authenticity.

The theory of *Sources of the Self* also allows for greater rigor in examining those parts of *Fight Club* that satirize the alienating quality of corporate employment. The very facelessness of the job disconnects Joe from his labor and prevents him from making sense of his work activity. He is therefore unable to create a meaningful narrative of his life. This confusion leads him to call his father repeatedly as the years pass, asking him for advice: "When I got a job and turned twenty-five, long distance, I said, now what? My dad didn't know, so he said, get married. I'm a thirty-year-old boy, and I'm wondering if another woman is really the answer I need" (51). When this advice proves unhelpful, Joe questions and eventually abandons altogether the advice and wisdom of older generations.

As the novel unfolds, however, Tyler begins to exert an increasingly tyrannical charisma over Joe—just as Fight Club and Project Mayhem require an increasingly straitjacketed conformity in order to "liberate" members from the oppressions of work and social mores. To explain the paradoxical conformity required by liberation in the novel, therefore, I turn to the work of Bourdieu.[6] Another lecture introduces students to the way Bourdieu envisions the dynamic interaction as the individual as *habitus* (the individual and her economic, cultural, and social *capital*) navigates *fields* according to the *doxa* or rules that govern each field.[7] When we turn to *Distinction*, we study the argument that taste works within larger sociological contexts. Where Taylor sees identity as innate, Bourdieu explains the ways that individuals both classify and are classified according to "behaviours that are intended to bring real being into line with official being" (25). Such behaviors, like Tyler's rebellion against imprisonment within blue-collar servitude, are the product of *educational capital* plus the *social class of the father*. *Distinction*, therefore, is a pun: it marks both class—a *distinguished* gentleman—and the manner that *distinguishes* him, that activity that produces, expresses, and justifies individual tastes within the pull of various *doxa*. Class distinction largely depends on possessing enough economic freedom to avoid necessity: any work is less free than being at home or on holiday, industry is less free than art, and the active acquirement of cultural capital is inferior to inheriting it (just as schooled knowledge is inferior to knowledge absorbed without question from the family background). For Bourdieu, therefore, consumption is a field where "cultured" selves establish and legitimate their tastes by opposing middlebrow and popular choices (as in, for example, the descending hierarchy of classical, jazz, and pop music). Legitimate tastes reproduce themselves while insisting on their essential authenticity—both distinct and distinguished—from lower choices, disguising their contingent and class-based origins in a myth of singularity that is belied by conformity to class norms.

Joe begins *Fight Club* with confessions of his love for the distinguishing markers of white-collar taste. In the confession already mentioned ("It took my whole life to buy this stuff"), Joe suggests that the price for these items has indeed been something of a Mephistophelean bargain. His "nesting instinct" to own IKEA furniture takes on pornographic qualities: where he had once read men's magazines in the bathroom, he now reads furniture catalogs. And just as pornography had defined his adolescent longing for adulthood, his lust for furniture defines his adult masculinity: "The Vild hall clock . . . oh, I had to have that" (43). Only the arrival of Tyler undermines the distinctive solace of upper-middle-class tastes. Tyler takes working-class jobs and pushes Joe to do the same, because these jobs allow for free and fearless expression: equivalent jobs are always available, after all, so no sacrifice is required to obtain them. Tyler also speaks fearlessly against the materialism of the members of Fight Club and Project Mayhem, all of whom are struggling in a variety of Bourdieuvian registers to distinguish themselves economically and culturally. Fighting becomes a kind of nostalgia for manliness, one that offers a different kind of success, but ultimately the members of Fight Club and Project Mayhem simply ape Tyler's words rather than following the broad example of his gestures and seeking their own idiosyncratic freedom. A line spoken by Joe in the novel echoes many of Tyler's sentiments: "The things you used to own, now they own you" (44). (Appropriately enough, in the film version that line is given to Brad Pitt as Tyler rather than Edward Norton as Joe.) These words announce the revolt against the tastes of the upper middle class, and the origin of Fight Club seems to offer an escape toward what Taylor calls greater authenticity and a more genuine individuality than would have been possible in either corporate or blue-collar shackles.

Yet Fight Club and later Project Mayhem can be reduced to an infamous set of rules, or *doxa* in Bourdieu's terminology, created and policed by Tyler. Every meeting begins with their repetition, a kind of deprogramming from the assumptions of capitalist culture even as they reprogram the speaker into the new norms of the underground. The members of Fight Club and Project Mayhem have abandoned the dominant hierarchy and orphaned themselves from the comforts of acceptability in order to search for something more satisfying—but the end result of both organizations is not freedom and autonomy but rather the acceptance of a new *doxa*. Project Mayhem intends to combine the newly shared *doxa* that creates Fight Club members and move these ideas onto the world stage of political action: "It's Project Mayhem that's going to save the world. . . . Like fight club does with girls and boys, Project Mayhem will break up civilization so we can make something better out of the world"

(125). Tyler repeatedly calls Joe a "space monkey" (e.g., 12, 78) and the members of Project Mayhem adopt the usage. One space monkey informs another, as blithely as if such usage is entirely his own, "Individually, we are nothing" (134). The repetition of Tyler's dogmas creates a new *doxa*, endlessly intoned until any possibilities for dissent—and therefore originality and selfhood, in Taylor's sense of the term—have been ruthlessly eliminated: "Tyler's words coming out of my mouth" (98); "This is all Tyler Durden dogma" (141); "The mechanic starts talking, and it's pure Tyler Durden" (149). These ideas are reproduced until the climax, when Joe says, "Everybody in Project Mayhem is part of Tyler Durden, and vice versa" (155). No one, not even Tyler, has a separate identity. The newly corporate body of Project Mayhem reproduces and polices its *doxa* with the same ruthless privilege, the same attempt to disguise its origin in class structure, as the endless ideological effacement and enforcement performed by dominant culture.

By using two contrasting views, Taylor's authentic self against Bourdieu's socially constructed one, this pedagogical exercise resolves none of the basic paradoxes either of the text as satire or of the ideology of possessive individualism. Taylor and Bourdieu can give us as readers only a critical purchase on Joe and Tyler and on the corporate culture that is imposed both by the automotive industry and by Fight Club and eventually Project Mayhem. Many of the ironic juxtapositions of the text itself can be articulated clearly in the theoretical distance between Taylor and Bourdieu. Like *The Catcher in the Rye* (1951), *Fight Club* takes an adolescent view of life; this quality may explain its appeal for college-age students. But students who have read this novel with the exercise suggested by this essay in mind will not easily be seduced by the *doxa* of either Joe or Tyler. They will read it as fiction, and any correlative between the text and things or ideas in their lived experience will be seen more clearly as satirical representations—and better examined from a cool, critical distance instead of an admiring but undiscerning proximity.

As a *reader* of satire, I take as axiomatic Swift's comment: "Satire is a sort of glass, wherein beholders do generally discover everybody's face but their own; which is the chief reason for that kind of reception it meets in the world, and that so very few are offended with it" (Swift 1). Following Swift, *teachers* of satire can decide that we should maximize the offense that satire does to its beholders—to help them see every blemish fully magnified in its representation. But teaching satires of possessive individualism, I feel compelled to help students realize that the mirror of satire contains at best a static representation and therefore reveals ideology for what it is when reading satire: a starting point.

Notes

1. I borrow the term "possessive individualism" from C. B. MacPherson's classic study but do not incorporate any substantial aspects of his theory. Rather, I use the term as a kind of shorthand for individualism predicated on private property.

2. Just taking texts that have been on my syllabus in the past decade as examples, I can easily picture adapting the basic idea of this essay to the analysis of recent works like *Office Space* (1999), *The Office* (2005–13), *Stuff White People Like* (2008), and *How to Be Black* (2012).

3. This definition has undergone significant revision by later criticism, particularly Fredric V. Bogel's trenchant observation that it straddles formalist and historicist models of criticism. See commentary in Bogel (7–8) and also Griffin (esp. 29–30, 36).

4. The narrator is the protagonist and is never named in the novel. In the 1999 film adaptation of *Fight Club* he is called Jack, after a name used in a series of *Reader's Digest* articles that he reads somewhat obsessively while living in the Paper Street house with Tyler. In the book these articles use the name Joe, which links him with the average Joe of contemporary myth and reinforces his everyman status in the text—his issues are meant to be our own. I refer to him as Joe in this essay.

5. In this summary of Taylor's arguments, I have relied throughout on Ruth Abbey's chapter "Interpreting Selfhood" in her excellent introduction to his thought, *Charles Taylor* (55–100), and on George Scialabba's review of Taylor's book, as well as *Sources of the Self*.

6. In this summary of Bourdieu's ideas, I have relied on Richard Jenkins's fine introductory study *Pierre Bourdieu* (esp. 128–51), as well as Bourdieu's *Distinction*.

7. I show a brief *YouTube* video that very quickly introduces these ideas (Reynolds); I also ask students to study the video (and to find others like it) at home until the difficult terms of Bourdieu's critique become familiar. This homework is meant to reinforce the ideas introduced in class.

Works Cited

Abbey, Ruth. *Charles Taylor*. Princeton UP, 2000.

Bogel, Fredric V. *The Difference Satire Makes: Rhetoric and Reading from Jonson to Byron*. Cornell UP, 2001.

Bourdieu, Pierre. *Distinction: A Social Critique of the Judgement of Taste*. Translated by Richard Nice, Harvard UP, 1984.

Griffin, Dustin H. *Satire: A Critical Reintroduction*. UP of Kentucky, 1994.

Jenkins, Richard. *Pierre Bourdieu*. Routledge, 1992.

MacPherson, C. B. *The Political Theory of Possessive Individualism: Hobbes to Locke*. Oxford UP, 1962.

Palahniuk, Chuck. *Fight Club*. W. W. Norton, 1996.
Reynolds, Cheryl. "Simple Introduction to Bourdieu." *YouTube*, 28 Mar. 2014, youtu.be/1W_IkfGg2nU.
Rosenheim, Edward W. *Swift and the Satirist's Art*. U of Chicago P, 1963.
Scialabba, George. "The Modern Mind." *Dissent*, Fall 1990, pp. 534–37.
Swift, Jonathan. *Major Works*. Edited by Angus Ross and David Wooley, Oxford UP, 2003.
Taylor, Charles. *Sources of the Self: The Making of the Modern Identity*. Harvard UP, 1989.

Peter Schmidt

Menippean Satire in the Digital Era: Gary Shteyngart's *Super Sad True Love Story*

In *Menippean Satire Reconsidered: From Antiquity to the Eighteenth Century*, Howard Weinbrot argues that Menippean satire tends to be produced in eras of "broken or fragile national, cultural, religious, political, or generally intellectual values" (7). It protests cultural decadence and decline by incorporating contradiction into its form, using "at least two other genres, languages, cultures, or changes of voice to oppose a dangerous, false, or specious and threatening orthodoxy" (6). Although it may feature memorable characters, the Menippean mode primarily targets diseased and dangerous ideas or habits. It is encyclopedic in range and ambition, absorbing and parodying different discourses and genres while constructing a narrative via debates, fantasies, annotations (either within the text or in footnotes and/or appendices), and other rhetorical devices. The result is an anxious, angry, labyrinthine, fragmented, stubbornly contrarian text.

Some satires also feature a dramatic moment Weinbrot calls a *Menippean incursion*, which "appears when necessary, penetrates the action, [and] offers a new voice or point of view [about the] threat of a dangerous orthodoxy" (275). In this extreme form of textual violence, the invasive voice enacts the arrogance of a particular discourse and worldview, interrupting and then disappearing and leaving a textual wound. The violated text thus stands as a scathing protest (and perhaps also a failed or despairing one) against the powers represented by the incursion.

Supplementing Weinbrot, I'd add the following general points. A satire that mainly lampoons a target, however cleverly, cannot be Menippean, for the boundary between what's mocked and the voice doing the mocking is too clear and stable: it offers us the chance to side with the primary speaker and laugh at someone or something from a secure, superior location outside or elsewhere. As Freud suggested in *Jokes and Their Relation to the Unconscious*, jokes and satire commonly inoculate us with power over another and/or something that tormented us. Examples of satires featuring a primary character engaging in comic revenge are Nora Ephron's *Heartburn* and Philip Roth's *Sabbath's Theater* (two very different novels in other ways). A rarer mode, Menippean satire is energized by outrage too, but it never focuses primarily on one speaker and its purpose is more ambiguous. It immerses us, sometimes terrifyingly so, within fear and culture clash, with no "safe space" available. Not only does the Menippean incursion signify such danger, but the whole of the form enacts invasion and vulnerability on every page. It becomes really difficult to construct what a speaker's (or the author's) "intent" was, much less to figure out the meaning of particular passages or the work as a whole. Interpretive and formal instability, brokenness, and ambiguity bristle at both the smallest and largest scales; the work seems amalgamated of one aporia piled upon another, causing vertigo, puzzlement, impasse. Affectively, this can make viewers or readers feel a kind of emotional free fall, generating exhilaration and terror, laughter and immense unease.

Menippean elements well describe the texture and structure of Gary Shteyngart's fiction and the crisis in US imperial confidence at the end of the American Century that Shteyngart anatomizes. In his 2010 novel *Super Sad True Love Story* (hereafter *Super Sad*), utopian narratives of technological progress, the triumph of neoliberalism, and American Restoration are roiled by anxious visions of decline, invasion, and loss occurring within the psyches of individual characters, their relationships, and the nation-state itself. Menippean satire is basically schizophrenic, marked by clashing voices, languages, worldviews, and values. So too is Shteyngart's text, split between the contrapuntal narratives of two protagonists from recent immigrant families, Lenny Abramov and Eunice Park. Shteyngart, however, updates the Menippean mode for an era that witnesses not just the atrophy of the nation-state (and the immigrant "success" story) but also of the print book and the practices of interpretation and empathy it encouraged. He slyly adds a strong contemporary instance of Menippean incursion, a supplement-epilogue, that in a rather Derridean (or a *Tristram Shandy*-an?) way reframes and unsettles all that we've just read.

This essay offers not so much a lesson plan for teaching *Super Sad* as a set of topics and tensions from which a lesson plan may be generated. It also seeks broader conclusions about why satire's historically most heterogeneous and nihilistic mode now has renewed prominence. Earlier US writers adept at the Menippean include Mark Twain (*Pudd'nhead Wilson*), Nathanael West (*Miss Lonelyhearts* and *The Day of the Locust*), and George Schuyler (*Black No More*). West's precedent is important for Shteyngart because of the ways in which he skewers "cures" for modernity's malaise offered by commerce, technology, and the "fine arts." Twain and Schuyler are important for showing how the Menippean may engage with race. They parody both biological and cultural arguments for racial difference, while simultaneously making farcical the ways that "difference" has repeatedly been commodified. In Twain's text, the guilt is said by the narrator to lie with the "erroneous inventory" of the murderer's racial identity rather than his actual actions, yet once his "real" "black" self is exposed he is promptly sold to pay for debts he created when "white" (121). Twain's novel definitively solves its murder mystery, but it gives thoroughly contradictory answers about the *cause* of the murder. (Was it Tom's "black" blood or his "white" privileges that corrupted him?) In Schuyler's novel, the best satire to emerge out of the Harlem Renaissance, a seeming reversal in race/power relations is marked by skin-darkening creams suddenly becoming best sellers: Americans remain obsessed with minute skin-color differences.

Since the 1960s—perhaps as a response to even more heightened uncertainty involving race, class, gender, sex, and the future of human identity—the Menippean mode in fiction has revived like some Frankensteinian patchwork monster. Thomas Pynchon, of course (most notably *Gravity's Rainbow*), but also Fran Ross (*Oreo*), Maxine Hong Kingston (*Tripmaster Monkey: His Fake Book*), David Foster Wallace (*Infinite Jest*), Philip Roth (*The Counterlife*; *The Ghost Writer*; *Operation Shylock*), and Paul Beatty (*The White Boy Shuffle*; *The Sellout*) are standout examples. Yet the rebellious return of Menippean satire is arguably global: consider the farcical nihilism and linguistic inventiveness countering capitalism's new colonialism in Emile Habiby's *The Secret Life of Saeed the Pessoptimist* (1974), set in Israel/Palestine, or Valeria Luiselli's *The Story of My Teeth* (2015), set in Mexico.

Why should the electroshock resurrection of Menippean satire occur now? Perhaps because of this savage irony: Menippean disruptive energies have been appropriated by postindustrial multinational capitalism, all in the name of selling "freedom" and "development." Creative destruction by the god of the market is perhaps the most profound Menippean "incursion" of all. What can sellers of mere fiction do in the face of such corporate power, which can invent infinite "shell" avatars while manipulating governments and shifting money from one location to another in milliseconds? Hypothesis: Menippean satire by writers rises in eras (such as the Gilded Age, the Depression, and the present) when elites engage in their own forms of violent social disruption in order to secure their power.

Shteyngart's gambit is to turn neoliberalism's appropriation of the Menippean against itself. What neoliberalism's new colonialism fears most is skeptical laughter, an emperor-has-no-clothes and we're-being-robbed moment. Shteyngart imitates its workings in order for us to notice what is erased in the name of the new. In the twilight of the Gutenberg era of the print book, Shteyngart has produced a text that identifies, parodies, and counters narratives that promote digital technology as offering a brave new world of "Post-Human" information analysis ("scanning") that supposedly will be vastly superior to old-school book- and individual-centered reading and interpretation. Shteyngart ironically binds such a commodified future *to* literary history and its representations of our fallible, nonquantifiable human tragicomedy. In the process, Shteyngart proves to be one of contemporary satire's most inventive practitioners, both funny and frightening at once.

I have taught *Super Sad* several times in a post–World War II fiction survey course popular with both majors and nonmajors. In my experience, students of the millennial generation immediately connect to the novel's adroit parodies of high-tech utopian gizmos and the pressures of contemporary social media. They identify with the conflicts experienced by the novel's primary protagonists, Lenny and Eunice, and eagerly dissect the novel's examples of the market's overwhelming power, including its effects on identity and the ways in which an Orwellian world of top-down surveillance has now morphed to include a horizontal network of "voluntary" sharing and competitive status acquisition. They are also struck by Shteyngart's suggestion that the United States, far from "exceptional," has basically become a third-world country with first-world pretensions, characterized by immense wealth inequities, social strife, decaying infrastructure, oligarchical rule, and mass-media narratives of "unity," "restoration," and "taking back" the country.

Some students will be made uneasy or even offended by the novel's intense pessimism, violence, and explicit language. To address these concerns, set up a class debate about the function of satire. Is satire's negativity and use of exaggeration—especially in its extreme Menippean mode—merely destructive and irresponsible, or do its painful truths perform a healthy function? If so, what? Such a discussion will to some degree reproduce the historical debate (begun by the Greeks) over whether allowing satire such liberties is a threat to society or necessary for its health. Apocalyptic fears about the end of the United States or even the end of the world are rife at present. So too is unease with social media and the commodification and hypersexualization of bodies and selves. How can this novel help us understand these anxieties and respond to them? Lesson plans should also not ignore the novel's exploration of gender, class, and race tensions or its sly rewriting of the American immigrant narrative. Examples of all the above may provide rich topics for discussion.

Do your students agree that *Super Sad* well captures the ambivalence we have regarding social media and technological "advances"? We feel they give us unprecedented power, yet we also fear their power *over* us. Why is it important to give doubts or ambivalence a voice, either in literature or in some other medium?

An innovative text should generate innovative assignments. As well as (or in place of) requiring a conventional analytic paper, consider having students write a reader-response diary in Lenny's voice or text their thoughts the way Eunice does. I also highly recommend a digital annotation assignment, which will help them explore how linguistic inventiveness is essential to Shteyngart's satire. Choose a number of invented terms or phrases key to *Super Sad*—such as "äppärät" or "American Restoration Authority"—and let students nominate some too. Give them models for good annotation, then let them go to work singly or in small groups. After they present their annotations to the full class, broaden the discussion to consider why such microreadings help deepen our understanding and enjoyment of the novel as a whole. It's also possible (with their permission) to publish revised and vetted student annotations or other guides on the internet, to assist a global community of readers.[1]

Using digital humanities to deepen students' engagement with *Super Sad* may seem counterproductive, even perverse, given the novel's satire of the dangerous allure of digital culture's reproduction of the human. But Shteyngart vividly shows how posthuman narratives repress ironies and doubts that art and religion have long explored. His Menippean incursions are sharply relevant precisely at this historical moment, when the humanities are obsessed with theorizing the posthuman while embedded within academic institutions that each year seem to function more and more on the corporate model. Could trying to become posthuman be a dangerous and self-defeating gambit, especially when administrations are all too happy to shrink or make "post" the humanities?

Super Sad allows us to resist either/or choices between nostalgic notions of the human and utopian narratives claiming new technologies will somehow *in themselves* make the humanities relevant again. It's the Menippean satiric way to audaciously cause such trouble while making us laugh uneasily (and sometimes uproariously) about our dilemmas. Just as Shteyngart deploys Menippean satire to absorb capitalism's phantasmagoria of identity branding and then open it up to parody and critique, so too does his novel make a very pleasurable case for the dangerous relevance of satiric fiction in the age of Images, Retail, Credit, and global universities promoting neoliberalism as the one true way to freedom.

Other indispensable elements for a *Super Sad* teaching plan should be a focus on close-reading skills and an analysis of the novel's primary protagonists, followed by broader questions that will allow students to use this particular text to think about historical and cultural issues. Some basic comments and questions follow below, to help structure one or more class sessions based on this approach. I begin with character analysis and then move on to historical and cultural topics that have been of lively interest to my students.

The novel's text juxtaposes Lenny's handwritten journals and Eunice's digital missives, and it is not until the final chapter that it's revealed why we can read these two voices braided together, as well as contemplate the grotesque ways the story of "Lenny <3 Euny" now has global pop culture buzz. Lenny is a product of Jewish-Russian comic pessimism and irony; both he and his family, recent émigrés from the last years of Soviet communism, cast a cold eye on utopian narratives of progress. Yet Lenny desperately wants to achieve immortality through new technologies that his literary influences and his own experience warn him offer false hope. How should we understand such a contradiction?

Lenny of course has financial incentive to believe tech hype: he's a mid-level employee for Post-Human Services, a Manhattan company selling "dechronification" products that supposedly reverse aging. Have students read closely a representative passage or two from Lenny's diary, such as this one:

> I gave Barry the willingness-to-live test. . . . The Infinite Sadness Endurance Test. . . . He was saddened by life, by the endless progression from one source of pain to another, but not more than most. . . . I knew already that this perfectly reasonable, preternaturally kind fifty-two-year-old would not make the cut. He was doomed, like me. And so I smiled at him, congratulated him on his candor and patience, his intellect and maturity, and with a tap of my finger against my digital desk threw him onto the blazing funeral pyre of history. (125)

Ask students to consider how we should interpret this passage. Is Lenny boasting, proud of his superiority and power? What words imply that is so? Or do some students sense Lenny is conflicted about his role in the company, perhaps confessing secret doubts here in his private diary? What evidence supports that different reading? Other questions: What is an "Infinite Sadness Endurance Test" and what would "passing" it mean? (Would you pass if you just denied you ever felt sad?) Do students think taking and passing such a test would be a good thing? Why or why not? Also, discuss the connotations of the words and the historical resonance of this dramatic moment: "[I] threw him onto the blazing funeral pyre of history."

Eunice majored in "Images" and minored in "Assertiveness." She turns to GlobalTeen text-messaging and social media to escape an abusive and authoritarian patriarch and America's economic and social collapse. Like Lenny, she desperately searches for a protective father figure in technology and postfamily social connections, yet she too is consumed by doubts. Have students analyze a text such as this one:

> I broke up with Ben. It was too much. He is so beautiful physically, so smart and such a rising star in Credit that I am completely intimidated by him. I can never reveal who I really am to him because he would just vomit. I know a part of him must be disgusted by my fat, fat body. . . .
>
> The weird thing is I've been thinking about Lenny, the old guy. I know he's gross physically, but there's something sweet about him, and honestly I need to be taken care of too. I feel safe with him because he is so not my ideal and I feel like I can be myself because I'm not in love with him. (74)

Later Eunice reflects, "I guess what I'm saying is I'm not as turned off by Lenny's vulnerabilities anymore . . . I think it's a very Korean thing, to be able to sense someone so sweet and gentle and appreciate him for who he is" (199).

Ask students how they respond to Eunice's confusions. What different forces in her family history and in American culture do they think have caused her insecurities? How should we interpret her comment "I feel safe with [Lenny] because he is so not my ideal"? (Note also how that one word, *so*, perfectly captures Eunice's teenage voice.) Does it make sense to students that Eunice would turn to Lenny for a sense of absolution, of unconditional love, even though as she admits he is "gross" and hardly her romantic ideal?

I encourage teachers to take similar approaches to their own favorite passages in the novel, so that students learn to dive deep into a passage's literary texture, not merely paraphrasing its content. Some other broader topics are the following:

Make a list of three to six features of Menippean satire as defined in the first pages of this essay. How many of these elements do students find in Shteyngart's novel? Weinbrot's book on Menippean satire is not pitched at a level accessible to most undergraduates, but if teacher and student want to explore further, a decent place to start is *Wikipedia*'s page on the subject.

Why do students think the more violent and disjointed Menippean form of satire—which focuses on diseased ideas and their social repercussions and doesn't allow a reader or viewer to enjoy a "safe space" free of those ideas' influence—has become popular again in the present era? Can students think of other satiric works (texts or other media) that they would call Menippean? What are some examples of other works (texts or other media) featuring a Menippean incursion or violent interruptions or juxtapositions? Consider, for instance, Childish Gambino's apocalyptic 2018 music video, "This Is America."

Note

1. For one class's annotations of *Super Sad True Love Story* key words and neologisms, see Schmidt.

Works Cited

Gambino, Childish (Donald Glover). "This Is America." *YouTube*, 5 May 2018, www.youtube.com/watch?v=VYOjWnS4cMY. Accessed 8 June 2018.

"Menippean Satire." *Wikipedia*, en.wikipedia.org/wiki/Menippean_satire. Accessed 3 Mar. 2018.

Schmidt, Peter. "Key Terms in Gary Shteyngart's *Super Sad True Love Story*." *Peter Schmidt@English Literature*, *Swarthmore XPress*, 2010, blogs.swarthmore.edu/pschmid1/?page_id=544.

Shteyngart, Gary. *Super Sad True Love Story*. Random House, 2010.

Twain, Mark. Pudd'nhead Wilson, *and* Those Extraordinary Twins*: Authoritative Text, Textual Introduction, Tables of Variants, and Criticism*. Edited by Sidney E. Berger, 2nd ed., W. W. Norton, 2005.

Weinbrot, Howard D. *Menippean Satire Reconsidered: From Antiquity to the Eighteenth Century*. Johns Hopkins UP, 2005.

Aaron Santesso

Satire and Elitism

Here are some words my students used in a survey that asked them to describe satire: *fun*, *cool*, *familiar*, *comforting*.[1] These terms accord with the general sense of satire I often notice in the classroom: a mode that students know something about, are predisposed to enjoy, and do not consider intimidating. And yet the very familiarity of satire can be an obstacle to real intellectual engagement with it: it is comfortable, funny, unchallenging. I will argue here that there are benefits to defamiliarizing satire and, in so doing, restoring its difficulty—the trickiness of writing it, the unpredictability of its effects, and its various paradoxes.

On one level, of course, it is odd that satire would need to be made discomforting. Any number of high-profile cases attest to the fact that satire can still be offensive (*Charlie Hebdo*) or disturbing (*Salo*; *Man Bites Dog*) or both (Michel Houellebecq). Why is it, then, that students so often view satire as something of a safe space—familiar and friendly? Likely it is because the actual consumption of much popular satire today, at least in America, is generally a low-risk proposition: the targets are usually innocuous or predictable, and the point is usually clear.[2] Many students worry about misinterpreting epic; few worry about misinterpreting satire—and why would they? What network television show, for example, would risk exposing its audience to a satire that might be completely misinterpreted or, worse, missed altogether? Even those parodies that are praised as "perfect imitations" of their targets are anything but: *The Colbert Report* (to take the most obvious example) was celebrated for its "pitch-perfect" impersonation of a conservative program and described as a "doppelgänger" of *The O'Reilly Factor*—but it was hardly that, and there was very little chance that it would be taken seriously.[3]

And yet on those rare occasions when a politician or celebrity did seem to take Stephen Colbert at his word, he or she was instantly rounded upon in a way that would not have happened if the person in question had misinterpreted an ode or a western. When the FIFA official Jack Warner, not long after he was indicted by American officials on charges of corruption and bribery, took literally a story from *The Onion* claiming that an impromptu World Cup had been hastily awarded to America, he was castigated and laughed at, his inability to distinguish satire from truth used as evidence of his flawed moral compass. There is a very real risk inherent in satire, in terms of the likelihood of misinterpretation and the reaction to that misinterpretation. Someone who gets a sonnet horribly wrong is unlikely to face public ridicule; someone who misses the point of a satire very much does and becomes another casualty of the genre, as it were.

When I teach satire (often eighteenth century, but also nineteenth century and modern) I try to reintroduce students to the risks, dangers, and challenges inherent in satire—and not just those faced by the satirists themselves (though the story of Dryden's cudgeling is a reminder that those risks are not new). I encourage students to think of satire not as a welcoming and jovial genre but as manipulative and, for the wrong reader, hostile. When satire is appealing, it is usually because the satirist flatters his or her chosen audience, implicitly complimenting their intelligence and discernment. The satirist treats the audience as part of an elite—a group intelligent or virtuous enough to see through irony. Colbert did not need to break character in *The Colbert Report*; indeed, it would have hurt the show if he had, since the appeal of the program was based partly on the notion that educated liberal viewers were intelligent enough to be in on the joke. The program, for all its progressive content, is ultimately predicated on a belief in an elite and that this group is the only one worth communicating with. Those who "get" such a satire are sharp, canny insiders, part of a select audience; those who miss the point or mistake the satire for reality are slow-witted, deluded, undereducated—rubes, basically.

This particular theory of satire as inherently elitist is most relevant to printed works. Visual, communal forms of satire (from eighteenth-century satiric drama up to live-audience television shows like *The Daily Show*) do not hold quite the same risks for the consumer: watching a satiric offering as part of a group changes the nature of satiric interaction, in that it greatly lessens the chance of missing out on the satiric nature of a production, on the satiric "cues."[4] Reading print satire by oneself presents a vastly different experience, in which missing the point is a real danger.[5] Historians of reading like Robert Darnton and Roger Chartier have traced a reading shift, from social to silent, in the late seventeenth and early eighteenth centuries; this shift to silent, private reading, according to other theorists, allowed for the emergence (or at least recognition) of two types of readers: naive and sophisticated (see Kent 19–21). The naive reader read literally, or purely for meaning, and was generally unaware of or incurious about context or various inflections that might affect meaning. The sophisticated reader—a figure who in the eighteenth century would have been called a "reader of taste"—read in a genre-aware and irony-conscious way.[6] Indeed, satire, perhaps above all other genres, ultimately functions as a kind of test, an exercise in discernment: if you know the code, if you are sensitive to context, you should be able to see the truth. If you do not, you have fallen short. Most satiric works have some policing function: failure to recognize the satire is an identifier of failure of some other sort (moral, intellectual, social, etc.). This policing exists in numerous forms, with various political inclinations, from the bitterly sarcastic praise of "civilization" in Twain's anti-imperialist "To the Person Sitting in Darkness" to the lighthearted dialogue of John Betjeman's "How to Get On in Society" and its game of "spot the gaucherie" (which my students always fail miserably, to their irritation). But if Twain's righteously outraged piece feels a long way from the humorous snobbery of Betjeman's (or from the straight-laced absurdity of a *ClickHole* article), the underlying logic is much the same: to miss the point is to reveal yourself as flawed and unworthy, not just as a reader but as a member of society. A thought to put to students comfortable with the gentle liberalism of modern popular satire: most satire is monologic and dedicated to identifying improper behaviors, and its ends, no matter how progressive its motivations and arguments, are therefore fundamentally conservative.

Parodic Satire and Close Reading

The ultimate test of this sort of policing satire is the parody, and in my experience it is parody that rewards classroom attention most richly. Broadly speaking, parodic satire exists in two forms: that which is evidently not serious (though it maintains numerous epic conventions, no one would take *Rape of the Lock* to be an earnest epic) and that which comes close enough to the target that it could be mistaken for it (e.g., Daniel Defoe's *The Shortest Way with the Dissenters*). The former is aligned more closely with poetry, largely for formal and structural reasons. John Gay's *The Shepherd's Week* is technically imitation, but it is virtually impossible to take seriously the overwrought singing contest, with its absurd character names and archaic vocabulary. Virtually impossible for trained scholarly readers, that is—these distinctions are less obvious to inexperienced student readers, who are often surprisingly willing to accept parodies at face value. But the giveaways are there, and this provides an excellent opportunity for close reading exercises. Lord Byron's "The Vision of Judgment" is a good case study, given its numerous (relatively) obvious signs that it is not in earnest. At first the language can seem much of a muchness to undergraduates. But asked to find the telltale moments, they land on something quickly enough. Sometimes it is the low vocabulary (e.g., the references to "Bob Southey" as "raving" and "multo-scribbling" [Byron 321, 332]). Sometimes it is the casual, familiar tone: "Let's skip a few short years of hollow peace" (314). Sometimes it is the triple-rhymed or slant-rhymed couplets that conclude many of the stanzas: "circumscribing, with some slight restriction, / The eternity of hell's hot jurisdiction" (316). Sometimes it is a combination of all the above:

> He potter'd with his keys at a great rate,
> And sweated through his apostolic skin:
> Of course his perspiration was but ichor,
> Or some such other spiritual liquor. (320)

Cumulatively, these moments make it clear that no one should take this as genuine—and yet even a work this bluntly ridiculous is part of the testing satiric tradition, if only in that it challenges the reader to recognize the elements being imitated, violated, and exaggerated.

The other model of parodic satire—parody that does not instantly signal its mockery—is more associated with prose and calls for different teaching exercises. Many of the most prominent examples are eighteenth-century ones: "A Modest Proposal," "Argument against Abolishing Christianity," "Mr. Collins's Discourse." Some ("Modest Proposal") were fundamentally ironic efforts, which are almost inevitably recognized as such sooner or later (the test lies not in simply recognizing the irony but rather in how long it takes to do so). Others (*Shortest Way*) were less obviously ironic and more perfect, consistent imitations of a flawed viewpoint. Among the latter is a work (or rather series of short works) that I often read with my students: Swift's Bickerstaff Papers, which imitate the ubiquitous prediction-filled almanacs put out by "astrologers" during the early eighteenth century. "Bickerstaff's" initial entry into the market, *Predictions for the Year 1708*, offers up no immediate indications of satire—the title page gives very little away—and when compared with Byron's "Vision" contains fewer verbal and structural red flags. For a modern audience, the humor is subtle; missing the satire altogether would be a real possibility. What helps is to compare the original predictions of Swift's primary target, the astrologer John Partridge, with modern horoscopes or fortune cookies. It is quickly apparent that Partridge, in his almanacs and works like *Merlinus Liberatus*, operates very much in fortune-cookie mode: most of the time he simply claims that one thing may happen and, if not, then another thing will happen. The closest he comes to clear predictions are suggestions that certain things may eventually materialize down the road: "things will do well, and there is such a thing as General Peace at hand, but not on a sudden" (qtd. in Rumbold 84).

Placed alongside such equivocations, the Bickerstaff Papers suddenly snap into focus. This will be no careful and vague set of pseudopredictions: now we hear that on April 4 the archbishop of Paris will die, and that on the seventh an insurrection will break out. And so on until we reach the prophecies for June, which begin with Paris being ravaged by fire and culminate with the most attention-grabbing prediction imaginable—the sudden death of Louis XIV from the gout—all delivered with a casual, almost bored confidence.[7] The masterstroke of the satire, however, is not in these over-the-top predictions but in the opening of the piece, in which one victim in particular is singled out:

> My first Prediction is but a Trifle, yet I will mention it, to show how ignorant those sottish Pretenders to Astrology are in their own Concerns: It relates to *Partridge* the Almanack-Maker; I have consulted the Stars of his Nativity by my own Rules, and find he will infallibly die upon the 29th of *March* next, about eleven at Night, of a raging Fever:

> therefore I advise him to consider of it, and settle his Affairs in Time. (Swift, *Bickerstaff Papers* 145)

Swift corners Partridge in brilliant and merciless fashion: if he ignores Bickerstaff's claims, he identifies himself as the kind of astrologer either unbothered by faulty predictions or uncertain as to whether they are accurate (precisely the kind of "pretender" Bickerstaff rails against); if he responds, he reveals himself as unable to distinguish between satiric and authentic prose and becomes the "ignorant" and unlearned pseudoilliterate that Swift accuses him of being. Essentially, Swift, in full policing mode, is daring Partridge to show himself as the kind of dunderhead who misses the point of a satire. Of course Partridge, in one of the least wise decisions imaginable, did respond, which naturally led to Swift's evisceration of Partridge's public protestations that he did not actually die on the promised day ("he is the *only* Person, from whom I ever heard that Objection offered" [*Bickerstaff Papers* 161]).

The broader significance of the Bickerstaff Papers does not lie in the destruction of one minor fraud, obviously, but, through the condemnation of an entire field and indeed of all "pretenders" to authority, in its depiction of Swift's regularly stated understanding of satire as a "rod" to beat back vulgar aspirants.[8] In Bickerstaff's opening attack upon the "gross abuse of astrology," he does not "lay the fault upon the art" but upon the astrologers themselves:

> I know several learned Men have contended that the whole is a Cheat; that it is absurd and ridiculous to imagine, the Stars can have any influence at all upon human Actions, Thoughts, or Inclinations: And whoever has not bent his Studies that Way, may be excused for thinking so, when he sees in how wretched a Manner that noble Art is treated by a few mean illiterate Traders between us and the Stars; who import a yearly Stock of Nonsense, Lyes, Folly, and Impertinence, which they offer to the World as genuine from the Planets, tho' they descend from no greater a Height than their own Brains. (141)

From the outset, the narrator is clear about where he and his targets lie on the social scale: he spends his time with "learned men," while the average astrologer belongs to the community of "mean, illiterate traders" who are no proper practitioners of any "noble art." Here again close reading can open up fuller meanings. I ask my students to find words in Swift's opening salvo that have additional connotations. The initial description of

Partridge as a "sottish pretender," for example, has two valences: *sottish* can mean "dull" or "stupid"—perhaps drawing upon the well-known use in Jeremiah 4.22: "my people is foolish, they have not known me; they are sottish children, and they have none understanding"; it can also mean "drunken," a common slur at the time, hinting at Partridge's vulgar and undignified nature. Similarly, to speak of these astrologers' "impertinence" suggests not merely that their work is "irrelevant" (an early meaning of the word) but also that they are intrusive, trespassing in areas beyond their purview or proper sphere. Partridge—a self-educated shoemaker who taught himself Latin and eventually earned an MD in Leiden—was precisely the sort of interloper upon the grounds of proper learning that Swift despised (we recall his regular attacks on "rabble" writers and his description of Defoe as a "stupid, illiterate scribbler" [Swift, *Irish Tracts* 85]), and the Bickerstaff Papers are saturated with the kind of language designed to slap down those uneducated strivers grasping for scholarly, political, or social relevance. Ultimately, it is worth reminding students used to seeing themselves as always on the "inside" of satiric jokes that, in a different age, their own position might have been more like Partridge's.

Not all satire is openly elitist, of course, nor does every satire mock the common man. But it is worth pushing the darker and less liberal side of satire in order to make it less familiar, less taken for granted. Genres really come alive only when one gets the sense that there is something at stake and that one isn't simply being told a joke. Satire can be funny; it can be familiar; it can be progressive. But in its operation and its intent it is ultimately, quite literally, discriminatory. This is—and should be—discomforting.

Notes

1. Approximately seventy students responded to this online survey; they were able to choose from a list of words and identify which they associated with various genres.

2. Not one student surveyed chose the word *risky* to describe satire.

3. See, for example, Stanley.

4. In this spirit, Web sites like *Funny or Die* alert viewers to the success of the piece before they even view it (pieces are organized by popularity and include a rating meter showing the current level of audience approval or disapproval).

5. Radio satire—without a live audience or laugh track—offers an interesting parallel.

6. Occasionally, satirists openly make this distinction—often when they feel their satire has been misunderstood. In the preface to *Bays's Opera*, for example,

Odingsells complains about the "superficial Readers" who missed the satire, as opposed to the "Persons of Taste" who were able to "discern a Moral couch'd under the extravagance of Fabulous Representations" (i).

7. "[T]hat which will make this Month memorable . . . is the Death of the *French* King, *Lewis* the Fourteenth, after a Week's Sickness at *Marli*, which will happen on the 29th, about six o'Clock in the Evening. It seems to be an Effect of the Gout in his Stomach, followed by a Flux" (Swift, *Bickerstaff Papers* 154).

8. The best repository of such language is the preface to *A Tale of a Tub*.

Works Cited

Byron, Lord (George Gordon). *Lord Byron: The Complete Poetical Works*, edited by Jerome J. McGann and Barry Weller, vol. 6, Clarendon Press, 1991.

Kent, Thomas L. *Interpretation and Genre: The Role of Generic Perception in the Study of Narrative Texts*. Bucknell UP, 1986.

Odingsells, Gabriel. *Bays's Opera. As It Is Acted at the Theatre-Royal, by His Majesty's Servants*. London, 1730.

Rumbold, Valerie. "Burying the Fanatic Partridge: Swift's Holy Week Hoax." *Politics and Literature in the Age of Swift: English and Irish Perspectives*, edited by Claude Rawson, Cambridge UP, 2010, pp. 81–115.

Stanley, Alessandra. "A Talking Head Meets His Comic Doppelgänger, and Sparks Fail to Fly." *The New York Times*, 19 Jan. 2007, p. A21.

Swift, Jonathan. *The Bickerstaff Papers and Pamphlets on the Church. The Prose Works of Jonathan Swift*, edited by Herbert Davis, vol. 2, Blackwell, 1957.

———. *Irish Tracts 1720–1723 and Sermons. The Prose Works of Jonathan Swift*, edited by Herbert Davis, vol. 9, Blackwell, 1963.

Nicholas D. Nace

Interactive Satire: The Reality of Fiction

I cannot but think you have said the thing which is not.
—Jonathan Swift, *Gulliver's Travels*

There's a minor variety of humor that consists of one person telling another something untrue only to see if this untruth is believed. If believed, the joke is then ready for its punch line, which simply consists of a revelation that the statement was not to be, and should never have been, believed. Thus the sincere party who follows the implied contract of conversation is deemed laughably credulous. This amounts to a special form of irony that disguises itself only as light incredibility; and though not precisely a joke, it clearly has a butt: the listener. For a time, in the 1990s, such humor attained its most epigrammatic and viral form with the "not" joke—a formula in which you would toss out an untrue observation and, after pausing for a nibble of belief, simply reel in what you'd just said. At the first possible moment of retrospection, the negation comes in the simplest form: "Not." What was said suddenly reveals itself as not merely untrue but fictional, and irony retroactively consumes any of the claim's residual information in one gulp. The record has been set right, but it's too late. Fiction has been released into the world, and we must forever be skeptical or be victims.

One of the enabling conditions of satire is that such a clarifying "not" never comes. Once satiric irony is deployed, our ability to know how the real links up with the fictional becomes questionable. Except in their engagement with certain *à clef* forms, students generally don't know precisely how a satire's fiction relates to the world they inhabit, though in standing outside the fiction, they can easily feel that they likewise stand outside its critique. But if they can't tell what's real and what's not, they may themselves be the butt of the joke. Or at least that's the dire way I frame my unit "Fiction and Reality" eight weeks into my upper-level English course covering satire from antiquity to the present. As fiction and reality grow harder to keep separate, satire increasingly situates itself in newly gray areas by becoming interactive. Not only can you get your news from a satirical persona, but you can purchase an artisanally sharpened pencil from one or even get your morning cappuccino from a "Dumb Starbucks," a business briefly established by the television show *Nathan for You* and enabled by a loophole that exempts parody from copyright law, even when that parody is a business. While the law may be clear, the line between audience and victim in such interactive satire may not be.

But when audiences are drawn within a satire, the concept of audience itself splits between the diegetic and extradiegetic, between those who participate, however ironically, and those who watch others participate, however ironically. I find that this split misleads students who breezily assume that the boundary between the satirical work and its audience doubles as the boundary between fiction and reality. Students may find it easy to laugh at an inscribed or conscripted audience but still not be inclined to look past such a response for signs of their own complicity. They can get the joke and still not appreciate how they've been gotten by it. And in satire, "getting it" is often a matter of recognizing fiction when you see it, whether that fiction is an exaggeration, a literalization, or a stereotype. This issue of recognizing fiction can be effectively addressed by introducing students to what I deem the most complex interactive satire, that orchestrated by Sacha Baron Cohen. While Baron Cohen has refined many of his techniques for the Trump era in his 2018 series, *Who Is America?*, the 2006 film *Borat: Cultural Learnings of America for Make Benefit Glorious Nation of Kazakhstan* offers the clearest example of his interactive methods.

In my course, *Borat* is both a summation of early satiric methodologies and an expansion into filmic satire. With it we can discuss parody, persona, and the question of satiric affect. It can pull together earlier discussions of Juvenalian xenophobia, the parodic deceptions of Daniel Defoe's *The Shortest Way with the Dissenters*, the logical disingenuities of "A Modest Proposal," and the naive peregrinations offered by the film's early ancestor *Gulliver's Travels*. But *Borat* also marks our shift into satire's filmic techniques, where, increasingly, hidden camera, docu-reality, and guerrilla-style theatrics disintegrate any comfortable boundary between fiction and reality. *Borat*'s unique blend of reality and fiction can, if carefully separated out in the centrifuge of classroom discussion, help students situate themselves in relation to satire and the world it critiques. This essay offers an analysis of *Borat* designed to help students appreciate the distinction between fiction and reality, between persona and player, between Borat and Baron Cohen.

But as I point out to students, even academics are not exempt from confusion in this matter. In an article in the *Slavic Review*, two Canadian scholars claim that Borat the character "desecrates the American anthem and laughs at the Pentecostal church's way of praising God" (Kononenko and Kukharenko 12). While both Borat and Baron Cohen do the first of these, only Baron Cohen can be said to do the second, and even then only through the ridicule implied by his behavior seeming laughable. What this conflation overlooks is the mechanism of the film's critique, which turns precisely on the issue of who believes what. Borat in fact takes seriously the Pentecostalists' charismatic forms of praise (speaking in tongues, faith healing) and in the process learns to forgive the real Pamela Anderson for not being as virginal as her fictional *Baywatch* character. If in such cases we fail to see the constructedness of a fictional character, we are pulled unwittingly into the scope of both the fiction and its critique. Without clarifying what's fiction and what's not, we cannot know precisely what we're laughing at when satire makes us laugh.

All Persons Fictitious

Before viewing the film, I ask students to write down everything they know about Kazakhstan. Then I ask them to write down everything they imagine to be different in Kazakhstan when compared with the United States: culture; clothing; religion; and views on race, sexuality, gender, and politics. Watching the film with their own limited knowledge in one hand and their longer list of assumptions in the other, my students see a not-too-distant reflection of their expectations in the form of the boorish, sexist, anti-Semitic, homophobic, and possibly homicidal Borat. They can and do laugh at him even while—especially while—feeling their stereotypes confirmed. They see Borat's creator as perpetrating a fiction in the guise of a documentary but claim no share in the fictions by which the internal audience apprehends and understands him.

Approaching *Borat* as a documentary reveals the several ways it stands apart, most notably as a hosted documentary, one that blurs the line not between fiction and nonfiction but between fiction and reality. The watch-what-happens-to-me-style documentary has been a fairly high-profile form since at least Morgan Spurlock's *Super Size Me* (2004). So what, I ask, is the difference? At a certain point students will say, "Borat's not real," leaving it up in the air whether they're talking about the character or the film. So I press on. "It's not true but it's real," I'll say. But my point is that *true* is not the wrong synonym for *nonfiction* but the wrong antonym for *fiction*. Films can be nonfiction and, by virtue of being "composed," in a sense not true. What *Borat* shows is that they can also be fictional and true, satirizing above all the ways real people handle certain fictions. In fact, through his travels, Borat, who himself has trouble telling fiction from reality, functions as a kind of phosphorescent dye that shows the paths through which a fiction, however outlandish, can pass as reality in the United States.

Of course, one of the pedagogical hazards of satire is its propensity to proclaim its fictionality in order to disclaim responsibility. So we begin our discussion at the end of *Borat*, freezing the screen on its disclaimer:

> No real person or entity depicted or appearing in the film has sponsored or otherwise endorsed its contents. The same applies to the government and people of Kazakhstan, none of whom are involved in this film or have approved it in any way. Nothing in this film is intended to convey the actual beliefs, practices or behavior of anyone associated with Kazakhstan.

This may get Baron Cohen off the hook, as students point out. But one generally "endorses" what one says, and without the ability to formally retract—to deliver a "not," in other words—any speech caught on film is ipso facto endorsed. And to the extent that Borat's behavior dislodges unseemly attitudes by the people who interact with him, not only are those attitudes endorsed, so is the fiction of Borat himself.

Borat calls the film he's making, the one that provides the explanation for the presence of a camera, a "documentary," and this generates in his interlocutors a self-consciousness about how one treats someone they perceive as other. As a journalist traveling to the United States in order to learn its customs and "make reportings" for Kazakhstan, Borat is both fictional and real. However, those who engage with him in the "documentary," as an internal audience to Borat's antics, seem to be only real and bear real-life consequences of their statements and actions in a way that Baron Cohen does not.[1]

Having read *Gulliver's Travels* with an eye toward questions of self and society, my students are ready for the inevitable question: who is Borat? He is, in the film's insistent faux Cyrillic, ВОЯДТ (as opposed to Борат), and this subterfuge is meant to suggest Baron Cohen's dedication to being in character even through the film's paratexts. He speaks a combination of Hebrew and Polish to his compatriot Azamat, who replies in Armenian; and he is confused by certain aspects of English, such as its endless recession into euphemisms when describing the appropriate place for defecation (*restroom* and *bathroom* being too metaphorical to offer the precision Borat requires).

Though Borat's crassness sometimes prompts disgusted distance from students, I urge them to pay attention even to Borat's small-scale miscommunications, which reveal the art of Baron Cohen's puppetry. *Borat* offers political commentary in the guise of carefully broken English, as in the character's public declaration of enthusiastic support for "George Bush's war *of* terror" (emphasis added). So too with the repeated reference to the "U, S, *and* A," which hints at the fractured nature of American society seen throughout the movie (particularly at a dinner party on "Secession Drive," at which Borat is indulged but his African American companion is not). Some subcultures are even at odds with themselves, as we see when Borat outrages a group of feminists by sniggering at their "theory" of gender equality and, in a final indignity, referring to one of them by Helen Gurley Brown's favorite term of endearment, *pussycat*. At the same time, things that Americans believe to be divided, such as church and state, turn out not to be, as we see when a congressman and state supreme court justice praise their "Christian nation" at a Pentecostal service.

Stereotyping Fictions

Thus the film satirizes America, students will say, as Borat himself becomes victim to American pretensions and inconsistencies. But this is precisely where students need to be pushed further to account not just for what Borat discovers but what he is made of. Borat is interpreted within the film not as an individual but as a collection of stereotypes about his country. Whether these stereotypes are specifically held by any American, once vivified by Borat, they appear to exist as potentialities in the American psyche. As viewers, we are treated to a ridiculous depiction of Kazakhstan (filmed in Romania) in which Kazakhs keep the mentally challenged in cages, joyously dance what looks to all purposes like the Running Man, and participate in the Running of the Jew, in which children must smash papier-mâché "Jew eggs" before they hatch. Those who interact with Borat in the movie, however, judge Kazakh culture solely by his example. When a Kazakh arrives in America, he just might ceremoniously eat cheese made from human milk or spend three hours watching the hotel television channel that's about the hotel. *Borat*'s audience is privy to a narrative whereas Borat's audience must, in adapting to him, construct one based on his behavior, often enlisting the mechanism of stereotyping in the process.

So I focus first on the internal audience by urging students to consider what happens when ignorance yields to fiction. Here I follow two steps: first, I encourage them to identify specific satiric targets in the film and test how accurately those targets are constructed by the film; second, I urge them to see how American ignorance, itself a target, in fact enables the entire film to work. The first step helps students assess the fictive component of stereotypes; the second helps them see that stereotyping is the very thing that allows Borat to demonstrate the process of othering, of breaking off an "us" from a "them," whether along national, social, or racial lines—or even those that generally divide external and internal audiences. During this process I (or occasionally a student) will upend the discussion of stereotypes to include those Baron Cohen might be said to perpetuate about Americans through his deployment of Borat. After attempting to come to terms with *Borat*'s depiction of southerners, a complex issue further distorted by the film's faked geography, students identify main stereotypes perpetuated by the film: the Salesman, the Teacher, and the Believer.

Salespeople come across the worst, which for students contributes to a satire on American greed. A car salesman unblinkingly recommends a speed at which Borat could kill Gypsies with a Hummer (35–45 mph), and a gun salesman helps Borat choose the best gun for killing Jews (a gold 9mm) before running into a legal technicality that prevents him from selling a gun to a foreigner. A woman holding a yard sale seems used to make a point that selling belongings in one's front yard is something Americans do that, from an ethnographic perspective, may not be so different from the stereotypes Americans have about commerce in central Asian villages.

Those who presume to teach also appear to be targeted but come out looking fairly decent (though students do not). Borat of course needs to learn American customs, so he hires a good-natured driving instructor, who along the way teaches a lesson about sexual consent, and an unflappable manners teacher, who calmly advises Borat against showing pictures of his naked son, Hooeylewis. Most important, however, is the humorless humor coach, who finds he cannot explain away the nastiness encoded in the mother-in-law joke when he encounters Borat's malformed version of it. What he finds most difficult is explaining the "not" joke to a man too naive for fiction. We can only sympathize when the humor is lost on Borat, though his final use of the joke (still not right) will signal the end of his quest for a stereotypical male American dream and his succumbing to the pressures of didacticism that come with his chosen documentary genre. And he does not forget his own role as a teacher, learning lessons for Kazakhstan: "But," he poignantly asks, "what had *I* learned?" Without pausing, he offers his lesson about stereotypes: "If you chase a dream, especially one with plastic chest, you miss the real beauty in front of your eyes," meaning Luenell, the woman with whom he was earlier ejected from a painstakingly "civilized" dinner party.

What a Fool Believes

The Believer is the most interesting stereotype suggested by students, largely because belief yields a way to negotiate the fiction vs. reality mismatch. While Judaism seems to be the target of Borat's anger, we of course interpret this against our knowledge that Baron Cohen is a practicing Jew. The targeted faith within the film instead seems to be Pentecostalism. If Pentecostalist beliefs are ridiculed, we must understand that *Borat* accomplishes this precisely by making Borat a believer. As a stereotype, Borat is what he believes. In terms of religion, Borat is none of the big three; his Kazakhs "follow the hawk" (presumably the one on their flag). And his professed beliefs are influenced by a crude form of science, as when he reiterates a Kazakh government scientist's claims that women have brains the size of a squirrel's. Personally, he believes a jar of Gypsy tears will protect him from AIDS, a Barbie doll is a woman shrunken by a Gypsy spell, and an old Jewish man and woman can shift their shapes into cockroaches.

But what do Americans believe about Borat? Here we come to the roots of stereotyping. The belief in difference precedes evidence that such a difference exists. Borat is a fiction, but he's a fiction that's believed by those who engage with him. When the owner of a Confederate memorabilia store is proffered a bag of pubic hair as payment, his response is "We don't use that stuff in this country." When a car salesman has to tell Borat that "there's no such thing as a 'pussy magnet' in this country," he makes the same slip and reveals what's viewed as possible in Kazakhstan, a piece of central Asia even the bourgeois traveler might dismiss with a vague gesture to the map and a *hic sunt dracones*. Over there—somewhere—are the benighted, the intransigent, the wretched refuse yearning to be sexist, racist, and homophobic.

Even though Borat attempts to learn about America, he is seldom met with reciprocal curiosity about his nation or customs. The only exceptions to this are when purveyors of a certain kind of white identity politics of endangerment hope to find in Borat's Kazakhstan—a country they would assume backward in all other ways—a model for the resubjugation of women and elimination of homosexuals. For example, three "scholars" on spring break wax nostalgic for a form of female slavery they assume exists in present-day "old Russia" but that America would do well to adopt. And when Borat volunteers his description of his nation's policy of executing homosexuals, the homophobic rodeo manager affirms, "That's what we're trying to get done here."

Borat is an exaggeration of otherness itself. What proves disturbing is not the precise lineaments of Borat's caricature, but the fact that Americans are so culturally uninterested in the non-Western world as to believe the caricature might exist—enough to engage with Borat in ways that reveal the underlying sense of American supremacy. As a result, many Americans can fathom Borat only through a narrative of cultivation as assimilation. The "cultural differences are vast," according to the dinner party hostess, but Borat could receive enough polish to "become Americanized." The rodeo producer feels that Borat would be accepted as "maybe an Italian" by shaving his mustache and looking less like a "terrorist." What feels most satirical to students are instances in which Borat doesn't have to adapt. They notice that he likes *Married with Children* and yuks along with the show's laugh track as the husband jokes about murdering his wife, and they question his ability to tell that what he's laughing at is a joke.

Before he demonstrates just how radical his alterity is, however, Borat straddles the line between assimilable and unassimilable. This is a boundary delineated, as in so much of Swift's satire, by the handling of human waste. But having brought a bag of his own ordure to his host's dinner table, Borat proves remarkably able to overstep even this line with only a patient lecture. In fact, what students tend to miss is that Americans stop Borat in very few situations. Though he is threatened with violence on the subways and streets of New York, forcibly ejected from two hotels, and wrestled to the ground in a Los Angeles parking lot, most Americans come across as very accepting, which only serves to help further identify the issue as what motivates such extreme tolerance. In a scene cut from the theatrical release, Borat persistently asks a grocery-store employee about each variety of cheese in his store's dairy section, to which the employee patiently answers "It's cheese" a total of fifty-two times.

As an other, Borat is evidently capable of any and all manner of incomprehension, crudity, and barbarity, and he revels in it not as an individual but as a stereotype, and as a stereotype he is indulged until he can be assimilated. In the end, he doesn't need to assimilate. On the contrary, Borat returns to Kazakhstan and Westernizes it, teaching his village to crucify Jews instead of exterminating them.

Guilty Bystanders

Is any act of speaking to Borat an act of endorsing a belief in the possibility of him? If one rejects him, that person becomes the target of a critique of intolerance; if one tolerates him, he or she is vulnerable to the critique of excessive tolerance. As in the "not" joke, insincerity may prove to be the solution. It is the only defense against coming within the compass of participatory satire and is used by the film's true hero: Borat's driving instructor. When asked if he would be Borat's boyfriend, his initial answer is no. Almost immediately, however, he dismissively accepts by saying, "Yeah, I can be your boyfriend." He has happened upon the insincerity that can counterbalance Borat's fiction, the utterance that could be followed by a "not."

To those who interact with him, Borat was a possibility before he became a fictional inhabitant of the real world. While it's unlikely that many Americans consider what Kazakhstan is like, they retain Borat's Kazakhstan as a possibility. The problem is not so much that Americans don't know but that they don't care to know.

So is the student moviegoer likewise a guilty bystander? To return to the language of *Borat*'s disclaimer: In the age of globalization, are we not all "associated" with Kazakhstan enough to be responsible for knowing something about its "actual beliefs"? When Baron Cohen opens his satire up to reality, do we as spectators—and in the case of most of my students, Americans—become targets? After our week dedicated to *Borat*, the final question I put to my students is whether anyone was moved to look up anything about Kazakhstan. In the five times I've taught this film, nobody ever was.

Note

1. This is manipulative for sure, though not as literally misleading as an earlier appearance of the Borat character on *Da Ali G Show*. Here Borat leads a sing-along of "In My Country There Is Problem," where Tucson bar patrons follow his lead even after the song becomes anti-Semitic, with its chorus, "Throw the Jew down the well."

Works Cited

Baron Cohen, Sacha, performer. *Borat: Cultural Learnings of America for Make Benefit Glorious Nation of Kazakhstan*. Directed by Larry Charles, Twentieth Century Fox, 2006.

Kononenko, Natalie, and Svitlana Kukharenko. "Borat the Trickster: Folklore and the Media, Folklore in the Media." *Slavic Review*, vol. 67, no. 1, Spring 2008, pp. 8–18.

Part VI

Satire across the Curriculum

Robin Runia

Satire in Composition: Writing toward Social Justice

Xavier University of Louisiana is a private, four-year, historically black institution located in New Orleans, which serves approximately three thousand students from across the United States. Two semesters of composition are standard (Composition and Rhetoric; Composition and Literature), and students work to establish mastery of the following department-required outcomes: to demonstrate comprehension of literary texts, including plot and character; to demonstrate comprehension of literary terms; to apply literary terms; to craft analytical arguments in response to literary texts (including thesis, evidence, and logical development); to gain knowledge of literary form and genre; and to incorporate credible sources, both primary and secondary, in writing.

In addition to these standard requirements, Xavier students are encouraged to engage more broadly with the university's distinct mission:

> Xavier University of Louisiana, founded by Saint Katharine Drexel and the Sisters of the Blessed Sacrament, is Catholic and historically Black. The ultimate purpose of the University is to contribute to the promotion of a more just and humane society by preparing its students to assume roles of leadership and service in a global society.

As an instructor also in service of this mission, in the fall of 2014 I took the opportunity offered by a composition course to test the hypothesis that reading, analyzing, and writing satire serves social justice.

The unfamiliar vocabulary, obscure literary allusion, and specific historical context of such texts often thoroughly, if not completely, alienate students. Unfortunately, many students encountering satire for the first time do not immediately recognize that "like all great literature it deals with matters of compelling power for all those engaged in hoping to better the world around them" (Weinbrot 26). Instead of this reverence for social justice, satire often elicits what William George calls a "knee-jerk, naïve response" in the form of a rejection of the dark imagination that produced it (38). Many scholars agree that the first step in helping students nuance their response involves examination of the "indirect ironic manner and style of writing" and "rhetorical procedures and devices utilized" by satirists (Mabe 85). In addition, as George has also demonstrated, engaging students in the writing of satire enables them to develop a more complete and sophisticated understanding of such satiric technique. The question remains however, whether engaging students in the writing of satire also might enable them to develop a more complete and sophisticated understanding of satire's social-justice imperative.

Accordingly, in my composition and literature course, one unit focused entirely on satire. First, we read Jonathan Swift's "A Modest Proposal" and Jane Collier's *An Essay on the Art of Ingeniously Tormenting*. With "A Modest Proposal," we spent much time with the archaic vocabulary and historical context. Especially important was helping the students to understand the complex relationship of the "projector" to his subject matter and his readers. The *OED*'s definition of *projector* for the eighteenth century—"A schemer; a person who lives by his or her wits; a promoter of bogus or unsound business ventures; a cheat, a swindler"—provided an entry point, and the examination of his deployment of supposedly "civilized" and "savage" behaviors did much to show just how topsy-turvy the projector's values are. We then delved more deeply into terms associated with satirical technique such as *irony*, *parody*, *hyperbole*, *incongruity*, and *caricature*, and we practiced recognizing them at work in Swift's text. Historical context proved essential at this point as well, and we spent a class period sorting out how Swift's biographical details and the economic state of Ireland set the stage for recognizing the humanitarian message of the text. As a result of this process, students were easily able to recognize, as one wrote, "This business proposal is far from being modest. It is outright selfish and inequitable."

While the essay's confrontation with social injustice became clear to my students, the question of whether satire could actually help right wrongs remained unanswered. Thus, armed with some of the vocabulary and historical context of the early eighteenth century, I introduced them to Collier's *Essay.* Collier's text is based upon Swift's "Directions to Servants" and opens with instructions, from a servant's perspective, "To Masters and Mistresses, concerning their Servants." The rest of the first portion is filled with "To the Patronesses of an humble Companion," "To Parents," and "To the Husband." The second part is divided into four sections: "To Lovers," "To the Wife," "To the Friend," and "To your Good Sort of People; being an Appendage to the foregoing Chapter." While each of these sections is explicitly described as essential to inflicting pain, each also deploys a variety of satirical techniques in addition to offering a formal narrative persona who speaks directly to the readers. In a challenge to the efficacy of the professed values of Xavier's historically black Catholic mission, Collier's narrator asks:

> Who is there, that having received a blow on one cheek, will turn the other, while revenge can be had from the law of assault and battery? Are there any who exercise the virtues of patience and forgiveness, if they can have legal means of punishing the aggressor, and revenging themselves tenfold on the person who gives them the most slight offence? Innumerable are the instances that could be given to shew, that the doctrine of the Gospel has very little influence upon the practice of its *followers*; unless it be on a few obscure people, that ***nobody knows.*** (45)

This introductory exaggeration of the narrator's universal indictment of "who" and "any," combined with the dismissal of the "few obscure" morally upright nobodies, initially produced that knee-jerk rejection of the narrator's dark and flawed nature. Nevertheless, once the narrator begins to detail her instructions for the vengeful torment between lovers, many of my students began to agree with the validity of her perspective. They enthusiastically embraced the narrator's claim that "Teazing and Tormenting is the sustenance, the breath, the very life, of most young women who are sure of the affections of their lovers. Nor are the men less expert at the practice of Teazing, when they know themselves to be the objects of a woman's love" (82). For my students, the propensity of both men and women to manipulate their lovers proved accurate. From there, however, the students disagreed with some of the irony of recommending what seemed to them outdated and thus ineffectual misogyny. For example, they refused the description of courtship by a man as "making [his female lover] completely and immoveably in love with—herself" (83). They also refused the antifeminist recommendations of an economically dependent wife to torment a husband: "If you bring a large fortune to your husband, custom and example will justify you in being as insolent as you please. . . . But my advice is, that if you bring no fortune to your husband, you should be as insolent as if you had increased his store by thousands" (84). In this case the obvious injustice of a historical system in which women had little to no economic independence proved too serious a problem for satire. Thus the efficacy of Collier's satire in promoting their more just awareness and attitudes proved uneven.

In order to deal with this failure and investigate the potential for satire to speak more consistently in favor of the students' more modern views of equality, I asked them to compose their own *Essay on the Art of Ingeniously Tormenting*. Preparing the students to write their own satire required us to engage in discussion of both what Collier's text says and what it does. We paid close attention, for example, to the instructions to masters and mistresses concerning their servants. Collier's narrator's literal message encourages these employers to injudiciously scapegoat and blame their servants while yelling and screaming as well as threatening and disappointing. She drives this message home, however, by flattering the reader, inflating her narrator's expertise and qualifications, and refuting critics. This deployment of an ironic message with nonironic rhetorical ploys is one of the key challenges the students mastered in order to effectively craft their own satires. In addition, editor Audrey Bilger provided a helpful focal point in her introduction to the edition of the text that we used. For Bilger, the effectiveness of satire in general and Collier's in particular lies in its ability to highlight two apparently contradictory impulses of human nature: the tendency to take pleasure in causing others pain and the capacity to feel sympathy for fellow sufferers. After thorough discussion of the extent to which the students felt this accurately described the power of Collier's text, I asked my students to craft their own *Essay*. In five hundred words, their satire had to incorporate at least three of the satiric techniques discussed in class as well as clearly expose a recognizable injustice and imply a recommended alternative.

Based on their own experiences with power differentials and inequality rooted in age, race, gender, or economic status, the students demonstrated their understanding of irony, sarcasm, ironic juxtaposition, hyperbole, caricature, etc. Their satires ranged in focus to reflect the variety of their interests and concerns, including instructions for the tormenting of second-generation American children by their overprotective parents and for the tormenting of unsuspecting young black men by bigoted police officers. Romantic relationships became the target of most of the students. In "To the Inconsiderate Lover," for instance, one young woman wrote,

> Exercise your power over her by doing the exact opposite of whatever she asks or expects of you. For example, she may ask you to be present for special events such as her sporting events, performances, etc. When she does so, express to her that you would not miss it even if the world came tumbling down because she means that much to you. However, when the time comes for her special event, by all means, DO NOT GO! You must make her feel insignificant by simply "forgetting to go" or having something of greater importance arise.

This example employs both hyperbole and understatement in recommending the lover set up his victim's expectations for disappointment. But it also, significantly, betrays the capacity to feel sympathy for fellow sufferers in its focus on "special events." In addition to encouraging the reader to follow the narrator in imaginatively identifying the kind of events that could possess great significance for the victim, these instructions also simultaneously manifest the pleasure of the tormentor through their use of capital letters and scare quotes.

By using such contradictory movements, the power and humor of these pieces was palpable to all when we read them aloud in class. The students clearly and easily recognized one another's felt injustices even while they also understood the impediments to their remedy.

Finally, to more definitively answer the question of whether satire actually promotes social justice, I asked the students to respond to a survey considering their experience with satire in the class and its relationship to the mission. I asked them the following: "To what extent do you believe your experience reading satire, writing satire, and writing about satire has enabled you to assume roles of leadership and service in a global society? Please be as specific as you can and consider your participation in various communities—friends, family, campus, city, the Web, etc." What I found after the semester's end was, at the very least, suggestive and encouraging.[1] The students explained that, for the most part, they valued satire for its particular power to manipulate the emotions of its readers in the presentation of another person's or group's perspective. One student noted, for example, how satire can exaggerate the perspective of victims, giving light to the wrongs they suffer. Satire's strength lies in its clear representation of the underrepresented. Nevertheless, I also noted that the multiple verb tenses deployed in many of the students' responses reflected more reserve. For example:

> Being prompted to study satire using several different methods has helped me to better understand the types of behaviors a leader should exhibit. Besides doing the opposite of the torment encouraged in Jane Collier's *An Essay on the Art of Ingeniously Tormenting*, the depiction of the victim's desires illustrated through specific methods of torment used against them inspires me to more seriously consider the goals and desires of those I lead or serve. These experiences push me to think of others, rather than only myself, and make me realize that to be a leader or to serve others, I need to respect and compromise with the people I work with to generate a positive and productive atmosphere. Such a respect for my colleagues would also generate a bond between us, making everyone more willing to work and providing healthier encouragement than fear.

From "has helped" to "inspires" and "need" to "would also generate," reading, writing, and writing about satire seems to have stopped just short of promoting a more just and humane society. The aid it offers is simultaneously in the past and hypothetical.

Ultimately, and perhaps not surprisingly, the students' beliefs in the power of satire to promote social justice seem to come down to the students' individual belief systems and commitments. For one student, satire's power was its imperative to think of others before herself:

> To a large extent, I believe that my experience with satire has made me more aware of the needs of others. Many of the satires I have read in this course have been written so leaders and people in higher positions will pay attention to the needs of those they are leading. In relationship to my leadership experiences, I hope to be able to make sure that I never lose sight of why I am trying to help.

Satire's power lies in consciousness-raising. Yet its weakness lies in the imperviousness of power to having its consciousness raised.

At the same time, for another student, satire's power lay in its demand that she interrogate her own behaviors before those of others:

> I have always believed in working for the greater good of mankind, promoting equality and tolerating nothing less. However, I believe the recent satires we've studied, and especially the satire I wrote myself, have shown me that justice, respect, etc. are not standards you can overlook in personal relationships. I've realized that to be a great

leader and to truly serve a global society [justice] must start in your personal life.

Satire's weakness and power lie in its intolerance of injustice. They also lie in its necessarily unstable oscillation between the private and the public, the personal and the social.

The optimists in the class, as well as the pessimists, loved their experience with satire, which they came to see as a means of uniting a critique of injustice with the ideal of a leadership mission. The relationship between satire and social justice can get lost in the challenges of teaching technique and context. And even when these obstacles are overcome, the relationship between satire and social justice may prove temporary, illusory, and a matter of personal idiosyncrasy. Nevertheless, if even one of my students of satire transforms her awareness of injustice into aims for its amelioration or eradication, as seems to have been the case, it does indeed also seem that satire actually works as a vehicle of reform.

Note

1. While I was able to generate participation from only a small sample (sixteen students), the size of which clearly impinges on any scientific validity the results of this survey might have, I did distribute the surveys through a third party along with forms for the students to grant permission for me to use their satires and survey responses. In an attempt to mitigate any sense of coercion the students might feel, the students were also informed that I would not receive their surveys and permissions, had they granted them, until after the end of the semester and final grades were calculated.

Works Cited

Collier, Jane. *An Essay on the Art of Ingeniously Tormenting*. Edited by Audrey Bilger, Broadview Press, 2003.

George, William. "Teaching Satire and Satirists." *The English Journal*, vol. 78, no. 3, Mar. 1989, pp. 38–43.

Mabe, Cassandra. "On Teaching the Ironical Satire of *Candide*." *Approaches to Teaching Voltaire's* Candide, edited by Renée Waldinger, Modern Language Association of America, 1987, pp. 83–87. Approaches to Teaching World Literature 15.

"University Mission Statement." *Xavier University of Louisiana*, www.xula.edu/mission/fullstory.html.

Weinbrot, Howard D. "Teaching Eighteenth-Century Satire." *Teaching Eighteenth-Century Poetry*, edited by Christopher Fox, AMS Press, 1990, pp. 25–46.

David Mazella

Satire in the Gateway Course

Sometime in the 1990s, many English departments noticed that their populations of majors had dramatically changed and in ways that forced them to rethink existing curricula. One department after another discovered that entering students had much more experience with standardized tests than literature, literary history, or academic writing. This meant that the writing instruction so urgently needed by students never ended, while the accumulation of an organized literary and historical understanding—the ultimate goal of most curricula at the time—never even began (*Report* 4–8). Faculty believed that students needed more systematic experience with literature and literary studies if they were to move from composition courses into more advanced forms of reading, writing, and research. To address this gap, many departments, including my own, created "gateway courses" focusing on both advanced disciplinary research and writing skills and specific literary content (Mazella). Depending on their level, these courses tended to be either sophomore surveys of major genres or more intensive, research-based "anti-survey" courses, designed to offset the broad coverage models found in the rest of the curriculum by focusing on a particular author, genre, or work.

Typically, students' still-developing reading skills meant that these courses concentrated on the lyric or other brief poetic or prose genres. From an institutional perspective, though, they also represented departments' first attempts to differentiate and sequence the typically ad hoc organization of their majors. Nonetheless, judging from the few essays subsequently published about these courses, most English departments have continued to struggle with the organization of their majors into something besides "a gumbo of courses thrown together to add up to thirty credit hours or thirty-six credit hours or whatever" (Shepard; Klein).

It is worth reflecting then about this curricular "gumbo" and how departments might make it more palatable for students just entering the major, or perhaps less like the disgusting goop prepared for Samuel Beckett's Mr. Knott in *Watt*, which consists of "all the good things to eat, and all the good things to drink, and all the good things to take for the good of the health[, which] were inextricably mingled and transformed into a single good thing that was neither food, nor drink, nor physic, but quite a new good thing" (87).

This essay will explore how grounding the gateway course in the peculiar demands of satire can help address two related issues: first, the singularly open, uncentered, and nonsequential disciplinary structures of literary studies; second, the problem of finding the most effective point of entry into literary studies, given these amorphous structures. A gateway course in satire can respond to this sometimes baffling complexity by focusing on three aspects of literary studies often left unaddressed in introductory courses: its open-ended definition of literature and literary inquiry; its demand that writerly and readerly motives be factored into the interpretation and discussion of texts; and the pivotal role of discussion and disagreement to reach provisional understanding and to advance knowledge in the field.

When trying to identify the specifically disciplinary difficulties of literary studies for novice learners, experienced faculty immediately face the problem of remembering their initiation into the field some decades earlier, long after those difficulties have been erased by subsequent practice. Adding to that distance and that amnesia is the fact that tenured faculty increasingly teach student populations that are increasingly nontraditional, first generation, and diverse, while being less economically secure than college students were during their school years. Yet these difficulties, relevant to any discipline's gateway course, become that much more urgent when the gateway takes students not toward a single, clearly delineated sequence of steps, but one set after another of further choices and additional directions for those who might want to advance. For this reason, the next few paragraphs will draw upon not just my experience but the academic ethnography of Janet Donald, who has systematically studied the epistemological structures of inquiry in a number of disciplines in order to compare their research and teaching cultures (232–70). In essence, this line of inquiry asks what students must learn and do in order to begin thinking and acting like practicing literary scholars, historians, psychologists, etc.

According to Donald, one of the most striking difficulties that literary studies poses for outsiders is the sheer diversity and open-endedness of both the objects studied and the research approaches taken toward those objects (232).[1] Moreover, a discipline is "divergent" to the extent that the methodological approaches it uses to study its varied objects are similarly unrestricted or undefined in advance, with plenty of internal disagreement about the most appropriate method of approaching problems and lots of overlaps and boundary disputes with other fields (like history, philosophy, sociology, and so forth). This means that senior scholars practice, and novices must learn, a kind of freewheeling synthesis of old and new information and methods that allows them to transfer knowledge from one kind of literary domain to another, though these initially may seem to share nothing in common. All the conceptual aids to synthesis and accumulated knowledge in literary studies, in the form of meta-terms like *period*, *genre*, *style*, *form*, and so forth, are only partial solutions to this problem and need to be given further substance by the text itself and surrounding contexts.

A second set of difficulties surrounds the problem of verification, wherein the practitioner must demonstrate the soundness of an interpretation, insight, or evidentiary argument to her scholarly peers for approval and agreement, to produce what Donald calls "consensual knowledge," rather than the "empirical testing of theories" found in the hard sciences. In a discipline like English, this verification cannot be done through any single, agreed-upon predefined or empirical method but only through a recursive cycle of interpretation, argument, and counterargument governing first the formation of one's own argument in a series of close readings and then the aggregation of subsequent debates among scholarly interpreters. This double set of verification practices, at the individual and collective level, makes "conflict and challenges to reputation" a routine part of how literary studies conducts interpretation and discussion, resolves arguments, and advances knowledge (236). This means that experienced scholars take for granted, while novices must learn, the disciplinary demand that scholars not merely produce and justify coherent and plausible interpretations, but they must also compare and evaluate those interpretations in relation to others (261–63).

A third type of difficulty is produced by the form in which interpreters must argue, verify, and provide evidence for their readings of literature. Disciplinary practices demand that interpretations be conveyed in close readings that leave most of their background operations in the realm of tacit knowledge, the better to reach agreement on a chosen, specific problem. This form of tactical selection is yet one more disciplinarily defined aspect of argumentation that novices can get wrong, either by trying to prove too much or too little as they confront the details of the texts before them.

Donald's description emphasizes features like English studies' uninterrupted curricular growth, proliferating methodologies, permeable boundaries, theoretically unlimited contention, and strategically tacit knowledge and argumentation. These features have the effect of ensuring that key concepts are not learned or refined in any common sequence but only in the course of a single student's inquiries, as an incidental effect of encountering and mastering the complexities of specific texts, contexts, genres, periods, and critical debates. Students do indeed advance in their understandings and skills, but their advancement is registered in their ability to engage in and persuasively argue the complexities of an ever broader and more comprehensive set of texts and contexts than their less experienced peers or, alternatively, in students' deepening knowledge and understanding of a particular text, context, author, genre, or period.

In essence, students in literary studies must learn not just how to perform their analyses at the micro and macro levels but also to toggle back and forth between those two scales in their interpretations and arguments. Thus one approach to the problem of initiating students might be to study and argue over a text, genre, or set of historical and critical contexts that mark out the open-ended, social, intrinsically argumentative nature of literary studies, often conveyed in a style designed to leave unsaid what is most important to understand. And what genre exhibits these qualities better than satire, in all the variety of its forms?

From the perspective of pedagogy, satires like *Gulliver's Travels* or *The Satanic Verses* help students confront and master the complexities of literary interpretations by beginning squarely with authorial motive: Why did the author write this? And what situation helped motivate the writing of this work or shape this particular passage? This is because the satirist takes up parodic literary forms to plunge readers into competing arguments in moral, political, or aesthetic controversy, forcing readers to cut through the clutter and distinguish between participants' stated and actual positions. Readers are then forced to respond to the dissonant situations just described with their own reductive yet *morally clarifying* judgments. These judgments amount to correctives or redescriptions of the satirist's ironic presentation of people and events. To make this kind of judgment, readers of satire must learn to move beyond misleading appearances or descriptions, bring forward what is left tacit or ironically omitted, and correctly attribute to the actors (and the author) their genuine roles or motives. In at least its own historical-cultural moment, satire has a readily recognizable target and purpose, and its meaning cannot be meaningfully discussed without establishing, at least provisionally, some concrete rhetorical situation of the author, her motivations, her target(s), and her intended audience. This is the most basic level of inference demanded by satire.

In this respect, satire operates within the social dynamic of the "tendentious joke" famously outlined by Freud: there is "the one who makes the joke," the one "who is taken as the object of [its] hostile or sexual aggressiveness," and a "third in whom the joke's aim of producing pleasure is fulfilled," meaning the "inactive listener" (118). In other words, satire, to be understood or enjoyed as such, demands that its readers be able to distinguish among satirist, target, and audience; to sense and attribute their motives correctly; and to rehearse the grounds of the controversy or situation that inspired the satire.

Satire's judgments, which often take the form of obscene jokes exhibiting "hostile or sexual aggressiveness," demand a response from its audience, either immediate or delayed, and the audience is consequently judged by its ability to follow the joke and come to the proper (or improper?) conclusion: explosive laughter. This is because of the fundamental nature of the genre: even when addressing generalized societal follies, vices, or abuses, satirists direct their anger toward specific human or institutional targets as examples of such abuses, though of course with enough distortion, exaggeration, or indirection to mislead the clueless part of the audience (Freud 125). It is hard to imagine a successful satire whose target, in at least a general sense, could go long unrecognized by the knowing part of the audience, though of course the precise nature of the target or the audience may remain a matter of debate.

At the same time, satire's persistent mockery of clueless readers pushes students (and their teachers) to feel that they have some personal stake in understanding what's going on, if only to get in on the joke. Students' interest in getting even the tacit dimensions of the joke, and their fears of becoming the butt of the joke, help motivate and direct the contextualization that all literature—especially historical literature—demands from its readers. Thus satire demands even from novice readers or audiences the focus and follow-through that allow some kind of concluding "illumination" to their momentary "bewilderment" (Freud 8–11).

For this reason, classroom discussions of satire may sidestep the problem of what Gerald Graff terms *pseudoargument* (9) or what Sheridan Blau calls *pseudoliterary discourse* (102) in literature classes, which occurs when novice readers generate abstract interpretations without ever considering the literary work as the product of specific human circumstances, intentions, interactions, or audience. Hence, whether we are talking about Lucian's *Dialogues of the Dead*, Dorothy Parker's poems, Ishmael Reed's *Mumbo Jumbo*, or Paul Beatty's *The Sellout*, satire raises all the usual questions of literary interpretation, but in illuminating and concrete ways for the student (and teacher) trying to move beyond high school–level questions of comprehension or theme. Problems of authorship, intention, irony, reception, judgment, contextualization—all these issues arise when discussing the meaning of a particular satiric episode in its relation to its intended target(s) or audience(s). The social nature of satire, however, makes the process of inquiry less a matter of untethered psychological or historical speculation and more one of contextualization, serving what Blau calls "evidentiary reasoning." It is not just a matter of "What is this about?" and more like "Why was this written? Who was it written for? And how can we tell?"

Once the reader of a satire understands it well enough to identify its author's targets, however, contextualizing the satire opens up further challenges of inferential reasoning: What, more precisely, is the situation that inspired the satire? What forms of abuse or folly are getting pointed out? What were the expected or unexpected responses? Especially when faced with historical satires featuring copious topical references (like, say, Lord Byron's "The Vision of Judgment"), students may initially feel unsure of where to begin, without quite understanding how the satirist has shaped the presentation to assist their inferences, while other kinds of biographical, historical, or generic cues may also assist them in making progressively better inferences.

To demonstrate how satirists can provide precisely the contexts and information that allow their satire to be enjoyed by nonscholarly audiences, I sometimes show my students a clip from Jon Stewart and Stephen Colbert's 2012 super PAC series on campaign finance. This series of skits, performed on both men's shows across their 2011–12 election coverage, spelled out the intricacies and "loop-chasms" of American campaign finance law in compelling ways. They did this by having Colbert create and legally register Colbert Super PAC with the Federal Election Commission; the PAC was eventually transferred to Stewart so that Colbert could run for "President of South Carolina" (McClennen and Maisel 36–45).

So, for example, on 17 January 2012 Stewart rolled clips of Newt Gingrich publicly urging his super PAC to stop libeling his opponents, along with Mitt Romney claiming that he could never coordinate with his super PAC without "going to the Big House." Then Stewart and Colbert made a joint phone call on the air with Trevor Potter, an actual campaign lawyer and expert, to see if their supposed noncoordination remained within the law. The two stayed cheek to cheek throughout, telling Potter of Stewart's outrageous, misleading ad buys in South Carolina and always assuring Potter, "We're not coordinating!" Every time Potter confirms that they've remained within the law, the two jump up and high-five each other, thrilled with their naughtiness.

Every time I've taught this, I've asked students how much campaign finance law they knew before they watched it and how much they understood the law after they had viewed it. Students can usually give a decent summary of the noncoordinating rule as it emerges from the skit, and they are much more willing to believe that a historical audience of Jonathan Swift's era might go through a similar process of learning about the salient contexts just from being exposed to the satire and its various cues. After all, much of the humor of these episodes comes from combining genuinely shocking yet real abuses with only slightly exaggerated parodies, and this basis in realism (e.g., legally registering Colbert Super PAC, the presence of real-life attorney Potter) helps inform audiences and focus their attention on the salient issues. Moreover, the genuine clips of Gingrich and Romney faux-worrying about violating campaign laws prepare audiences for the Colbert-Stewart "noncoordination" singsong, so audiences can understand the comedians as engaged in an only slightly exaggerated version of Gingrich and Romney's song and dance.

Keeping in mind the three underdiscussed aspects of literary study that began this essay, I would offer a few principles I have found useful for teaching such a gateway course. These principles will help students of satire better understand the formal openness, flexible contextualization, and argumentative procedures of literary studies.

The first principle is to avoid at the outset too narrow or prescriptive a definition of the genre and its features. Instead, begin with the students' own varied definitions and examples of satire, let them witness and explore its full range of meanings from the past and present, and collectively elaborate and refine the definitions as you proceed in the course readings and discussions. This will help them to understand that their definitions and examples—of not just satire but any literary genre—will always be incomplete, a selection from a broader set of possibilities. In sum, treat the class as a semester-long pursuit of the questions "What is a satire?" and "What motivated X to write *this* satire in *this* form?" Use the genre's formal messiness, its boundary problems, its reliance on excess and obscenity, its topicality, and its occasionally frustrating opacity and indirection to show that it is precisely these features that make it compelling. Use your open-ended questions and discussions as the basis for the class to clarify its nature and purpose. Make it clear that you are sometimes as baffled by the material as they are. Since authorities of all kinds, including intellectual authorities like academics, experts, or critics, are often rendered suspect or ridiculous in satires, students should become extra alert to the dangers of becoming learned fools themselves and insist instead on solving this genre's intellectual puzzles without asking for outside assistance from Professor Pangloss.

Second, resist the temptation to pre-interpret the satiric work with your own lectures or assigned critical readings, but instead throw the responsibility of contextualization onto the students, as part of their process of reading, rereading, and marking up the text for difficulties or discoveries and to help them compare and assess rival interpretations. Make their reflective reading process, with all its false starts and dead ends, the basis for all subsequent research and writing. This is in keeping with our first principle, which is to encourage students to distrust others' solutions to the questions they develop and therefore to become more reliant on their own powers of questioning and investigation in their reading.

Third, and most important, remember that the social nature of both the classroom and the satiric work are sometimes expressed in heated disagreements, unsettling confrontations, noisy disavowals, and quiet, retrospective alterations of one's views. In this regard, satire acknowledges the jagged, sometimes disruptive and painful aspects of intellectual transformation and the price paid by those unable or unwilling to learn. Honoring that social impulse—which assumes that any so-called consensual or achieved knowledge attained will always be partial, contingent, hard-won, and fleeting—will also honor what is most valuable about satire itself.

Note

1. The sheer variety and incommensurability of objects studied (texts, forms, genres, media, etc.) and categories of specialization (period, nation, area, race, ethnicity, sexuality, intersectionality, etc.) are usually taken for granted in literary studies, but they can seem baffling to outside observers. In Donald's terms, a discipline like English literature is also labeled "soft" and "unbounded" to the extent that the objects or problems it studies cannot be restricted to a single or unique set of things or phenomena.

Works Cited

Beckett, Samuel. *Watt.* Grove Press, 1970.

Blau, Sheridan D. *The Literature Workshop: Teaching Texts and Their Readers.* Heinemann, 2003.

Donald, Janet Gail. *Learning to Think: Disciplinary Perspectives.* Jossey-Bass, 2002.

Freud, Sigmund. *Jokes and Their Relation to the Unconscious.* Translated and edited by James Strachey, Norton, 1989.

Graff, Gerald. "The Unbearable Pointlessness of Literature Writing Assignments." *The Common Review*, vol. 8, no. 2, Fall 2009, pp. 6–12.

Klein, Scott W. "'Everyone Has Their Reasons': Planning English Department Curricular Reform." *ADE Bulletin*, vol. 154, 2015, pp. 62–67.

Mazella, David. "Some Implications of Curricular Change at the University of Houston." *Profession*, 1998, pp. 89–103.

McClennen, Sophia A., and Remy M. Maisel. *Is Satire Saving Our Nation? Mockery and American Politics.* Palgrave Macmillan, 2014.

Report to the Teagle Foundation on the Undergraduate Major in Language and Literature. Modern Language Association, Feb. 2009, www.mla.org/content/download/3207/81182/2008_mla_whitepaper.pdf.

Shepard, Alan. "Gumbo? On the Logic of Undergraduate Curricula in English Studies." *ADE Bulletin*, vol. 133, Winter 2003, pp. 25–28.

Stewart, Jon, and Stephen Colbert, performers. "Colbert Super PAC—Not Coordinating with Stephen Colbert." *The Daily Show*, 17 Jan. 2012. *Comedy Central*, www.cc.com/video-clips/3pwzi5/the-daily-show-with-jon-stewart-colbert-super-pac---not-coordinating-with-stephen-colbert.

Edward Wesp

Satire in the Survey

By its nature, the survey course presents instructors with a set of competing concerns. The imperative to provide "coverage" inevitably competes for attention with approaches that would emphasize closer reading of individual texts. In part this is simply practical—more time spent on any text means less time for a wider survey—but there is also a more substantial pedagogical tension at work.

Even if the tenor of debate has cooled over the years, there are still pertinent theoretical questions about the roles of aesthetic and formal criticism alongside culturally grounded readings in the literature classroom. This tension is further complicated by the needs of many incoming college students in terms of their development as subtle readers and writers, for whom the survey course that becomes something closer to cultural history may not be a good fit. To the extent that literature courses often justify part of their value institutionally by highlighting the development of reading and writing skills, the drive to emphasize close work with texts has motivations other than a call to resume New Criticism.

In the context of this dilemma, satirical literature can play a valuable role in linking close reading and cultural analysis. By its nature, satire points outward from the text to critique issues of social and political relevance. At the same time, understanding the operation of satirical writing demands a close look, as it makes its meaning by indirection. Satire can break the pattern of survey readings that appear as indexical or symptomatic markers of cultural context, requiring active and inferential reading as well as attention to literary form. Moreover, this kind of active reading can provide a livelier and more accurate view of the cultural ideas texts reveal to students, emphasizing sites of contention and the uneven development of cultural ideals.

The examples that follow are taken from an early American literature survey course (precolonial to the Civil War) that is principally organized around a set of major cultural or ideological themes traced across the period covered by the course.

As part of our study of the ways that slavery brought dominant strains of American self-imagination to contradiction and crisis, I assign John Greenleaf Whittier's poem "The Hunters of Men," a satirical antislavery poem published in 1834. Though simple in form, with a meter and refrain akin to popular song, the biting irony of the poem mounts a critique that expands students' understanding of how slavery was understood in antebellum America. Importantly, though, for students to arrive at that understanding requires that they read the poem carefully—and more than once—in order to substantiate their interpretation.

These lines from the opening stanza reflect the overall pattern of the poem, which is only gradually revealed to be thoroughly ironic:

> HAVE ye heard of our hunting, o'er mountain and glen,
> Through cane-brake and forest,—the hunting of men?
> The lords of our land to this hunting have gone,
> As the fox-hunter follows the sound of the horn;
> . . . .
> So speed to their hunting, o'er mountain and glen,
> Through cane-brake and forest,—the hunting of men! (lines 1–4, 9–10)

The cheerful encouragement of those final lines sets the stage for what follows, as the speaker of the poem celebrates the heroic practice of slave hunting. By the end, the speaker addresses the reader directly, calling for the reader to provide "alms for our hunters" as their spirit begins to falter: "Alms, alms for our hunters! why will ye delay, / When their pride and their glory are melting away?" (41–42).

There is no obvious break in the voice of the poem, such that a superficial reading could regard the poem as a rather melodramatic proslavery celebration of the labors of those tracking down fugitive slaves. Even prepared with the foreknowledge that Whittier was, in fact, writing against slavery, students are faced with the task of reconciling that context with the words on the page. I typically ask them to do so in the form of a short response essay, since writing will encourage the kind of attentive reading necessary to come to terms with the poem. I ask two basic questions: How would you support the claim that the poem actually satirizes the position it seems to espouse? Why would Whittier have pursued his critique through the indirect route of the poem's irony?

The first of these questions can be answered only by a careful review of the text, looking for the clues by which Whittier tips his hand to the reader. For instance, while a cursory reading of the second stanza will note that priests, statesmen, and women ("wife, widow, and maid") have joined the hunt, a more probing rereading may lead students to note the troubling fact that "The saint and the sinner, with cursing and prayer, / The drunk and the sober, ride merrily there" (15–16). The equal mingling of saint and sinner, drunk and sober, all met by the same cheery praise of the speaker casts doubt on the presumed respectability of the gentlemen and ladies listed elsewhere in the stanza. Students should find the inability of the hunters, or indeed the speaker of the poem, to distinguish between the moral and immoral as support for the notion that all is not as it seems.

Likewise, students will often point out the speaker's apparently unconscious slippage between the patriotic invocation of "this 'land of the brave and this home of the free'"(22) and its modified repetition in the next stanza: "What right have they here in the home of the white, / Shadowed o'er by our banner of Freedom and Right?" (37–38). Attending to this poetic repetition with difference, students are well positioned to argue that Whittier has purposely allowed his proslavery speaker to make a case that strains the contradiction of American liberty and American slavery to its breaking point.

In these and other instances, students find themselves doing more than explication or summary, building a case to read the text against its superficial meaning. This work also positions them to answer the second key question of why Whittier might have chosen his indirect approach. There are a number of interesting directions this can go, including a fairly common—but insightful—observation that there is something pretty shocking about seeing the grim subject of hunting fugitive slaves transformed into a jaunty ballad. But this is another occasion to send students back to the text, prompting them to take note of the character Whittier depicts as the poem concludes. It is the "politic statesman" who "looks back with a sigh / There is doubt in his heart, there is fear in his eye" (45–46). Inasmuch as the "politic statesman" remains a recognizable type in contemporary political life, written responses and class discussion will get the class to the closing notion that slavery's political future is, in the end, dependent on the support of the people, without which the government might willingly change course. In this way, the conceit of the poem implicates readers as supporters of slavery unless they resist—generally accepted by students to be a pretty neat trick for such a simple-seeming poem, and all emerging from a careful, critical reading of the text's literary operation.

In seeing that Whittier's poem criticizes not just slavery in the abstract but rather the many northerners whose ambivalence or apathy toward slavery allowed it to persist, students also gain a sharper and more lively understanding of how slavery was understood and debated. A similar revelation is made possible by other satirical texts I teach in the survey, texts that reveal positions that often surprise student readers. Several such texts are those written by Fanny Fern, the pen name of the popular nineteenth-century writer Sarah Willis Parton.

Fern's newspaper columns regularly appear in lists of students' favorite readings from the semester. Her style strikes students as refreshingly modern and accessible, and the issues of gender equality she addresses have a continued relevance. While it is readily clear that her work makes a case for women's rights in marriage, work, and public life, the particular value of her satirical writing is the way that it helps students move beyond commonplace responses to such material. By tracing the details of the criticisms she levels, students gain a much better feel for the contours of the world facing women in the antebellum United States.

Fern's early sketch "Hints to Young Wives" presents itself as an alternative to the more conventional conduct manuals published under similar titles. Beginning with a declaration that she would like to see such books burned (along with their authors), Fern depicts an exaggerated image of the woman these books produce: "The minute she sees her husband coming up the street, she makes for the door, as if she hadn't another minute to live . . . then chases round (like a cat in a fit) . . . warms his slippers and puts 'em on, and dislocates her wrist carving at the table for fear it will tire him" (2464). Students will certainly catch the general critique of wives' roles within marriage, but Fern, like so many satirists who win the admiration of their audience, won her fame with a keen eye for the manifest contradictions and absurdities that provide the openings exploited by her critique.

Asking students to carefully document the specific target of Fern's critique in "Hints to Young Wives" will typically surprise student readers who have noted only Fern's generally feminist themes. Retrograde advice books and insensitive husbands get their share of disdain, but it turns out that neither is the central target of Fern's satire. It is, instead, compliant wives who come in for the greatest ridicule, as is revealed by having students really focus on the text. The whole sketch is but four paragraphs long, so it's not unreasonable to have students take it on paragraph by paragraph, a project that is well suited to in-class group discussion. Read with this care, students should find that each paragraph is in fact devoted to a chiding caricature of the wife who is too desperate to please her husband.

This can strike students as odd or even as blaming the victim of inequality. But some prompting to consider the formal construction of the text clarifies Fern's approach and, with it, some of the cultural ideas that inform her critique. Short and conversational as it is, the text does develop a compelling female narrator who explicitly addresses a female audience, both within the fiction of the sketch and outside it. With this in mind, students may accept the idea that while the text does ridicule women who succumb utterly to cultural demands, it also constructs a feminine subjectivity that is the space within which Fern calls for change. The complexity of the rhetorical and narrative situation Fern creates forces students beyond a rote assessment that Fern is "for women's rights" and challenges them to think more carefully about the situation with which the text engages.

The fact that men's attitudes are presented as an unchangeable fact marks the force against which Fern imagined herself working: a patriarchal culture so well entrenched that it may as well be taken as given. (This is emphasized comically when the narrator drops her baby and reflects that "it was a *female*, and I thought it just as well to put her out of future misery" [2465].) In response, Fern's remedy is to urge women to claim what power they do have within the confines of this system, by directly acknowledging the power relations built into marriage and forcing their husbands to do the same. Though students may miss it the first time through, they are generally surprised and amused by Fern's knowing suggestion that "[i]f you have made the interesting discovery that you were married for a sort of upper servant or housekeeper, just *fill that place and no other*" (2464–65). As class discussion reveals that the "other" places Fern describes include romantic and, yes, sexual availability, students get an approachable and engaging sense of how this issue was discussed in the period we are studying. While Fern's decision to approach the subject with oblique humor confirms that her sketch emerged out of a more traditional time, the very fact that Fern raises these issues, and that her large, mainstream audience was clearly expected to get the joke, jars the class out of an enervated attitude toward older literature as the product of a distant, bygone age.

In this example from Fern, satirical forms invite enough attention to the text to complicate preconceived expectations about cultural meaning, but in other cases, asking students to follow the logic of satire can help clarify the meaning of an otherwise baffling text. Students' affection for Edgar Allan Poe as an author of gothic horror may encourage their interest in his political satire, but it takes some guided, attentive reading to fully recognize the target of his critique. In the case of Poe, the issue is not just finding the nuance of his position, as with Whittier's particular aim at passive support for slavery or Fern's call for tactical maneuvering within the strictures of marriage; Poe's work confronts readers with a critique of democracy itself, a position that most will not expect from the otherwise familiar presence of Poe's work.

At first read, Poe's "The System of Doctor Tarr and Professor Fether" evokes a standard Poe milieu, recounting a trip to an uncannily off-kilter insane asylum that eventually erupts into a concluding tumult of violence and destruction. In that sense, the story is like Whittier's "Hunters of Men," in that the first step toward an understanding of the story is identifying the fact that it is indeed satirical in the first place. The strongest clue is that the story is about the narrator's effort to evaluate the madhouse's system of psychiatric treatment. Over the course of the tale, the narrator learns that the fabled "soothing system" used at the hospital—in which patients are to be granted great liberty, even including the indulgence of their delusional fantasies—is a catastrophic failure. But it is hard to take a particularly satisfying meaning out of this narrow reading of the story, leaving readers with a superficial critique of a psychiatric treatment that Poe has simply exaggerated into absurdity.

A more revealing way into the story is provided in part by the context of the survey course, which can be used to encourage students to pursue a reading that uncovers indirect connections to the thematics that structure the semester's work. In the case of an early American literature survey, it doesn't feel too forced to push students to find some way of connecting this odd tale with the surrounding discourses of liberty, bondage, and progress. Given this direction, students are more likely to focus on an otherwise odd detail at the end of the story: the band of madmen who play "Yankee Doodle" as the inmates and wardens fall into the climactic melee. Why does this American patriotic tune accompany a riot of madmen in the South of France?

The incongruity of the detail is an opening that can lead to a revelatory reenvisioning of Poe's tale in a classroom discussion. Getting students to start with even the most commonplace associations with "Yankee Doodle" begins a chain of associations that turn out to be pretty straightforward but are surprisingly inverted in terms of cultural valuation. If that song is meant to evoke the battles of the American Revolution and is played here by a lunatic band as the tarred and feathered wardens (they having suffered the titular punishment at the hands of the inmates) are about to reclaim control of the madhouse, the seemingly inevitable parallel recasts that original American struggle in an unusually unflattering and confused light.

By the end of the story it becomes clear that the initial "revolution," in which the inmates gained control, was precipitated not by the burden of tyrannical authority, but rather the dangerous freedom of the "soothing system." As Monsieur Maillard (the former chief doctor, who has gone mad and becomes the patient who leads the inmates' revolt) points out, "A lunatic may be 'soothed,' as it is called, for a time, but, in the end, he is very apt to become obstreperous" (1018). It can take a bit of prodding, but by working carefully through the associations Poe has set up, we can get to the point where the story reads as a satirical retelling of the American Revolution as foundational myth, one that recasts it as the chaos of madmen run amok—a story of too little, rather than too much, governmental control. Though the class would have encountered some other more explicitly political readings that critiqued the assumptions of liberal democracy, it is a different experience for students to encounter the idea that a popular author would expect an appreciative audience for a story that adopts such an irreverent stance toward principles that no mainstream American voices today would dare to mock.

In the classroom, satire's critical aims sharpen cultural focus, while the snap of humor and transformations of irony and mockery beckon the reader to read closely. If the goal of the survey course is to connect students to living positions that reflect the nuanced complexity of other times and places, and if the goal of literary study is the particular examination of how that experience is conveyed through written art, satire fits both goals admirably.

Works Cited

Fern, Fanny. "Hints to Young Wives." Lauter, pp. 2464–65.

Lauter, Paul, general editor. *The Heath Anthology of American Literature: Early Nineteenth Century, 1800–1865*. Vol. B, 7th ed., Houghton Mifflin, 2013.

Poe, Edgar Allan. "The System of Doctor Tarr and Professor Fether." *Collected Works of Edgar Allan Poe: Tales and Sketches, 1843–1849*, edited by Thomas Ollive Mabbott, vol. 3, Belknap Press, 1978, pp. 997–1024.

Whittier, John Greenleaf. "The Hunters of Men." Lauter, pp. 1929–31.

Darryl Dickson-Carr

Making Wit, Irony, and Satire the Foundations of American Literature

Something funny happened to American literature on the way from its production to its place in the higher education classroom. Like a certain chicken crossing the road, it lost its humor and irony to get to the side of respectability, despite bad clichés, mixed metaphors, and sheer dullness. Emily Dickinson became deadly serious in our estimation, instead of a wry observer. Walt Whitman and Ralph Waldo Emerson became creators of grand narratives about American democracy, rather than subversive critics of that democracy. We seldom credit Frederick Douglass, the formerly enslaved abolitionist and civil rights activist, as a master not only of the jeremiad but also of withering irony and invective. Of major nineteenth-century American authors, only Mark Twain and occasionally Herman Melville get recognized for their rich irony and allegorical flair, with Twain earning the title of satirist most often. As a result, we forget that American literature was and is ironic, as American life has always been rife with irony. Douglass identified and delineated America's central irony perfectly in "What to the Slave Is the Fourth of July?" (1852), as he spoke of the inherent hypocrisy within a nation professing liberty as its greatest virtue while holding 15 percent of its population in bondage: "At a time like this, scorching irony, not convincing argument, is needed. Oh! Had I the ability, and could I reach the nation's ear, I would to-day pour out a fiery stream of biting ridicule, blasting reproach, withering sarcasm, and stern rebuke. For it is not light that is needed, but fire" (444).

Is this fire any less necessary in teaching American literature? I do not advocate histrionics for our pedagogical methods but for the materials we assign. We have shed light on literary history, but we need more fire in the belly, the same belly whence we might even find ourselves laughing, painfully, as we try to digest a history of slavery in the land of freedom, of democracy competing with capitalism, of pornography traipsing and trysting with Puritanism, of modernity ever in jeopardy of its cruel older sibling, feudalism, rolling over and smothering it in the bed they share. Both reading and teaching American literature should be a riot of wit and irony. I hope to show in this essay how we can ignite the American literature classroom by returning irony to it.

Before I go any further, I should pull back from the rhetorical precipice on which I now stand. I do not argue that instructors of American literature are unaware of or fail to teach satire and irony, nor do I argue American history's contradictions are invisible to us. Twain is a cornerstone of American literature. Those teaching early American literature are obligated to include Washington Irving in their offerings. Any course on modernism or postmodernism requires numerous novels, stories, and poems that rely on parody and pastiche. My claim, instead, is more limited: using literary texts authored by African Americans as my crucial evidence, I aim instead to situate satire and irony at the center of the American literature classroom, rather than at its margins as a virtual afterthought.

Novelist Paul Beatty argues in the introduction to *Hokum: An Anthology of African-American Humor* (2006) that two canons exist within the African American literary tradition. Beatty writes:

> One canon consists of songs, folktales, and insider apothegms that are deeply and invariably funny, whereas the other . . . comes out of a tradition of abolitionist "And ain't I an intellect?" activism aimed, then as now at whites. Save for Langston Hughes, Ralph Ellison, George Schuyler, Zora Neale Hurston, and a select group of others, the defining characteristic of the African-American writer is sobriety—moral, corporeal, and prosaic. (11)

Beatty's argument arises from a particular encounter with African American literature when he was young and assigned Maya Angelou's *I Know*

Why the Caged Bird Sings (1969), a cornerstone of contemporary African American literature. Beatty finds Angelou's depiction of racist oppression and tragedy itself oppressive, made more so by the fact that the Los Angeles Unified School District saw fit to adopt and assign Angelou's memoir, thereby cementing its place as *the* representative example of African American experiences (7).

Beatty's skepticism highlights the grim solemnity that surrounds public perceptions of not only African American lives but also American life in general. In Beatty's words, "there has never been a colored Calvin Trillin, Bennett Cerf, or Mark Twain. Hell I'd settle for a cornball Dave Barry," one willing to write pithy, folksy, humorous bromides regularly (11). Beatty obviously does not argue that African American humorists do not exist; his anthology highlights the fact that humor is everywhere in African American writings, from fiction, to poetry, to addresses, to press conferences, to impromptu interviews with celebrities. That humor alternately eschews, embraces, chews, swallows, or expunges stereotypes about African Americans, all in the name of asserting black humanity and foibles. In the process, African Americans become more human. Satire, it would seem, has a humanizing effect, yet we have deracinated it from the nourishing field of American literary studies.

If we are to replant humor, we might begin with the American Renaissance (c. 1830–1860), the period in which such authors as Emerson, Melville, Whitman, Hawthorne, Dickinson, and many others explicitly advocated for or otherwise helped develop an American literary tradition. As David Reynolds argues, "The typical literary text of the American Renaissance . . . provides an especially democratic meeting place for numerous idioms and voices [that] often conflict to create paradox and irony" in pursuit of social and literary reform (9). Yet this pursuit was fraught with ambivalence; what gives the reformer and innovator the right to dictate morality and progress to others?

African American authors had a less ambivalent attitude toward American contradictions than many of their peers. Eradicating slavery and achieving freedom for all were indisputable ends for African American authors in the American Renaissance era, to say nothing of Reconstruction and subsequent stages of American history. Abolitionists, of course, fiercely debated the form freedom should take, with many conflicts over moral suasion, armed rebellion, and migration to Africa and other destinations causing disputes among Douglass, William Lloyd Garrison, Henry Highland Garnet, Sojourner Truth, Martin Delany, and many others. But for these authors the question of slavery's absurdity in the face of American democratic ideals was settled. Their discussions of the slavery question allow avenues for critical responses to American literature and culture through irony and satire.

But let us pause for a couple of quick definitions. Although satire cannot be easily defined, I depend here upon a basic understanding: satire criticizes ideas, institutions, and people through humor, irony, indirection, and invective, often for the sake of improving the objects of its derision. A more traditional definition based on satire's rhetorical strategies might replace *improving* with *correcting*—a small but significant distinction. Satire does more than simply criticize interminably; it frequently upbraids individuals or institutions to accept models for morally or ethically just behavior. In texts central to American literary traditions, satire retains its role as a corrective.

Irony, for its part, defends or attacks a particular position by seeming to argue another while hoping the reader will appreciate the distance between the surface and hidden meaning. It may simultaneously be a muted expression of anger and aggression toward an authority and a sign of contempt for those unable or unwilling to pick up the clues the speaker/writer lays out for irony to be understood. In some cases, it may be nearly impossible to say what the ironist/satirist means, or appears to mean, depending upon the discursive communities in which the irony exists.

In the eyes of early African American writers, the distance between the American Christian's status and the oppressed may very well have determined the degree to which these ironies were clear and therefore whether scathing, ironic speeches and writings by Douglass, Truth, David Walker, or other champions of reform and civil rights may have had their intended effects. The allegiance among abolitionists, the early women's movement, and the temperance movement in the 1840s and 1850s was hardly accidental. These movements shared similar causes and perceived similar hypocrisies that stood in reform's way. These causes still resonate with our students.

But students may still struggle with reading irony and satire into these texts. Properly decoding irony requires a common cultural literacy or shared outlook, and in the United States, such a common outlook is most uncommon. If it were possible to read American history from a shared perspective, this issue would be moot, but sectional divisions—between the North and South, the East and West Coasts, the Midwest and everyone else—obviate the common. Descendants of slavery's proponents may read southern history according to a narrative that depends upon celebrating mythologies of Lost Causes and Wars of Northern Aggression over fact. This difference has been the source of both strife and considerable opportunities for satirical critiques, especially in Twain; satire frequently lampoons humanity's love for credulity immune to correction and reason.

We may also attribute students' struggles partially to a disciplinary issue. In the recent past, teaching satire seemed a province best reserved for scholars and instructors specializing in eighteenth-century British literature (Swift, Pope, Dryden, etc.) or in individual authors known specifically for their satirical writings: Erasmus, Voltaire, Twain, Mencken, Nathanael West, George Bernard Shaw, Kurt Vonnegut, and so on. Authors from other national or ethnic traditions simply would not appear within the satirical canon, frequently because scholars studying satire had little incentive to veer outside of it. Thanks to a rich catalog of work since the late 1980s, though, American literary studies scholars have made it possible to diversify and further enrich courses specifically in satire, to say nothing of American literature courses in general.

Irony returns to the American literature classroom when we demonstrate how it informed texts as fundamental to American social and political discourse as *The Autobiography of Benjamin Franklin*, Thomas Jefferson's *Notes on the State of Virginia*, Irving's "Rip Van Winkle," Walker's *Appeal to the Coloured Citizens of the World*, Truth's "Ar'n't I a Woman?," and Douglass's *Narrative of the Life of Frederick Douglass* and "What to the Slave Is the Fourth of July?" By tracing the legacies of these works' techniques in such later texts as Melville's "Bartleby, the Scrivener" and *Moby-Dick*, Twain's *Pudd'nhead Wilson*, W. E. B. DuBois's "The Comet," Schuyler's *Black No More*, Don DeLillo's *White Noise*, and David Foster Wallace's "A Supposedly Fun Thing I'll Never Do Again" and *Infinite Jest*, students might learn not only how to identify irony and satire but also to place them in a broader American intellectual tradition, one that values continuous critique, whether as part of the American Renaissance, the Progressive era, the New Negro movement, modernism, or postmodernism.

In the *Narrative of the Life of Frederick Douglass*, Douglass uses the basic components of American democracy and daily life to show how slavery not only undermines democracy but also parallels it, thereby allowing Douglass to question democratic practice itself. In chapter 2 of *Narrative*, Douglass recounts how his fellow slaves cherished their election to work at owner Colonel Lloyd's farm:

> They regarded it as evidence of great confidence reposed in them by their overseers. . . . He was called the smartest and the most trusty fellow, who had this honor conferred upon him the most frequently. The competitors for this office sought as diligently to please their overseers, as the office-seekers in the political parties seek to please and deceive the people. The same traits of character might be seen in Colonel Lloyd's slaves, as are seen in the slaves of the political parties. (30)

Douglass aligns slavery with American political parties to underscore the peculiar institution's inseparability from the rest of American life. Slavery corrupts not only the enslaved and the enslaver but also the very idea of democracy and democratic voices. Slavery could not exist one day without the consent of American politicians, North and South; slavery and political sycophancy are close cousins, caught in a perverse, incestuous relationship. In American life, the only division between the enslaved and the political candidate seeking campaign donations is that one is legally deprived of his freedom, while the other is blind to his effective enslavement to narrow readings of the law.

This blindness finds its way into Douglass's "What to the Slave Is the Fourth of July?" and Walker's *Appeal*, wherein each author expresses dismay that Americans remain obtuse regarding their own democratic principles.[1] Walker extracts the Declaration of Independence's introduction and its most famous phrase—"We hold these truths to be self evident—that all men are created equal"—to note that the principle bears no argument. Yet, Walker writes, "[c]ompare your own language . . . with your cruelties and murders inflicted by your cruel and unmerciful fathers and yourselves on our fathers and on us—men who have never given your fathers or you the least provocation!!!!!!" (75).

The same might be said of Truth's "Ar'n't I a Woman?" address, in which she berates men for denying women's rights out of self-evident fear of losing their superiority. She effectively demonstrates that men have a sacred duty to remedy the inequality that original sin brought into the world, to execute and embody the *felix culpa* ("happy fault") by raising women from ignorance and oppression: "Den that little man in black dar, he say women can't have as much rights as man, cause Christ want [wasn't] a woman. Whar did your Christ come from? . . . From God and a woman. Man had nothing to do with him" (92).[2] By arguing that men had no role in the creation of Christ, she parallels an argument that Walker and others present regarding whites and Europeans generally: their superior position has nothing to do with any inherent qualities but instead willful misreading of Scripture and misprision of their own democracy.

Compare these passages to the prologue of Beatty's 1996 debut novel, *The White Boy Shuffle*, in which protagonist Gunnar Kaufman muses upon his reluctant ascent to ersatz "Leader of the Black Community," one inspiring African Americans to commit suicide en masse: "In the quest for equality, black folks have tried everything. We've begged, revolted, entertained, intermarried, and are still treated like shit. Nothing works, so why suffer the slow deaths of toxic addiction and the American work ethic when the immediate gratification of suicide awaits?" (2). This rather jarring juxtaposition of texts separated by 140 years or more serves a particular purpose: throughout his novel, Beatty rejects every conventional narrative used to contain or control African Americans' will to democracy and equality. Every path, every argument that promised liberation, from moral suasion to various forms of violent rebellion, has failed to obtain because of the most intractable of American problems: blindness; lack of historical circumspection and knowledge (with the possible exception of Confederates and their neo-Confederate descendants); lack of detailed, theologically informed religious practice; lack of civic knowledge.

To take Beatty's point then, how do we teach American ironies when many of our students lack a common cultural and historical knowledge? It is clearly necessary to start with some basic definitions that allow one to identify wit, irony, and satire, but I suggest also teaching about the jeremiad, about invective, about *reductio ad absurdum*, about *post hoc, ergo propter hoc* reasoning, about parody, picaros and picaresque narratives, tricksters, signifying, allegory, and so on. Early satirists such as Irving might help, with his portraits of American society reminiscent of Juvenal, full of chaotic, absurd crowds of the grotesque and infamous. Yet I remain convinced that "What to the Slave Is the Fourth of July?" contains examples of nearly all these elements or otherwise mocks them.

Douglass's address, delivered 5 July 1852, presents itself initially as an entry in July 4 speeches: encomia meant to praise the infinite wisdom of the United States' founders in their desire for freedom. The genre's grandiosity is beyond Douglass's abilities, as he avers: "A feeling has crept over me, quite unfavorable to the exercise of my limited powers of speech. . . . The papers and placards say, that I am to deliver a 4th July oration. This certainly sounds large, and out of the common way, for me" (117). After several more instances of *diminutio* directed toward his own rhetorical craft,

Douglass turns this strategy to the nation itself, which is "now 76 years old," a "young" age for a nation, a "mere speck" in its life (118). Douglass begins building a trope that will cast the United States as childish in its perverse lust for slavery despite its love of liberty. He speaks of the British Crown as "parental," caring properly for its young colonial charges, who rebelled at the parent's tyrannical overreach. As he begins to praise the bravery and wisdom of the founding fathers—"great men"—and their resistance to tyranny, close reading finds that these are fathers only in an ironic sense; they founded a nation but were mere children who "felt themselves the victims of grievous wrongs," rather than victims in fact (119).

Yet in Douglass's words we find a contradiction. Douglass's perspective may not be favorable, but he praises the founders. He describes them and the nation they founded as children, yet they were great men. They championed justice and freedom bravely and beyond reproach, yet "Americans are remarkably familiar with all facts which make in their own favor . . . I shall not be charged with slandering Americans, if I say I think the American side of any question may be safely left in American hands" (122). Douglass moves seamlessly between encomium and mock encomium so subtly that in this part of his address, he damns the founders and the nation they founded as often as he praises them—and therefore praises them almost not at all.

I do not wish to trace all of Douglass's address. Suffice to say that Douglass blasts the proslavery members of his audience with a beautiful instance of *apodioxis*:

> Would you have me argue that man is entitled to liberty? That he is the rightful owner of his own body? You have already declared it. Must I argue the wrongfulness of slavery? . . . Is it to be settled by the rules of logic and argumentation, as a matter beset with great difficulty, involving a doubtful application of the principles, hard to be understood? (126)

From this point, Douglass's mock encomium shifts into a classic jeremiad, employing invective and anticlimax to destroy verbally Americans' sense of exceptionalism. Americans are not the elect in a Calvinist universe, Douglass avers; they are the preterite, or will soon be:

> What to the American slave, is your 4th of July? I answer: a day that reveals to him, more than all other days in the year, the gross injustice and cruelty to which he is the constant victim. To him, your celebration is a sham; you boasted liberty, an unholy license; your national great-

> ness, swelling vanity; your sounds of rejoicing are empty and heartless; your denunciations of tyrants, brass fronted impudence; your shouts of liberty and equality, hollow mockery; your prayers and hymns, your sermons and thanksgivings, with all your religious parade, and solemnity, are, to him, mere bombast, fraud, deception, impiety, and hypocrisy. (127)

Just as the king of Brobdingnag concluded that the natives of Lemuel Gulliver's England were "the most pernicious Race of little odious Vermin that Nature ever suffered to crawl upon the Surface of the Earth" (Swift, *Travels* 108), so does Douglass, like Walker, damn Americans for hypocrisies and brutality that align them with those they consider inferior.

This criticism rests at the heart of the jeremiad, whose purpose is to demonstrate that those blessed by God shall soon be cursed due to their sins. In this sense, Douglass's address shares its ancestry as much with John Winthrop's "A Modell of Christian Charitie" (1630) as it does with Jonathan Swift. In Winthrop's most famous words,

> [F]or wee must Consider that wee shall be as a Citty upon a Hill, the eies of all people are uppon us; soe that if we shall deale falsely with our god in this worke wee have undertaken and soe cause him to withdrawe his present help from us, wee shall be made a story and a by-word through the world, wee shall open the mouthes of enemies to speake evil of the wayes of god, and all professours for Gods sake. (131)

Winthrop's sermon, of course, is one of the defining documents of American identity. The idea of the colonies and later the republic being a "Citty upon a Hill" resonates to this day. Although the sermon's focus overall is upon Christians showing love and charity, its political purpose was to condemn the Massachusetts Bay Colony's denizens for disunity and strife. These conditions, Winthrop argues, result from a lack of charity and have led to the colony's vulnerability to its environment, its Indian neighbors, and history's judgment.

At this moment, it may appear that we are veering too far afield of satire. Winthrop has no home in any glossary of satirists. Yet both the form and idealism contained within this jeremiad offer students a way to see the poles that mark two crucial boundaries of American discourse. The distance between American moral ideals and realities forms the basis for American literature's most devastating works.

One semester several years ago I had the opportunity to teach a lower-level course devoted to satire from Juvenal to the present. It posed a challenge for a number of reasons, with the first being the lack of shared perspective noted above. The second reason could be easily anticipated, if not resolved. Defining satire is tremendously difficult without resorting to oversimplified crib notes. I began by showing students that satire is criticism through humor, but I was immediately confronted with two questions that we never settled: Why do satirists criticize at all? Isn't this criticism inevitably harsh and cruel? Several students in the course rejected the notion that satirists *should* satirize simply because they can. The reason was clear.

"Satyr is a sort of Glass," Swift writes, "wherein beholders do generally discover every body's Face but their Own; which is the chief Reason for that kind Reception it meets in the World, and that so very few are offended with it" (*Tale* 375). Swift, of course, means the last part of the sentence ironically, but the misapprehension that follows irony and satire is quite real; readers are unlikely to see their own faces in the mirror. Nevertheless, satire and irony in American literature allow us to see that moral imperatives run throughout the American literary tradition, even after modernism and postmodernism's rejection of specific moralities. This is the common bond, the common cause, and how one may begin to teach American students to read and value satire.

Notes

1. Ralph Ellison riffs on these principles and this trope in the epilogue to *Invisible Man* (1952), published a century after Douglass's speech.

2. The text of Truth's speech comes from the "Book of Life" section of *Narrative of Sojourner Truth*, as recounted by Lydia Maria Gage. Biographer Nell Irvin Painter points out that Truth did not speak anything resembling the so-called Negro dialect commonly represented in literature. Born Isabella in Ulster County, New York, circa 1797, Truth's first language was Dutch; she did not speak English until much later. While Painter allows "[i]t is not possible to know exactly how Sojourner Truth spoke," her daughter, Gertrude Dumont, "protested that Truth's speech was nothing like the mock-southern dialect that careless reporters used" (Painter 7). The passage is therefore controversial, and we should read it for rhetorical effect rather than syntactical accuracy. A more accurate or at least dialect-free version was published in the *Anti-Slavery Bugle* on 21 June 1851.

Works Cited

Beatty, Paul. Introduction. *Hokum: An Anthology of African-American Humor*, edited by Paul Beatty, Bloomsbury, 2006, pp. 1–12.

———. *The White Boy Shuffle*. Houghton Mifflin, 1996.

Douglass, Frederick. *Narrative of the Life of Frederick Douglass, an American Slave, Written by Himself.* 1845. Edited by William L. Andrews and William S. McFeely, W. W. Norton, 1997.

———. "What to the Slave Is the Fourth of July?" Douglass, *Narrative*, pp. 116–27.

Painter, Nell Irvin. *Sojourner Truth: A Life, a Symbol.* W. W. Norton, 1996.

Reynolds, David S. *Beneath the American Renaissance: The Subversive Imagination in the Age of Emerson and Melville.* Harvard UP, 1988.

Swift, Jonathan. *A Tale of a Tub.* 1704. Swift, *Writings*, pp. 263–420.

———. *Travels into Several Remote Nations of the World.* 1726. Swift, *Writings*, pp. 1–260.

———. *The Writings of Jonathan Swift.* Edited by Robert A. Greenberg and William B. Piper, Norton, 1973.

Truth, Sojourner. *Narrative of Sojourner Truth: A Bondswoman of Olden Time, with a History of Her Labors and Correspondence Drawn from Her "Book of Life"; Also, a Memorial Chapter.* 1850. Edited by Nell Irvin Painter, Penguin, 1998.

Walker, David. *David Walker's Appeal, in Four Articles; Together with a Preamble, to the Coloured Citizens of the World, but in Particular, and Very Expressly, to Those of the United States of America.* 1829. Edited by Sean Wilentz, Hill and Wang, 1996.

Winthrop, John. "A Modell of Christian Charitie." *Colonial American Writing*, edited by Roy Harvey Pearce, 2nd ed., Holt, Rinehart, and Winston, 1969, pp. 116–31.

Part VII

Resources

Evan R. Davis and Nicholas D. Nace

Definitions

Bredvold, Louis I. "A Note in Defence of Satire." *ELH*, vol. 7, no. 4, Dec. 1940, pp. 253–64.

Briggs, Peter M. "Notes toward a Teachable Definition of Satire." *Eighteenth-Century Life*, vol. 5, no. 3, 1979, pp. 28–39.

Dasenbrock, Reed Way. "An Absurd Century: Varieties of Satire." *The Cambridge Companion to the Twentieth-Century English Novel*, edited by Robert L. Caserio, Cambridge UP, 2009, pp. 238–50.

Elkin, P. K. *The Augustan Defence of Satire.* Clarendon Press, 1973.

Elliott, Robert C. "The Definition of Satire: A Note on Method." *Yearbook on Comparative and General Literature*, vol. 11, 1962, pp. 19–23.

Feinberg, Leonard. *The Satirist: His Temperament, Motivation, and Influence.* Introduced by Brian A. Connery, Transaction, 2009.

Frye, Northrop. "The Nature of Satire." *University of Toronto Quarterly*, vol. 14, no. 1, Oct. 1944, pp. 75–89.

Hodgart, Matthew. *Satire: Origins and Principles Transaction.* Introduced by Brian A. Connery, Transaction, 2010.

Hume, Robert D. "'Satire' in the Reign of Charles II." *Modern Philology*, vol. 102, no. 3, Feb. 2005, pp. 332–71.

Jackson, Wallace. "Satire: An Augustan Idea of Disorder." *Proceedings of the Modern Language Association Neoclassicism Conferences, 1967–1968*, edited by Paul J. Korshin, AMS Press, 1970, pp. 13–26.

Kernan, Alvin B. "Robert C. Elliott 1914–81." *English Satire and the Satiric Tradition*, edited by Claude Rawson, Basil Blackwell, 1984, pp. 1–5.

Mack, Maynard. "The Muse of Satire." *The Yale Review*, vol. 41, 1951, pp. 80–92.

Nilsen, Don L. F. "Satire—The Necessary and Sufficient Conditions—Some Preliminary Observations." *Studies in Contemporary Satire*, vol. 15, 1988, pp. 1–10.

Randolph, Mary Claire. "Thomas Drant's Definition of Satire, 1566." *Notes and Queries*, vol. 180, 1941, pp. 416–18.

Rosenheim, Edward W. *Swift and the Satirist's Art.* U of Chicago P, 1963.

Russell, Frances Theresa. *Satire in the Victorian Novel.* Russell, 1964.

Spacks, Patricia Meyer. "Some Reflections on Satire." *Genre*, vol. 1, 1968, pp. 13–20.

———. "Uncertainties of Satire." *Modern Language Quarterly*, vol. 40, no. 4, 1979, pp. 403–11.

Sutherland, James. *English Satire*. Cambridge UP, 1962.

Test, George A. *Satire: Spirit and Art*. U of South Florida P, 1991.

Weinbrot, Howard D. *The Formal Strain: Studies in Augustan Imitation and Satire*. U of Chicago P, 1969.

Anthologies

Bakalar, Nick, editor. *American Satire: An Anthology of Writings from Colonial Times to the Present*. Meridian, 1997.

Brown, Ashley, and John L. Kimmey, editors. *Satire*. C. E. Merrill, 1968.

Clark, John R., and Anna Motto, editors. *Satire—That Blasted Art*. Putnam, 1973.

Falk, Robert P., editor. *American Literature in Parody: A Collection of Parody, Satire, and Literary Burlesque of American Writers Past and Present*. Twayne, 1955.

Fischer, Hermann, editor. *English Satirical Poetry from Joseph Hall to Percy B. Shelley*. Niemeyer, 1970.

Fitz Gerald, Gregory, editor. *Modern Satiric Stories: The Impropriety Principle*. Scott, Foresman, 1971.

Furlong, Norman, editor. *English Satire: An Anthology*. Harrap, 1946.

Gransden, K. W., editor. *Tudor Verse Satire*. Athlone Press, 1970.

Grigson, Geoffrey, editor. *The Oxford Book of Satirical Verse*. Oxford UP, 1980.

Gross, John, editor. *The Oxford Book of Parodies*. Oxford UP, 2010.

Heaney, Peter, editor. *An Anthology of Eighteenth-Century Satire: Grub-Street*. Edwin Mellen Press, 1995.

Kernan, Alvin B., editor. *Modern Satire*. Harcourt, Brace and World, 1962. Harbrace Sourcebooks.

Kiley, Frederick T., editor. *Satire from Aesop to Buchwald*. Odyssey Press, 1971.

Lucie-Smith, Edward, and J. M. Shuttleworth, editors. *The Penguin Book of Satirical Verse*. Penguin, 1967.

Miller, Paul Allen, editor. *Latin Verse Satire: An Anthology and Critical Reader*. Routledge, 2005.

Neilsen, Philip, editor. *The Penguin Book of Australian Satirical Verse.* Penguin, 1986.

Ogborn, Jane, and Peter Buckroyd. *Satire.* Cambridge UP, 2001.

Queenan, Joe, editor. *The Malcontents: The Best Bitter, Cynical, and Satirical Writing in the World.* Running Press, 2002.

Rousseau, George S., and Neil L. Rudenstine, editors. *English Poetic Satire: Wyatt to Byron.* Holt, Rinehart and Winston, 1972.

Smeaton, William Henry Oliphant, editor. *English Satires.* Books for Libraries Press, 1971.

Vines, Sherard, editor. *Georgian Satirists.* Wishart, 1934.

———, editor. *Whips and Scorpions: Specimens of Modern Satiric Verse, 1914–1931.* Wishart, 1932.

Wells, Carolyn, editor. *A Satire Anthology.* Scribner's Sons, 1905.

Winokur, Jon. *The Big Book of Irony.* St. Martin's Press, 2007.

Essay Collections

Connery, Brian A., and Kirk Combe, editors. *Theorizing Satire: Essays in Literary Criticism.* St. Martin's Press, 1995.

Davis, Jessica Milner, editor. *Satire and Politics: The Interplay of Heritage and Practice.* Palgrave Macmillan, 2017. Palgrave Studies in Comedy.

Gill, James E., editor. *Cutting Edges: Postmodern Critical Essays on Eighteenth-Century Satire.* U of Tennessee P, 1995. Tennessee Studies in Literature 37.

Hudson, Nicholas, and Aaron Santesso, editors. *Swift's Travels: Eighteenth-Century Satire and Its Legacy.* Cambridge UP, 2011.

Paulson, Ronald. *Satire: Modern Essays in Criticism.* Prentice-Hall, 1971. Prentice-Hall English Literature Series.

Quintero, Ruben, editor. *A Companion to Satire: Ancient and Modern.* Blackwell, 2007. Blackwell Companions to Literature and Culture 46.

Rawson, Claude, editor. *English Satire and the Satiric Tradition.* Blackwell, 1984.

Teaching

Beaty, Frederick L. "Teaching Satire in English Bards and 'The Vision of Judgment.'" *Approaches to Teaching Byron's Poetry*, edited by

Frederick W. Shilstone, Modern Language Association of America, 1991, pp. 83–88.

Bogel, Fredric V. "Teaching Pope Today: Satire, Resistance, Theory." *Approaches to Teaching Pope's Poetry*, edited by Wallace Jackson and R. Paul Yoder, Modern Language Association of America, 1993, pp. 64–72.

Caron, James E. "Parody and Satire as Explorations of Culture in *The Innocents Abroad*." *Making Mark Twain Work in the Classroom*, edited by James S. Leonard, Duke UP, 1999, pp. 65–87.

Clark, John R. "Desolation and Decorum: The Teaching of Modern Satire." *Studies in Contemporary Satire*, vol. 4, 1977, pp. 1–13.

Creaser, Wanda J. "Teaching Satire on the Border: It's a Journey Back to the Eighteenth Century." *Teaching the Eighteenth Century*, edited by Mary Ann Rooks, Cambridge Scholars, 2009, pp. 49–61.

Goodhue, Elizabeth K. "Satire, Sentimentalism, and Civic Engagement: From Eighteenth-Century Britain to the Twenty-First-Century Writing Course." *Service Learning and Literary Studies in English*, edited by Laurie Grobman and Roberta Rosenberg, Modern Language Association of America, 2015, pp. 93–103.

Modia, María Jesús Lorenzo, and Begoña Lasa Álvarez. "Teaching Eighteenth-Century Poetic Satire with a Competency-Based Approach: Jonathan Swift and Lady Mary Wortley Montagu." *International Education Studies*, vol. 4, no. 5, 2011, pp. 25–32.

Pullen, Charles. "Swift's Letters in Teaching Tone and Technique in *Gulliver's Travels*." *Approaches to Teaching Swift's* Gulliver's Travels, edited by Edward J. Rielly, Modern Language Association of America, 1998, pp. 89–95.

Real, Hermann Josef, editor. *Teaching Satire: Dryden to Pope*. Carl Winter Universitätsverlag, 1992.

Weinbrot, Howard D. "Teaching Eighteenth-Century Satire." *Teaching Eighteenth-Century Poetry*, edited by Christopher Fox, AMS Press, 1990, pp. 25–46.

Wesp, Edward. "'Some Words with a Mummy': Teaching Satire and the Democratic Threat in Poe's Fiction." *Approaches to Teaching Poe's Prose and Poetry*, edited by Jeffrey Andrew Weinstock and Tony Magistrale, Modern Language Association of America, 2008, pp. 48–54.

Theories

Bakhtin, M. M. *Problems of Dostoevsky's Poetics.* Edited and translated by Caryl Emerson, U of Minnesota P, 1984. Theory and History of Literature 8.

Bloom, Edward Alan, and Lillian D. Bloom. *Satire's Persuasive Voice.* Cornell UP, 1979.

Bogel, Fredric V. *The Difference Satire Makes: Rhetoric and Reading from Jonson to Byron.* Cornell UP, 2001.

Castle, Terry J. "Why the Houyhnhnms Don't Write: Swift, Satire and the Fear of the Text." *Critical Essays on Jonathan Swift*, edited by Frank Palmeri, G. K. Hall, 1993, pp. 57–71.

Gilmore, John T. *Satire.* Routledge, 2017. The New Critical Idiom.

Griffin, Dustin H. *Satire: A Critical Reintroduction.* UP of Kentucky, 1994.

Guilhamet, Leon. *Satire and the Transformation of Genre.* U of Pennsylvania P, 1987.

Highet, Gilbert. *The Anatomy of Satire.* Princeton UP, 1962.

Knight, Charles A. *The Literature of Satire.* Cambridge UP, 2004.

Phiddian, Robert. "Satire and the Limits of Literary Theories." *Critical Quarterly*, vol. 55, no. 3, Oct. 2013, pp. 44–58.

History

Beasley, Rebecca. "Wyndham Lewis and Modernist Satire." *The Cambridge Companion to the Modernist Novel*, edited by Morag Shiach, Cambridge UP, 2007, pp. 126–36.

Bricker, Andrew Benjamin. "Libel and Satire: The Problem with Naming." *ELH*, vol. 81, no. 3, Fall 2014, pp. 889–921.

Carpenter, Humphrey. *A Great, Silly Grin: The British Satire Boom of the 1960s.* PublicAffairs, 2002.

Dyer, Gary. *British Satire and the Politics of Style, 1789–1832.* Cambridge UP, 2006.

Gérin, Annie. *Devastation and Laughter: Satire, Power, and Culture in the Early Soviet State, 1920s–1930s.* U of Toronto P, 2018.

Greenberg, Jonathan. *The Cambridge Introduction to Satire.* Cambridge UP, 2018.

Hoffmann, George. *Reforming French Culture: Satire, Spiritual Alienation, and Connection to Strangers.* Oxford UP, 2018.

Jones, William. *Satire in the Elizabethan Era: An Activistic Art.* Routledge, 2017. Routledge Studies in Renaissance Literature and Culture 41.

Kernan, Alvin B. *The Cankered Muse: Satire of the English Renaissance.* Yale UP, 1959. Yale Studies in English 142.

Marshall, Ashley. *The Practice of Satire in England, 1658–1770.* Johns Hopkins UP, 2013.

Matz, Aaron. *Satire in an Age of Realism.* Cambridge UP, 2013.

Miller, Tyrus. *Late Modernism: Politics, Fiction, and the Arts between the World Wars.* U of California P, 1999.

Puchner, Martin. "The Aftershocks of Blast: Manifestos, Satire, and the Rear-Guard of Modernism." *Bad Modernisms*, edited by Douglas Mao and Rebecca L. Walkowitz, Duke UP, 2006, pp. 44–67.

Rogers, Pat. *Documenting Eighteenth-Century Satire: Pope, Swift, Gay, and Arbuthnot in Historical Context.* Cambridge Scholars, 2011.

Simons, Jay. *Jonson, the Poetomachia, and the Reformation of Renaissance Satire: Purging Satire.* Routledge, 2018. Routledge Studies in Renaissance Literature and Culture.

Vivier, Eric D. "John Bridges, Martin Marprelate, and the Rhetoric of Satire." *English Literary Renaissance*, vol. 44, no. 1, Winter 2014, pp. 3–35.

Wood, Marcus. *Radical Satire and Print Culture, 1790–1822.* Clarendon Press, 1994.

Classical and Medieval Backgrounds

Branham, R. Bracht. *Unruly Eloquence: Lucian and the Comedy of Traditions.* Harvard UP, 1989.

Freudenburg, Kirk, editor. *The Cambridge Companion to Roman Satire.* Cambridge UP, 2005.

Frost, William. "English Persius: The Golden Age." *Eighteenth-Century Studies*, vol. 2, no. 2, Dec. 1968, pp. 77–101.

Hendrickson, G. L. "*Satura Tota Nostra Est.*" *Classical Philology*, vol. 22, Jan. 1927, pp. 46–60.

Hudson, Nicola. "The Beast at the Feast: Food in Roman Verse Satire." *Food, Culture and History*, edited by Gerald Mars and Valerie Mars, London Food Seminar, 1993, pp. 204–20.

Kaplan, Carter. *Critical Synoptics: Menippean Satire and the Analysis of Intellectual Mythology*. Fairleigh Dickinson UP / London Associated UP, 2000.

Kendrick, Laura. "Medieval Satire." *European Writers: The Middle Ages and the Renaissance*, edited by William T. H. Jackson, Scribner, 1983, pp. 337–75.

Kupersmith, William. *Roman Satirists in Seventeenth-Century England*. U of Nebraska P, 1985.

Kupersmith, William, and W. B. Carnochan. "Juvenal as Sublime Satirist (An Exchange)." *PMLA*, vol. 87, 1972, pp. 508–11, 1125–26.

Mann, Jill. *Chaucer and Medieval Estates Satire*. Cambridge UP, 1973.

Nelsestuen, Grant A. *Varro the Agronomist: Political Philosophy, Satire, and Agriculture in the Late Republic*. Ohio State UP, 2016.

Parsons, Ben. "'A Riotous Spray of Words': Rethinking the Medieval Theory of Satire." *Exemplaria*, vol. 21, no. 2, 2009, pp. 105–28.

Pinkus, Philip. "The New Satire in Augustan England." *University of Toronto Quarterly*, vol. 38, 1969, pp. 136–58.

Plaza, Maria. *The Function of Humour in Roman Verse Satire: Laughing and Lying*. Oxford UP, 2006.

Rudd, Niall. *Themes in Roman Satire*. U of Oklahoma P, 1986.

Spacks, Patricia Meyer. "From Satire to Description." *The Yale Review*, vol. 58, 1969, pp. 232–48.

Sullivan, J. P., editor. *Satire: Critical Essays on Roman Literature*. Indiana UP, 1963.

Tucker, Samuel Marion. *Verse Satire in England before the Renaissance*. Columbia UP, 1908.

Weinbrot, Howard D. "History, Horace, and Augustus Caesar: Some Implications for Eighteenth-Century Satire." *Eighteenth-Century Studies*, vol. 7, no. 4, Summer 1974, pp. 391–414.

Yona, Sergio. *Epicurean Ethics in Horace: The Psychology of Satire*. Oxford UP, 2018.

Rhetoric and Philosophy

Carnochan, W. B. "Augustan Satire and the Gates of Dreams: A Utopian Essay." *Studies in the Literary Imagination*, vol. 5, no. 2, 1972, pp. 1–18.

———. "Satire, Sublimity, and Sentiment: Theory and Practice in Post-Augustan Satire." *PMLA*, vol. 85, no. 2, Mar. 1970, pp. 260–67.

Cope, Kevin. "Satire: The Conquest of Philosophy." *Literature as Philosophy / Philosophy as Literature*, edited by Donald G. Marshall, U of Iowa P, 1987, pp. 175–84.

Ker, Ian. "Newman the Satirist." *Newman after a Hundred Years*, edited by Ian Ker and Alan G. Hill, Clarendon Press, 1990, pp. 1–20.

More, Nicholas D. *Nietzsche's Last Laugh:* Ecce Homo *as Satire*. Cambridge UP, 2014.

Rhodes, Neil. "Nashe, Rhetoric and Satire." *Jacobean Poetry and Prose: Rhetoric, Representation and the Popular Imagination*, edited by Clive Bloom, St. Martin's, 1988, pp. 25–43.

Seidel, Michael. "Satire and Metaphoric Collapse: The Bottom of the Sublime." *Satire in the Eighteenth Century*, edited by J. D. Browning, Garland, 1983, pp. 116–23.

Terry, Richard. "'Ill Effects from Good': The Rhetoric of Augustan Mockery (with Illustrations from Pope and Fielding)." *Journal for Eighteenth-Century Studies*, vol. 17, no. 2, Sept. 1994, pp. 125–37.

Techniques

Aden, John M. "Pope and the Satiric Adversary." *Studies in English Literature, 1500–1900*, vol. 2, no. 3, Summer 1962, pp. 267–86.

Eddings, Dennis W., editor. *The Naiad Voice: Essays on Poe's Satiric Hoaxing*. Associated Faculty Press, 1983.

Farrell, Maurice. "Satiric 'Subversion' and the Continuity of Doublethink." *The British Journal of Aesthetics*, vol. 16, no. 4, 1976, pp. 370–75.

Hile, Rachel E. *Spenserian Satire: A Tradition of Indirection*. Manchester UP, 2017.

Jump, John D. *Burlesque*. Methuen, 1972.

Kernan, Alvin B. "Aggression and Satire: Art Considered as a Form of Biological Adaptation." *Literary Theory and Structure: Essays in Honor *of William K. Wimsatt*, edited by Frank Brady et al., Yale UP, 1973, pp. 115–29.

Kropf, Carl R. "Libel and Satire in the Eighteenth Century." *Eighteenth-Century Studies*, vol. 8, 1974–75, pp. 153–68.

———, editor. *Reader Entrapment in Eighteenth-Century Literature.* AMS, 1992.

Mookerjee, Robin. *Transgressive Fiction: The New Satiric Tradition.* Palgrave Macmillan, 2013.

Nichols, James W. *Insinuation: The Tactics of English Satire.* Mouton, 1971.

Irony

Booth, Wayne C. *A Rhetoric of Irony.* U of Chicago P, 1974.

Colebrook, Claire. *Irony in the Work of Philosophy.* U of Nebraska P, 2002.

Dentith, Simon. *Parody.* Routledge, 2000.

Enright, D. J. *The Alluring Problem: An Essay on Irony.* Oxford UP, 1986.

Fish, Stanley. "Short People Got No Reason to Live: Reading Irony." *Doing What Comes Naturally: Change, Rhetoric, and the Practice of Theory in Literary and Legal Studies*, Duke UP, 1989, pp. 180–97.

Frye, Northrop. *Anatomy of Criticism: Four Essays.* Princeton UP, 1957.

Hutcheon, Linda. *Irony's Edge: The Theory and Politics of Irony.* Routledge, 1995.

———. *A Theory of Parody: The Teachings of Twentieth-Century Art Forms.* Methuen, 1985.

Knox, Norman. *The Word* Irony *and Its Context, 1500–1755.* Duke UP, 1961.

Kreuz, Roger J., and Richard M. Roberts. "On Satire and Parody: The Importance of Being Ironic." *Metaphor and Symbolic Activity*, vol. 8, no. 2, 1993, pp. 97–109.

Lear, Jonathan. *A Case for Irony.* Harvard UP, 2011.

Muecke, D. C. *The Compass of Irony.* Methuen, 1969.

Poirier, Richard. "The Politics of Self-Parody." *Partisan Review*, vol. 35, no. 3, Summer 1968, pp. 339–53.

Winokur, Jon. *The Big Book of Irony*. St. Martin's Press, 2007.

Wood, Allen G. *Literary Satire and Theory: A Study of Horace, Boileau, and Pope*. Garland, 1985.

Humor

Burke, Kenneth. "Comic Correctives." *Attitudes toward History*, New Republic, 1937, pp. 166–75.

Connery, Brian A. "Inside Jokes: Familiarity and Contempt in Academic Satire." *University Fiction*, edited by David Bevan, Rodopi, 1990, pp. 123–37.

Dagnes, Alison. *A Conservative Walks into a Bar: The Politics of Political Humor*. Palgrave Macmillan, 2012.

de Sousa, Ronald. "When Is It Wrong to Laugh?" *The Philosophy of Laughter and Humor*, edited by John Morreall, State U of New York P, 1987, pp. 226–49.

English, James F. "The Laughing Reader: A New Direction for Studies of the Comic." *Genre*, vol. 19, 1986, pp. 129–54.

Langer, Susanne K. "The Great Dramatic Forms: The Comic Rhythm." *Feeling and Form: A Theory of Art Developed from Philosophy in a New Key*, Scribner, 1953, pp. 326–50.

Legman, Gershon. *Rationale of the Dirty Joke: An Analysis of Sexual Humor*. Grove, 1968.

Lockwood, Thomas. "The Augustan Author-Audience Relationship: Satiric vs. Comic Forms." *ELH*, vol. 36, no. 4, Dec. 1969, pp. 648–58.

Rosso, Michela. *Laughing at Architecture: Architectural Histories of Humour, Satire and Wit*. Bloomsbury Visual Arts, 2018.

Simpson, Paul. *On the Discourse of Satire: Towards a Stylistic Model of Satirical Humor*. John Benjamins Publishing, 2003.

Gender and Sexuality

Gatrell, Vic. *City of Laughter: Sex and Satire in Eighteenth-Century London*. Atlantic, 2006.

Hedrick, Elizabeth. "Robin Morgan, Jane Alpert, and Feminist Satire." *Tulsa Studies in Women's Literature*, vol. 33, no. 2, Fall 2014, pp. 123–50.

Johns-Putra, Adeline. "Satire and Domesticity in Late Eighteenth-Century Women's Poetry: Minding the Gap." *Journal for Eighteenth-Century Studies*, vol. 33, no. 1, 2010, pp. 67–87.

Lewis, Jayne. "Compositions of Ill Nature: Women's Place in a Satiric Tradition." *Critical Matrix*, vol. 2, 1986, pp. 31–69.

Mannheimer, Katherine. *Print, Visuality, and Gender in Eighteenth-Century Satire: "The Scope in Ev'ry Page."* Routledge, 2011.

Melzer, Sondra. *The Rhetoric of Rage: Women in Dorothy Parker*. Peter Lang, 1997.

Nussbaum, Felicity A. *The Brink of All We Hate: English Satires on Women, 1660–1750*. UP of Kentucky, 1984.

Webster, Jeremy. "The 'Lustful Buggering Jew': Anti-Semitism, Gender, and Sodomy in Restoration Political Satire." *Journal for Early Modern Cultural Studies*, vol. 6, no. 1, Spring–Summer 2006, pp. 106–24.

Wilcoxon, Reba. "Mirrors of Men's Fears: The Court Satires on Women." *Restoration: Studies in English Literary Culture, 1660–1700*, vol. 3, no. 2, Fall 1979, pp. 45–51.

Williams, Carolyn. *Gilbert and Sullivan: Gender, Genre, Parody*. Columbia UP, 2012.

Race and Ethnicity

Balce, Nerissa S. "Laughter against the State: On Humor, Postcolonial Satire, and Asian American Short Fiction." *Journal of Asian American Studies*, vol. 19, no. 1, Feb. 2016, pp. 47–73.

Ball, John Clement. *Satire and the Postcolonial Novel: V. S. Naipaul, Chinua Achebe, Salman Rushdie*. Routledge, 2003.

Carpio, Glenda R. *Laughing Fit to Kill: Black Humor in the Fictions of Slavery*. Oxford UP, 2008.

Dickson-Carr, Darryl. *African American Satire: The Sacredly Profane Novel*. U of Missouri P, 2001.

———. *Spoofing the Modern: Satire in the Harlem Renaissance*. U of South Carolina P, 2015.

Doty, Benjamin J. "Satire, Minstrelsy, and Embodiment in *Sheppard Lee*." *Early American Literature*, vol. 51, no. 1, 2016, pp. 131–56.

García-Caro, Pedro. *After the Nation: Postnational Satire in the Works of Carlos Fuentes and Thomas Pynchon*. Northwestern UP, 2014.

Hernández, Guillermo E. *Chicano Satire: A Study in Literary Culture.* U of Texas P, 1991. Mexican American Monographs 14.

Leonard, James S., et al., editors. *Satire or Evasion? Black Perspectives on* Huckleberry Finn. Duke UP, 1992.

Maus, Derek C., and James J. Donahue, editors. *Post-Soul Satire: Black Identity after Civil Rights.* UP of Mississippi, 2014.

Thompson, William R. "The American Indians' Attempt to Get the Last Laugh." *Studies in Contemporary Satire*, vol. 16, 1989, pp. 1–10.

Satire and the Public

Bertelsen, Lance. *The Nonsense Club: Literature and Popular Culture, 1749–1764.* Clarendon Press, 1986.

Connery, Brian A. "'Wild Work in the World': The Church, the Public Sphere, and Swift's Abstract of Collins' Discourse." *Swift as Priest and Satirist*, edited by Todd C. Parker, U of Delaware P, 2009.

Knight, Charles A. "The Images of Nations in Eighteenth-Century Satire." *Eighteenth-Century Studies*, vol. 22, no. 4, Summer 1989, pp. 489–511.

Maus, Derek C. *Unvarnishing Reality: Subversive Russian and American Cold War Satire.* U of South Carolina P, 2011.

McRae, Andrew. "Renaissance Satire and the Popular Voice." *Imperfect Apprehensions: Essays in English Literature in Honour of G. A. Wilkes*, edited by Geoffrey Little, Challis Press, 1996, pp. 5–17.

Rabb, Melinda Alliker. *Satire and Secrecy in English Literature from 1650 to 1750.* Palgrave Macmillan, 2007.

Film, Television, and Media

Chedraui, Carmen Irabien. "The Perfect Dictatorship: Political Satire in Contemporary Mexican Cinema." *Cineaste*, vol. 41, no. 3, Summer 2016, pp. 44–45.

Colletta, Lisa. "Political Satire and Postmodern Irony in the Age of Stephen Colbert and Jon Stewart." *The Journal of Popular Culture*, vol. 42, no. 5, Oct. 2009, pp. 856–74.

Courtemanche, Eleanor. "Satire and the 'Inevitability Effect': The Structure of Utopian Fiction from *Looking Backward* to *Portlandia*." *Modern Language Quarterly*, vol. 76, no. 2, 2015, pp. 225–46.

Dale, Timothy M., and Joseph J. Foy, editors. *Homer Simpson Marches on Washington: Dissent through American Popular Culture*. UP of Kentucky, 2010.

Day, Amber. *Satire and Dissent: Interventions in Contemporary Political Debate*. Indiana UP, 2011.

Ezell, Silas Kaine. *Humor and Satire on Contemporary Television: Animation and the American Joke*. Routledge, 2016.

Gillingham, Paul, Michael Lettieri, and Benjamin T. Smith, editors. *Journalism, Satire, and Censorship in Mexico*. U of New Mexico P, 2018.

Gournelos, Ted. *Popular Culture and the Future of Politics: Cultural Studies and the Tao of* South Park. Lexington Books, 2009.

Gournelos, Ted, and David J. Gunkel, editors. *Transgression 2.0: Media, Culture, and the Politics of a Digital Age*. Continuum, 2012.

Gournelos, Ted, and Viveca Greene, editors. *A Decade of Dark Humor: How Comedy, Irony, and Satire Shaped Post-9/11 America*. UP of Mississippi, 2011.

Henry, Matthew A. The Simpsons*, Satire, and American Culture*. Palgrave Macmillan, 2012.

McCaffrey, Donald W. *Assault on Society: Satirical Literature to Film*. Scarecrow Press, 1992.

McClennen, Sophia A. *America According to Colbert: Satire as Public Pedagogy*. Palgrave Macmillan, 2011. Education, Politics, and Public Life.

McClennen, Sophia A., and Remy M. Maisel. *Is Satire Saving Our Nation? Mockery and American Politics*. Palgrave Macmillan, 2014.

Newitz, Annalee. "What Makes Things Cheesy? Satire, Multinationalism, and B-Movies." *Social Text*, vol. 18, no. 2, Summer 2000, pp. 59–82.

Nilsson, Johan. *American Film Satire in the 1990s: Hollywood Subversion*. Palgrave Macmillan, 2013.

Palmeri, Frank. "Cruikshank, Thackeray, and the Victorian Eclipse of Satire." *SEL: Studies in English Literature, 1500–1900*, vol. 44, no. 4, Autumn 2004, pp. 753–77.

Thompson, Ethan. "Good Demo, Bad Taste: *South Park* as Carnivalesque Satire." *Satire TV: Politics and Comedy in the Post-Network Era*, edited by Jonathan Gray et al., New York UP, 2009, pp. 213–32.

Torres, Luis A. "Bilingualism as Satire in Nineteenth-Century Chicano Poetry." *An Other Tongue: Nation and Ethnicity in the Linguistic Borderlands*, edited by Alfred Arteaga, Duke UP, 1994, pp. 247–62.

Zoonen, Liesbet van, et al. "Performing Citizenship on YouTube: Activism, Satire and Online Debate around the Anti-Islam Video *Fitna*." *Critical Discourse Studies*, vol. 7, no. 4, 2010, pp. 249–62.

Visual Arts

Beirne, Piers. *Hogarth's Art of Animal Cruelty: Satire, Suffering and Pictorial Propaganda*. Palgrave Macmillan, 2015.

Berger, Arthur Asa. Li'l Abner*: A Study in American Satire*. Twayne, 1970.

Elleström, Lars. *Divine Madness: On Interpreting Literature, Music, and the Visual Arts Ironically*. Bucknell UP, 2002.

Flood, Catherine, and Sarah Grant. *Style and Satire: Fashion in Print, 1777–1927*. V&A Publishing, 2014.

Hallett, Mark. *The Spectacle of Difference: Graphic Satire in the Age of Hogarth*. Yale UP, 1999.

Hardy, Dominic, et al., editors. *Sketches from an Unquiet Country: Canadian Graphic Satire, 1840–1940*. McGill-Queen's UP, 2018. McGill-Queen's / Beaverbrook Canadian Foundation Studies in Art History 24.

Harvey, John. "Graphic Satire and Illustrations." *The Cambridge Guide to the Arts in Britain: Romantics to Early Victorians*, edited by Boris Ford, vol. 6, Cambridge UP, 1990, pp. 172–83.

Levine, Edward. "The Inflated Image: Satire and Meaning in Pop Art." *Satire Newsletter*, vol. 6, no. 1, 1968, pp. 43–49.

Mansfield, Elizabeth C., and Kelly Malone, editors. *Seeing Satire in the Eighteenth Century*. Voltaire Foundation, 2013.

McCreery, Cindy. *The Satirical Gaze: Prints of Women in Late Eighteenth-Century England*. Clarendon Press, 2004.

McPhee, Constance C., and Nadine M. Orenstein. *Infinite Jest: Caricature and Satire from Leonardo to Levine*. Metropolitan Museum of Art, 2011.

Pierce, Helen. *Unseemly Pictures: Graphic Satire and Politics in Early Modern England*. Yale UP, 2008.

Sampson, Grant. "Hogarth and the Traditions of Satire." *Humanities Association Review*, vol. 31, nos. 1–2, 1980, pp. 67–85.

Soper, Kerry D. *Garry Trudeau:* Doonesbury *and the Aesthetics of Satire*. UP of Mississippi, 2008.

———. *We Go Pogo: Walt Kelly, Politics, and American Satire.* UP of Mississippi, 2012.

Thompson, Todd Nathan. *The National Joker: Abraham Lincoln and the Politics of Satire.* Southern Illinois UP, 2015.

Verse

Arner, Robert D. "Wit, Humor, and Satire in Seventeenth-Century American Poetry." *Puritan Poets and Poetics: Seventeenth-Century American Poetry in Theory and Practice*, edited by Peter White, Pennsylvania State UP, 1985, pp. 318–36.

Lockwood, Thomas F. "On the Relationship of Satire and Poetry after Pope." *Studies in English Literature*, vol. 14, no. 3, Summer 1974, pp. 387–402.

———. *Post-Augustan Satire: Charles Churchill and Satirical Poetry, 1750–1800.* U of Washington P, 1979.

Love, Harold. *English Clandestine Satire, 1660–1702.* Oxford UP, 2004.

Rawson, Claude. *Satire and Sentiment, 1660–1830: Stress Points in the English Augustan Tradition.* Cambridge UP, 1994.

Ryzhik, Yulia. "Complaint and Satire in Spenser and Donne: Limits of Poetic Justice." *English Literary Renaissance*, vol. 47, no. 1, Winter 2017, pp. 110–35.

Selden, Raman. *English Verse Satire, 1590–1765.* Allen and Unwin, 1978.

Weinbrot, Howard D. *Alexander Pope and the Traditions of Formal Verse Satire.* Princeton UP, 1982.

———. *Eighteenth-Century Satire: Essays on Text and Context from Dryden to Peter Pindar.* Cambridge UP, 1988.

Yu, Christopher. *Nothing to Admire: The Politics of Poetic Satire from Dryden to Merrill.* Oxford UP, 2003.

Novels

Ball, John Clement. *Satire and the Postcolonial Novel: V. S. Naipaul, Chinua Achebe, Salman Rushdie.* Routledge, 2009.

Bosco, Mark, and Kimberly Rae Connor, editors. *Academic Novels as Satire: Critical Studies of an Emerging Genre.* Edwin Mellen Press, 2007.

Colletta, Lisa. *Dark Humor and Social Satire in the Modern British Novel.* Palgrave Macmillan, 2003.

Cook, Jonathan A. *Satirical Apocalypse: An Anatomy of Melville's* The Confidence-Man. Greenwood Press, 1996.

Dickson-Carr, Darryl. *African American Satire: The Sacredly Profane Novel.* U of Missouri P, 2001.

Greenberg, Jonathan. *Modernism, Satire, and the Novel.* Cambridge UP, 2011.

Greenblatt, Stephen Jay. *Three Modern Satirists: Waugh, Orwell, and Huxley.* Yale UP, 1966.

Gregson, Ian. *Character and Satire in Post-War Fiction.* Continuum, 2006.

Harris, Jocelyn. *Satire, Celebrity, and Politics in Jane Austen.* Bucknell UP, 2017. Transits: Literature, Thought and Culture, 1650–1850.

Hume, Kathryn. "Diffused Satire in Contemporary American Fiction." *Modern Philology*, vol. 105, no. 2, Nov. 2007, pp. 300–25.

Kharpertian, Theodore D. *A Hand to Turn the Time: The Menippean Satires of Thomas Pynchon.* Fairleigh Dickinson UP, 1990.

Lewis, Wyndham. *Satire and Fiction.* Arthur Press, 1930.

Milthorpe, Naomi. *Evelyn Waugh's Satire: Texts and Contexts.* Fairleigh Dickinson UP, 2016.

Palmeri, Frank. *Satire, History, Novel: Narrative Forms, 1665–1815.* U of Delaware P, 2003.

———. *Satire in Narrative: Petronius, Swift, Gibbon, Melville, and Pynchon.* U of Texas P, 1990.

Paulson, Ronald. *The Fictions of Satire.* Johns Hopkins UP, 1967.

———. *Satire and the Novel in Eighteenth-Century England.* Yale UP, 1967.

Seidel, Michael. *Satiric Inheritance: Rabelais to Sterne.* Princeton UP, 1979.

Weinbrot, Howard D. *Menippean Satire Reconsidered: From Antiquity to the Eighteenth Century.* Johns Hopkins UP, 2005.

Weisenburger, Steven. *Fables of Subversion: Satire and the American Novel, 1930–1980.* U of Georgia P, 1995.

Womack, Kenneth. "Academic Satire: The Campus Novel in Context." *A Companion to the British and Irish Novel, 1945–2000*, edited by Brian Shaffer, Blackwell, 2013, pp. 326–39.

———. *Postwar Academic Fiction: Satire, Ethics, Community*. Palgrave, 2002.

Yazdani, Saeed. *Jack London: Literature of Protest through Satire*. Common Ground Publishing, 2013.

Drama

Ballaster, Ros. "Satire and Embodiment: Allegorical Romance on Stage and Page in Mid-Eighteenth-Century Britain." *Eighteenth-Century Fiction*, vol. 27, nos. 3–4, Spring–Summer 2015, pp. 631–60.

Griffin, Alice, and John Griffin. "Satire in the New York Theatre." *Satire Newsletter*, vol. 2, no. 1, 1965, pp. 41–46.

Griffith, Katherine, moderator. "What's So Funny: The Use of Humor, Comedy, Satire." *International Women Playwrights: Voices of Identity and Transformation*, edited by Anna Kay France and P. J. Corso, Scarecrow Press, 1993, pp. 96–104.

Kinservik, Matthew J. *Disciplining Satire: The Censorship of Satiric Comedy on the Eighteenth-Century London Stage*. Bucknell UP, 2002.

Macey, Samuel. "Theatrical Satire: A Protest from the Stage against Poor Taste in Theatrical Entertainment." *The Varied Pattern: Studies in the Eighteenth Century*, edited by Peter Hughes and David Williams, A. M. Hakkert, 1971, pp. 121–29.

Schechter, Joel. *Eighteenth-Century Brechtians: Theatrical Satire in the Age of Walpole*. U of Exeter P, 2016.

Snider, Rose. *Satire in the Comedies of Congreve, Sheridan, Wilde, and Coward*. Phaeton Press, 1972.

Yearling, Rebecca. *Ben Jonson, John Marston and Early Modern Drama: Satire and the Audience*. Palgrave Macmillan, 2016.

Notes on Contributors

David Alff is associate professor of English at the University at Buffalo, the State University of New York, where he teaches and researches the literature and culture of eighteenth-century Britain. He is the author of *The Wreckage of Intentions: Projects in British Culture, 1660–1730* (2017).

John Clement Ball, professor and chair of English at the University of New Brunswick, is author of *Satire and the Postcolonial Novel: V. S. Naipaul, Chinua Achebe, Salman Rushdie* (2003) and *Imagining London: Postcolonial Fiction and the Transnational Metropolis* (2004) and editor of *Twentieth-Century World Fiction* (2011).

Danielle Bobker is associate professor at Concordia University in Montreal. Her research on the eighteenth-century architecture of intimacy has most recently appeared in *Digital Defoe* and *History of the Present*. Her latest project explores the relationships among humor, anger, and other affects in satire and satire criticism.

Fredric V. Bogel, professor of English at Cornell University, teaches eighteenth-century literature, satire, critical theory, and the history of poetry. His most recent book is *New Formalist Criticism: Theory and Practice* (2013). He is currently working on "The Matter of Emotions: Affect and Mechanism in Eighteenth-Century Literature," a study of literature, philosophy, aesthetic theory, and acting that explores materialist and volitional accounts of affective and aesthetic experience.

Kirk Combe is a professor of English at Denison University in Ohio. He teaches and researches in the areas of early modern British satire and drama, literary and cultural theory, and popular culture. Along with his scholarly publications, he also writes fiction and screenplays.

Michael J. Conlon is emeritus associate professor of English, rhetoric, and general literature at Binghamton University, the State University of New York. He has published articles on John Dryden, Alexander Pope, and Jonathan Swift and on the subjects of performance, parody, and satire in early modern English literature.

Evan R. Davis is Elliott Professor of English and assistant dean of the faculty at Hampden-Sydney College. He has published essays on Jonathan Swift, Alexander Pope, and Daniel Defoe and edited the Broadview Press edition of *Robinson Crusoe*. He is currently coediting, with Nicholas Nace, *The Broadview Anthology of Eighteenth-Century British Satire*.

Amber Day is professor in the Literary and Cultural Studies Department at Bryant University. She is the author of *Satire and Dissent: Interventions in Contemporary Political Debate* and editor of *DIY Utopia: Cultural Imagination and the Remaking of the Possible*. She has published on parody news shows, satiric documentaries, ironic activism, viral videos, community art, and comedians in the public sphere.

Helen Deutsch has been teaching and writing about eighteenth-century satire at the University of California, Los Angeles, for the past twenty years. She is the author of *Resemblance and Disgrace: Alexander Pope and the Deformation of Culture* (1996) and *Loving Dr. Johnson* (2005). She is currently working on a study of Jonathan Swift and Edward Said tentatively titled "The Last Amateur."

Darryl Dickson-Carr is professor and chair of English at Southern Methodist University. He is the author of *Spoofing the Modern: Satire in the Harlem Renaissance* (2015), *The Columbia Guide to Contemporary African American Fiction* (2005), and *African American Satire: The Sacredly Profane Novel* (2001).

Darryl P. Domingo is associate professor of English at the University of Memphis. He has published widely on eighteenth-century literature, including satire, and is the author of *The Rhetoric of Diversion in English Literature and Culture, 1690–1760* (2016). He is working on a study of advertising and the arts of persuasion in eighteenth-century Britain.

Joe B. Fulton is professor of English at Baylor University in Waco, Texas, where he has been honored as a Baylor University Class of 1945 Centennial Professor. Fulton has published five books on Mark Twain, most recently *Mark Twain under Fire: Reception and Reputation, Criticism and Controversy, 1851–2015* (2016).

Jonathan Greenberg is professor and chair of English at Montclair State University, where he specializes in modernism. He is the author of *Modernism, Satire, and the Novel* (2011) and *The Cambridge Introduction to Satire* (2018) and the editor, with Nathan Waddell, of *Brave New World: Contexts and Legacies* (2016).

Matthew Henry is a faculty member at Richland College, where he teaches courses in composition, cultural studies, and African American literature. From 2010 to 2011, he was a Fulbright scholar in American studies at the University of Potsdam in Germany. He has published numerous academic journal articles and one book, The Simpsons, *Satire, and American Culture* (2012).

James Horowitz, an assistant professor of literature at Sarah Lawrence College, has published on topics such as John Dryden's Jacobitism, Samuel Johnson's parliamentary reporting, and the eighteenth-century reception of

Ovid. His book project is tentatively entitled "Divided Bodies: Performing Gender, Sexuality, and Partisanship in England, 1675–1730."

Nicholas Hudson, professor of English at the University of British Columbia, is the author of *Writing and European Thought, 1600–1830*; *Samuel Johnson and the Making of Modern England*; and *A Political Biography of Samuel Johnson*. Along with publishing many essays on the history of race, theories of language, social class, and the novel, he coedited *Swift's Travels: Eighteenth-Century British Satire and Its Legacy* with Aaron Santesso.

Catherine Ingrassia is professor of English at Virginia Commonwealth University. Her publications include *Authorship, Commerce, and Gender in Early Eighteenth-Century England: A Culture of Paper Credit* (1998) and *"More Solid Learning": New Perspectives on Alexander Pope's* Dunciad (2000). She edited Eliza Haywood's *Anti-Pamela* (2004) and *The Cambridge Companion to Women's Writing in Britain, 1660–1789* (2015) and coedited *A Companion to the Eighteenth-Century English Novel and Culture* (2005) and *British Women Poets of the Long Eighteenth Century* (2009).

David Mazella is associate professor of English at the University of Houston. He is the author of *The Making of Modern Cynicism* (2007), and he is currently working on a literary history of the year 1771, from the perspective of four imperial cities: London, Edinburgh, Philadelphia, and Kingston, Jamaica.

Sophia A. McClennen is professor of international affairs and comparative literature at Penn State University and founding director of the Center for Global Studies. She studies the relationship between satire and politics, and her most recent book is *Is Satire Saving Our Nation? Mockery and American Politics*, coauthored with Remy Maisel.

Nicholas D. Nace is assistant professor of rhetoric at Hampden-Sydney College. He is the editor of several volumes of essays on close reading and, with Evan Davis, *The Broadview Anthology of Eighteenth-Century British Satire* (forthcoming). His work on Restoration satire has appeared in *The Review of English Studies* and *The Book Collector*.

Frank Palmeri, professor of English and Cooper Fellow in the Humanities at the University of Miami, is the author of *Satire in Narrative* (1991); *Satire, History, Novel: Narrative Forms, 1665–1815* (2003); and *State of Nature, States of Society: Enlightenment Conjectural History and Modern Social Discourse* (2016). His current book project is entitled "The Decline and Return of Radical Satire: Fiction, Caricature, and the Political Imaginary in Nineteenth-Century England."

Anne Lake Prescott is the Helen Goodhart Altschul Professor of English, emeritus, at Barnard College. The author of *Imagining Rabelais in Renais-*

sance England and other studies of Anglo-French relations, she has written essays on satire and polemics and has taught courses on the Menippea and their cousins at Barnard and Columbia.

Adam Rounce is associate professor in English literature at the University of Nottingham. He has written extensively on various seventeenth- and eighteenth-century writers, is coediting two volumes of the writings of Jonathan Swift for Cambridge University Press, and is the author of *Fame and Failure, 1720–1800: The Unfulfilled Literary Life* (2013).

Robin Runia is associate professor of English at Xavier University of Louisiana. She has published explorations of spirituality, race, and sexuality in *Restoration and Eighteenth-Century Theatre Research* and *Religion in the Age of Enlightenment*. Her current monograph project is titled "Displaced Britons: Africans and Creoles in the Works of Maria Edgeworth."

Aaron Santesso is professor of literature at Georgia Tech. He is the coauthor, with David Rosen, of *The Watchman in Pieces: Surveillance, Literature, and Liberal Personhood*, which received the James Russell Lowell Prize from the MLA. He has authored or edited several other books, including, with Nicholas Hudson, *Swift's Travels: Eighteenth-Century Satire and Its Legacy.*

Peter Schmidt teaches American literature and literary history at Swarthmore College. He is the author of books on William Carlos Williams, Eudora Welty, and the literature of the early New South, including *Sitting in Darkness: New South Fiction, Education, and the Rise of Jim Crow Colonialism, 1865–1920*, and *Making and Unmaking Whiteness in Early New South Fiction after the Civil War*. He coedited *Postcolonial Theory and the United States* with Amritjit Singh.

Kerry Soper, professor in the Department of Comparative Arts and Letters at Brigham Young University, writes about the history of comedy and satire in comic strips, television, film, and other popular media. His books include *Garry Trudeau:* Doonesbury *and the Aesthetics of Satire*; *We Go Pogo: Walt Kelly, Politics, and American Satire*; and a forthcoming study of Gary Larson's *The Far Side.*

Anne H. Stevens is professor of English and chair of the Department of Interdisciplinary, Gender, and Ethnic Studies at the University of Nevada, Las Vegas. She is the author of *British Historical Fiction before Scott* (2010) and *Literary Theory and Criticism: An Introduction* (2015).

Matthew Stratton is associate professor of English at the University of California at Davis. His book *The Politics of Irony in American Modernism* was awarded an honorable mention for the 2015 Modernist Studies Association Book Prize. His current book project is titled "Uncommon Sense: Dictatorship and the Political Imagination of Anglo-American Fiction."

Christopher Vilmar is associate professor of English at Salisbury University, where he teaches widely in British literature. In addition to publications on Samuel Johnson, John Arbuthnot, and other figures, he coedited, with Adam Rounce, the poetry entries of *The Encyclopedia of British Literature, 1660–1789* (2015).

Howard D. Weinbrot is Ricardo Quintana Professor of English and William Freeman Vilas Research Professor emeritus in the College of Letters and Science, University of Wisconsin, Madison. His books on satire include *The Formal Strain: Studies in Augustan Imitation and Satire*, *Alexander Pope and the Traditions of Formal Verse Satire*, *Eighteenth-Century Satire: Essays on Text and Context from Dryden to Peter Pindar*, and *Menippean Satire Reconsidered: From Antiquity to the Eighteenth Century.*

Edward Wesp is associate professor of English and chair of the English Department at Western New England University. He teaches and writes primarily on the subjects of nineteenth-century American literature and contemporary digital media.

Index